501
MUST-READ BOOKS

501
MUST-READ BOOKS

BB Bounty
Books

Publisher: Polly Manguel
Project Editor: Emma Beare
Contributing Editor: Joanna Smith
Publishing Assistant: Jo Archer
Designer: Ron Callow/Design 23
Picture Research Head of Department: Liz Fowler
Picture Researchers: Emma O'Neill, Sophie Delpech
Production Manager: Neil Randles

First published in Great Britain in 2006 by Bounty Books,
a division of Octopus Publishing Group Limited
Reprinted five times

This paperback edition published in 2014 by Bounty Books,
a division of Octopus Publishing Group Limited
Endeavour House, 189 Shaftesbury Avenue, London WC2H 8JY
www.octopusbooks.co.uk

An Hachette UK Company
www.hachette.co.uk

Copyright © 2006, 2014 Octopus Publishing Group Limited

A CIP catalogue record is available from the British Library

ISBN: 978-0-753726-97-6

Printed and bound in China

Cover photography: front, main, Interfoto/Alamy; above, Joseph Clemson/Alamy;
back, Image Asset Management Ltd/Alamy

Contents

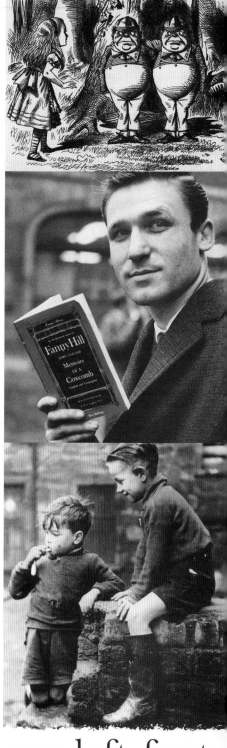

my left foot

CHRISTY BROWN

'One of the literary greats of the modern age'
Irish Times

Introduction

501 Must-Read Books is like the wisest, cleverest, best-read and trusted friend you have ever had. The recommendations for inclusion in this comprehensive book were made by a bibliophile and writer with a peerless reputation, but the reviews themselves were compiled by lecturers, writers and book lovers, sharing their pleasure or surprise or even indignation with the rest of us. Reading is of course subjective, but the reviewers have set aside their personal preferences to share their thoughts and impressions with book lovers everywhere. This comprehensive guide will inspire you to read more widely than you could have imagined and to explore previously untrodden paths in your bookstore or library. In these pages you will find travel rubbing shoulders with memoir, modern and classic fiction, nestling together, sci-fi and thrillers, children's books and history all gathered and reviewed in sometimes surprising but always stimulating essays.

Many factors apply when it comes to choosing a book you will enjoy, or by which you will be educated, informed and entertained. We can rely on the recommendations of friends, or join a book group to broaden our horizons, or read the book reviews in the Sunday newspapers. But there is a limit to the amount of time most of us can spend in bookstores reading the first page of the millions of titles published every year, in every conceivable category and genre, attracted by the brilliant covers (remember too that you can't judge a book…) and two-line opinions of the critics. Many bookstores have bright, intelligent assistants who will take the time to talk about the books that they and their other customers have enjoyed and on-line you will get interesting recommendations based on the titles you have ordered in the past. But if like me you often order books for friends or for research on line, their computerized system becomes thoroughly confused by what, I often imagine its little computer chip judges to be my wildly eclectic tastes. You may have enjoyed a particular author's work, but he or she only wrote three books and you have read those. Perhaps you used to like fantasy literature but now find you are interested in the tales of other more earthbound cultures, or you enjoy the lives of real people but want to test the deep waters of modern fiction. Maybe you have just discovered the tantalising literature of other people's travels and adventures and want more. Our tastes change over time and sometimes we long for someone to say 'Read this, it's fantastic', and sit us down in a cosy armchair, by a roaring fire, or under an apple tree in a lazy hammock and leave us to dive into the world of another's imagination or experience.

In this book the reviewers, who come from all walks of life and different age groups, have spent many hours absorbing the works that they have been asked to review and each has expressed pleasure and surprise at where their reading has taken them. Sometimes, one may have thought they knew the body of work of a classic or modern fiction author like F. Scott Fitzgerald, or Kingsley Amis, only to find that our lists included a book with which they were unfamiliar or had long forgotten. The pleasure in reading this novel or short story has all the piquancy of meeting an old friend after a long separation, reminding one of why you had become friends in the first place. It is refreshing too, to see the whole world of literature represented rather than just the Western European titles with which we are all familiar. Reading some of the recommendations in modern fiction, for example, Chinua Achebes' *Things Fall Apart* or Gabriel Garcia Marquez's masterpiece *100 Years of Solitude*, opens our eyes to the cultural heritage of Africa and South America as well as being extraordinarily stimulating and entertaining novels. AS Byatt's *Possession* or Robertson Davies' *Fifth Business* lead us into the realms of poetry and magic as well as being enthralling reads, beautifully written.

The history section encompasses titles as diverse as Herodotus' *The Histories* and Rosalind Miles' *A Woman's History of the World* as well as Howard Zinn's *A People's History of The United States* and T.E. Lawrence's *Seven Pillars of Wisdom*. So different in terms of style and context and yet, if you were to read every title recommended here you would have a phenomenal understanding of, and perspective on the known history of the world and our 21st century place in its continuum.

The travel section allows us to visit the exotic and the distant shores of many lands but also to share in the passion and motivation of the writers who offer their experiences; from Jan Morris's pieces for *Rolling Stone* magazine in which she set out to visit countries and cities where major events in modern times had just happened and monitor their effects, to *The Travels of Marco Polo*, arguably the first modern travelogue and an illuminating account of his monumental expeditions in the East and the effects of cultural exchange. The flora and fauna, the temperature and climate changes, the vivid impressions and humourous accounts of journeys undertaken and hardships endured, all add up to a rich confection of delight for the armchair traveller.

If real travel is not your cup of tea, then perhaps the fantastic and imaginative experiences of science fiction will take you to places you have never been and of which you couldn't conceive. Futuristic landscapes, technological wonders, bizarre social structures and travels through time and space, the recommendations here have it all. Once again it is the diversity of the works that is so astonishing from Anthony Burgess' Dystopian nightmare *A Clockwork Orange* to Douglas Adam's wry and amusing *Hitchhiker's Guide to the Galaxy*; William Gibson's modern classic *Necromancer* to Sci Fi master Ray Bradbury's *Martian Chronicles*. Science Fiction allows us to take another look at the human race and our social mores and the perceived threats to our way of life from an entirely different perspective, from once upon a time in a galaxy far, far away...

The children's book list reminds us that this rich genre has long offered titles other than the masterly Harry Potter books, from classics such as Joanna Spyrii's *Heidi* and *The Happy Prince* by Oscar Wilde to new treasures like *Charlotte's Web*, we can relive the magic of our own childhoods or share in the joy of discovery in those of our children and grandchildren. Memoir, Fiction, Thrillers all offer this same eclectic mix of modern and traditional literature that would thoroughly confuse that computer chip in the online bookstore but offers you the reader, hours if not years of unalloyed pleasure.

Incidentally, the reviews never spoil the plotline or ruin the anticipation of any book, and offer useful suggestions for other works by each author which you might enjoy, although space does not always allow for a full list, so there are often more unknown pleasures ahead if you follow these recommendations.

The best analogy for choosing a book might be that of the personal ads and lonely heart's columns. A typical ad might read:
'Smart inquisitive mind, imaginative, restless, open to new experiences, good sense of humour, seeks similar, compassionate, knowledgeable, surprising, intellectually stimulating, emotionally uplifting, thought provoking, distracting, colourful, rich, unusual, eccentric, globally aware, historically smart, with the innocence of a child, thrill seeking, techie, partner or partners for lifetime commitment to fun, adventure and new experiences.' It is with some degree of envy that I can truly say that with the help of *501Must-Read Books* you need look no further, your perfect partner is just waiting to meet you and for you to live together, happily ever after.

CHILDREN'S FICTION

Little Women

LOUISA MAY ALCOTT
1832 – 1888
Nationality: American
First Published: Roberts Brothers, 1868
Other Selected Titles:
Flower Fables
Good Wives
An Old Fashioned Girl
Little Men: Life at Plumfield with Jo's Boys
Aunt Jo's Scrap-Bag
Under the Lilacs
Jo's Boys and How They Turned Out: A Sequel to Little Men
A Garland for Girls

The heart-warming story of the March sisters – Meg, Jo, Beth and Amy – is one of the most popular books of 19th-century American fiction. It is set during the American Civil War, when their father is away serving as a chaplain with the Union Army. The family have fallen on hard times, and the girls have to grow up fast. Helped by their ever-loving, ever-patient Marmee and through Bible study, each of the girls learns to shoulder some of the family's burdens and overcome her own particular character flaws: literary Jo her temper and outspokenness, domesticated Meg her greed and envy of other people's wealth, musical Beth her overwhelming shyness, and artistic Amy her vanity and selfishness. Alcott's characters are more believable, and more likeable, for their imperfections. As the story follows them through their months of worries about their father and about Beth's health, there are moments of both laughter and joy, as well as sadness.

Lighter notes often arrive in the form of Laurie, the irrepressible scamp who lives next door with his stern, unapproachable grandfather. He eventually helps Beth to overcome her shyness through a shared love of music. Their lessons are not always learned so easily: Meg sees that her friend Sallie's wealth has not brought her happiness; an outspoken remark by Jo destroys her chances of being taken to Europe by rich Aunt March and teaches her that privileges must be earned and that her temper has to be curbed; while Amy learns that helping others is rewarding. Despite the tragedies and hardships that befall the family, this timeless book is an optimistic, charming exploration of growing up.

A scene from Little Women.

Fairy Tales

Originally published as individual stories in Denmark from 1827 and in collections between 1835 and 1872 under the general name of *Eventyr*, Anderson's fairy tales and other stories have delighted generations of children. Ranging from the comedy of *The Emperor's New Clothes*, to the poignancy of *The Little Mermaid* and the joyful ending of *The Ugly Duckling*, they are charming reminders of a more innocent past. There are more than 200 tales, and while many have a moral theme, this is never heavily emphasized and they can be enjoyed as simple stories.

In *The Ugly Duckling* we learn that beauty is only skin deep and it is wrong to treat someone badly just because they are different, while *The Emperor's New Clothes* is a lesson in both the rewards for vanity and the stupidity of not challenging what is manifestly untrue just to follow the crowd. Among the best known are *The Princess and the Pea* (which is sometimes called *The Real Princess*), in which the girl proved she was a real princess because one pea under a hundred mattresses and a hundred coverlets kept her awake at night; and *The Snow Queen*, in which the little boy is lured away from what is right by the queen, but soon tires of luxurious boredom and longs to be back with his family and friends. Other favourite fairy tales include *The Tinder Box*, *The Fir Tree*, *The Swineherd*, *The Phoenix*, *The Ice Maiden*, *The Little Match Girl*, *Thumbelina*, *The Red Shoes*, *The Wild Swans* and *The Marsh King's Daughter*.

HANS CHRISTIAN ANDERSEN
1805 – 1875
Nationality: Danish
First Published: George Routledge & Sons, 1890 (first English translation)

Danish fairy tale writer, Hans Christian Andersen.

Peter Pan

J.M. BARRIE
1860 – 1937
Nationality: British
First Published: Hodder &
Stoughton, 1911
Other Selected Titles:
The Little White Bird
Peter Pan in Kensington Gardens

Adapted from part of an earlier novel, *The Little White Bird,* and a stage play, *Peter Pan, or The Boy Who Wouldn't Grow Up, Peter Pan* is both an exciting adventure and an exploration of growing up. Peter and the lost boys are chiefly based on the boys of the Llewelyn Davies family, whom J.M. Barrie knew well and eventually unofficially adopted.

In the book, Peter invites Wendy to come to Neverland to be

mother to his lost boys. She and her brothers fly with Peter to an island populated by pirates (including, of course, Peter's sworn enemy Captain Hook), a crocodile with a taste for human flesh, Tiger Lily, and Tinkerbell, the irritable fairy who is a rival with Wendy for Peter's affections. This is seen much more clearly in the book than any of the film adaptations. Peter isn't interested at all: that sort of thing is for grown-ups, like caring and responsibility.

The delight of the book lies in the magical adventures, flying above the trees, and the fights with Captain Hook. And behind it all is the never-stopping, ever-present

Sir James Barrie in 1902. He originally called the book Peter and Wendy.

Book illustration of Peter Pan with Wendy sewing his shadow on, by Mabel Lucie Atwell.

tick of the crocodile's clock.

Written around a century ago, in places the story is not as politically correct as we might like in the 21st century. Yet Barrie's understanding of children – their fears, their hopes and how their imaginations work – allowed him in this story to capture the innocence of childhood and the magical world of a child's imagination. Adults can read the symbolic sub-text that underlies Peter's desire to remain in the enchanted realm of Neverland, but for children it is simply a ripping good story.

The Wonderful Wizard of Oz

L. FRANK BAUM
1856 – 1919
Nationality: American
First Published: Geo M. Hill
Co., 1900
Other Selected Titles:
Mother Goose in Prose
Father Goose: His Book
A New Wonderland
The Master Key: an Electric Fairy Tale
The Life and Adventures of Santa Claus
The Enchanted Island of Yew
Dorothy and the Wizard in Oz
The Emerald City of Oz

Dorothy lives on a Kansas farm with Uncle Henry, Aunt Em and Toto the dog. When a cyclone strikes before she can make it to the storm cellar, she and Toto are swept up with the house and dropped in the land of the Munchkins, accidentally killing their despotic ruler – the Wicked Witch of the East – as they land.

Despite it appearing a magical land, all Dorothy wants to do is to get back to Kansas, so the Good Witch of the North gives her the other witch's silver shoes and sends her along the yellow-brick road with a protective kiss, to find the Wizard of Oz. On her way, she encounters many dangers, as well as a scarecrow who wants a brain that isn't filled with straw, a cowardly lion who wants courage and a tin man who wants a heart. The terrifying wizard in the emerald city sets them a further challenge, which will enable them all to achieve their desires. After all their hardships, encounters with goodies, baddies, evil witches and funny animals, will Dorothy get back to Kansas?

As well as being a wonderful and exciting adventure for children, *The Wonderful Wizard of Oz* contains the lesson that all of us possess the resources we need to attain what we want if only we have the self-confidence to try. Each of the four travellers faces challenges in turn and overcomes them, not though by being special, but by co-operating and helping each other along the way.

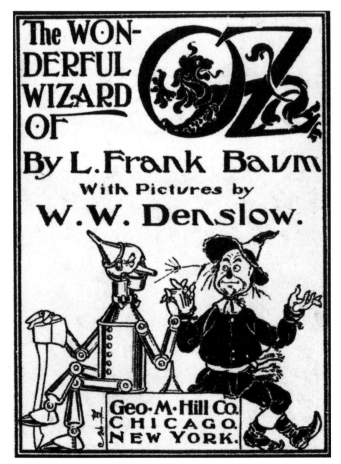

The original title page from the 1900 edition illustrated by W.W. Denslow.

The Last Unicorn

A unicorn lives alone in a lilac wood, where she has been for centuries. One day she overhears two hunters discussing whether unicorns exist, and she decides to set off to see whether she is the last of her kind. Hearing from a feather-brained butterfly that an evil creature called the Red Bull, under the command of King Haggard, is responsible for their disappearance, she determines to find them and bring them back. So few people believe in unicorns that her horn escapes notice and she travels unmolested until she is caught by a witch who puts her on display in a carnival – with an illusory horn.

One person who does recognize her identity is Schmendrick, an incompetent wizard, and they escape to carry on with her quest. They are joined by Molly Grue, a young woman who still believes in legends. Together they travel to the lands of King Haggard, where the unicorn must face the demonic Red Bull, and the characters come to terms with who they are. What dangers must she face in her quest to find what has happened to all of the other unicorns?

Beagle's transcendent use of the English language in his lyrical prose-poetry and songs is as enchanting as the story. Unlike many fantasy novels, this one does not take itself too seriously. Cully, the wannabe Robin Hood, and his grumpy men are brilliant comic creations, and Beagle deliberately introduces such anachronisms as Tex-Mex food into his medieval world. While children will enjoy this magical tale at face value, for adults the underlying idea of the cost of humanity being mortality is equally fascinating. It is in the incidental details that Beagle draws parallels between his fantasy world and reality, and reminds us that without dreams, our world would be a dull place indeed.

PETER S. BEAGLE
1939 –
Nationality: American
First Published: Viking Press, 1968
Other Selected Titles:
A Fine and Private Place
Lila the Werewolf
The Folk of the Air
The Unicorn Sonata
Tamsin
Two Hearts
The Line Between

The Last UNICORN a novel by Peter Beagle

The Secret Garden

Frances Hodgson Burnett.

FRANCES HODGSON BURNETT
1849 – 1924
Nationality: British
First Published: Frederick A. Stoker Co., 1909
Other Selected Titles:
Little Lord Fauntleroy
Sara Crewe

When Mary Lennox's parents die of cholera, the lonely, sickly child, who has been spoiled by the servants but neglected by her parents, is sent to England to live at her Uncle Archibald's house. She finds the bleak Yorkshire moors in winter a very different place to India. Used to her orders being obeyed, Mary is astonished by servants who answer back. However, she is soon intrigued by the tales that the maid Martha tells her of her life at home in a large, poor family, especially about her brother, Dickon, and his animals.

When Martha tells her about the garden that was locked ten years ago by her absent uncle after his wife's death there, Mary determines to find both it and the key. As spring approaches and she spends more time skipping in the gardens and talking to the elderly gardener Ben Weatherstaff, she begins to become a happier, nicer and healthier child.

When her uncle comes home briefly, she asks him if she may have a bit of earth to care for; it marks a turning point for both of them. But Missenthwaite Manor holds another secret: just who can Mary hear crying in the night?

Written at a time when middle-class children were expected to behave as miniature adults, this magical story is an exaltation of the beauty of nature and its beneficial effects on the human spirit, the need for human companionship and for children to be allowed to be children. The author has captured in prose the beauty of the Yorkshire moors in springtime so completely that the reader can almost smell the flowers.

Alice's Adventures in Wonderland ✓

Usually known as *Alice in Wonderland*, this is the fantasy tale of a little girl who follows a white rabbit down its hole and has a series of adventures, each weirder than the last. She encounters a hookah-smoking caterpillar, a duchess who gives her baby pepper and calls it a pig (so it turns into one), a cat that disappears leaving only its smile, a mad hatter, an equally mad March hare, a dormouse, a gryphon, a mock turtle and a dodo, among others.

Alice drinks potions and eats cakes and toadstools to change size, attends a bizarre endless teaparty, plays a game of croquet with an unmanageable flamingo for a croquet mallet and is a witness at the trial of the knave of hearts, where she risks the queen shouting 'Off with her head!'.

The story was originally told to the three Liddell sisters on a picnic because the middle sister, Alice, was bored. The author understands how children's minds work and the way he turns logic on its head appeals to their sense of the ridiculous. In the riddles and the poems – such as 'how doth the little crocodile...?', 'you are old Father William' and 'the mouse's tail' – he reaches even more absurd heights, and even mocks school lessons. In the sequel, usually just called *Through the Looking Glass*, Alice encounters more absurd people, such as the squabbling twins Tweedledum and Tweedledee. Although some references, such as mock turtles, may be dated, this is rightly still among the most popular of children's books, nearly 150 years after it was first published.

**LEWIS CARROLL
(CHARLES LUTWIDGE DODGSON)**
1832 – 1898
Nationality: British
First Published: Macmillan, 1865
Other Selected Titles:
*Alice's Adventures in Wonderland
Through the Looking Glass and What
Alice Found There
Jabberwocky
The Hunting of the Snark*

*'Tweedledum and Tweedledee'.
Illustration from the original
edition by John Tenniel.*

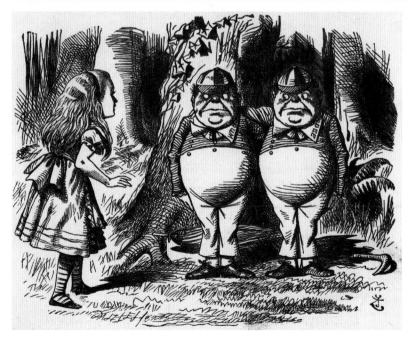

**CARLO COLLODI
(CARLO LORENZINI)**
1826 – 1890
Nationality: Italian
First Published: T. Fisher Unwin,
1891 (first English translation)

Pinocchio

Although it is probably most famous now from the 1940 Disney film, the original story of the little marionette who wanted to be a real boy is well worth reading. Geppetto, the poor woodcarver, is lonely and wants a little boy, so he carves himself a puppet out of a block of wood, but even before Geppetto has taken the wood home, Pinocchio has started to cause trouble, provoking a fight between his father and his old best friend Antonio the carpenter. The blue fairy takes pity on the old man and brings the puppet to life. Almost at once he's cheeky and disobedient, telling lies and being naughty. He desperately wants to be a real boy, but the blue fairy tells him that he is too naughty.

The book is darker than the film and Pinocchio is a lot more selfish and aggressive, but there is also some humorous slapstick that is absent from the Disney version. Going his own way, ignoring the advice of his father, the blue fairy and his conscience, the cricket (whom he kills), Pinocchio soon falls in with a variety of bad company, including the fox, the cat and the assassins. Like many Tuscan folk tales, of which it follows the tradition, this is a story with very important moral lessons for children: disobedience does not pay, and boys who love and take care of their parents will get the reward that they deserve. Despite the moral point, it is thoroughly enjoyable. Children will love the gruesome bits, and identify with his naughtiness.

Chapters 1–15 were originally published in Italian in serial form in *Il Giornale dei Bambini* between 1881 and 1882, while chapters 16 on were added for the book, published in 1883 as *Le Avventure di Pinocchio*.

Charlie and the Chocolate Factory

Like children everywhere, Charlie Bucket adores chocolate but, sadly, his family is so poor that they can only afford to buy him one bar a year, on his birthday. What makes poor Charlie's longing even worse is that he has to walk near the best chocolate factory in the world – the secretive Willy Wonka's – every day. When Charlie's father loses his job, things go from bad to worse.

One day, Willy Wonka announces that he has hidden golden tickets in five Wonka Bars, with the prize of a tour of the factory for the five lucky winners. The sale of Wonka Bars rockets, Wonka-mania encircles the globe, and one by one the tickets are found: by greedy Augustus Gloop, bratty Veruca Salt, gum-chewing Violet Beauregard and television addict Mike Teavee. But there is still one golden ticket to find. Charlie's desperation to be able to buy a Wonka Bar and hopefully find the final golden ticket is a feeling that all children (and their parents) know.

The inside of the chocolate factory is magical, with its themed rooms, amazing chocolates and sweets, the Oompa-Loompas and, of course, Willy Wonka himself. The well-deserved, weird fates of the naughty children are hilarious, and the gruesome methods that have to be used to squeeze or stretch them back to normal are graphically illustrated. The Oompa-Loompahs are like some surreal Greek chorus as they regularly break into verse to comment on the children's misbehaviour. As in all of his books, Dahl shows a deep understanding of how children think and feel; although the moral message is strong, the ridiculous consequences of being naughty make it easy to take, while the reward for being good is beyond any child's wildest dreams.

ROALD DAHL
1916 – 1990
Nationality: Norwegian-British
First Published: Alfred A. Knopf, 1964
Other Selected Titles:
James and the Giant Peach
Danny the Champion of the World
The Enormous Crocodile
The Twits
The BFG
Revolting Rhymes
Charlie and the Great Glass Elevator
The Witches

Sophie's World

A NOVEL ABOUT THE HISTORY OF PHILOSOPHY

JOSTEIN GAARDER
1952 –
Nationality: Norwegian
First Published: Farrar, Straus &
Giroux, 1994
Other Selected Titles:
The Christmas Mystery
The Solitaire Mystery
Hello? Is Anybody There?
That Same Flower
Through a Glass, Darkly
The Frog Castle
Maya
The Orange Girl

Fourteen-year-old Sophie Amundsen has just enrolled on a philosophy correspondence course when she discovers a letter in the post asking her such questions as 'Who are you?' and 'Where does the world come from?'. The novel has two parallel streams: the day-to-day life of Sophie herself, and the lessons from Alberto Knox that guide Sophie through some 30 schools of philosophy from the pre-Socratics to the present day. She learns to ask the questions that philosophers were asking in their own times, to understand how they were thinking, to actively question the origins of the universe and why we are here, as well as the truth behind myths and religions.

Soon, Sophie also starts to receive cards written to a girl of her own age called Hilde Moller Knag from her father. Sophie becomes so engrossed in the philosophy and the mystery of Hilde that she becomes divorced from reality, and as the lessons approach the 20th century, both she and Alberto start to question whether they are just characters in a book written by Mr Knag for Hilde, through whose eyes part of the book is seen. As Sophie and Alberto start to work out ways to discover the truth, and if necessary escape, things begin to get really weird, and the reader may end up wondering just who are the real characters in the book. In addition to being a mysterious story, this is a good, gentle introduction to the history of philosophy for older children with questioning minds.

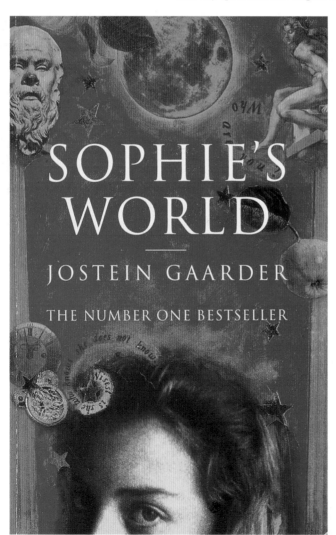

The Weirdstone of Brisingamen

In *The Weirdstone of Brisingamen* and its sequel, *The Moon of Gomrath*, the worlds of man and magic collide. Sent to stay near Alderley Edge in Cheshire with Gowther and Bess Mossock on their farm, Susan and Colin have no sooner arrived than they are embroiled in the eternal struggle between the forces of dark and light. Selina Place tries to force them into her car with a strange incantation and Susan notices that the stones on her bracelet – her 'tear' – went cloudy while they were near the woman.

The children's curiosity soon leads them into danger in the form of hundreds of goblin-like svarts, from whom they are rescued by Cadellin, the wizard of Fundindelve. Cadellin tells them that the forces of evil – the Morthbrood – have had the upper hand since a local farmer stole the magical gemstone Firefrost – the Weirdstone of Brisingamen – from its throne in Fundindelve. When Bess recognizes Susan's tear as having been in her family for generations, the children realize that it must be Firefrost and set out to return it to Cadellin, but it is taken from them and falls into the hands of Selina Place.

When they tell him the story, Cadellin is in despair and orders the children not to meddle further. Of course they disobey, and the final desperate chase is the stuff of nightmares: spied on by birds, hunted by the blood-curdling Mara and not sure whom they can trust, the children must crawl, creep and skulk their way to the final meeting place. Set in the spectacular landscape that Garner knows and loves, this gripping tale, peopled by witches, wizards, dwarves, elves and goblins, is far better than any sword and sorcery novel.

ALAN GARNER
1934 –
Nationality: British
First Published: Collins, 1960
Other Selected Titles:
The Moon of Gomrath
Elidor
The Owl Service
Red Shift

PENGUIN CLASSICS

KENNETH GRAHAME

The Wind in the Willows

KENNETH GRAHAME
1859 – 1932
Nationality: British
First Published: Methuen, 1908
Other Selected Titles:
The Reluctant Dragon

The Wind in the Willows

When Mole decides to go to the river bank one morning rather than do his spring cleaning, it is the beginning of a magical adventure. He and Ratty, the water rat, bump into the irrepressible, boastful Mr Toad, owner of Toad Hall and possessor of large amounts of money and not much brain. Set in the peaceful countryside of early 20th-century England, the three enjoy a paradisiacal life picnicking on the river bank, messing about on boats and driving around in a horse and cart, until Toad is almost run over by a motor car.

Naturally, being speed-obsessed, he is instantly lost and wants one, but unlike in the Disney film, he neglects to pay for it and so ends up in jail. His escape, and his flight from the forces of justice, eventually reunite him with his friends, but has he learned humility? Or is he the same outrageous, wayward braggart as before? Only the much-tried loyalty of Ratty, Mole and Badger stands between him and complete disgrace, so has Mr Toad at last learned his lesson?

For children, it is a story of friends and the exciting adventures that they can have together, set in an imaginary, but somehow totally believable world, and the morals are well disguised. For adults, it is like a distant, idyllic childhood dream. The story is beautifully written, with evocative descriptions of the countryside interspersed with adventures such as the ride on the gipsy caravan, the scary night-time search for Otter's baby, the climactic battle against the weasels for Toad Hall, and funny episodes such as Toad's first glimpse of a motor car. It is deservedly one of the classics of children's literature.

Children's and Household Tales

These stories were originally published in German as *Kinder-und Hausmärchen* in two volumes in 1812 and 1814, and are often known in English as the *Brothers Grimm Fairy Tales*. Collected as part of their research into linguistics, the Grimms' folk tales include some 200 of the best-loved children's stories in Western literature, including *Cinderella*, *Red Riding Hood*, *Hansel and Gretel*, *Rumpelstiltskin*, *Rapunzel* and *Snow White*. With most of the violence and earthiness of the original stories removed, they are so well-known and widely loved that many of their characters and concepts such as sleeping beauty, the needle in a haystack, and the frog prince have crossed into a wider culture. Many of the stories were collected from the German and French countryside and reflect folk beliefs and superstitions: woods are dark and evil places inhabited by witches and wolves; townsfolk are untrustworthy, whereas peasants and woodsmen are honest and hardworking; and misfortunes are caused by witches and goblins.

The stories about royalty are populated by beautiful princesses, wicked stepmothers and kings who set impossible tasks for their daughters' suitors. Animals, too, conform to character-types. The stories are often highly moralistic, with goodness being rewarded and wickedness punished. Because they derive from long-told folk tales, these simply-told fairy stories about talking animals, bargains with the devil, changelings, princesses, peasants, goblins, elves and witches still have a universal appeal and remain perennial favourites with younger children and are particularly good for parents to read to them.

JACOB GRIMM
1785 – 1863
WILHELM GRIMM
1786 – 1859
Nationality: German
First Published: G. Bell & Sons, 1884
(first English translation)

Illustration from Snow White *by Jesssie Willcox Smith.*

The Curious Incident of the Dog in the Night-Time

MARK HADDON
1962 –
Nationality: British
First Published: Jonathan Cape, 2003
Other Selected Titles:
The Talking Horse and the Sad Girl and the Village Under the Sea

Mathematical genius Christopher Boone is 15 and suffers from Asperger's Syndrome (a form of autism in which everything is overwhelming because of the lack of the mental and emotional filters that most people possess). One night, he discovers his neighbour's poodle, Wellington, impaled on a garden fork. Wrongly blamed for the killing, he decides to imitate one of his literary heroes, Sherlock Holmes, and investigate the murder using similar deductive logic, and to write about it as he does so.

During his investigation, he also uncovers facts closer to home and, believing himself to be in danger from the killer, runs away to London.

The author's work with sufferers of Asperger's Syndrome means that he is able to portray Christopher's world view in accurate, believable detail, understanding what it is like to be terrified of yellow or of shaking hands, but not to be aware of, or disturbed by, the danger of being on the tracks in front of an underground train.

By turns funny and sad, but always moving, Christopher's literal-minded observations of the world around him – where adults shout at him for not obeying arbitrary rules that he doesn't understand or know the need for, and he has to impose pattern and routine on the chaos that confronts him – make him a character to be admired, not pitied. Mark Haddon's skill lies in writing so that although Christopher is unaware of emotional undercurrents and nuances of mood, the reader is made aware of them. It is a beautifully written book, suitable for older children and adults alike.

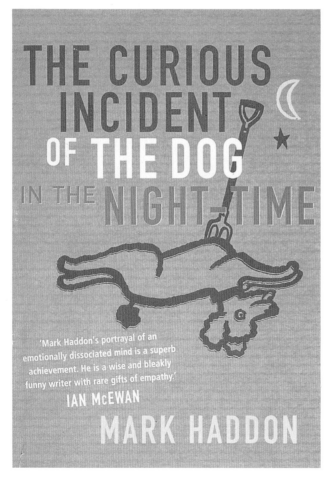

THE CURIOUS INCIDENT OF THE DOG IN THE NIGHT-TIME

'Mark Haddon's portrayal of an emotionally dissociated mind is a superb achievement. He is a wise and bleakly funny writer with rare gifts of empathy.'
IAN McEWAN

MARK HADDON

Emil and the Detectives

Emil is on a train journey to visit family in Berlin when he wakes up to find that the desperately needed large sum of money that he was taking to his grandmother, and which was pinned inside his coat pocket, has gone, as has the friendly stranger who gave him a bar of chocolate. Was he drugged and robbed? Nothing daunted, Emil spots the man at the station and follows him, acquiring help along the way in the form of Gustav and his 50 or so street-wise friends. The thief doesn't stand a chance of escaping as he is watched by the inventive and ingenious children, who have an organization as sophisticated and efficient as Sherlock Holmes's Baker Street Irregulars.

This is an exciting adventure, full of mystery, and the crime-doesn't-pay moral is sugared because the story is so funny. The author includes an absurd introduction, in which he relates how difficult it is to come up with a plot, even if you are lying on the floor under the dining table (which explains Emil's surname: Tischbein is German for table leg; and there are similar puns in some other children's names). The children in the story have a great sense of mischief, making them human and thoroughly believable, while their bravery and sense of justice lead them into several hair-raising and unforeseen situations.

Versions with the original illustrations by Walter Trier add to the enjoyment of the book because he captured the spirit and individuality of the children so well.

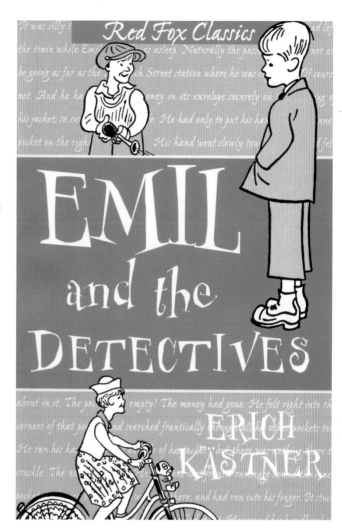

ERICH KASTNER
1899 – 1974
Nationality: German
First Published: Doubleday, 1930
Other Selected Titles:
Annaluise and Anton
Emil and the Three Twins
Three Men in the Snow
Lottie and Lisa
Simpletons
Little Man
The Flying Classroom
Little Man and the Little Miss

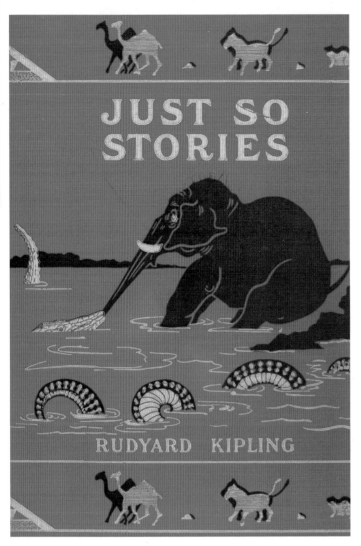

Just So Stories

Kipling's *Just So Stories* are ideal for parents to read with children. In eight of them he devises fantastical explanations for natural phenomena such as the leopard's spots, why the tides follow the Moon, the armadillo's scales and why the rhinoceros has crumpled, scratchy skin and such a bad temper. *The Cat That Walked By Himself* is a brilliant evocation of the relationship between cats, dogs and humans, while *The Butterfly That Stamped* could come straight out of *One Thousand and One Nights*. *How the First Letter Was Written* and *How the Alphabet Was Made* are comically knowing: not only do the Neolithic tribesmen call themselves that, they know what writing's called even though they haven't yet invented it.

The ridiculously pompous language – with its repetitions, rhymes, alliterations and rhythm – such as 'the great grey-green greasy Limpopo River' is perfect for reading aloud. The stories were originally written for Kipling's eldest daughter, the best-beloved who is often addressed in such asides as '...That meant just the same thing, but the Ethiopian used long words. He was a grown up.' Kipling was known in his own time chiefly as a poet, and he paints vivid word-pictures, such as when the whale opens his mouth until it nearly touches his tail in order to swallow the sailor and his raft, the struggle on the river bank between the crocodile and the insatiably curious elephant's child, and the chase half-way across Australia between Old Man Kangaroo and Yellow Dog Dingo. Each story has a nonsense poem as a tailpiece.

RUDYARD KIPLING
1865 – 1936
Nationality: British
First Published: Macmillan, 1902
Other Selected Titles:
The Phantom Rickshaw
Wee Willie Winkie
Life's Handicap
The Jungle Book
Kim
Just So Stories for Little Children
Puck of Pook's Hill
Rewards and Fairies

The Complete Nonsense Books

Lear's first *Book of Nonsense* appeared in 1846, under the pseudonym of Derry Down Derry and contained 112 limericks. He wrote four more books of limericks, songs, alphabets and verse over the next 30 years, but the 1912 collection was the first time that they all appeared in print together. As well as more than 200 limericks (including the old man with a beard, the young lady of Ryde, and the old person of Slough), it contains such favourite longer verses as the Owl and the Pussycat, the Pobble who has no toes, the Jumblies (who went to sea in a sieve), the Dong with a luminous nose, Quangle Wangle's Hat and Calico Pie. Lear was an accomplished artist and the line drawings that accompany the text add to the mayhem, as do instructions on where to shout in some of the verses, such as the Akond of Swat.

Less well-known are the nonsense alphabets, which smaller children enjoy, and botanies, in which plants such as Phattifacia stupenda and Enkoopia chickabiddia can be found. The nonsense cookery section has a terrifying recipe for Amblongus Pie, which finishes with the instruction 'serve up in a clean dish, and throw the whole out of the window as fast as possible.' Even with the made-up words, Lear keeps the language simple and plays with the sounds of words, so that younger children can enjoy the nonsense. The limericks appeal to children's quirky sense of humour while the stories contained in the longer verses remain firm favourites.

EDWARD LEAR
1812 – 1888
Nationality: British
First Published: Duffield & Co., 1912
Other Selected Titles:
Book of Nonsense
Nonsense Songs, Stories, Botany and Alphabets
More Nonsense, Pictures, Rhymes, Botany, etc.
Laughable Lyrics. A Fourth Book of Nonsense Poems, Songs

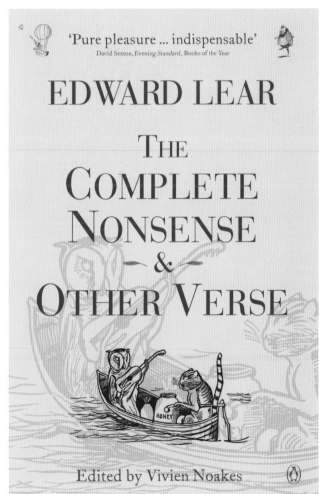

'Pure pleasure ... indispensable'
David Sexton, *Evening Standard*, Books of the Year

EDWARD LEAR

THE COMPLETE NONSENSE & OTHER VERSE

Edited by Vivien Noakes

A Wrinkle in Time

MADELEINE L'ENGLE
1918 –
Nationality: American
First Published: Ariel Books, 1962
Other Selected Titles:
The Arm of the Starfish
A Wind in the Door
Dragons in the Waters
A Swiftly Tilting Planet
A House like a Lotus
Many Waters

Thirteen-year-old Meg Murry is a misfit: apparently bright, she is lazy at school. Her five-year-old brother Charles Wallace Murry is bullied at school for seeming stupid and the town's gossips are saying that their father has left their mother. On a dark, stormy night, Mrs Whatsit, one of the three old women who have moved into the allegedly haunted house nearby, arrives and explains to them and their mother what has really happened to their father. A brilliant scientist, he was working on faster-than-light travel using tesseracts (wrinkles in the fabric of space and time through which spacecraft can take shortcuts) and has been captured on the planet Camazotz by a great force of evil that is darkening the universe one planet at a time.

Only the children can rescue their father. The three old women (who turn out to be something very different from the witches the townspeople take them for) whisk the children, with their friend Calvin O'Keefe, across space and time to find their father. Once there, they have to confront IT, a disembodied brain that controls the entire population: IT's method of domination is to offer people complete security in return for giving up their freedom and individuality.

As well as being an exciting fantasy novel, the book is imbued with religious allegory and moral themes, such as the value of kindness, the evils of discrimination and malicious gossip, and the destructiveness of vanity. In their perilous quest to find their father, the children have to look deep into their characters and rely on their own strengths, as well as those of their companions, in order to succeed in their perilous quest.

The Lion, the Witch and the Wardrobe

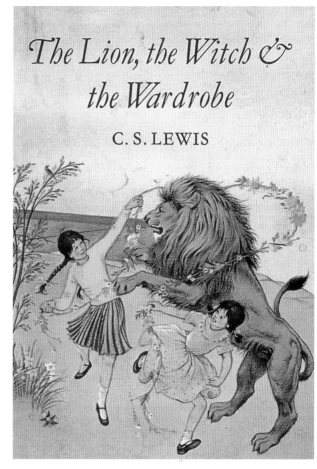

Peter, Susan, Edmund and Lucy have been sent to a house in the country during the war to avoid the air raids. While exploring, Lucy steps into a large wardrobe full of fur coats and finds herself in a snowy wood, where she meets a faun, who invites her home for tea. When Lucy decides that it is time to go home, Mr Tumnus the faun bursts into tears and confesses that he is meant to kidnap her and hand her over to the White Witch, who rules Narnia and keeps it in a permanent state of winter. He relents and takes her back to where they met, from where she makes her way back to the wardrobe. The others refuse to believe her (to them, she has only been gone a few seconds) and accuse her of lying.

During a game of hide and seek, when she decides to hide in the wardrobe, Edmund follows her and he too finds himself in Narnia. He, however, encounters the White Witch and through flattery is persuaded to return, bringing the others with him. When, eventually, the four children make it through the wardrobe together, Mr Tumnus' home has been wrecked and he is under arrest. The children encounter kindly Mr and Mrs Beaver, from whom they first learn about Aslan, the rightful King, who is on the verge of returning. At some point, Edmund slips away to find the witch and the others have to flee for their lives to the stone table, where Aslan and the witch will do battle.

The story is an allegory of Christianity, with Aslan's sacrifice mirroring that of the beginnings of Christianity. The magical world of Narnia and the characters that inhabit it, in this and the other books in the series, are enchanting.

C.S. LEWIS
1898 – 1963
Nationality: British
First Published: Geoffrey Bles, 1950
Other Selected Titles:
Prince Caspian
The Voyage of the Dawn Treader
The Silver Chair
The Horse and His Boy
The Magician's Nephew
The Last Battle

Pippi Longstocking

ASTRID LINDGREN
1907 – 2002
Nationality: Swedish
First Published: Viking Press, 1950
(first English translation)
Other Selected Titles:
Pippi Goes on Board
Pippi in the South Seas
Pippi's After Christmas Party

Pippi is a truly original character: nine years old, with red plaits that stick out sideways, she lives by herself in a large house – the Villa Villekulla – with her monkey and her horse. Her mother died when she was a baby, and her father is lost at sea, but he left her with a suitcase full of gold pieces and she is cheerfully optimistic that he will be back one day. She is highly unconventional and very assertive.

Pippi's complete lack of adult supervision delights children, as do the episodes where she outwits grown-ups (as she does frequently). This is shown when she dances with the burglars and they leave without stealing anything, or when she plays tag on the roof with the policemen who come to take her to a children's home before carrying them to their car, on each hand. Her wacky adventures often involve the two children next door, Tommy and Annika, to whom she is a superhero.

Whether Pippi is dealing with bullies, beating up the strongest man in the world, rescuing children from fires, or making up absurd tales about people she says she has known, including her grandmother's servant who never swept under the beds, she is always hysterically funny.

Pippi's unique take on life – not bothering with all the usual problems that children have (mainly inflicted by their parents), as she cheerfully rights wrongs, plays with her horse, dances and eats pancakes – is a joy to read.

Dr Dolittle

Dr John Dolittle lives in Puddleby-in-the-Marsh with his sister and dozens of pets. Because he prefers animals to human beings, his practice is failing and he is becoming very poor. One day, the cat's-meat man suggests that he would be more successful as an animal doctor and, much to his surprise, his parrot Polynesia tells him the same thing. She also teaches him to understand and to talk to animals.

One of his first patients is a horse which the vet has been treating for lameness when what it actually needed was spectacles. Soon, all the people who were avoiding him as a doctor are bringing their sick animals to him, and wild animals are flocking to his door. However, the presence of a crocodile in the fish pond scares all his clients, and his sister, away and he ends up poor again.

One cold night, Chee-chee the monkey tells him that there is a terrible sickness among the monkeys in Africa, so he decides to sail to Africa in a borrowed boat with Jip the intelligent dog, Dab-Dab the duck, Gub-Gub the drippy pig, Too-Too the owl, Polynesia, the monkey, the crocodile and the swallow who brought the news about the monkeys.

Their adventures on their journey include shipwreck, being imprisoned by the king of Jolliginki, and an encounter with Barbary pirates who like the idea of roast duck and pork for dinner. The doctor's ability to talk to such animals as lions, sharks and porpoises, and his friends' ingenuity, save the day.

This lovely story, which was originally written as letters home from the trenches in the First World War, has delighted generations of children. Older versions contain an uncomfortably racist episode, but this has been amended in later editions.

HUGH LOFTING
1886 – 1947
Nationality: British
First Published: Cape, 1920
Other Selected Titles:
The Voyages of Dr Dolittle
Dr Dolittle's Post Office
Dr Dolittle's Circus
Dr Dolittle's Caravan
Dr Dolittle's Zoo
Dr Dolittle's Garden
Dr Dolittle in the Moon
Dr Dolittle's Return

At the Back of the North Wind

GEORGE MACDONALD
1824 – 1905
Nationality: British
First Published: Strahan, 1871
Other Selected Titles:
Dealings with the Fairies
Ranald Bannerman's Boyhood
The Princess and the Goblin
Gutta Percha Willie
The Wise Woman
The Princess and the Curdie
Cross Purpose and the Shadows
An Acceptable Time

Diamond is a small boy in the rough world of Victorian London. His family has fallen on hard times, and he has to sleep in the hayloft over the stable. He is visited by a beautiful fairy-like woman, who calls herself North Wind and takes him on fantastical journeys flying over Britain and teaching him about herself. She takes him to the enchanted land where she lives, at the back of the north wind, and through all the trials of his young life, he longs to be back there.

Diamond is a personification of goodness, a pure and innocent soul, uncomplaining and unworldly, and somehow under the protection of North Wind. When he shares the knowledge that he has brought back from her enchanted land with the people around him, their preconceptions and values are challenged, as are those of the reader. While not disguising the ills caused by the grinding poverty of the age, the author makes plain his belief that our deepest need is for love, not material wealth.

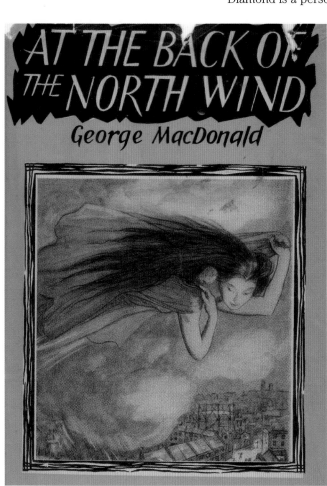

He uses language in a unique way, and includes poems, songs and stories within the main story to introduce new ideas. Macdonald had spent some time as a minister, and his belief that goodness is truth shines through the book. The full meaning and beauty behind the story only becomes apparent as the identity of North Wind emerges.

At times moving, at others funny, this book is thoroughly enjoyable and will both inspire the reader's imagination and challenge their values.

Nobody's Boy

Remi Barbarin is a poor peasant boy, who discovers one day that the couple he has always thought of as his parents had in fact rescued him when he was a baby after they found him abandoned in silk clothes. However, times are desperately hard and against his adoptive mother's wishes his 'father' sells him at the tender age of eight to a street musician called Vitalis, and so he begins a life on the road.

The two of them make a living by travelling round France with three performing dogs and a monkey called Jolie-Coeur. Vitalis soon becomes more of a friend than a master, and teaches the boy his trade. When tragedy strikes, Remi is left alone and has to make his own way in the world. He decides to find his real family. As he hunts for his relatives, he finds clues to their identity that lead him all over France, and even to England.

The plot has twists and turns as success is followed by setbacks, while the descriptions of life on the streets in 19th-century France are vividly written, as he encounters almost everything that life can throw at him. It is a heart-warming tale of one boy's journey to manhood and his determination to reach his goal.

Originally published in France in 1878 as *Sans Famille*, the translation by Florence Crew-Jones is the best-known English version. The story is also known as *No Family* from a US television series.

HECTOR MALOT
1830 – 1907
Nationality: French
First Published: Headley Brothers, 1916 (first English translation)
Other Selected Titles:
Nobody's Girl
Little Sister
Anie
Conscience
The Woman in the Cast
Romain Kalbris, His Adventures by Sea and Shore

Hector Malot.

Winnie-the-Pooh

These much-loved tales of a boy and his honey-eating bear were originally written for the author's own son, Christopher, and are set in the countryside of the Ashdown Forest near their home in southern England. Pooh, a bear of very little brain, gets himself into all kinds of sticky situations, whether it is trying to get honey from a bees' nest up a tree by disguising himself as a cloud, getting stuck in Rabbit's doorway because he's eaten too much, or falling down the trap he has built to catch the very scary Heffalump. But he is also a kind bear, when he restores Eyeore's missing tail, and brave when he and Christopher Robin set off in an upturned umbrella to rescue Piglet from the flood.

From gloomy old Eyeore to timid little Piglet, the animals that accompany Christopher Robin and Pooh on their adventures all have their own charm, even bossy Rabbit and Owl, who is not as clever as he would like to think he is. In the eternal summer of a magical childhood in the Hundred-Acre Wood, Christopher, Pooh and the others have such adventures as an expotition to the North Pole, and Pooh and Piglet hunt, and very nearly catch, a Woozle.

The stories are simply written, to appeal to young readers, and full of comic moments, such as Eyeore falling over every time he puts one hoof up to his ear in order to hear better, and Christopher Robin shooting Pooh out of the sky with a pop-gun, as well as silly verses to join in with. E.H. Shepherd's original illustrations add to the charm of this perennially popular book.

A.A. MILNE
1882 – 1956
Nationality: British
First Published: Methuen, 1926
Other Selected Titles:
When We Were Very Young
Now We Are Six
The House at Pooh Corner

Above: Christopher Robin and his father A.A. Milne, around the time of publication of Winnie-the-Pooh, *in 1926.*

Left: An illustration from the original edition showing Christopher Robin taking Pooh downstairs.

Anne of Green Gables

Matthew and Marilla Cuthbert, an elderly brother and sister who live in Avonlea on Canada's Prince Edward Island, need help on the farm, so they apply to adopt a boy. What greets Matthew at the station is Anne Shirley, a red-haired, freckle-faced 11-year-old girl. Reluctantly, the couple decide to keep her and gradually the joyless lives of shy Matthew and prim Marilla are transformed by the lovable chatterbox.

Anne's lively imagination helps her to make up fantastical stories to amuse her friends, and to transform the mundane and ordinary into things of beauty, such as when she renames Barry's Pond the Lake of Shining Waters. But not everything about Avonlea is idyllic, and Anne has two nemeses: hyper-critical Mrs Rachel Lynde, who she wins over, and Gilbert Blythe, who starts out badly by calling her 'carrots' and receives a slate over his head and eternal hatred as just reward.

Other deeply funny moments include Anne's overblown apology to Mrs Lynde for losing her temper, Matthew's attempts at the store to buy Anne a new dress, and the results of Anne's experiment in colouring her hair. Marilla is at first impatient of Anne's faults, but as Anne grows and learns to curb her temper and think less about her appearance, the older woman softens to her. Whether she is getting her best friend Diana Barry drunk by accident, falling off the roof after being dared to walk across it by the irritating Josie Pye, or having to be rescued from the bridge by Gilbert, Anne is an engaging scamp.

Like all lives, Anne's has its hardships and she learns some hard lessons, but when tragedy strikes her loving nature is at its best. Set in the beautiful landscape where the author had grown up with her own grandparents, this story is a charming and enjoyable coming-of-age novel.

L.M. MONTGOMERY
1874 – 1942
Nationality: Canadian
First Published: L.C. Page & Co., 1908
Other Selected Titles:
Anne of Avonlea
Anne of the Island
Anne's House of Dreams
Anne of Windy Poplars
Anne of Ingleside

Lucy Maud Montgomery, based her Anne of Green Gables *books on this house.*

Five Children and It

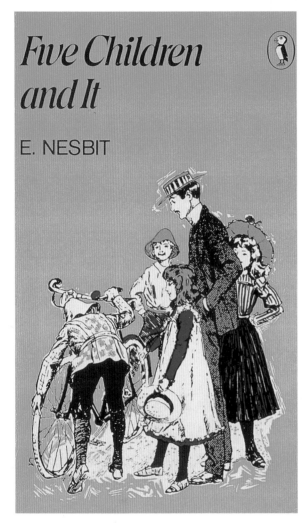

Five Children and It

E. NESBIT

E. NESBIT
1858 – 1924
Nationality: British
First Published: T. Fisher Unwin,
1902
Other Selected Titles:
The Story of the Treasure Seekers
The Wouldbegoods
The Phoenix and the Carpet
The New Treasure Seekers
The Story of the Amulet
The Railway Children

Five children – Cyril (Squirrel), Anthea (Panther), Robert (Robs), Jane (Pussy) and baby brother Hilary (the Lamb) – are sent to the White House by the Kent seaside. One day, while exploring a nearby gravel pit, they dig up a strange creature with eyes like a snail, bat's ears, rat-like whiskers, hands and feet like a monkey and a spider-shaped body covered with thick fur. It is distinctly tetchy, but tells them that it is a Psammead (pronounced Sammyad, and the It of the title) or sand fairy, and lets on that he can grant wishes.

What follows is a hilarious series of mishaps as none of the childrens' wishes is granted in quite the way they hoped. When Anthea wishes that they could all be as beautiful as the day, they become so, but no-one recognizes them, the servants chase them from the house and they have to go without dinner. When they finally turn back into themselves at sunset and return home, they get a good scolding from the servants.

When they ask for money beyond their wildest dreams, it turns out to be almost impossible to spend and they get questioned by the police. Further wishes result in the Lamb becoming the victim of various kidnap attempts, Robert becoming 11 feet tall, an invasion of red Indians, and the children having to eat an invisible dinner while the house is under siege by a party of distinctly angry knights. Most of the episodes end with them being sent to bed without supper.

This timeless tale of the children's mishaps and adventures is not only very funny, but contains the important lesson: be careful what you wish for, because it might just come true.

Tom's Midnight Garden

When, at the beginning of the summer holidays, Tom's brother Peter contracts measles, Tom is disgusted to learn that he is to be sent to stay with his Aunt Gwen and Uncle Alan, in their dull, gardenless flat in an old converted building. Confined indoors in case he is infectious, he is rude, lonely, bored and restless and has trouble sleeping.

The only thing that marks the passing of the monotonous days is the chiming of the grandfather clock that belongs to the landlady, Mrs Bartholomew. One night, he hears it chime 13 times at midnight. When he gets downstairs, he opens the back door and instead of the alley full of dustbins, there is a beautiful, ethereal garden. Over the ensuing nights, as he explores farther, he discovers that the people he comes across cannot see him, and realizes that the garden is the perfect place to escape from his aunt and uncle. However, he has a nagging feeling that someone in the garden is aware of his presence, and eventually he meets a girl called Hatty, a girl who is as lonely as himself and who, unlike her relations, can see him.

After a great deal of confusion, they work out that he has gone back to the end of the 19th century. But why? What is the tie that pulls him back to the past? The two children spend enchanted days together, playing in the sun. When Tom's time with his aunt and uncle is nearly over, he has to decide whether to go home or to stay in the garden forever.

In addition to being a beautifully written story about love and friendship, the book has a more melancholy theme: the need to leave childhood behind and the sadness of friends who grow apart with age.

PHILIPPA PEARCE
1920 – 2006
Nationality: British
First Published: Oxford University Press, 1958
Other Selected Titles:
Still Jim and Silent Jim
From Inside Scotland Yard
The Children of the House
The Way to Sattin Shore
Bubble and Squeak
Freddy
Old Belle's Summer Holiday
The Ghost in Annie's Room

The War of the Buttons

LOUIS PERGAUD
1882 – 1915
Nationality: French
First Published: Walker, 1968
(first English translation)

Originally published in French as *La Guerre des Boutons* in 1912, this is a joyfully comic novel about the children (mainly the boys) of two neighbouring villages. The adults of the villages have been feuding for centuries and the boys continue the tradition in their own unique way. They fight each other in large gangs and the captives have their buttons, braces and laces sliced off and have to return home half-naked in shame to their mothers, sometimes also having suffered a good smacking at the hands of their tormentors. The inventive ways the boys think up to avoid losing their buttons are deliciously funny, as are the results, and will leave the reader laughing at the same time as feeling pity for their poor victims. Despite the coarse language the boys and adults often use, and the bawdy humour, the book retains an innocence.

As well as being deeply funny, the story is also a social satire: the children are unwittingly playing out in their games the narrow-minded prejudices of their parents in a feud of which no-one can remember the cause. There is a strong anti-war message, but, ironically, the author died on the battlefields of northern France three years later. Pergaud really understood children, how they play, how alien the world of adults seems and the heartaches and joys of being young.

The book is filled with tender nostalgia: for childhood, when everything was so much simpler, and for the landscape of home. But it still remains one of the funniest children's books ever written.

Louis Pergaud
La Guerre des boutons

folio

Fairy Tales

Originally published in French in 1697, and later in English as *Histories, or tales of past times, with morals*, but also known as *Mother Goose's Tales*, this collection contains eight of the best-loved fairy tales. Like the Grimm brothers a century later, Perrault adapted his stories from folk tales. Eight stories – *Cinderella, Sleeping Beauty, Tom Thumb, Puss in Boots, Riquet of the Tuft, Bluebeard, The Fairies*, and *Little Red Riding Hood* – were included in the original, and some editions also have the creepy *Donkey Skin* and *Ludicrous Wishes*.

Perrault's version of *Sleeping Beauty* is darker than many modern versions as it follows her to her life with her mother-in-law, and the ending to *Red Riding Hood* is rather different to more sanitized modern versions.

Perrault wrote his tales for a sophisticated, literary and aristocratic audience, not for children, and removed some of the coarser details such as the Ugly Sisters cutting off bits of their feet in order to fit into the glass slipper, but he is slightly subversive in *Puss in Boots* when he implies that anyone could be an aristocrat given the right clothes.

In *Tom Thumb, The Fairies* and *Cinderella*, the rewards of being good are highlighted, while the tale of *Bluebeard* emphasizes the importance of wifely obedience. However, all the stories are enchanting tales in their own right, peopled with memorable characters from the clever cat who makes his master's fortune and Cinderella's step-mother, to scary Bluebeard and Red Riding Hood's wolf.

CHARLES PERRAULT
1628 – 1703
Nationality: French
First Published: T. Sabine & Son, 1729 (first English translation)

A scene from the tale of Sleeping Beauty.

The Tale of Peter Rabbit

BEATRIX POTTER
1866 – 1943
Nationality: British
First Published: Frederick Warne &
Co., 1902
Other Selected Titles:
The Tale of Squirrel Nutkin
The Tailor of Gloucester
The Tale of Mrs. Tiggy-Winkle
The Tale of Mr. Jeremy Fisher
The Tale of Tom Kitten
The Tale of Jemima Puddle-Duck
The Tale of Ginger and Pickles
The Tale of Mrs. Tittlemouse

Beatrix Potter's most famous character is the hero, or perhaps anti-hero, of her first children's book: Peter, the naughty little rabbit. Like many of her characters, he is based on her observations of the animals she kept at home or saw in the wild on holiday. Peter is far more adventurous than Flopsy, Mopsy and Cottontail, and almost as soon as their mother has told them to avoid Mr McGregor's garden while she is out shopping because their father had an 'accident' there and ended up in a pie, the wicked little rabbit is squeezing himself under the garden gate to gorge himself on Mr McGregor's vegetables while the others obediently go up the lane to pick blackberries from the hedgerows. Inevitably, Mr McGregor eventually spots Peter near the cucumber frame, and chases the terrified young rabbit all over the garden, where he manages to lose both his shoes and his little blue coat.

This short tale was originally written for private amusement, but her friends encouraged her to look for a publisher. Like the other books in the series, it was originally published in a small format that is easy for children to hold. Each short episode of the story is accompanied by a beautiful illustration, making it easier for young children who are just learning to read.

THE TALE OF PETER RABBIT

BY BEATRIX POTTER

F·WARNE & C?

The Colour of Magic

The first novel in Terry Pratchett's Discworld series, *The Colour of Magic* is the story of the hapless failed wizard Rincewind, a man who always manages to be in the wrong place at the wrong time. When Twoflower, an archetypal blundering tourist who stops to take pictures every 100 yards, arrives in Ankh-Morpork, Rincewind is given the task of making sure that he comes to no harm. This is not easy as the naive Agatean manages to land them in a succession of perilous situations, chiefly surrounding his seemingly bottomless supply of money, from which they are regularly rescued by Twoflower's Luggage – an overprotective travelling trunk with legs, teeth and the ability to locate its master anywhere on the Disc. They have encounters with dragons that exist only in the imagination and can only hurt you if you believe in them, Death personified, trolls, terrifying monsters, dryads and astronomers who want to throw them off the edge of the Disc so that they can find out whether Great A'Tuin, the giant turtle on whose back the four elephants that support the Disc stand, is male or female.

Pratchett's surreal world, where not possessing fire insurance almost guarantees that your home will be burned down, is a deeply satirical, but very witty spoof on the fantasy genre, with quests, mad scientists, running gags, barbarians, slapstick, assassins, appalling puns, cameras operated by imps and gods who decide the fate of individuals with the throw of a dice.

Writer Terry Pratchett in London, 2000.

TERRY PRATCHETT
1948 –
Nationality: British
First Published: Collin Smythe, 1983
Other Selected Titles:
The Light Fantastic
Wyrd Sisters
Equal Rites
Mort
Sourcery
Reaper Man
Small Gods
Jingo

Northern Lights

PHILIP PULLMAN
1946 –
Nationality: British
First Published: Scholastic Limited, 1995
Other Selected Titles:
The Subtle Knife
The Amber Spyglass
The Ruby in the Smoke
The Tiger in the Well
Thunderbolt's Waxwork
The Tin Princess
The Gasfitter's Ball
The Firework-Maker's Daughter

Philip Pullman.

This is the first in Pullman's His Dark Materials trilogy. *Northern Lights* is set in a parallel universe, with different technology and natural laws, where everyone is closely accompanied by a daemon, a manifestation of their soul, and the world is ruled by a strict church. Lyra Belacqua is a rebellious young girl who lives at Jordan College, Oxford. One evening, hidden in a wardrobe, she spies on her uncle, Lord Asriel, as he displays photographs of a mysterious substance called 'Dust' to the college's scholars.

Rumours abound among the children that a group of evil people called Gobblers is kidnapping children. When Lyra's friend Roger is taken by a woman with a golden monkey daemon, she decides to rescue him, but is persuaded by Mrs Coulter – who has a golden monkey daemon – to move in with her. Before she goes, the Master gives Lyra an alethiometer, a device that aids decision-making. Lyra's discovery that Mrs Coulter is the leader of the General Oblation Board of the church (the children's Gobblers) who are taking the kidnapped children to the far north leads her to escape and she meets up with her friends the Gyptians. They have also been losing children and agree with her to head north. But why is Mrs Coulter kidnapping children? The horrifying truth is revealed to Lyra in the course of her quest.

This exciting, and spellbinding story for older children has been seen as an attack on Christianity, but it is in fact a condemnation of dogma and the way it can lead people to do terrible things in the name of their religion. Lyra, unsure who she can trust, and betrayed by those who should love her the most, must not only save Roger and rescue Lord Asriel, but make decisions on which the fate of the universe rests.

Swallows and Amazons

The four Walker children – John, Titty, Susan and Roger – spend their summer holidays staying at a farm in the Lake District of northwest England. Borrowing a dinghy, *Swallow*, they spend their days sailing, fishing and exploring. Allowed by their parents to camp on an island near the farm, they are angered by the invasion of 'their' island by pirates, Nancy and Peggy Blackett, owners of another dinghy, the *Amazon*, who claim that the land is theirs. After lots of dastardly deeds on either side, including kidnapping and boat stealing, the two groups decide to join forces, especially against the terrifying ber-pirate, Captain Flint (in reality the Blacketts' uncle Jim), who ends up having to walk the plank from his own ship.

The background to the children's adventures is the lovely landscape of the lakes, of which Ransome paints lyrical images as he describes the farmland and such traditional crafts as charcoal-burning. The imaginative children rename all the towns and geographical features, so the local town becomes Rio and the island, Wild Cat Island, while grown-ups become natives.

While there is no complicated plot, what the author does do is to identify completely with the children and depict the world through their eyes so perfectly that readers can lose themselves in a vanished, innocent world where youngsters can be let loose, unfettered by concerns for their safety, and anyone with a healthy imagination can amuse themselves with no need for a television, computer games or structured play.

ARTHUR RANSOME
1884 – 1967
Nationality: British
First Published: Jonathan Cape, 1930
Other Selected Titles:
Swallowdale
Peter Duck
Winter Holiday
Coot Club
Pigeon Post
The Big Six
Missee Lee
The Picts And The Martyrs

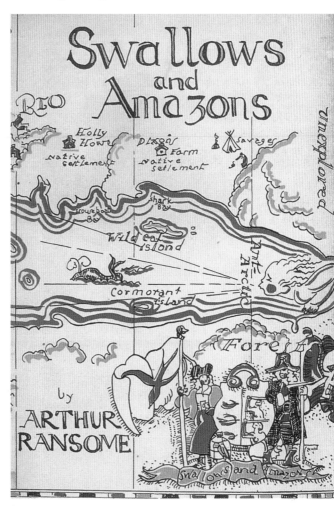

Jacob Two-Two Meets the Hooded Fang

MORDECAI RICHLER
1931 – 2001
Nationality: Canadian
First Published: McClelland & Stewart, 1975
Other Selected Titles:
Jacob Two-Two and the Dinosaur
Jacob Two-Two's First Spy Case

Jacob Two-Two is small and quiet, so he has to say everything twice just to be heard over his four brothers and sisters. Sent out on his first errand at the age of six (or 2+2+2, as he thinks of it), he asks the greengrocer for two pounds of firm red tomatoes twice, and the greengrocer thinks he's being insolent deliberately. Before Jacob Two-Two knows what has happened, he is up in court in front of the horrific Justice Rough, who

sends him to the children's prison in a castle on Slimer's Isle as a prisoner of the Hooded Fang. There, he and his fellow prisoners are put into a work gang to do such horrid labours as making rain for picnics and weeds to ruin swimming holes. Jacob manages to send a letter asking for help, but what form will his hoped-for rescue from the foggy, wolverine-infested island take?

This hilariously funny, action-packed book pokes fun at the hypocrisy of adults and is full of wacky settings, and jokes that will make children giggle, like the Hooded Fang (who thinks that he's mean but is actually warm-hearted and kind) crying for his mummy. Richler's straightforward, human story is vividly told, and his understanding of how children's logic works means that the plot is superb, with a great build-up of suspense as it leads up to a real swashbuckling rescue attempt.

Underlying this delightful story is a strong message about how every child should be equally loved, even if they can't do things that their older siblings can do, and that being little doesn't make you any less valued.

Harry Potter and the Philosopher's Stone

Ten-year-old Harry Potter is an orphan, who lives with his uncaring Aunt Petunia, loathsome Uncle Vernon and (worst of all) his spoiled cousin Dudley. Always in trouble for things that are not apparently his fault, condemned to a life of drudgery and forced to sleep under the stairs, Harry is astonished to receive a letter from the Hogwarts School of Witchcraft and Wizardry.

Before he can open the letter, Uncle Vernon takes it, but the house is soon plagued by letters and surrounded by owls. On Harry's 11th birthday, a giant called Rubeus Hagrid appears at their island hideaway with another copy of the letter. Harry rapidly finds that it is an offer of a place at Hogwarts, that he is a wizard himself and that he acquired the scar on his forehead in the fight when his parents were killed by 'you know who'. Hagrid deals with Uncle Vernon, and with Dudley, and soon Harry finds himself in the magical world of Hogwarts under the care of headmaster Albus Dumbledore.

Harry's eventful first year at the school – with its successes and failures, friendships and enmities, Quidditch matches and potions lessons – is overshadowed by dark thoughts of his parents' murder and the dawning knowledge that one day he may have to meet 'you know who' again. Harry's curiosity is destined to lead him and his friends into trouble, even danger, before they discover the truth about the mysterious Philosopher's Stone.

The enthralling start of Harry's journey towards coming to terms with his past and facing his future is peopled by believable characters with whom it is easy to identify. By turns funny, sad, mysterious and a bit scary, this is a compelling story for readers of all ages.

J.K. ROWLING
1965 –
Nationality: British
First Published: Bloomsbury, 1997
Other Selected Titles:
Harry Potter and the
Chamber of Secrets
Harry Potter and the Prisoner
of Azkaban
Harry Potter and the Goblet of Fire
Fantastic Beasts and Where
to Find Them
Quidditch Through the Ages
Harry Potter and the Order
of the Phoenix
Harry Potter and the
Half-Blood Prince

The King of the Golden River

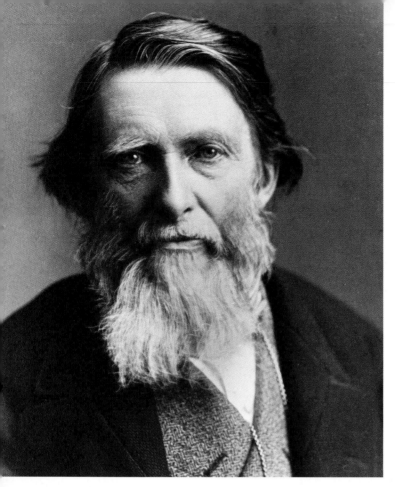

John Ruskin around 1900.

JOHN RUSKIN
1819 – 1900
Nationality: British
First Published: Smith Elder, 1851
Other Selected Titles:
The Two Paths
Unto This Last
Cestus of Aglaia
The Crown of Wild Olive
Time and Tide
The Queen of the Air
The Eagle's Nest
Love's Meinie

Schwartz, Hans and Gluck are three brothers who live on a farm in a beautiful valley, at the head of which is a waterfall so high that it remains glowing in the sunlight after sunset, so it is known as the golden river. The valley is blessed with an ideal climate because of the benign south west winds.

One wet day, Gluck hears a knock at the door, and reluctantly (because he knows his evil, mean brother will beat him) lets a curious-looking old man dry off near the fire. His brothers return and turn the old man out rudely; he threatens that he'll return that night, for the last time. At midnight, he blows off half the roof of the house, and floods the house and the valley, washing all the precious soil away. He leaves a calling card, inscribed 'South West Wind, Esquire'. The wind makes good his threat and no more south west winds come, so the valley becomes a desert.

Schwartz and Hans decide to melt down their gold into spoons to make money. The last bit of gold is an heirloom of Gluck's, a mug with a face at the bottom. Gluck is desolate, but the King of the Golden River, who had been imprisoned in the mug, appears in the furnace. He tells Gluck that anyone who drops three drops of holy water into the cataract at the top of the mountain will restore his fortune, but unholy water would turn him into black stone.

One by one the three brothers make the arduous journey across the glacier to the top of the mountain. Will any of them succeed? Set in the Alps that Ruskin loved, this charming tale illustrates the triumph of kindness and goodness over evil.

The Little Prince

In this enchanting, allegorical tale, the narrator finds himself trying to mend his crashed aeroplane in the Sahara Desert when he is interrupted by a small boy who asks him to draw a sheep. Although taken aback, he does so and thus begins a series of conversations between himself and the Little Prince. The latter explains that he travels through the universe from asteroid to asteroid, each populated by only one inhabitant.

ANTOINE DE SAINT-EXUPERY
1900 – 1944
Nationality: French
First Published: William Heinemann,
1944 (first English translation)
Other Selected Titles:
Southern Mail
Night Flight
Wind, Sand and Stars
Flight to Arras
Letter to a Hostage
The Wisdom of the Sands

As well as being a lovely, poetical story that children adore because it depicts the world from their point of view, it is a criticism of the absurdities of adults. Each grown-up the Little Prince meets, whether a businessman, a lamplighter or geographer, embodies a flaw possessed by adults, such as greed, or pursuing futile, meaningless tasks. The Little Prince also encounters a fox, who asks to be tamed, and from him the prince learns that responsibilities should not be assumed without thought because once started, they have to be seen through.

Saint-Exupéry believed firmly that children see the important things in life – such as the bonds of friendship and responsibility – more clearly than adults do because they see with their hearts not just with their eyes. Children see with awe what adults look at with cynicism and in the conversations between the pilot and the Little Prince the former is reminded of what childhood was like. By the end of the book he has been changed totally by the encounter. Younger children love this gentle story, while older readers will be touched by its meaning.

The Human Comedy

WILLIAM SAROYAN
1908 – 1981
Nationality: American
First Published: Harcourt Brace &
Co., 1943
Other Selected Titles:
*The Daring Young Man On the
Flying Trapeze
Tracy's Tiger
The Summer of the Beautiful
White Horse
My Name Is Aram*

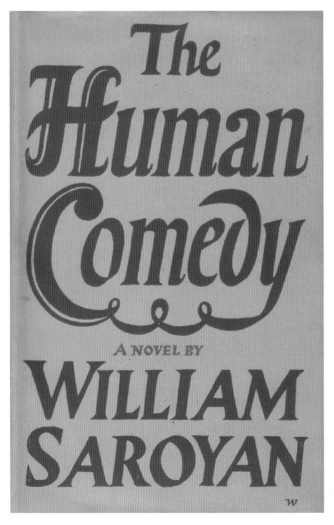

Set in a fruit- and wine-growing area of California (based on his own home town of Fresno), Saroyan's exploration of the struggles of day-to-day family life for those left at home during World War Two was written to bring a note of hope. Homer Macauley is a 14-year-old boy who lives with his mother, his older sister, Bess, and his four-year-old brother, Ulysses. Their father is dead and the older brother, Marcus, is about to embark for war. Although he should still be in school, Homer takes a job as a telegram delivery boy because he feels that he now should assume responsibility for the family.

This job brings him into contact with the naked emotions of love and pain, as among the telegrams he delivers are those from the War Department telling people he knows that their sons are missing in action or dead, which he finds difficult to cope with.

The story is told from the viewpoint of different characters in turn, as each deals with and surmounts the hardships of the time. Although the novel is bittersweet and poignant, just as in reality, there are lighter moments, such as when the adorable Ulysses has to be rescued from a humane animal trap. As the reader follows Homer's early, sometimes painful, journey towards adulthood, the author emphasizes the need for the simple human truths – love, faith, dreams, compassion and the importance of family bonds.

The bittersweet ending holds the lesson that no matter what tragedy strikes, there is always hope and life does go on. Although Homer's world is completely different to that lived by most children his age today, they can still identify with his growing pains and absorb values from this heart-warming story.

The Misfortunes of Sophie

Four-year-old Sophie lives in a large chateau in the French countryside with her parents and her cousin Paul. She is a lively, adventurous little girl who repeatedly gets into trouble for her misbehaviour. She never intends to be bad, but like many children, she never thinks about the consequences of her actions for either herself or other people.

A loving child, Sophie wishes to care for her beautiful wax doll, but the poor thing ends up blind, bald, footless, with a broken arm and finally, headless. Each time she is remorseful about her faults and promises not to do it again, but then quickly manages to get into trouble a different way.

Other misdeeds include cutting up her mother's goldfish and putting salt on them, a crime to which she confesses when she sees that Simon the servant will lose his job; cutting up a bee, for which her mother takes away her knife and makes her wear the bee's remains on a ribbon round her neck as punishment; and scratching Paul, which she admits to out of a sense of guilt.

Mme de Ségur wrote this story for her own grandchildren, and it contains strong moral lessons. When she does not admit to her mistakes, Sophie is punished, but when she owns up and says she is sorry, her mother is gentler with her.

However, the sheer silliness of Sophie's misdeeds, her lively character and her overblown squabbles with her cousin Paul make this book a true delight to read.

Comtesse de Ségur
LES MALHEURS DE SOPHIE

COMTESSE DE SEGUR
1799 – 1874
Nationality: French
First Published: D.C. Heath & Co., 1901 (first English translation)
Other Selected Titles:
Inn of the Guardian Angel
Adventures of a Donkey
Dream Drops
Old French Fairy Tales
Happy Surprises

Where the Wild Things Are

MAURICE SENDAK
1928 –
Nationality: American
First Published: Harper & Row, 1963
Other Selected Titles:
Kenny's Window
Very Far Away
The Sign on Rosie's Door
Seven Little Monsters
Outside Over There
Dear Mili
In the Night Kitchen
The Nutshell Library

Max is naughty, ignoring rules and chasing the dog with his fork, and when he is cheeky to his mother, she calls him a 'wild thing' and sends him to bed with no supper to learn his lesson. Dressed in his favourite wolf suit, Max is in such a rage that as his bedroom starts to turn into a jungle and the walls dissolve, he makes for a sailing boat on the edge of the ocean.

He sails for more than a year to the land where the wild things are: huge monsters with claws, fangs and big scary eyes. But Max is not frightened of anything, not even wild things, and he stares them down and orders them to 'Be still'. The wild things agree that he is the wildest of all of them, so they make him their king and give him a crown and sceptre. Max decrees 'Let the rumpus begin', and he and the wild things dance in the moonlight, hang from the trees and generally run riot, until Max realizes he misses his mother's love and wants to go home.

Despite what some critics said when it was first published, the book is not encouraging young children to be naughty, but shows them that even if they sometimes want to be wild things, a home with loving discipline is the best place to be.

On a practical level the book helps to explain the purpose of 'time out', assists children with anger management, teaches them to channel their tempers creatively and come to terms with who they are. Above all, Max's adventurous in this enthralling story show that a child's imagination is a wonderful thing as it can take them anywhere they want to go.

50

And To Think That I Saw It On Mulberry Street

The first of Dr Seuss' books for children is less fantastical than some of the more famous ones from later years, but it is still thoroughly enjoyable. Marco, a small boy who has an over-active imagination, has been set a task by his father – to tell him truthfully what he sees on Mulberry Street on his way to and from school. As his father puts it: 'Your eye's much too keen. Stop telling such outlandish tales. Stop turning minnows into whales.' One day, all he sees is a horse and a broken-down wagon, which he thinks is boring, and soon his imagination is working overtime. Wouldn't it be more fun if the horse was a zebra and the wagon was in fact a beautiful chariot?

Bit by bit, his wild flights of fancy lead him to such unlikely sights as an elephant pulling a brass band, reindeer, Eskimos, a Chinese boy eating with sticks and planes dropping confetti. Dr Seuss' trademark rhyming and meter are already fully formed in this book: he developed the idea for the format while listening to the engine of an ocean liner.

The simple rhymes make this a great book for children to read along with, and the silly situations and ideas that Marco dreams up will have them in giggles. Dr Seuss here is encouraging children to think creatively, while retaining the ability to tell the difference between reality and imagination. But he also wants their parents to allow them to enjoy the magic of being a child.

**DR SEUSS
(THEODOR SEUSS GEISEL)**
1904 – 1991
Nationality: American
First Published: The Vanguard Press, 1937
Other Selected Titles:
*How the Grinch Stole Christmas!
The 500 Hats of Bartholomew Cubbins
The King's Stilts
The Seven Lady Godivas
Horton Hatches the Egg
McElligot's Pool
Thidwick the Big-Hearted Moose
Bartholomew and the Oobleck*

Black Beauty

ANNA SEWELL
1820 – 1878
Nationality: British
First Published: Jarrold's, 1877

Originally written to educate people who worked with horses in animal welfare, this book quickly became a children's classic. It is the autobiography of a horse, from his earliest memories of being taught by his mother to be good and kind, to his eventual retirement.

In the 19th century, animals were given no respect, and were badly mistreated. At first petted as a young lady's carriage horse, after he nearly dies through the ignorance of a young man and is too badly scarred to stay in that job, Beauty is sold on to work as a cab horse in London: back breaking work for a cruel master.

Unsentimental in her attitude to horses, Sewell portrays their treatment at the hands of humans with a clear eye. A particular hatred of hers was the 'bearing rein', which held a horse's head up at an unnatural, cruelly painful angle. *Black Beauty* was instrumental in the abolition of this monstrosity and in improving animal welfare in general in Britain at the time.

Each part of the book holds different trials for the horses and different lessons for the reader on kindness, humanity and respect, which it is easy to transfer to how to treat humans as well. Beauty's goodness and patience are in stark contrast to his friend Ginger's wilfulness and temper and their differing fortunes hold morals on behaviour and obedience.

The author's real understanding of horses allows her to give Beauty such qualities as bravery and loyalty while avoiding the slushiness of so many other books that anthropomorphize animals. It is a beautiful, moving, at times harrowing, story that all children, not just pony-mad little girls, can enjoy.

The Golem

The golem is a creature out of ancient Yiddish legend. Formed from clay and imbued with almost limitless power through cabalistic ritual, it is virtually indestructible. It is sent, or summoned, to help the Jewish people in time of their direst need.

One such time of need is in the Czechoslovak capital, Prague, during the late 1930s and early 1940s. The golem is sent to help Rabbi Reb Lieb. Lieb, who is in a fair amount of trouble, decides to use the golem's power for his own ends, an action that he has specifically been warned against. This attempted misuse of power breaks his control over the golem and it starts to disobey him.

The immensely strong being has no emotional maturity and rampages around in a manner reminiscent of a thwarted, overgrown two-year-old. Eventually, it ends up in the service of the Emperor. Singer's retelling of the classic legend does nothing to hide the obscenity of the persecution of Jewish people in eastern Europe before the Second World War, or the absurdity of the accusations thrown at them. This means the book is best reserved for older children with some awareness of what went on. Singer uses the story to explore the idea of what it is to be human, to be vulnerable and mortal, and to ask questions about the nature of absolute power and the limits to what can be done to preserve peace.

In this ultimately tragic modern retelling, there are notes of irony, ludicrousness and the downright grotesque, but it is told with such wisdom, warmth and humour that the ideas it contains stay in the memory and the heart.

Isaac Bashevis Singer in 1978.

ISAAC BASHEVIS SINGER
1904 – 1991
Nationality: Polish-American
First Published: Farrar, Straus & Giroux, 1982
Other Selected Titles:
The Topsy-Turvy Emperor of China
The Wicked City
Naftali and the Storyteller and His Horse, Sus Shosha
A Young Man in Search of Love
The Penitent
Yentl the Yeshiva Boy
Why Noah Chose the Dove

JOHANNA SPYRI

JOHANNA SPYRI
1827 – 1901
Nationality: Swiss
First Published: T.Y. Crowell, 1902
(first English translation)
Other Selected Titles:
Moni the Goat Boy and Other Stories
Rose Child
What Sami Sings with the Birds
Little Miss Grasshopper
Tiss, a Little Alpine Waif
Vinzi, a Story of the Swiss Alps
Dora
Critli's Children

Heidi

Orphaned as a baby, Heidi lives with her Aunt Dete, but when the latter gets a new job that means she can no longer keep the little girl, she is only too happy to dump her on her reclusive, grumpy old grandfather, a goatherd who lives high in the Swiss Alps. Despite the worries of everyone in the village about leaving the girl there, the odd couple – after some initial reluctance on grandfather's part – are happy together.

Away from her aunt's oppression, the little girl's spirits soar and her goodness and faith soften the old man's heart. Playing with the goats and Peter the goatherd, and sleeping nestled in the hayloft in her grandfather's cabin, Heidi is happier than she has ever been.

But then Dete reappears and persuades Grandfather that the position she has found Heidi in Frankfurt as a companion to a wheelchair-bound girl, Clara, is for her own good and will help her to get on in life. Although Heidi learns to love Clara, the servants – particularly the cold-hearted, stern Fraulein Rottenmaier – make her unhappy and she desperately misses the mountains, until a friendly doctor realizes the cause of her sleep-walking and intervenes.

This is a heart-warming tale, set in the stunning landscape of the high Alps. The vivid descriptions of the mountain pastures, Grandfather's cabin and Heidi's simple life are some of the most evocative ever written. Like many writers of the time, Spyri believed in letting children be children, away from the restraints of adult rules and expresses this in the events that necessitate Heidi's return to the mountains and Clara's astonishing recovery.

Treasure Island

Although not the first book about pirates, *Treasure Island* is counted by many people as being the best, and introduced to a broad audience such indispensable concepts as one-legged seamen, black-sailed ships, the black spot, parrots yelling 'pieces of eight', and 15 men on the dead man's chest singing 'Yo ho ho and a bottle of rum'.

In the book, Jim Hawkins helps his father to run the Admiral Benbow, an inn near Bristol. One day, a desperate-looking ruffian, Billy Bones, appears cursing people and demanding drink. When he suffers a stroke, they have no choice but to allow him to stay. They cannot keep him away from the rum and while drunk he tells Jim that he is a pirate and he has a treasure map but is in danger from other pirates. When the blind pirate, Pew, catches up with him and tips him the black spot, he suffers a second stroke and dies. Jim retrieves Bones' map before the pirates and takes it to Dr Livesey and Squire Trelawny. The three decide to mount an expedition to Skeleton Island to find the treasure. Sadly, they are fooled into hiring some of Billy's former shipmates among their crew.

What follows is a rip-roaring tale of mutiny, treachery, sword-fights and murder as Jim, Dr Livesey and the squire are forced to live on their wits in order to survive against ruthless enemies.

Stevenson's text, in such episodes as Jim and his mother listening to Pew's stick tap-tapping the ground as he approaches the inn, or Jim's terror when he is first grabbed by Ben Gunn, is so vivid that the reader is transported there with them.

ROBERT LOUIS STEVENSON
1850 – 1894
Nationality: Scottish
First Published: Cassel & Co., 1883
Other Selected Titles:
The New Arabian Nights
Prince Otto
Kidnapped
The Strange Case of Dr. Jekyll and Mr. Hyde
The Black Arrow: A Tale of the Two Roses
The Master of Ballantrae
The Wrong Box
Catriona

The Fellowship of the Ring

J.R.R. TOLKIEN
1892 – 1973
Nationality: British
First Published: George Allen &
Unwin, 1954
Other Selected Titles:
The Two Towers
The Return of the King
The Hobbit, or There and Back Again
Farmer Giles of Ham
The Homecoming of Beorhtnoth
The Adventures of Tom Bombadil
Tree and Leaf
Smith of Wootton Major

The first book in the trilogy that forms The Lord of the Rings begins in the Shire, where the lovable Hobbit, Bilbo Baggins, is having his eleventy-first birthday. When he slips on the ring that makes him invisible in order to escape from his guests, neither he nor they realize that it is calling the dark forces of Lord Sauron to their peaceful land. He departs from the Shire that night, leaving his home and the ring (the latter somewhat reluctantly) to his nephew Frodo.

Years later, Gandalf the wizard reappears, troubled about the long-lasting effects of the ring on Bilbo, and shocks Frodo by throwing it in the fire. There, his worst fears are confirmed: on it is written two lines of a verse '*One Ring to rule them all, One Ring to find them, One Ring to bring them all and in the darkness bind them*'. Frodo's is the most powerful of the 20 rings that Sauron created in order to gain domination over the world and he must travel to the heart of Sauron's empire in order to destroy it.

So begins Frodo's quest, as he and his friends flee the evil Ringwraiths, being joined by other members of the fellowship on the way, until there are nine of them to balance the nine wraiths and represent all the free races: hobbits Frodo, Merry, Sam and Pippin, humans Aragorn and Boromir, Legolas the elf, Gimli the Dwarf and Gandalf.

Their perilous quest leads them over and under mountains and into fights with creatures of evil until the ring's power begins to corrupt other members of the Fellowship and Frodo and Sam decide to strike out on their own. This epic adventure and its sequels form one of the classics of English literature.

Mary Poppins

The Bank children – Jane and Michael, and twin babies John and Barbara – live at 17 Cherry Tree Lane with their parents. When their nanny leaves, her replacement arrives from the clouds one evening borne on the east wind on a parrot-headed umbrella. What follows is a series of magical adventures, some exciting, some just plain silly: from flying round the Earth in a minute to having tea bouncing round on the ceiling.

The Mary Poppins of the book is not like Julie Andrews in the Disney version: she's vain and sometimes irritable and very unlikely to sweeten medicine with a spoonful of sugar. But she is also magical, and within her stern exterior lurks all kinds of delightful nonsense. She can slide up banisters, float in the air, step into pictures, stick stars on the sky, talk to animals and make cows dance. However, Mary also firmly believes in good behaviour: disobedience causes nasty results, including one of the children being turned into the decoration on a plate.

However, the children adore her: she is not distant and neglectful like their parents; they know that she will not let them down; they feel safe within the caring discipline that she brings to their lives and she is exciting to be with. When Mary's birthday coincides with a full Moon, the children dream that they visit the zoo and the cages are full of people while the animals wander around looking at them – to adults an absurd idea, but one that children will enjoy. Australian writer P.L. Travers' sly mocking of the way the British middle classes brought up their children is as appealing today as when it was first written.

Written more than 70 years ago, the book's attitude towards black, oriental and Inuit people is appalling; some modern versions have had the offending section (part of Bad Tuesday) removed, but it will still be found in older editions.

P.L. TRAVERS
1899 – 1996
Nationality: Australian
First Published: Reynal & Hitchcock, 1934
Other Selected Titles:
Mary Poppins Comes Back
Mary Poppins Opens the Door
Mary Poppins in the Park
Mary Poppins From A to Z
Mary Poppins in the Kitchen
Mary Poppins in Cherry Tree Lane
Mary Poppins and the House Next Door

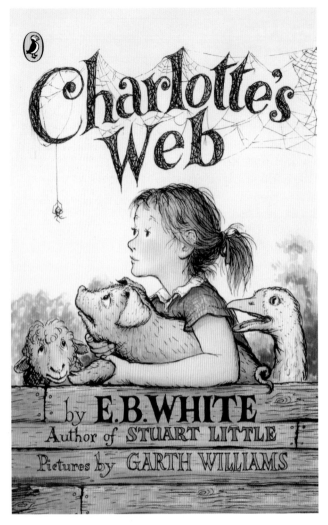

E.B. WHITE
1899 – 1985
Nationality: American
First Published: H. Hamilton, 1952
Other Selected Titles:
Stuart Little
The Trumpet of the Swan

Charlotte's Web

Fern Arable is devastated when she hears that her father's pig's new litter has a runt and that as it is not worth saving her father is going to kill it. Persuading him that the piglet has a right to life and promising to look after it, she saves it and calls it Wilbur.

When Wilbur becomes too large, Fern is forced to sell him to her uncle, Homer Zuckerman, where he will one day meet the fate of all farm pigs. When he discovers this, Wilbur is distraught, and sits in the corner crying, 'I don't want to die,' so Charlotte – the big, hairy orb-web spider who lives in the rafters above his sty – decides to help him.

With the help of Templeton the sneaky rat, and some of the other animals in the barn, she writes a message in her web: 'Some Pig'. Soon people from miles around are visiting to see this strange phenomenon, and the pig that inspired it. But will the messages work?

The book contains several messages. For example, Fern's caring for Wilbur teaches her responsibility, and she realizes that if she stands up for what she believes in she can make a difference in the world. Charlotte and Wilbur's friendship, despite their differences in nature, teaches tolerance. As he grows up, like any child Wilbur learns to cope with fear, loss and loneliness. However, and as importantly, this life and death story is full of warmth, with silly characters such as the geese and the snobby sheep and a wealth of detail on creepy-crawly spiders which will delight children.

The Sword in the Stone

This is the first book of the tetralogy that forms *The Once and Future King*, reinterpreting Thomas Malory's *Le Morte d'Arthur*. The classic version of the legend of King Arthur, *The Sword in the Stone* tells of Arthur's childhood hidden far from view of his enemies. While out hunting with Kay, Sir Ector's ward Wart (Arthur) encounters a strange old man called Merlyn, who becomes the boys' tutor. Soon Arthur is involved in an amazing series of adventures, being turned into a fish, an owl, an ant, a badger and a hawk so that he can experience life from different points of view. He also encounters Robin Wood and his Merry Men, gets captured by a giant, meets King Pellinore and his Questing Beast, rescues Friar Tuck and attends a meeting of trees. He also shares a more conventional education with Kay, learning hunting, jousting and falconry.

All of these experiences are designed to prepare Wart for his destiny, although he has no idea what that might be. This is pure fantasy, in a world that is a mixture of medieval and 20th-century England, where Merlyn lives backwards in time, animals talk and mustard pots have legs. White's story is peopled with memorable characters, including Wart himself, the eternally worried Sir Ector, the continually-confused and occasionally tetchy Merlyn and Archimedes the talking owl.

The children's exciting adventures, set in a world of medieval pageantry, allows the reader's imagination to take flight and remains a perennial favourite.

T.H. WHITE
1906 – 1964
Nationality: British
First Published: Collins, 1938
Other Selected Titles:
The Queen of Air and Darkness,
originally entitled *The Witch in the Wood*
The Ill-Made Knight
The Candle in the Wind
The Book of Merlyn

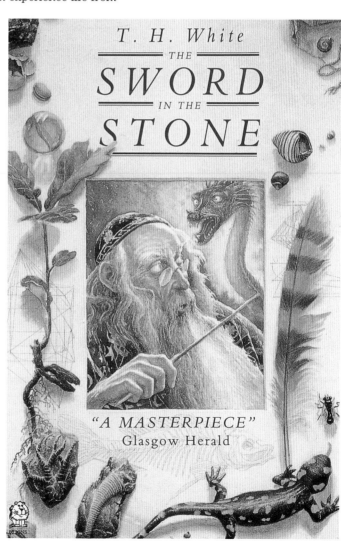

T. H. White
THE
SWORD
IN THE
STONE

"A MASTERPIECE"
Glasgow Herald

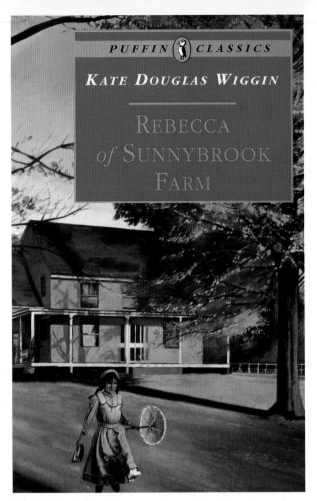

KATE DOUGLAS WIGGIN
1856 – 1923
Nationality: American
First Published: Houghton Mifflin,
1903
Other Selected Titles:
The Story of Patsy
The Birds' Christmas Carol
A Summer in a Canyon
Polly Oliver's Problem
The Village Watch-Tower
Penelope's Irish Experiences
The Diary of a Goose Girl
New Chronicles of Rebecca

Rebecca of Sunnybrook Farm

In order to help her mother (a widow with seven children) Hannah Randall's aunts offer to take her in, but Mrs Randall asks them to take the younger Rebecca instead. At the age of ten she moves from Sunnybrook Farm to their austere townhouse in Riverboro, Maine. Although she tries to be good, it seems that Aunt Miranda disapproves of her, although Aunt Jane is much more kind-hearted.

It is clear from the author's first description of her that Rebecca is an unusual child. She is bright, energetic and loving, and she has a very vivid imagination and a great flair for the dramatic. At first she is deeply unhappy in her new life and contemplates running away from her aunts, but gradually she settles into her new surroundings, learning to do her chores better and not answering back.

Whether she is charming the neighbours into buying soap to get the Simpsons a lamp, throwing her beloved parasol down the well in a fit of remorseful self-sacrifice, inviting missionaries to stay without her aunts' knowledge or borrowing a baby for Sunday, her aunts can never tell what mischief Rebecca will get herself into next.

Rebecca's special brand of magic works on most of the people of Riverboro, bringing joy and purpose to Aunt Jane's life and friendship to others such as Mr Ladd, a local boy made good.

The book traces the following seven years of Rebecca's life, with all its joys, sorrows and hardships, to her graduation from school and beyond as the sparky little girl grows into a loving and dutiful young woman.

The Happy Prince and Other Tales

As well as the title story, this short collection includes *The Nightingale and the Rose*, *The Selfish Giant*, *The Devoted Friend* and *The Remarkable Rocket*, which Wilde made up for his own children. Each contains a different moral, and despite the wit and humour he uses, they are in places very moving and sad. The happy prince is a decorated golden statue of the former ruler of a city, who persuades a swallow to remain in the cold north while he gives away his jewels and gold leaf to the poor of the city. When he was alive the prince was happy, but knew nothing of the suffering of the poorer people, but is now unhappy because he does see it.

The hard-hearted selfish giant excludes everyone else from his garden, so nature herself turns from him, Spring forgets to visit the garden and it remains locked in winter until he mends his ways because of a little boy and is redeemed. *The Remarkable Rocket* is a caution against arrogance and pride, couched in a very silly tale about a firework who is so puffed up in his own importance that he thinks the prince is marrying a princess just to honour him.

Wilde's use of language in these simple tales with deep meanings is brilliantly evocative and paints vivid pictures, whether he is describing the song of the Nightingale as she sacrifices herself to give the student a red rose, or Hail rattling on the roof of the castle for three hours until he broke most of the slates.

OSCAR WILDE
1854 – 1900
Nationality: Irish
First Published: David Nutt, 1888
Other Selected Titles:
The Canterville Ghost
The Happy Prince and Other Stories
The Portrait of Mr. W.H.
Lord Arthur Saville's Crime and Other Stories
Intentions
The Picture of Dorian Gray
House of Pomegranates
De Profundis

An illustration from The Selfish Giant.

CLASSIC FICTION

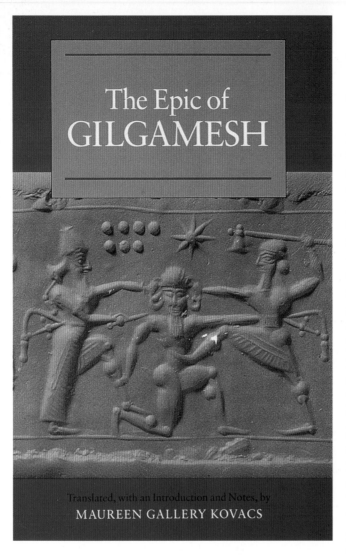

The Epic of
GILGAMESH

Translated, with an Introduction and Notes, by
MAUREEN GALLERY KOVACS

ANON
circa 2100 BCE
Iraq (Mesopotamia)

The Epic of Gilgamesh

The Epic of Gilgamesh tells the moving story of a King of Uruk from around 2700 BCE. The themes of the epic are common among other Babylonian and Sumerian poetry, namely that of a man who must suffer mortality as punishment for disobeying the gods. In the poem, Gilgamesh is pitted against the wild man Enkidu, who is outraged at the selfish and sexual excesses of Gilgamesh. They meet and fight for so long that they call a draw, becoming friends. On an adventure stealing cedar wood from a forbidden forest, the two meet the demon Humbaba, whom they kill. The goddess of sex, Ishtar, is overcome with corporeal desire for Gilgamesh who rejects her. For their transgressions, the gods decide that Enkidu must die. Terrified by his own death, Gilgamesh seeks out Utanapishtim who was granted immortality by the gods after surviving the flood. Gilgamesh finds the plant that will give him immortality but a serpent steals it from him. Gilgamesh returns to Uruk in the sanguine knowledge that he will die, but also knowing that humankind will live. The city that he had built and come to hate, he now sees as the closest thing to immortality that he will achieve.

Gilgamesh caused quite a stir when it was first discovered in Ottoman Iraq and translated in 1872, as the poem contains a number of Biblical stories that exist here about 1500 years before the book of Genesis was written. It is also humanity's oldest work of literature. Four translations of the poem are currently in print.

The Thousand and One Nights

The Thousand and One Nights comprises a series of folktales which were compiled from a variety of sources, the most common being Hazâr Afsâna, or the *Thousand Myths*. Around the 1300s, an ingenious framework for the stories was added: Scheherazade.

King Shahyar, disgusted by his wife's infidelity, has her executed. Convinced of the innate unfaithfulness of all women, he instructs his advisor to bring a new bride to him each night – the following morning they are also put to death. The advisor's daughter, Scheherazade, has an ingenious idea: becoming Queen Scheherazade, she entertains her new husband with a story, but at dawn she breaks off the narrative at a crucial point, to be continued the following evening and thereby stalling her execution.

Although the tales are lively and inventive, what is so astonishing about *The Thousand and One Nights* is the web of narrative that Scheherazade weaves, often telling several stories concurrently. The collection contains stories which have become commonplace: A*li Baba and the Forty Thieves*, *Sinbad the Sailor*, and *Aladdin*. It was first translated into English in 1835, and more famously so in 1884 by Sir Richard Francis Burton who did not censor the sometimes sexually explicit subject matter (he had translated the Kama Sutra the year before).

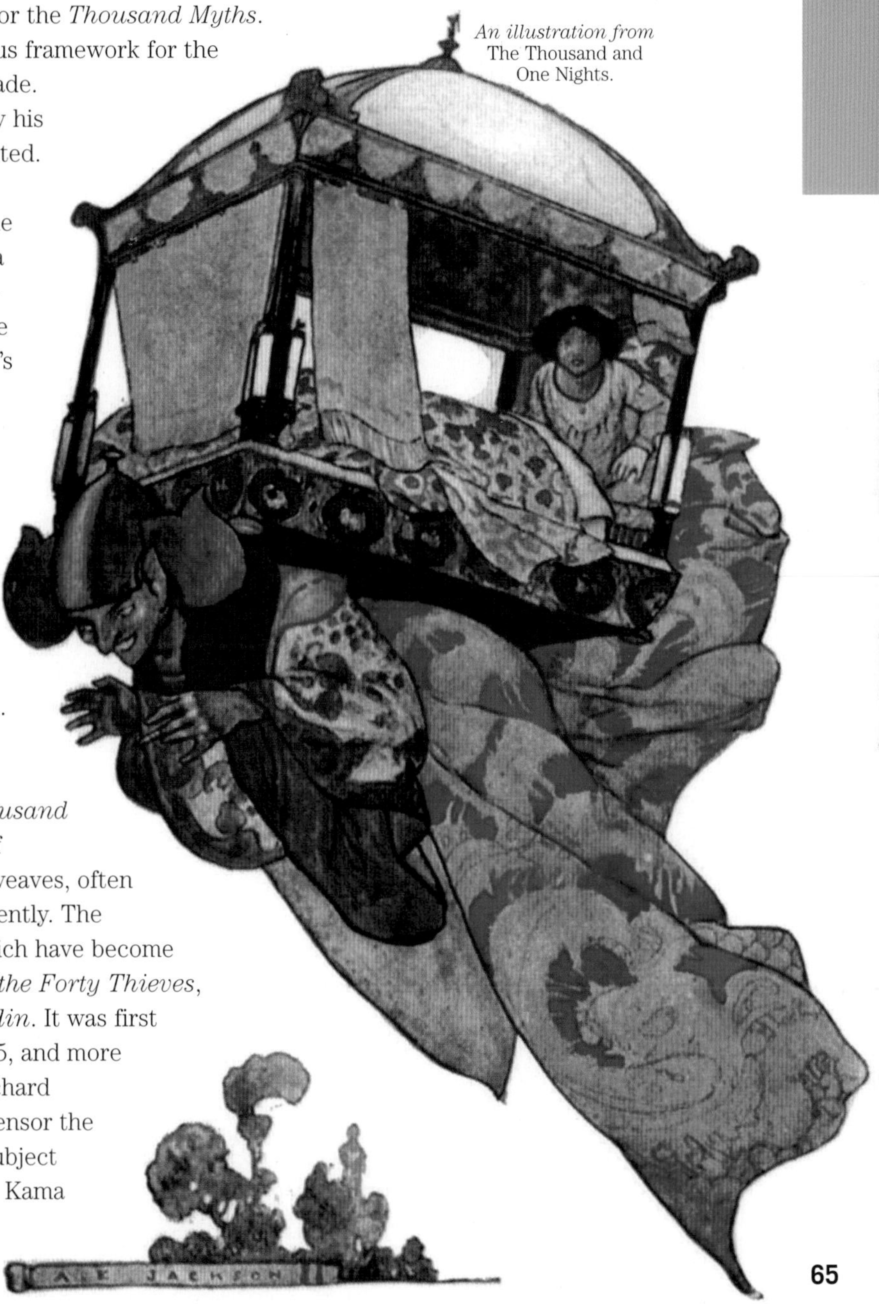

ANON
circa 900 – 1300 CE
Persia

An illustration from The Thousand and One Nights.

65

Sense and Sensibility

JANE AUSTEN
1775 – 1817
Nationality: British
First Published: T. Eggerton, 1811
Other Selected Titles:
Pride and Prejudice
Mansfield Park
Emma
Northanger Abbey
Persuasion

Jane Austen's *Sense and Sensibility* tells the story of two sisters, Elinor and Marianne Dashwood. On his death their father leaves them, their younger sister and their mother without a house, as it has been bequeathed to their stepbrother, John. Although instructed to take good care of his sisters, John is dissuaded of his duty by his wife. The family moves to Devonshire shortly after Elinor and Edward Ferrers have become attracted to one another.

In Devonshire, Marianne meets the dashing and unprincipled John Willoughby. Both men seem ideal suitors for the very different characters of the two women, but both men have secrets.

The novel had a long period of gestation. It was initially begun in 1795–6 as a sketch entitled *Elinor and Marianne* and was significantly revised by Austen in 1809. It was her first published novel, and in it are all the trademarks of her fiction that was to follow: insightful observation, astute characterization and dazzling wit.

Sense and Sensibility was filmed in 1995 by the Taiwanese director, Ang Lee. Emma Thompson won an Oscar for Best Adapted Screenplay.

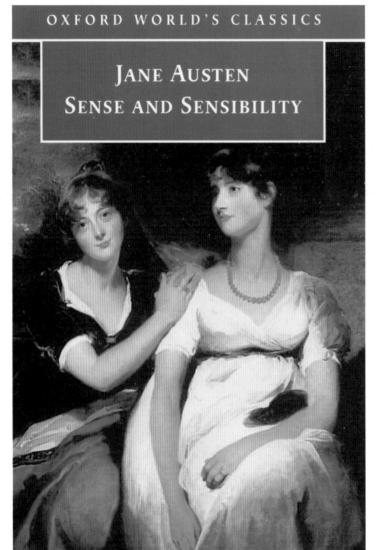

OXFORD WORLD'S CLASSICS

JANE AUSTEN
SENSE AND SENSIBILITY

Old Goriot

Balzac was an incredibly prolific writer; Old Goriot is the 41st of some 94 novels and collections of short stories that he completed before his death in 1850. Perhaps his best-known novel, *Old Goriot* was first published in serial form and is part of Balzac's immense Comédie Humaine.

It recounts the stories of Old Goriot and his relationships with the wanton daughters that he loves far too dearly, given their unpleasantnesses. When the young country lad, Eugene, finds rooms at a run-down boarding house, and meets two beautiful women who mysteriously visit his fellow lodger Old Goriot, he senses an opportunity to better himself socially and financially. But in the modern city, things are not always as they appear. It is a place where those unaware of the risks of temptation will find only a tragic end. Like much of Balzac's fiction, it is a story of obsession, love, hate and greed; it is drama on a grand scale that tells an exceptionally modern story of a man's ambition to make his way in the big city.

HONORÉ DE BALZAC
1799 – 1850
Nationality: French
First Published: Werclet, 1834–5
Other Selected Titles:
Les Chouans
La Rabouilleuse
Eugénie Grandet
La Cousine Bette

An illustration of old Goriot.

Vathek: an Arabian Tale

WILLIAM BECKFORD
1760 – 1844
Nationality: British
First Published: J. Johnson, 1786

Beckford's *Vathek* is a splendid hybrid of the Gothic and Orientalist traditions that were in fashion at the end of the 18th century. The novel recounts the adventures of the Caliph Vathek, who can kill with a glance.

Corrupted by a desire for power, he becomes a servant of Eblis (the Devil), committing terrible sacrifices to him. On a journey to see the treasures of the pre-Adamite sultans, he meets and falls in love with Nouronihar.

He eventually gains access to the treasures of Eblis, but sees only their worthlessness. The price that Vathek must pay for committing his many sins provides the novel with its terrifying and tremendously infernal conclusion.

William Beckford wrote Vathek *when he was just 21 years of age.*

The novel's sheer inventiveness, eccentricity and sumptuosity have made it an enduring classic of what is often deemed to be a minor genre. Sources that reference the dates of publication for the novel often disagree because of the scandal that surrounded its first release.

Beckford, a talented linguist, had first written the novel in French, but his translator, Samuel Henley, managed to release the English version first, and also claimed authorship of it – both Beckford and Henley are thought to have written incorrect dates on their manuscripts.

Lady Audley's Secret

What is Lady Audley's secret? Critics have been unable to satisfactorily answer this question since the publication of this weirdly wonderful adventure. Lady Audley is the bigamous wife of George Talboys, who abandons her and leaves for Australia. Consequently, she fakes her death and remarries. George returns and is promptly pushed down a well. Robert Audley, the inquisitive nephew of Lady Audley's husband is nearly killed in a deliberate fire at his lodgings. Lady Audley's secrets (namely murder and bigamy) are brought to light, and she is diagnosed with congenital insanity.

Critics, such as Elaine Showalter, though, have convincingly argued that Lady Audley's secret is that she is sane and her actions are those of a woman who is trapped and made a victim of her society.

The novel is a prime example of the Sensation fiction genre, which was renowned for its ability to titillate, shock and sometimes terrify its audience. Like its fellow Sensation shockers, critics and moralists hated this novel when it was published, but in the 1860s the public could not get enough of them. The Sensation genre, however, all but petered out after a decade in the spotlight.

The book was a runaway success for the young novelist, not only for its extremely effective plotting, but for the antics of its unforgettable villain that one can't help but cautiously cheer on.

MARY ELIZABETH BRADDON
1835 – 1915
Nationality: British
First Published: Thomas Hailes Lacy, 1861–2
Other Selected Titles:
Aurora Floyd
The Doctor's Wife

PENGUIN CLASSICS

MARY ELIZABETH BRADDON

Lady Audley's Secret

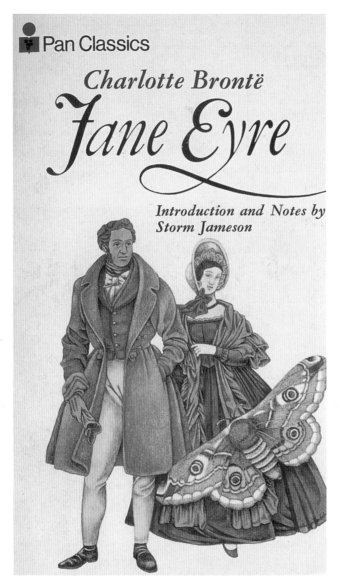

Pan Classics

Charlotte Brontë

Jane Eyre

Introduction and Notes by Storm Jameson

CHARLOTTE BRONTË
1816 – 1855
Nationality: British
First Published: Smith, Elder & Co., 1847
Other Selected Titles:
The Professor
Shirley
Villette

Jane Eyre ✓

This novel is a *bildungsroman* written by the fictional Jane Eyre. Born an orphan and brought up by a family uninterested in her well-being, Jane Eyre is sent off to the austere Loxwood School, where she is again unsympathetically treated by those into whose care she is entrusted. Although Jane's defiance is often roused at the school, she does find comfort in the friends she makes there. In early adulthood, she finds work as a governess at Thornfield Hall, where she meets her dashing and Byronic employer, Mr Rochester.

They fall in love and agree to marry. On their wedding day, Jane discovers Rochester already has a wife, a madwoman kept in the attic, explaining the strange noises Jane has been hearing. Jane flees from Thornfield.

She is taken in by some newly-discovered cousins and learns that she has inherited, and has become financially independent. Just before she leaves England to become a missionary with her cousin, she hears a mesmeric appeal from Rochester to return to Thornfield, where she discovers the house burned and Rochester blinded in his attempts to save his dying wife.

The novel has been filmed several times, but no adaptation captures the extraordinary narrative power and Jane's independence of spirit which made it both controversial and successful in the mid-Victorian period, but also have made it one of the most enduring stories of all classic fiction.

Wuthering Heights

The story of Heathcliff and Cathy, the doomed lovers of Emily Brontë's only novel, is nearly as popular throughout the world as that of Shakespeare's starcrossed lovers Romeo and Juliet.

EMILY BRONTË
1818 – 1848
Nationality: British
First Published: T.C. Newby, 1847

Narrated by the pompous Lockwood, a tenant of Heathcliff's Thrushcross Grange, the story begins with Lockwood's account of being terrified on his first night at Wuthering Heights, the home of his landlord.

The narrative is then taken up by Mrs Dean, servant to the Earnshaw family, who tells of Heathcliff's first arrival. Saved from the streets of Liverpool by Mr Earnshaw, Heathcliff is taken to Wuthering Heights to be brought up as one of his own children. Although there is a great deal of resentment among the children, Cathy and Heathcliff fall in love, despite Cathy feeling that Heathcliff is beneath her.

She eventually marries a more socially acceptable suitor, and Heathcliff's bitterness, malevolence and ultimately vengeance drive the novel with a ferocity that disturbed its Victorian readers.

The anti-hero's revenge burns within the affected families for generations to come. It is in part, Heathcliff's enigmatic characterization and his unrelenting violence and malice that has provided this utterly remarkable and sometimes disturbing book with its longevity.

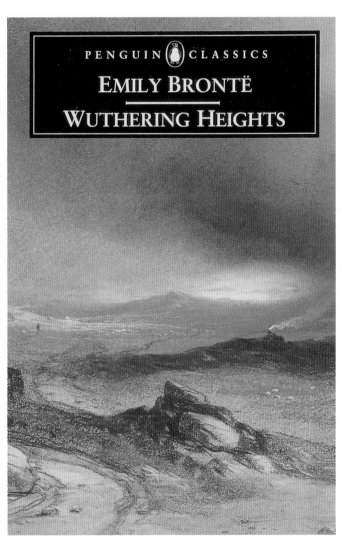

PENGUIN CLASSICS

EMILY BRONTË

WUTHERING HEIGHTS

The Pilgrim's Progress

JOHN BUNYAN
1628 – 1688
Nationality: British
First Published: N. Ponder, 1678
Other Selected Titles:
Grace Abounding

Frontispiece from the first edition.

Without doubt the most famous Christian allegory still in print, *The Pilgrim's Progress* was first published in the reign of Charles II and was completed while its author was imprisoned for offences against the Conventicle Act (which prohibited the conducting of religious services outside the bailiwick of the Church of England).

The book recounts a dream of the supernatural trials and adventures of Christian (an Everyman figure) from the City of Destruction, who is weighed down by a terrible burden after reading a book (an unspecified Bible). His heavy load threatens to drag him down to Hell, and Christian seeks out ways that he might rid himself of his burden (of sin).

The second part concerns Christian's wife, Christiana, and her journey (with her children) through the same pilgrimage in the company of her neighbour, Mercy.

The book is a Puritan conversion narrative, of which there are predecessors in Bunyan's own work (*Grace Abounding*), *Foxe's Book of Martyrs*, as well as other emblem books and chapbooks from the Renaissance. Nonetheless, *The Pilgrim's Progress* is laced with a kind of verve, charm and humour that one would not usually associate with puritanical works.

The Canterbury Tales

There is very little in the entire canon of English literature that can rival *The Canterbury Tales*' sheer creativity, linguistic mettle, and its sometimes ribald and passionately moving stories. The Prologue recounts the gathering of 31 pilgrims at Southwark's Tabard Inn. Twenty-four tales are then told as a kind of competition on the pilgrimage to Canterbury and they are linked by entertaining and insightful exchanges between the different storytellers.

Highlights include 'The Miller's Tale', a hilarious story of sexual deception and 'nether eye' kissing. 'The Wife of Bath's Tale' has generated a great deal of critical discussion because of its remarkably modern gender politics. A disgraced knight is offered freedom if he is able to answer a simple question: what it is that women most desire? The resolution of the tale is both intellectually satisfying and moving.

'The Pardoner's Tale' recounts how three thugs come to a sticky end when they squabble over the share of a treasure that they find in the forest; too late do they realize that the old man that directed them there was none other than Death himself.

Even though the cycle of tales is incomplete, the stories have depth and linguistic verve, and are perhaps so memorable for adding up to something far greater than the sum of their parts.

GEOFFREY CHAUCER
1343 – 1400
Nationality: British
First Published: 1387
Other Selected Titles:
Troilus and Criseyde

Illustrated page from the William Morris edition.

The Collected Stories

Russian short story writer Anton Chekhov.

ANTON CHEKHOV
1860 – 1904
Nationality: Russian
First Published: Chatto, 1916 (first English translation)
Other Selected Titles:
The Black Monk and Other Stories
The Kiss and Other Stories
The Bet and Other Stories

Anton Chekhov began his writing career in the mid-1880s and has since been recognized as the Russian master of the short story. The stories were first translated by Constance Garnett between 1916–22.

A Boring Story (From an Old Man's Notebook), his first masterpiece, took many risks for a writer so young. It is a complex story of different moods and textures that later influenced *The Seagull*. It is about the final months of an ageing and eminent professor's life. Feeling only regret for the mediocrity of the life that he has lived, he takes up with a young actress to whom he feels the need to fabricate his past. It is a remarkable story that leads to a thought-provoking conclusion about the mundanity of existence.

Other highlights in the collection include *The Grasshopper* (dramatizing the clash between empiricism and aestheticism), *Misfortune* (clearly influenced by Anna Karenina), and *Lady with Lapdog*, a love story that Chekhov's friend Gorky found so moving that he later wrote to Chekhov complaining that everything that he had written since felt 'coarse and written not with a pen but with a log'.

As is in evidence in these short stories, Chekhov's work is characterized by a humanity and subtlety not often found mixed with astute comedy and tragedy; his fine dramatic abilities, his keen observation and wit are renowned throughout the world.

The Man Who Was Thursday

The Man Who Was Thursday is truly a very odd novel; in parts it is a horror novel, detective novel, political thriller, comedy and romance. Subtitled 'a Nightmare', the novel is similar in theme to Conrad's *The Secret Agent*, insofar as it begins with the contemporary fears of anarchist bombings in London. But just at the point where the novel seems to be tying itself temporally to Edwardian England, it takes a trip into fantastic realms and throws one enigma after another at the reader.

Detective Gabriel Syme is elected – undercover – to the Central European Council of Anarchists where it is his task to prevent any further bombings. Each member of the Council is assigned a code name from the days of the week. As the novel progresses, Chesterton unwinds the strange entanglements that exist between the men through a bizarre and intriguing series of narrative twists and revelations that come so fast on the heels of one another that only the most attentive reader will keep up. All this in a book that also includes a hot-air balloon chase and a high-speed elephant pursuit – and it's only a novella.

G.K. CHESTERTON
1874 – 1936
Nationality: British
First Published: Benn, 1908
Other Selected Titles:
The Napoleon of Notting Hill
Manalive

G.K. Chesterton (back left) at a literary garden party with fellow authors.

London book distributor John Gold, who, in 1964, objected to his stock of Fanny Hill being confiscated under the Obscene Publications Act. Pictured here with an edition of the less successful Memoirs of a Coxcomb first published in 1751

Fanny Hill, or Memoirs of a Woman of Pleasure

JOHN CLELAND
1709 – 1789
Nationality: British
First Published: G. Fenton, 1749
Other Selected Titles:
Memoirs of a Coxcomb, or
The History of Sir William Delamere
The Surprises of Love

John Cleland's novel from the mid-18th century was the subject of an obscenity trial, both at the time of publication and as recently as 1963. It tells the story of Fanny Hill, a young and naïve country girl who, only recently arrived in the big city of London, soon falls into prostitution. She then explicitly narrates her sexual adventures in the whore houses of London in the two letters that comprise the novel. (The appropriation of the epistolary form was almost certainly a poke at Samuel Richardson.) But what is so utterly unique about this novel is that it is not the moralistic Hogarthian portrait that one might expect, it is instead an explicit celebration of a young woman's sexuality. Indeed the censure and anger that it has raised in the intervening years would not perhaps have existed if Fanny's tale had a moral lesson, but she does not end up a gin-supping disease-infested street crawler. Fanny manages to attain for herself the winnings of the best romantic heroines.

The Moonstone: a Romance

On her 18th birthday, Rachel Verrinder is endowed with the gift of an exceptional diamond, originally stolen from a Hindu temple in India. On the night of her birthday, some rather clumsy Indian jugglers suddenly arrive at the house to entertain the guests, and that night, Rachel's diamond is stolen from her. The Indian jugglers are obviously suspected of the theft, but are thought to be not guilty as there are others in the house acting suspiciously, most notably Rachel herself.

There then follows an investigation which reveals all kinds of adventures and dishonesties among Rachel's family, friends and suitors (among them Franklin Blake, the collector of the papers that make up the novel). The story and its conclusion are spectacular, but it is also Collins' sense of place and his ear for the nuances of voice among his cast of characters that really set this captivating novel apart.

The Moonstone is a noteworthy novel for so many other reasons, too. The memorable characters are too numerous to mention. On a structural level, it has neither a third- nor first-person narrator, but a series of characters who recount the sections of the story that they know best. Its portrayal of the Indians was incredibly generous and liberal in the context of the still-recent Indian Mutiny of 1857. Many have suggested that this novel single-handedly inaugurated the genre of the Detective Mystery and it certainly has many of the hallmarks of the genre yet to come. The principal criterion, though, must surely be a rivetting plot and *The Moonstone* certainly has that.

WILKIE COLLINS
1824 – 1889
Nationality: British
First Published: Tinsley Brothers, 1868
Other Selected Titles:
The Woman in White
No Name
Armadale

Wilkie Collins in 'The Novelist who Invented Sensation' by Michael Nicholson.

The Hound of the Baskervilles

SIR ARTHUR CONAN DOYLE
1859 – 1930
Nationality: Scottish
First Published: G. Newnes, 1902
Other Selected Titles:
A Study in Scarlet
The Sign of Four
The Adventures of Sherlock Holmes
The Memoirs of Sherlock Holmes
The Lost World
The Valley of Fear

Sir Arthur Conan Doyle relaxes at home with his pipe.

Originally serialized in *Strand* magazine, *The Hound of the Baskervilles* is probably Arthur Conan Doyle's best-known novel. Set on Dartmoor in 1889, this Sherlock Holmes adventure tells the story of a curse on the Baskerville family, that of a hound or demon dog that has returned after several hundred years to begin taking the lives of the Baskervilles once again.

The story is brought to Holmes and Watson by Dr James Mortimer, the doctor who declared Sir Charles Baskerville dead, and subsequently withheld from the official inquest his belief that there were the footsteps of a giant dog leading away from Sir Charles' body.

Doyle was certainly more mature as a writer in this novel. So confident is he, that he removes Holmes from the middle section of the novel entirely, and leaves Watson to recount his adventures. As the novel develops, the reason for Holmes' absence is revealed, and the solution to the crime is as ingenious as we would expect from the world's most famous detective.

Heart of Darkness

On a boat anchored in the Thames, the main protagonist, Marlow, tells of his adventures in African ivory country to find the famously successful and enigmatic Mr Kurtz.

Having made a trying journey to collect his steamboat from the Central Station in Africa, Marlow is distraught to discover it wrecked. Here he learns that Mr Kurtz is unwell, and sets off to find him. The long and slow passage through the African heartland fills Marlow with a growing sense of dread.

They are attacked by African natives and some of the crew are killed. At the Inner Station, Marlow hears more stories of Kurtz, of his strange power over the natives and the severed heads that surround his hut. Marlow tries to transport Kurtz back down river to safety, but Kurtz' enigmatic dying words are 'The horror! The horror!' Marlow returns to civilization and visits Kurtz's girlfriend but does not tell her what he witnessed.

This novella is astonishingly powerful and equally enigmatic. Its meaning, politics and status have all been hotly debated since its first publication in 1902.

Joseph Conrad himself travelled to Africa in 1890.

JOSEPH CONRAD
1857 – 1924
Nationality: Polish
First Published: W. Blackwood & Sons, 1902
Other Selected Titles:
Lord Jim
Nostromo
The Secret Agent
Under Western Eyes

Robinson Crusoe

DANIEL DEFOE
1660 – 1731
Nationality: British
First Published: W. Taylor, 1719
Other Selected Titles:
Moll Flanders
A Journal of the Plague Year

Considered by many to be the cornerstone of the English novel, *Robinson Crusoe* is also thought to be the first English novel. It is a prose romance that recounts the first-person narrative of a shipwrecked mariner stranded on a desert island. His resourcefulness enables him to survive there for nearly 30 years. The novel takes a sudden turn when Crusoe discovers a single footprint in the sand, not his own.

Later rescuing Man Friday, Crusoe then takes on the task of civilizing him and takes him to England when they are both rescued. The novel presents the now discomforting paradigm of the civilized West educating the savagery of man in the state of nature. In the sequel, *The Serious Reflections... of Robinson Crusoe* (1720), both men return to the island where Crusoe loses Friday.

The novel is thick with allegory derived from *Job*, *Jonah Everyman* and the *Prodigal Son*; the novel is also indebted to *The Pilgrim's Progress* and *Gulliver's Travels*. In many ways it is the proto-text of the English novel and has been reworked many times (in particular by the Booker Prize-winning J.M. Coetzee in *Foe*). It was the best-selling novel throughout the 19th century.

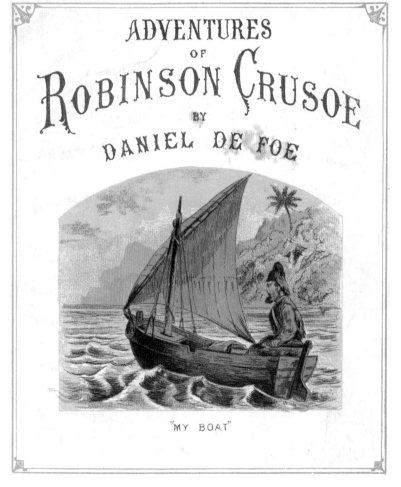

ADVENTURES OF ROBINSON CRUSOE BY DANIEL DE FOE

"MY BOAT"

The Christmas Books

Although there are technically five Christmas stories by Dickens, only two are actually set during the Christmas period (the others are New Year stories). These two enjoyable novellas are easily read in a single sitting.

A Christmas Carol, featuring the indomitable and miserly Ebenezer Scrooge, is known throughout the world. The story of Scrooge's conversion is both astonishingly powerful and moving and, as such, this must surely be the most famous Christmas story outside the Gospels.

The much less known *The Haunted Man* (1848) is also a story of the redemptive powers of memory. It is not as easy a read as Scrooge's story, but it is perhaps more thought provoking. The 'Haunted Man' is a figurative trope for a man haunted by the unhappy memories of his past. He is granted the wish of being able to forget these memories and Dickens' ingenious story then traces the terrible effects of this loss of memory. Without such memories, the characters in the story lose all their sense of compassion and they become unable to relate to their fellow man.

Both these novellas are astonishing in their perception and they are acutely affecting fables of modern life.

CHARLES DICKENS
1812 – 1870
Nationality: British
First Published: Chapman & Hall, 1843/8
Other Selected Titles:
Oliver Twist
David Copperfield
Bleak House
Great Expectations
Our Mutual Friend

An illustration showing Mr and Mrs Fezziwig dancing together at their ball.

Our Mutual Friend

CHARLES DICKENS
1812 – 1870
Nationality: British
First Published: Chapman & Hall,
1865
Other Selected Titles:
Oliver Twist
David Copperfield
Bleak House
Great Expectations

Dickens' last completed novel, *Our Mutual Friend* is considered to represent Dickens at his very best. It is a panoramic drama about the spectacle and sensation derived from the interactions between the highest and lowest of society.

It begins as a mystery story when a body is found drowned in the Thames and is identified as John Harmon, who was returning to London to collect his inheritance of his father's riches and his dust heaps. A suspicious man gives a false name at the morgue and the mystery is set in train.

From here the novel segues into a romance between Lizzie Hexam (a waterman's daughter) and the lawyer Eugene Wrayburn. Because their class difference is so extreme, Wrayburn's obsession can only lead to the fall of Lizzie. But Wrayburn, beaten nearly to death by a jealous suitor, is redeemed and is released from the bounds of his shallow society and is free to marry Lizzie.

The novel's dramatic scope, its all-encompassing satirization of contemporary society and its dissection of the insubstantiality of materialism make this novel one of Dickens' greatest.

Crime and Punishment

Raskolnikov's story is a tragic masterpiece of Russian literature. It is the disturbing and haunting tale of a young man's descent into criminality, horror, guilt and ultimately, of punishment. A former student, Raskolnikov lives in poverty and chaos and is eventually driven to murdering an aged woman (a pawnbroker) and her sister. He believes he has devised the perfect crime, as no one will regret the loss of his victims.

FYODOR DOSTOYEVSKY
1821 – 1881
Nationality: Russian
First Published: *Russkii Vestnik* periodical, 1866
Other Selected Titles:
Notes from the Underground
The Idiot
The Devils
The Brothers Karamazov

It is a crime novel without the mystery, as from the very outset of the novel Dostoyevsky draws us into the interior of Raskolnikov's mental life; we see his reasoning and can explain his actions. The novel, though about the terrible nature of the crime, is really about the nature of punishment and the toll it takes on one's conscience. It is one of the finest studies of the psychopathology of guilt written in any language and Dostoyevsky's sublime skill at observing the working of Raskolnikov's terror and remorse make it an uncomfortably memorable novel in which the palpable tension is sometimes unbearable.

George Eliot's home in 1800.

**GEORGE ELIOT
(MARY ANNE EVANS)**
1819 – 1880
Nationality: British
First Published: Blackwood & Sons
1871
Other Selected Titles:
*Adam Bede
The Mill on the Floss
Silas Marner
Daniel Deronda*

Middlemarch: A Study in Provincial Life

'One of the few English novels written for grown-up people' was how novelist Virginia Woolf described this stunning, momentous and moving novel.

Set in the 1830s, Middlemarch is a fictional village undergoing change. The novel recounts the stories of the village's inhabitants, principally that of Dorothea Brooke who mistakenly marries Dr Edward Casaubon because she believes him to be an intellectual of the highest nature. Too late does she discover his mediocrity and after his death she falls in love with Casaubon's nephew, the Byronic Will Ladislaw.

Dr Tertius Lydgate's story is that of a young man, an ambitious doctor, trying to make his way in the world. He marries the beautiful Rosamund Vincy and they become estranged as Lydgate struggles under the burden of terrible debt.

The rich and enterprising scope of the novel means there are many other strands of narrative that interconnect and they are all shaped by Eliot's sometimes breathtaking skills for insight and sympathy in her characterization. It is a humane and sincere examination of how communities shape individual life. The novel's ending is perhaps the most poignant and moving of any novel from any age.

Tom Jones

The novelty of structure, character, comedy and voice in this book is what made *Tom Jones* such a great success in its own day; it has also made it an enduring classic in ours.

The story of a foundling, the book tells the tale of Tom Jones, who is discovered one night in the bed of the beneficent Mr Allworthy, who takes him in and educates him. He has a rival in Allworthy's nephew and heir Blifil, and Tom's tutor Thwackum shares this resentment. Envy is fuelled when Tom falls for Blifil's intended, Sophia Western – who despises Blifil.

Mr Allworthy is eventually wrongly convinced of Tom's selfishness and poor conduct and banishes Tom from the house. Tom leaves for the adventures that the army may offer. Unable to bear the prospect of marriage to Blifil, Sophia runs away to London.

Tom sets off to the big city in pursuit of forgiveness but is soon drawn into an affair with the aristocratic Lady Bellatson. Jealousies abound among the women in Tom's life and Blifil returns to taunt Tom. The secrets of Tom's birth are eventually revealed, and he becomes the rightful heir to Mr Allworthy.

The novel was filmed in 1963 starring Albert Finney and Susannah York, with a screenplay by John Osborne.

HENRY FIELDING
1707 – 1754
Nationality: British
First Published: A. Millar, 1749
Other Selected Titles:
Amelia

The Penguin English Library

HENRY FIELDING
TOM JONES

The Great Gatsby

F. SCOTT FITZGERALD
1896 – 1940
Nationality: American
First Published: C. Scribner's Sons,
1925
Other Selected Titles:
Tender is the Night
The Last Tycoon

The narratorial voice of this novel is what makes it such a very impressive one. It is narrated by Nick Carraway, who rents a house at West Egg in Long Island across the water from his cousin, Daisy. His neighbour there is the enigmatic Jay Gatsby who lives the high life from the profits of his minor criminal activities. Gatsby's infamous parties are attended by many guests who do not know their host.

Nick becomes cynically fascinated and transfixed by Gatsby and their friendship nurtures many confidences. Carraway learns that Gatsby and Daisy had been in love, but that Daisy had not waited for him to return from the war and had married another. Nick arranges a meeting between the two, and Daisy finds herself impressed by the change in Gatsby's fortunes. Daisy's husband Tom, himself already involved in an affair with the garage-owner's wife Myrtle, becomes jealous of Gatsby's attentions to his wife. Then Myrtle is killed in an accident and Tom tells Myrtle's husband that Gatsby is responsible.

The novel is beautifully spare in its prose style and the voice of the narrator effectively captures the moral vacuity of a post-war America obsessed with wealth and status.

F. Scott Fitzgerald, his wife Zelda and daughter Scottie out on a drive.

Madame Bovary ✓

Where most 19th-century novels had been concerned merely to present plainly likeable stories that ended in a marriage, Madame Bovary navigated unknown territory by beginning with one. The nature of the novel as a form that is always undergoing change, and Flaubert's masterpiece is no exception to this rule.

Charles Bovary, a doctor, marries a simple farm girl. She is all set for a life of adventurous marriage, but her only excitement seems to derive from the novels that she reads. Her husband, though sanguine and kind, is both boring and stultifying. After the birth of their first child, Emma feels that her life is over. Grasping for intimacy, she begins an affair with a local landowner and makes enthusiastic plans for them to run away together.

Because he does not love her, their plans come to nothing. She takes up with another man, and her life becomes increasingly chaotic. Her debts spin out of control and she sees suicide as her only possible solution.

One particular aspect of the novel that drew attention when it was first published was its narrator's refusal to be drawn into the kinds of moral commentary that was the mainstay of so many other works of this period.

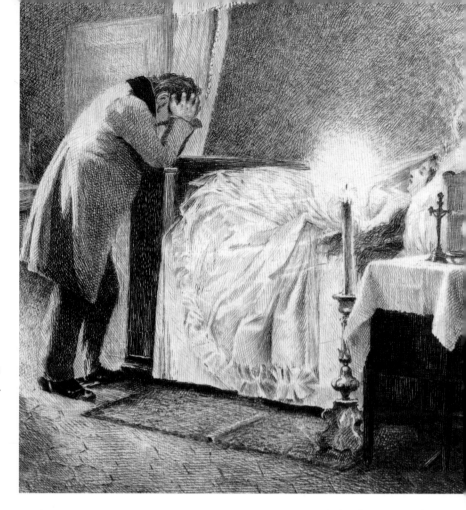

A dramatic scene from
Madame Bovary.

GUSTAVE FLAUBERT
1821 – 1880
Nationality: French
First Published: Charpentier, 1857
Other Selected Titles:
Sentimental Education
Three Tales

Howards End

E.M. FORSTER
1879 – 1970
Nationality: British
First Published: E. Arnold, 1910
Other Selected Titles:
Where Angels Fear to Tread
A Room with a View
Passage to India
Maurice

The Schlegel sisters are intelligent, independent and artistic women who become connected, by engagement and cautious friendship, to the Wilcox family – a family of hardened and successful businessmen. Mrs Wilcox befriends Margaret, becomes ill and dies. She bequeaths her house, Howards End, not to her family but to Margaret, whom she felt was its spiritual heir as her husband and sons saw it only in fiscal terms as 'property'. The family keep silent about Mrs Wilcox's wishes. Mr Wilcox, however, befriends Margaret, and eventually proposes to her. Margaret becomes the second Mrs Wilcox.

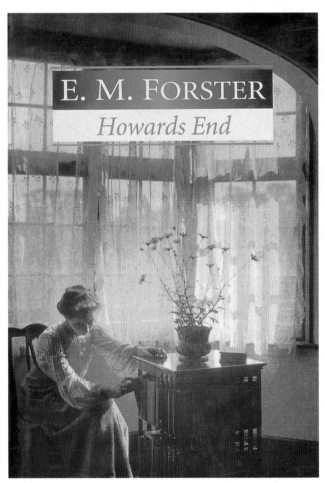

Her sister, on the other hand, takes up with – and later becomes pregnant by – a young insurance clerk, Leonard Bast. Mr Wilcox indirectly gives Leonard some poor business advice and impoverishes him. Where Helen Schlegel sees that Mr Wilcox must make amends, the new Mrs Wilcox is keen to approach the matter more cautiously. In trying to resolve the problem, terrible truths are learnt by all involved.

'Only connect' has become perhaps the most famous epigraph in western literature. It announces the philosophical driving force of liberal humanism that Forster used to dramatize this powerful account of the complexities of behaving morally in the modern world. Mr Wilcox does learn some compassion and humility in the story – the Wilcoxes and the Schlegels do 'connect', but all at a terrible cost.

The novel's conclusion is appropriately dramatic, but what is most enduring about this wonderful novel is the magic of Forster's prose. Though on rare occasions it is rather too whimsical, Forster's imagination endows the English landscape with a life of its own.

North and South

Originally published in Charles Dickens' periodical, *Household Words*, Elizabeth Gaskell's *North and South* is a lively novel of social and romantic reconciliation.

The Hales live in rural Hampshire. Margaret is the daughter of the village parson who is forced to resign his living because of his irreconcilable religious doubts. They move to the dirty and sooty industrial town of Milton (modelled on Manchester). Here, Margaret is shocked into sympathy by the poverty of the town's workers, and when she meets the Thorntons (new-monied local mill-owners) an immediate dislike ensues between her and the young John Thornton. She later risks her own life to protect him from a violent mob. Misunderstanding the reason for her impulse to protect a fellow human being, Thornton proposes to her almost out of duty and she rejects him. After Thornton sees her with another man (a secret meeting with her fugitive brother), he respects her honesty and remains silent despite legal pressures to reveal the truth. Believing that she has lost the affections of Thornton, she sees him in a new light and they are reunited.

Like many of Gaskell's novels, its fundamental theme is that of sympathy and feeling for one's fellow man. The theme has been reused by writers such as E.M. Forster (in *Howards End*) and later by David Lodge (in *Nice Work*).

ELIZABETH GASKELL
1810 – 1865
Nationality: British
First Published: Harper, 1855
Other Selected Titles:
Mary Barton
Cranford
Wives and Daughters

Elizabeth Gaskell was also acclaimed for her biography of Charlotte Brontë.

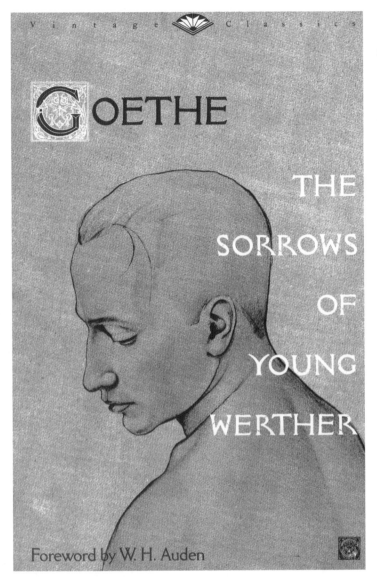

The Sorrows of Young Werther √E

A tragic story of a doomed love affair, *The Sorrows of Young Werther* was the novel that gained Goethe outstanding popularity as a writer.

A young, passionate and highly strung artist recounts in a series of letters a visit to the fictional village of Wahlheim. Here, he meets and falls hopelessly in love with the young and beautiful Lotte, who after the death of her mother has taken responsibility for her remaining family.

However, the existence of a fiancé, Albert, causes the young Werther considerable anguish but he decides to befriend him nonetheless as a means of getting closer to Lotte.

The novel's conclusion caused considerable controversy at the time of publication. In its absolute focus on the interiority and subjectivity of its anti-hero, the novel anticipated Romanticism. Goethe later remarked of the ending that he had 'shot his hero to save himself'.

JOHANN WOLFGANG VON GOETHE
1749 – 1832
Nationality: German
First Published: Freystadt, 1774
Other Selected Titles:
Roman Elegies
Faust
Willhelm Meister's Apprenticeship
Hermann and Dorothea
Effective Affinities
The Italian Journey

The Vicar of Wakefield

A TALE SUPPOSED TO BE WRITTEN BY HIMSELF

This influential novel, sold on behalf of the author by Dr Johnson, found its way into Goethe's *The Sorrows of Young Werther*, Jane Austen's *Emma* and Dickens' *A Tale of Two Cities*, and was the only one published by this poet, playwright, novelist, librettist, historian and essayist.

Told in the first person by Dr Primrose (the vicar), it begins on the evening of his son's wedding, which is cancelled when the Primroses' tranquil life is wrecked by the news of their bankruptcy. The son, George, is dispatched to make his way in the world and the rest of the family move to a more modest parish on the land of Squire Thornhill.

They meet Mr Burchell at an inn, and he later saves their daughter, Sophia, from drowning. She is smitten, but the ambitious Mrs Primrose won't have her daughter marry a pauper. Their relative stability at the new parish is only disturbed by the connivings of Squire Thornhill, who plans to have his way with

one of Primrose's daughters by marrying her in a sham ceremony (as he has done with other women). After rescuing Olivia, they return to find their house in flames. Despite their utter destitution, Thornhill still insists on payment of rent. The disasters and the dénouements stack up as the novel drives towards its ending which is as idyllic as its beginning.

OLIVER GOLDSMITH
1728 – 1774
Nationality: Irish
First Published: F. Newbury, 1766

A hand-coloured aquatint by Thomas Rowlandson, from the first edition.

The Power and the Glory

GRAHAM GREENE
1904 – 1991
Nationality: British
First Published: W. Heinemann, 1940
Other Selected Titles:
Brighton Rock
The Heart of the Matter
The End of the Affair
The Quiet American
Travels with My Aunt

Graham Greene was an experienced traveller and the setting of this novel derives from time that he had spent in Mexico in 1937, reporting on religious discrimination and persecution.

It recounts the tragic story of a priest whose faith is long lost in drink and lechery. The story is set in a fictional republic where the church and religious worship is illegal. The act of banning worship inspires and reignites the priest's faith in God and the church, and he decides to continue serving his parishioners until he is physically prevented from doing so. His irreligious antagonist in the novel is a kind and humane police lieutenant who is responsible for his capture and execution as a martyr. While the Christian metaphor of the Passion in the conclusion to this novel is not exactly subtle, it does nonetheless tease out the complexities of the debate with which the novel has been engaging, namely that of the relative values of Humanism set against the Christian faith.

What is so unique about this novel, and indeed much of Greene's work, is the comfortable co-existence of a thriller plot with the high, moral ambiguity of a modern drama.

King Solomon's Mines

H. RIDER HAGGARD
1856 – 1925
Nationality: British
First Published: Cassell & Co., 1885
Other Selected Titles:
The Witch's Head
Allan Quartermain
Jess
She

Only the third of some 57 novels that Rider Haggard would publish in his career, *King Solomon's Mines* was by far the most successful.

Strap-lined 'The most amazing book ever written', it narrates the adventures of Allan Quartermain. Living in Durban, South Africa, he is approached by the English aristocrat Sir Henry and Captain Good to assist on a rescue mission for Sir Henry's brother, last seen travelling north heading for the treasure trove of King Solomon's Mines. In possession of an old map to the mines, they set off with Umbopa, a strange native who seems different in some way to the other porters. Travelling through arid deserts and treacherous mountainscapes they meet the Kukuanas, a people ruled by a violent and belligerent king. However, the real enemy of the Kukuanas is a withered hag called Gagool. Umbopa is revealed as the true ruler of the Kukuanas. Gagool, as punishment, is forced to help the men find their way to their treasure, but she outwits them, sealing them inside the mountain with a boulder. Nonetheless, they find their much sought-after fortune, and are able to escape. The men return to Durban laden with riches.

This is a breakneck read, with the pace of a modern thriller. It was the first novel of its kind that spawned many imitators.

Prolific British novelist
H. Rider Haggard.

Jude the Obscure

THOMAS HARDY
1840 – 1928
Nationality: British
First Published: Osgood, McIlvaine
& Co., 1895
Other Selected Titles:
Far from the Madding Crowd
The Return of the Native
Tess of the D'Urbevilles
The Mayor of Casterbridge

*Thomas Hardy felt himself
to be a Dorset-born outsider in
literary London.*

This was the last novel that Hardy published in his lifetime. So bereft was he at the undeserving critical backlash against it – which attacked the novel on moral grounds rather than aesthetic ones – that he vowed never to publish another novel. And for the last two decades of his life he was true to his word and published only poetry. Like much of Hardy's work, *Jude the Obscure*, is a powerful, moving and tragic novel.

Young Jude Fawley is not made for the world in which he is living, that of a pauper. The novel begins in Jude's childhood with his pathetic attempts at earning money by being a live scarecrow. He is sacked because he feels sympathy for the crows, feeling they should be allowed a little feed.

The boy's aspirations are high. As he stands in the fields, he can see the university town of Christminster (a fictionalized Oxford) on the horizon and he longs to attend. Though intellectually capable, he is caught in the grips of a series of romantic and sexual wrangles that make his path to Christminster impossible.

Though he and his troubled family do eventually move to the city, they exist on the extreme economic and moral periphery of society. One of their sons, on hearing that his mother is again expecting a baby, makes the most terrible decision.

The Scarlet Letter

Born in Salem, Massachusetts, to a wealthy settler family, Nathaniel Hawthorne was a respected novelist and short story writer. He was troubled in later life by his ascendancy from John Hawthorne, who had judged at the Salem witch trials.

Published when he was 45 years old, *The Scarlet Letter* won instant critical and public acclaim. Set in neighbouring Boston in the 17th century, the story tells the tale of Hester Prynne whose husband was lost and presumed dead. After an affair with a local man which yields a child, she is vilified by her society and subjected to public interrogation conducted maliciously and virulently by the local minister Arthur Dimmesdale. Hester refuses to reveal the identity of her lover and she is forced to wear a scarlet letter 'A' (for adulterer) on her clothing at all times.

As the years pass, Hester earns some respect in her community by living well, but she is constantly reminded of her guilt. Unbeknownst to the community, her husband returns as the town's doctor to witness the public persecution of his wife. Revealing that Indians had captured him, he makes her swear to keep his true identity a secret. He discovers that none other than Dimmesdale was Hester's lover. Realizing that Dimmesdale's mysterious illness derives from his burden of guilt, Hester's husband offers him medical help and decides to exact his revenge by keeping him well physically but torturing him emotionally.

The novel's conclusion is far from ideal. Despite the death of Dimmesdale, Hester decides to continue wearing her scarlet letter as a mark of penance and endurance in a world of sin.

Nathaniel Hawthorne was a popular literary figure in his lifetime.

NATHANIEL HAWTHORNE
1804 – 1864
Nationality: American
First Published: Ticknor, Reed & Fields, 1850
Other Selected Titles:
The House of the Seven Gables
The Marble Faun

*The great whale capsizes a
boat full of fishermen.*

HERMAN MELVILLE
1819 – 1891
Nationality: American
First Published: Harper, 1851
Other Selected Titles:
Typee
Omoo
Redburn
White-Jacket
Pierre
Israel Potter

Moby-Dick, or, The Whale

Cast and set as part of a timeless and allegorical world, *Moby-Dick* is a novel rich in symbolism and metaphor. The names of the characters all have biblical resonances, and the Epilogue begins with a quotation from the *Book of Job*: 'and I only am escaped alone to tell thee'.

The novel's extraordinary oddness comprises an encyclopaedia of whaling lore, a Biblical meditation on the value of life, and a study of Man's relationship with both nature and his countrymen.

The adventures that take place in the novel are so well known that they have entered the American consciousness. 'Call me Ishmael', the novel begins, announcing its narrator, a young outcast who seeks to find real meaning by following a life at sea.

He joins the crew of The Pequod and sets sail on Christmas Day, mastered by the monomaniacal Captain Ahab whose sole desire is to capture and kill the monster of the sea, the whale known as Moby-Dick. Tension mounts on the ship until the whale is sighted and several other vessels enter the chase.

The whale's famous cunning wins out in the end and he destroys the ships. Captain Ahab is last seen accidentally pinioned to the whale and only Ishmael survives to tell this strange and fertile tale.

The Portrait of a Lady ✓

Isabel Archer, a young and independent-minded American visits her wealthy aunt and uncle. Here she meets her cousin, Ralph, who knowing of her penniless state encourages his father to provide for Isabel in his will.

After his death, Isabel inherits and travels to the continent with her aunt and her friend, Mrs Merle. In Florence, she is introduced to the widower Gilbert Osmond and his daughter. Osmond becomes the third man to have proposed to Isabel, and despite her previous desire to remain independent, she accepts. What is unusual about this novel is that Isabel's marriage is not the end of the novel, but marks its midpoint. Like George Eliot's Casaubon, Osmond turns out not to be the ideal husband. There is a chain of connections between her husband's intimates that Isabel discovers too late. The novel's final pages are among the most acutely moving ever written.

In its depth of character, its breadth of social commentary, its insight into the workings and motives behind the slightest and seemingly least significant of actions and events, this novel is among the very greatest. The story is notoriously difficult to adapt for any other medium but Jane Campion's 1996 film is a surprisingly successful one.

HENRY JAMES
1843 – 1916
Nationality: American
First Published: Macmillan & Co., 1881
Other Selected Titles:
Roderick Hudson
The Europeans
The Bostonians
What Maisie Knew
The Turn of the Screw

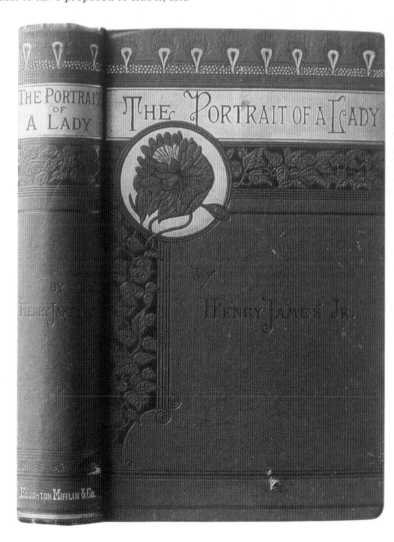

The Iliad

'Sing, O goddess, the anger of Achilles'. So begins the poem that would define the genre of Epic Poetry and become the cornerstone of Western Literature.

Divided into 24 books, the poem's title derives from Ilion (also known as Troy), and it begins ten years into the Trojan War. The action of the poem, though lasting only a few weeks, is representative of the decade-long war that began when Paris – the son of the King of Troy – stole Helen, wife of Menelaus. It follows the 'rage of Achilles' after he is insulted by the chief commander of the Greek (Achean) army, Agamemnon; Achilles refuses to fight with his allies and Agamemnon's army takes many casualties. Despite offering an admission of wrong-doing, Agamemnon's army suffers greater losses after Achilles arrogantly refuses to fight for the second time. Achilles' friend, Patroclus, is later killed in battle by Hector; the death of his friend rouses Achilles to fight and he kills Hector, violently mistreating the dead body and refusing to return it for burial. The poem ends in resolution when the body is returned and Hector is given an appropriate funeral.

There is still considerable speculation as to the identity of Homer. The poems have been ascribed a name, but it has no known identity. Some scholars believe that he was more than one man; others question whether he was the same poet that wrote *The Odyssey*. Some have persuasively argued that the poems' author was in fact a woman.

HOMER
First Published: circa 700 BCE
Other Selected Titles:
The Odyssey

LEFT: The wooden horse is offered as a gift at the gates of Troy.

Les Misérables (The Wretched)

VICTOR HUGO
1802 – 1885
Nationality: French
First Published: A. Lacroix &
Verboeckhoven, 1862
Other Selected Titles:
The Hunchback of Notre Dame
The Man Who Laughs

The funeral of Victor Hugo, Paris 1885.

Perhaps the greatest writer that France has produced, Victor Hugo published widely in fiction, prose, poetry, drama and many other genres. *Les Misérables* is his greatest achievement as a novelist, but it is perhaps better known to contemporary theatre-goers as one of the longest-running shows in the history of musicals.

Set in the early 19th century, this panoramic novel follows the fortunes, downfalls and histories of a number of its characters over two decades. The figure that draws the stories of its disparate characters together is the ex-convict Jean Valjean. Having been imprisoned for nearly 20 years for stealing food for his starving family, Valjean breaks his parole by committing a minor crime, and the novel then recounts Valjean's attempts to rid himself of his past and make his way in the world. Years later, his past returns to haunt him when the determined police inspector, Javert, arrests the wrong man in Valjean's place, drawing him out to face the shame of his previous life.

So ambitious is the novel in its narrative and philosophical scope, it is impossible to do it justice in such a brief introduction. And despite its prodigious length, the structure of the novel makes it somewhat more accessible than expected.

Three Men in a Boat

(TO SAY NOTHING OF THE DOG)

One of the funniest novels ever written, *Three Men in a Boat* has scarcely dated since its first publication when it was celebrated throughout Europe and bootlegged in America. It started life as a piece of travel writing. Jerome remarked in his *My Life and Times* that 'I did not intend to write a funny book... the book was to have been 'The Story of the Thames', its scenery and history', but as he began writing, it took on a life of its own.

Narrated by J., it is the hilariously chaotic story of a sojourn taken on the Thames from London to Oxford with his weary inept friends George, Harris, and the dog Montmorency.

The novel is a series of often very funny vignettes that recount the many scrapes the men get involved in. Rather than the situations, it is Jerome's prose that is the real attraction here. He finds humour in the most banal of objects from a tin of pineapple chunks that is impossible to open, to the description of his friend's day's work: 'George goes to sleep in a bank from ten till four each day except Saturdays, when they wake him up and put him outside at two.'

JEROME K. JEROME
1859 – 1927
Nationality: British
First Published: Arrowsmith, 1889
Other Selected Titles:
Three Men on the Bummel

Kim

Although he was best known for his children's fiction (especially the Disney adaptation of *The Jungle Book*), Rudyard Kipling was also a novelist of outstanding solemnity and perception. Nowhere is this more in evidence than in *Kim*.

The novel presents a lively picture of life on the roads and streets of India. In picaresque fashion, it is the story of the orphan, Kimball O'Hara, whose father was a sergeant in the Irish regiment.

Growing up on the streets of Lahore, Kim meets horse trader Mahbub Ali, who is connected with the British Secret Service. He also meets an old Tibetan Lama on a quest to be freed from the wheel of life, and he joins him to become his disciple.

On his travels, Kim is drawn back into the Irish Regiment, and he is sent away to school in Lucknow. His aptitude for espionage is there nurtured by the British he meets. On leaving school, Kim goes again on a spiritual quest with the Lama, but this time he also steals papers from his Russian counterparts as he goes.

The novel's ending sees Kim unsure whether to continue his spiritual journey, or to devote himself to the life of spying and espionage at which he is a natural. Kipling was the first English writer to receive the Nobel Prize for Literature in 1907.

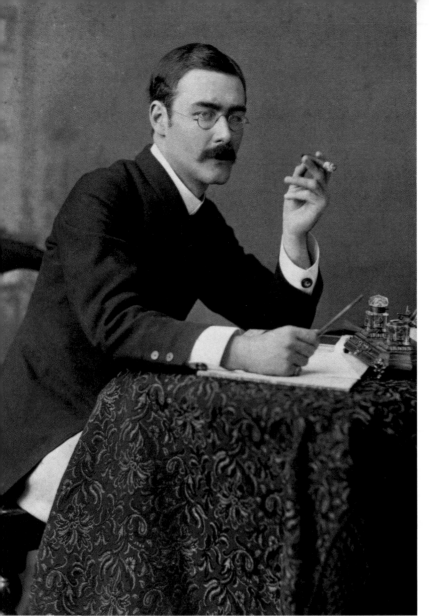

Rudyard Kipling was born in Bombay and later moved to Lahore, Pakistan.

RUDYARD KIPLING
1865 – 1936
Nationality: British
First Published: Macmillan, 1901
Other Selected Titles:
The Jungle Book
Just So Stories
Puck of Pook's Hill

Bliss and Other Stories

This collection, published in 1920, is a showcase for Katherine Mansfield's considerable talent. She was one of the 20th century's most gifted short story writers, much influenced by Chekhov, and enjoyed close friendships with DH Lawrence and Virginia Woolf. Something in her style is to literature what Impressionism is to painting. Her work features a wealth of stream-of-consciousness and interior dialogue, so that the reader experiences emotions and unfolding events at the same time as the protagonist. This is especially evident in the title story *Bliss*.

Bertha, a young, happily married woman, with money, fashionable friends and a beautiful baby passes her day in a mood of bliss. Everything from the fruit she arranges for her dinner party to the pear tree in the garden heighten her sense of acute happiness. She is especially pleased that a recent acquaintance, the enigmatic Pearl, is joining their party. She feels a special bond with Pearl, and experiences ardent desire for her husband Harry, for the first time. As her guests leave, she catches a glimpse of Harry's infidelity with Pearl – ignorance was indeed bliss.

A writer of peerless talent, Katherine Mansfield was as widely respected by her contemporaries in the Bloomsbury Group as she is today. She died of tuberculosis at the age of 34.

KATHERINE MANSFIELD
1888 – 1923
Nationality: New Zealand
First Published: Constable & Co., 1920
Other Selected Titles:
In a German Pension
Prelude
Collected Stories
The Garden Party and Other Stories
The Dove's Nest
Something Childish and Other Stories

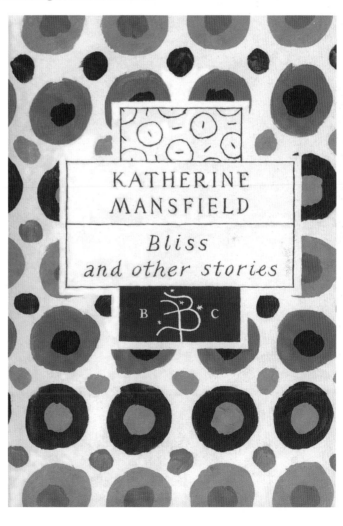

SIR THOMAS MORE
1477 – 1535
Nationality: British
First Published: Thierry Maartens, 1516

Utopia

Derived from the Greek for 'no place' (*ou topos*) and coined by Thomas More, a utopia is an imaginary and perfect world, an ideally organized state. More's was the first such exploration of a utopian world, and began a new genre of literature that is still as fresh today as it was in the 16th century.

First written in Latin, the book was later translated into other European languages – German, Italian and French editions appeared in 1550, the English edition was translated posthumously in 1551. Shakespeare is believed to have co-written a play about him in the 1590s.

A rewrite of Plato's *Republic*, *Utopia* is a satirical essay that describes the world in which there is total religious toleration (More was imprisoned and later executed for refusing to recognize Henry VIII's marriage to Anne Boleyn). His utopian state also has no notion of private property and provides free education to men and women alike. Consequently, the society lives in a state of complete pacificism, though they are prepared to take up arms if necessary. Neither is there any poverty or want. There are hardly any laws as each man and woman is morally self-governing.

The genre of Utopian Fiction is fascinating because it is only when an economic environment that is as stable as feudalism begins to decline, and introduces the idea that the life of the individual can be different, that such a genre can emerge.

Tales of the Grotesque and Arabesque

Probably published in 1839, this was the first collection of short stories that Poe produced. In two volumes, it comprised 25 tales, among them 'The Fall of the House of Usher', 'MS. Found in a Bottle', 'William Wilson' and 'The Assignation'.

The latter is set in Venice, where the narrator witnesses his friend rescue the drowning child of Marchesa Aphrodite, whose husband surreptitiously looks on as they arrange an assignation after midnight. The traces of a romance between the two are revealed to the narrator who later discovers they were both poisoned.

'The Fall of the House of Usher' is perhaps the most famous tale from the collection. It recounts the metaphoric and quite literal collapse of both the house and the family.

'MS. Found in a Bottle' is the bizarre story of a storm at sea which flings the narrator from one ship onto another. As the sole survivor of the first shipwreck, he now finds himself alone among the sailors on the ghostly vessel. He writes the manuscript of the title, whose last entry tells of a coming storm. 'William Wilson' is a classic *doppelgänger* story, of two William Wilsons whose presence disturbs one another at school and in adulthood until they fight in a duel where one dies proclaiming that the other is dead, too.

The stories are startlingly original, often disturbing and frequently macabre.

EDGAR ALAN POE
1809 – 1849
Nationality: American
First Published: W. Burton, 1839
Other Selected Titles:
Narrative of Arthur Gordon Pym of Nantucket
The Raven and Other Poems
Eureka: A Prose Poem

Poe was one of America's first true literary crtics.

Marcel Proust was neurotic and oversensitive like his main character.

MARCEL PROUST
1871 – 1922
Nationality: French
First Published: *Nouvelle Revue Française*, 1913–1927
Other Selected Titles:
Swann's Way
Within a Budding Grove
The Guermantes' Way
The Cities of the Plain
The Captive
The Sweet Cheat Gone
Time Regained
Jean Santeuil

In Search of Lost Time

In Search of Lost Time is an unparalled epic in Modernist Literature. Made up of six books, some 4000 pages in all, it describes what is in essence a plot that is almost comical in its simplicity.

The narrator, Marcel, wakes up and decides to become a writer. Of course, such a short, inane summary does no justice whatsoever to the temporal complexity of the plot, its exactness of characterization, and its ability to reveal the functions and illusions of memory.

Nowhere throughout the six books are these facets brought together with such integrity than in the 'Overture' of the first book. This 50-page chapter functions as the entire novel in miniature. The renowned taste of the Madeleine cake becomes the symbol for Proustian and Modernist notions of time where the narrator's sense of taste utterly usurps his linear experience of time and instead connects him directly to his childhood as if nothing had passed in the interim.

Instead of a thread of time, Proust created a model of narrative time that resembled a tightly-tied shoe lace: a continuous line that keeps looping back and wrapping around itself, bringing parts of the thread into contact with others that would usually remain separated.

Proust's fiction had considerable influence on many other Modernist writers, most notably Virginia Woolf.

A Sicilian Romance

Belonging in the Gothic tradition of the story where the sometimes distant past haunts the present, where its darkness encroaches on the enlightened present day, *A Sicilian Romance* takes as its basic premise the mystery of a haunted castle and the secrets that it keeps. It both shocked and thrilled in equal measure in its day.

ANNE RADCLIFFE
1764 – 1823
Nationality: British
First Published: P. Wogan, 1790
Other Selected Titles:
The Castles of Athlin and Dunbayne
The Romance of the Forest
The Mysteries of Udolpho
The Italian

The sisters Julia and Emilia Mazzini inhabit a dark and isolated mansion on the island of Sicily. After the return of their father, they begin to see and to hear evidence of a ghostly presence in a rundown wing of the old house.

After the author takes us deep into the cavernous womb of the island to explore hidden passageways where the secrets of the house are finally revealed, Julia and Emilia are compelled to finally face up to the family's shameful and indulgent past.

Author Ann Radcliffe had many literary admirers in her time (among them William Hazlitt, Sir Walter Scott and Jane Austen), who thrilled in the delightful excesses of her thrilling novels. Her portrayals of the rapturous terrors of the gothic still endure today, as their female characters are models of the emancipated and independent woman.

OXFORD WORLD'S CLASSICS

ANN RADCLIFFE
A SICILIAN ROMANCE

Clarissa ✓

SAMUEL RICHARDSON
1689 – 1761
Nationality: British
First Published: Samuel Richardson, 1747–8
Other Selected Titles:
Letters Written to and for Particular Friends (known as *The Familiar Letter*)
Pamela, or Virtue Rewarded
The History of Sir Charles Grandison

Samuel Richardson published Clarissa *himself.*

Among the very longest of novels written in the English language (over a million words), Samuel Richardson's *Clarissa* has secured a place in literary history for its tremendous psychological insight. Written in the then fashionable epistolary form, its main body consists of the letters of Clarissa Harlowe and her seducer, Lovelace (though there are many more correspondents throughout the novel).

Clarissa, a young woman who expects to marry well, is gravely disappointed by her parents' choice of suitor. The extremely wealthy, though ugly, Solmes is not Clarissa's idea of a good match. Instead she is drawn to a man who is as dashing and fashionable as he is lacking in moral character. He casts himself as Clarissa's rescuer from her intended and dreaded marriage by whisking her off to the apparent safety and anonymity of London.

With Clarissa now isolated from her family and friends in the city, Lovelace is free to force his intentions upon her, despite her attempts to resist him. Eventually, unable to bear the temptation that Clarissa presents him, Lovelace drugs and rapes her. Neither recovers: Clarissa suffers temporary insanity, while Lovelace, sick with guilt, is killed in a duel.

The novel's seeming narrative simplicity is not its strength; it is the sometimes devastating psychological insight that Richardson achieves that is its real forté.

Waverley

Waverley was Scott's 14th published work which solidified his reputation as Scotland's most famous novelist. He was a prolific writer, both in poetry and prose fiction.

Subtitled 'Tis Sixty Years Since', *Waverley* is a historical novel that was the first of its kind. Instead of using the historical setting as a mere backdrop to the novel (as the Gothic genre had done before), it sets its characters within the thrall of real events – in this case, the Jacobite uprising.

Edward Waverley, a fine young gentleman, obtains a commission in the army in 1745, and while on leave attracts the attentions of the Baron of Bradwardine's daughter, Rose. On his travels, he later meets and falls in love with Flora, the daughter of a Highland chieftain, putting Edward in a politically compromising position. Despite suffering the burdens of intrigues he does not marry Flora and instead returns to Rose. The Highland Chieftain is convicted of treason and Flora goes into a convent.

The fame that *Waverley* earned for Walter Scott was international and was such that Edinburgh's Scott Monument is the tallest literary effigy in the United Kingdom.

PENGUIN CLASSICS

WALTER SCOTT

Waverley

SIR WALTER SCOTT
1771 – 1832
Nationality: Scottish
First Published: A. Constable & Co., 1814
Other Selected Titles:
Guy Mannering, or The Astrologer
Rob Roy
Ivanhoe

Frankenstein, or The Modern Prometheus

MARY SHELLEY
1797 – 1851
Nationality: British
First Published: Lackington et al, 1818
Other Selected Titles:
The Last Man

Mary Shelley was the daughter of the radical feminist Mary Wollstonecraft.

Mary Shelley was the only daughter of the writers William Godwin and Mary Wollstonecraft. She eloped with the poet Percy Bysshe Shelley in 1814, and they were married two years later. It was during this time that they stayed for a few days at the Villa Diodati on Lake Geneva. It was here that they and their friends Byron and Polidori decided to devise stories to entertain themselves. It was the two lesser-known literary figures which produced the most memorable work. Polidori's *The Vampyre* was relatively successful in its day, but the story of *Frankenstein* has burned brightly in the popular imagination ever since its publication in 1818.

The story is told by an English explorer in the Arctic who assists Frankenstein on the final leg of his chase at the end of the novel. Frankenstein is a talented young medical student who strikes upon the secret of endowing life to the dead. He becomes obsessed with the idea that he might make a man. The resulting creature is lonely, miserable and an outcast who seeks murderous revenge for his condition. The creature flees with Frankenstein in pursuit. It is here that he meets the explorer and recounts his story, dying soon after. The novel has been filmed numerous times, but none has effectively conveyed the stark horror and philosophical acuity of the novel.

The Red and the Black ✓

The Red and the Black is the Hamlet of the 19th-century Realist novel. Just as Shakespeare's play is thought by many critics to have invented the notion of psychological interiority as a way of conveying narrative, it

Dubouchet inv sculp.

The Red and the Black *is set in France in the 1830s.*

did not become the mainstay for prose fiction to engage with the complex interior lives of its characters until Stendhal.

It is the story of Julien Sorel, a young and idealistic man eager to make his way in the world. He believes that his posturing, manners and machinations will endear him to his betters, and believes himself to be the possessor of social talent and intellectual insight. As the novel progresses, Stendhal's skill at revealing Sorel's mediocrity is evident.

The novel goes on to explore the ways in which his central character is merely a pawn in a much larger game conducted by those much more powerful than himself. The novel's main aim it seems was to satirize the aristocracy (the 'red' of the army uniform) and to ridicule the impetuousness of the Catholic Church (the 'black' of the cassock).

STENDHAL (MARIE-HENRI BEYLE)
1783 – 1842
Nationality: French
First Published: Hilsum, 1830
Other Selected Titles:
La Chartreuse de Parme
(*The Charterhouse of Parma*)

The Strange Case of Dr Jekyll and Mr Hyde

Robert Louis Stevenson suffered from respiratory illness all his life and died when he was only 44.

ROBERT LOUIS STEVENSON
1850 – 1894
Nationality: Scottish
First Published: Longmans, Green & Co.,1885
Other Selected Titles:
Treasure Island
Kidnapped
The Master of Ballantrae

Perhaps Stevenson's most successful novella, the story of Dr Jekyll and Mr Hyde explored the pathology of the split personality. Several characters within the book narrate the story, and they tell of Dr Henry Jekyll's experiments to separate the good and evil aspects of his personality.

Jekyll devises a drug that he has some success with. He is able at will to change into his evil counterpart, Mr Hyde, who gives way to uncontrollable urges on the streets and alleyways of London. While the respectable doctor initially finds no difficulty in returning from his rabid personality to the sanguine one, he soon finds himself slipping into Mr Hyde without recourse to his drugs. Unable to make any more of the drug because of an error in the formula, Jekyll's supplies soon run out. Having committed terrible crimes, Mr Hyde is now wanted in London for murder. Dr Jekyll takes his own life, but the body found at his house is that of Hyde's. It is only his confession that reveals the truth of the man's real struggle.

The story has been interpreted as a representation of the Victorians' sense of themselves. Jekyll is the public persona and in every way a gentleman, but just beneath the surface lie baser desires that remain unspoken.

Dracula

One of the most spectacular novels of the 19th century, *Dracula* still frightens its readers today just as it did over a century ago. The story, like that of *Frankenstein*, has become a modern myth and has been performed countless times on stage, radio, television and in film.

BRAM STOKER
1847 – 1912
Nationality: Irish
First Published: A. Constable & Co., 1897

Presented in a series of formats (such as letters, diaries, even news items), it tells the story of a London solicitor, Harker, recruited by Count Dracula to acquire property for him in England. Harker's journey to the Count's home in Transylvania is an ominous one, and after his arrival the sense of dread and fear is palpable as the tension rises and Harker slowly begins to realize his client's horrible eccentricities.

Perhaps the novel's most powerful moment is when Harker sees his employer crawling face-downwards on the outside wall of his castle, like a bat. Harker escapes and Dracula follows him to England where Harker's fiancée and her friend come into the count's line of sight.

Aided by Van Helsing – an expert in vampirism – Harker has to kill one of his own who has become a vampire after Dracula drained her veins. They then pursue Dracula back to Transylvania where his long life finally comes to an end.

PENGUIN CLASSICS

BRAM STOKER

DRACULA

Gulliver's Travels

(TRAVELS INTO SEVERAL REMOTE NATIONS OF THE WORLD BY LEMUEL GULLIVER)

JONATHAN SWIFT
1667 – 1745
Nationality: Irish
First Published: B. Motte, 1726

One of the keystones of English literature, *Gulliver's Travels* is an exceedingly odd book – part novel, part adventure, and part prose satire. Because it was one of the books that gave birth to the novel form, it inevitably did not yet have the rules of the genre to keep to because they had not yet been laid down.

Divided into four sections, the novel tells of four adventures of Lemuel Gulliver. In the first he is shipwrecked on the island of Liliput, which is inhabited by a people that are only a few inches tall, their smallness quite literally translates into small-mindedness as they spend their time indulging in ridiculous and petty debates. Brobdingnag is Gulliver's second destination; it is a place inhabited by giants who are horrified when Gulliver recounts the splendid achievements of civilization. The third adventure is not nearly as focussed; it mainly consists of disconnected vignettes that do not have anything near the philosophical or even the geographical unity that the first two have. The fourth sees Gulliver visiting the Houyhnhnms, a horse-like people who caringly govern the brutish Yahoos. Gulliver is ashamed to note that the Yahoos resemble humans.

Whether it is a novel, adventure or satire does not really matter; it is one of the most thought-provoking reads in any genre or language.

TRAVELS

INTO SEVERAL

Remote NATIONS

OF THE

WORLD.

In FOUR PARTS.

By *LEMUEL GULLIVER*,
First a SURGEON, and then a CAPTAIN of several SHIPS.

VOL. I.

LONDON·

Printed for BENJ. MOTTE, *at the Middle* Temple-Gate *in* Fleet-ftreet.
MDCCXXVI.

*Gulliver entertains the people
of Brobdingnag.*

Vanity Fair

WILLIAM MAKEPEACE THACKERAY
1811 – 1863
Nationality: British
First Published: Bradbury & Evans, 1848
Other Selected Titles:
The History of Pendennis
The History of Henry Esmond
The Newcomes

One of the most hilarious and viciously satirical novels of the Victorian period, *Vanity Fair* recounts the adventures of Becky Sharp – the orphaned daughter of a Parisian actress – who is more than determined to make her way in the world.

As a spirited and worldly-wise young woman, Becky aims to marry well. It does not matter to whom as long as he is wealthy. Her friend, Amelia, is a more ideal Victorian woman; she is submissive, restrained and unerringly polite – though as the novel progresses the reader sees how Amelia uses these aspects of her personality to manipulate others.

Becky is introduced to Amelia's hapless brother, Jos, and believes that she has captured him in agreeing to marry her, but he escapes her the following day. This event sets off what becomes nothing short of a panoramic social satire in which no character escapes Thackeray's merciless wit.

The novel was illustrated by Thackeray himself, and the pictures are key to understanding some of the novel's unanswered questions. Becky succeeds at the end of the novel in finally marrying Jos, but he dies soon after and there is an accompanying illustration which settles the question of whether Becky was responsible for the murder of Jos, something that Victorian propriety would not permit Thackeray to do in his text.

War and Peace

War and Peace is still a work of unrivalled scope and achievement; it is recognized as one of the world's greatest novels in any language. Its vast array of characters are set on the world stage and take part in both fictional and real events.

Set in the time of the Napoleonic wars, the book opens at a party given by Anna Pavlovna Scherer in July 1805 and the reader is introduced to the novel's cast of characters as the narrator pans around the room.

Pierre Bezukhov is probably the novel's principal character. He is the illegitimate son of a prosperous count. He is an irresponsible youth, but on inheriting his father's estate undergoes a profound philosophical conversion and becomes possessed by the idea of living a good life in an imperfect world (a common theme to Tolstoy's other works). The novel recounts this change with great subtlety, but it is the tragedy of Pierre's ultimate lack of success in effecting change, both for himself and for the peasants of his estate, which is the most moving element.

Pierre is later embroiled in the war when he witnesses the Battle of Borodino and, appalled by the consequent carnage that he witnesses, sets off to assassinate Napoleon. He is captured by the French, but later freed by the Russians. During this time, his selfish and immoral wife has died, and Pierre is free to make the right choice in a new marriage.

Tolstoy was revered as a hero in his native Russia.

LEO TOLSTOY
1828 – 1910
Nationality: Russian
First Published: *Russkii Vestnik* periodical, 1865–9
Other Selected Titles:
Anna Karenina
A Confession
The Death of Ivan Ilyich

Barchester Towers

ANTHONY TROLLOPE
1815 – 1882
Nationality: British
First Published: Smith, Elder & Co., 1857
Other Selected Titles:
The Warden
Framley Parsonage
The Small House at Allington
The Last Chronicle of Barset
The Eustace Diamonds
He Knew He Was Right
The Way We Live Now

Anthony Trollope was fascinated with everyday provincial life.

Anthony Trollope is a writer of rare abilities, brevity of characterization, and skill in maintaining the complexities of debate and argument (whether taking place between a married couple, or on the political stage). *Barchester Towers*, the second of the six novels that form *The Barsetshire Chronicles*, exhibits all the facets of this writer's wherewithal.

The Warden ended with the marriage of John Bold and Eleanor Harding, while *Barchester Towers* begins with Eleanor's sudden widowhood, and another death, that of the Bishop of Barchester. All expect Dr Grantly, the Bishop's son, to inherit the position, but instead it is given to Dr Proudie.

He arrives at Barchester, with his wife (surely one of the finest comic creations of any novel) and his unctuous and slithering chaplain, Obadiah Slope. What follows in the novel is a classic battle of wills in which the clashes between the old world and the new are eloquently dramatized by Trollope, a world in which all parties involved seek to get their own way without resorting to compromise.

Barchester Towers is one of many classic novels that Anthony Trollope produced in a prolific career, throughout which he also worked and travelled as a civil servant. Among his non-literary achievements, he is responsible for the introduction in England of the red pillar box in which letters are still posted today.

The Adventures of Huckleberry Finn

More politically and satirically engaged than its predecessor *The Adventures of Tom Sawyer*, *Huckleberry Finn* has earned its place in the canon of American literature. Narrated by its eponymous hero, Huck, the novel begins by explaining (in deepest-southern dialect) his escapades since *The Adventures of Tom Sawyer*.

Huck is now living in the home of Widow Douglas, and his contemptible and dishonest father kidnaps him to claim the money that he and Tom had stolen from Injun Joe's cave. Escaping, Huck runs away to Jackson's Island. On the island he meets another fugitive, Jim, a slave of the Douglas household. Tom discovers that his disappearance has been attributed to Jim, who is thought to be on the run for Tom's murder.

The two decide to escape on the Mississippi river. In picaresque fashion, the novel recounts their adventures as they travel downstream, encountering all kinds of dubious life. Jim is sold by petty criminals to another family, but is rescued by Huck and, latter, Tom Sawyer, who ingeniously pose as one another to free Jim. Jim has, however, unknowingly been freed already in the will of Widow Douglas' sister.

Its sometimes unsympathetic lampooning of life in Missouri and especially its views on slavery endowed the novel with a greater moral gravitas that some of Twain's other work lacked.

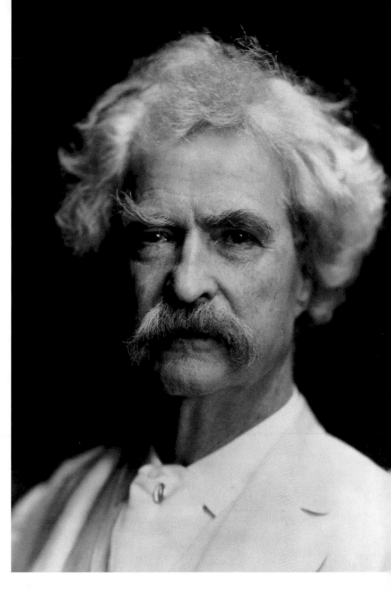

Mark Twain's skill lay in revealing injustice through the eyes of children.

**MARK TWAIN
(LANGHORNE CLEMENS)**
1835 – 1910
Nationality: American
First Published: Dawson, 1884
Other Selected Titles:
*The Adventures of Tom Sawyer
The Prince and the Pauper
A Connecticut Yankee in King
Arthur's Court
The Tragedy of Pudd'nhead Wilson*

Candide, or Optimism

**VOLTAIRE
(FRANÇOIS-MARIE AROUET)**
1694 – 1778
Nationality: French
First Published: G. & P. Cramer, 1759
Other Selected Titles:
Zadig

François-Marie Arouet.

It is the signal of a great novel where one of its characters' names enters the language as an adjective, in this case 'Panglossian'. Dr Pangloss' constant assertion that 'all is for the best in this, the best of all possible worlds' was a signifier of his unerringly excessive optimism in a world that clearly was dealing him a very bad hand indeed. Such was the philosophical dimension of Voltaire's funny, incisive and satirical novella that tells of the adventures of the young and naive Candide and his friends, Dr Pangloss (his tutor), the obscenely materialistic Cunégonde (Candide's belle) and Cacambo (Candide's servant).

In picaresque style, the novel satirizes the optimistic philosophy of Gottfried Liebniz by taking the reader through a gallery of the horrors of the 18th-century world, like the disastrous Lisbon earthquake of 1755, or the terrible conditions of slavery, or the stupidity of imperial war. The novel's adventures and misadventures are narrated at a whiplashing pace as the group travel internationally. But it is its unwavering humour and Voltaire's ability to never miss an opportunity to lampoon the unenlightened that make *Candide* such a memorable read.

The enjoyable story of *Candide* was successfully adapted for the operatic stage by Leonard Bernstein in 1956.

The Castle of Otranto

Arguably the first ever Gothic novel, *The Castle of Otranto* reads like a spoof of the genre that was to emerge in later years. So full is it of caves, animate statues, ghosts and ghouls, appearances and disappearances, terror, sorrow, love and loss, that Walpole was afraid of ridicule on publication and decided to publish it anonymously and pretend that the novel was a translation of a 16th-century Italian manuscript.

On his wedding day, Conrad, the son of Prince Manfred of Otranto, is killed when he is crushed beneath a giant black helmet that fell from a statue. Determined to have an heir, Manfred decides to divorce his wife and marry his son's intended, Isabella. She flees from the castle and is assisted by a man that she finds in the underground passageways. She escapes and is given sanctuary at a monastery, which she also flees.

A series of daring rescues and thrilling escapes ensues until the novel concludes with Prince Manfred accidentally murdering his daughter in place of Isabella and his sorrow for his loss is so terrible that the castle walls collapse. He and his wife (Hippolita) vow to lead a good religious life henceforth.

Horace Walpole

HORACE WALPOLE
1717 – 1797
Nationality: British
First Published: W. Bathoe & T. Lowndes, 1764

The House of Mirth

Edith Wharton was a wealthy society hostess.

EDITH WHARTON
1862 – 1937
Nationality: American
First Published: Macmillan & Co.,
1905
Other Selected Titles:
Ethan Frome
The Age of Innocence

Lily Bart – beautiful, confident and socially adept – is 29 years of age yet she is still unwed. Her ambitions for a worthy groom of sufficient wealth and position in society have, so far, not been fulfilled.

Her choice of husband lies between the affluent, though highly socially inept, Simon Rosedale, and a man she cannot marry: Lawrence Selden. Although the latter is a lawyer, she knows that she cannot live the life she so desires with him and never declares her feelings for him.

After a gambling party, Lily becomes indebted to Gus Trenor, whose suggestion that she repay him in sexual currency rather than money shocks her. On a boating trip, the wife of George Dorset, in order to conceal an assignation with her lover, accuses Lily of being her husband's mistress. The subsequent scandal drives Lily outside respectable society.

Lily goes on to become a milliner. After a final meeting with Lawrence Selden, she commits suicide. It is Selden who discovers her body, having come to ask for her hand in marriage. He also finds that her inheritance was to be used to pay her debt to Trenor.

Characterized by insightfulness, Wharton's harmonious and confident prose is such that she did not need to fill it with sensational event, and instead relied on the analysis of her characters' psychology and their desires and intentions to entertain the most demanding reader.

The Picture of Dorian Gray

Oscar Wilde's prosecution and imprisonment in 1895 eclipsed somewhat the power and sheer ingenuity of this modern fable. It is the story of three friends, Lord Henry Wotton, a decadent aesthete, Basil Hallward, a talented artist, and Dorian Gray their handsome young protégé.

Obsessed with his own beauty and its destined decay, Dorian sells his soul so that he may stay young, and the portrait that Basil painted of him may grow old instead.

Dorian descends into a life of excess, and becomes the subject of gossip among the chattering classes who report him as having been seen in the lowliest and most iniquitous parts of London. The portrait, bearing the scars of Dorian's debauched and immoral life, now depicts the horrific and deformed representation of his soul. Dorian's depravity culminates in, as he sees it, the necessary murder of Basil so that his secret is safe.

Meanwhile, the brother of Sybil Vane (an ex-lover of Dorian's), who had sworn revenge on him after Sybil's suicide, is accidentally killed at a shooting party. Released from this burden, Dorian swears to be good, and expecting to see his new morality depicted in a rejuvenated portrait, Dorian finds no trace of decency and kindness in the picture. In desolation, he stabs the painting and dies. His servants find only a bloated ugly corpse with a knife in its chest and a pristine and unmarked picture of Dorian Gray as he was 18 years ago.

The fact that Oscar Wilde's imprisonment and subsequent death prevented him from writing another novel was a grave loss to literature.

OSCAR WILDE
1854 – 1900
Nationality: Irish
First Published: Ward, Lock & Co., 1890
Other Selected Titles:
The Canterville Ghost
The Happy Prince and Other Stories
The Portrait of Mr. W. H.
Lord Arthur Saville's Crime and Other Stories
De Profundis

At the time of publication, Oscar Wilde was criticized for the immoral and unhealthy nature of the story.

To the Lighthouse ✓

VIRGINIA WOOLF
1882 – 1941
Nationality: British
First Published: Hogarth Press, 1927
Other Selected Titles:
The Voyage Out
Jacob's Room
Mrs Dalloway
The Waves
The Years
Between the Acts

Virginia Woolf and her husband set up Hogarth Press in 1917.

Although not explicitly autobiographical, *To the Lighthouse* borrowed extensively from Woolf's own experience of the family holidays of her childhood. In three sections it obliquely tells the story of the Ramsays' and their guests' efforts to go and see a nearby lighthouse while on holiday. The first section recounts the events of a single summer's day in which we are introduced to Mrs Ramsay (not dissimilar in character to Mrs Wilcox in *Howards End*), a matriarch whose understated personality, generosity and graciousness is valued by all around her, except perhaps for Mr Ramsay who is too involved in himself, his philosophy, and curt practicality to notice her.

The drama opens with the youngest child, James, whose desire it is to see the lighthouse, his mother's keenness to allow him to, and his father's insensitive remonstrance that the weather will never permit them to take the journey. Mr Ramsay is indeed correct and they do not go. In the second section, Woolf's extraordinary skill and lyricism as a writer recounts the death of Mrs Ramsay, and other family members, and soars through a decade of history. It is only in the final section of the novel that a very different kind of visit to the lighthouse is finally accomplished. It is a novel of rare significance, sumptuously written and executed.

La Bête Humaine

Despite having been together many years, Roubaud suspects Séverine of an infidelity with one of his superiors at the railway company. He manipulates her into tricking Grandmorin to meet her aboard a train where Roubaud murders him. The mentally disturbed Lantier sees him commit the murder but remains silent, and later takes up an affair with Séverine. As their relationship develops, Séverine's marriage deteriorates to the point that she plots with Lantier to kill Roubaud, but is unable to go through with it.

Lantier then falls victim to the jealousy of another woman, Flore, who decides to kill Lantier and Séverine, derailing their train. Although many are killed, Lantier is only injured and Séverine is unhurt. Flore, unable to suffer the burden of guilt, takes her own life. In his recuperation, Lantier's mania for murder returns and he kills Severine. Astonishingly, Roubaud is found guilty of the crime and given life imprisonment.

The novel concludes with yet another terrible crime when Lantier fights with the husband of his new lover, and both fall to their deaths from a moving train, leaving some drunken and jovial soldiers on board careering through the night to certain death.

Originally intended as two novels, one about the railways, the other about a man destined by heredity to become a murderer, *La Bête Humaine* is a strange, disturbing and memorable novel that depicts the chaos and corruption of the French legal system.

Zola wrote La Bête Humaine *as the 17th in a series of 20 novels.*

ÉMILE ZOLA
1840 – 1902
Nationality: French
First Published: Charpentier, 1890
Other Selected Titles:
Thérèse Raquin
L'Assommoir
Germinal

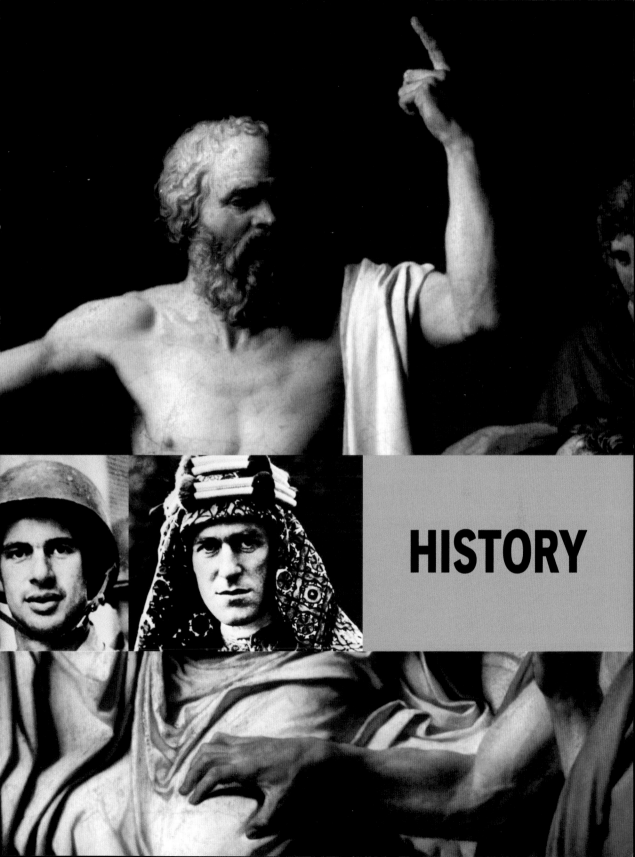

HISTORY

London – The Biography

PETER ACKROYD
1949 –
Nationality: British
First Published: Chatto & Windus, 2000
Other Selected Titles:
The Life of Thomas More
Albion: The Origins of the English Imagination
Shakespeare: A Biography
Voyages Through Time: Ancient Egypt

Readers of Ackroyd's *London: The Biography* will be disappointed if they expect a meticulous survey of the city's architectural development or a studied portrait of the famous men and women to have walked its streets over time. Instead what we receive is a swashbuckling and emotive commentary on the life of the city as an evolving organism, beginning with the violent impulse of Roman invasion and control in 55BC, and concluding with a vision of late 20th-century London, a city of 'prismatic blue glass' echoing with the mixed tones of chattering yuppies and resilient cockney banter.

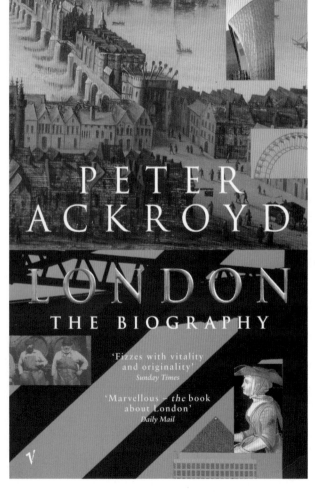

Ackroyd beckons the reader on a journey which incorporates histories of crime, dress, disease, politics and theatre, but refuses to get side-tracked into particular genres or theoretical frameworks that might alienate the reader or interrupt the story of chaotic but magnificent daily life within England's capital.

Ackroyd's style is striking for the way it expresses awe and loyalty to a metropolis he is clearly falling further in love with as he writes, but this passion is infused with scholarship too, as a cacophony of literary, philosophical and anonymous voices, both resident and visiting, commentate on the city in its various guises. The chapter Loud and Everlasting is the perfect epitome of Ackroyd's historical strategy, relaying hundreds of years of the city's evolution with reference to the sounds of bells, industrial machinery, traffic, conversation and cries, all contributing to the changing accent of the city over time.

The reader of this book may at times feel bewildered, harried and distracted by the diversity of information Ackroyd offers, but this is part of the book's objective and power – it is a text which performs the character of the capital, teeming with a complicated cast of 'Londoners', as it describes it.

Che Guevara: A Revolutionary Life

In the late 1970s, and for over a decade thereafter, the currency of Che Guevara's image was down-valued. That image still appeared – emblazoned on tourist and teen commodities across the West, and in many Cuban houses it still nestled beside images of the Virgen de la Guardia, the patron Madonna of Cuba. Compared to the worldwide sheer iconicity of that image following Che's murder in 1967, however, it seemed as if Che's moment was waning.

Yet his image re-emerged with powerful force in the 1990s. As a symbol of rebellion and defiance, it still graced commodities aimed at the dissatisfied but now the picture of a bearded man, gaunt face topped by a beret with a single star, also appeared on the banners of demonstrators in Italy and Venezuela, was carried proudly by the Zapatistas in Chiapas, and was flaunted by a newly beleaguered Cuban government. John Lee Anderson's ambitious biography can be thought of as both a symptom of and an attempt to explain our enduring fascination with Ernest 'Che' Guevara.

Anderson spent over five years researching Che's life; he travelled to Cuba, Argentina, Bolivia, Paraguay, Mexico, Moscow, Washington, Sweden and London; he managed to get an unprecedented level of access to Aleida March, Che's widow, and to several of the revolutionary's closest friends and advisors.

The result is the definitive biography of a man whose life was interwoven with some of the conflicts, movements and ideas which themselves defined the second half of the 20th century. There are bound to be omissions and inconsistencies in any work on a figure so central to, and so controversial within, 20th-century political culture. Even if it cannot please everyone all the time, however, Anderson's detailed work remains the most significant single volume on the life and times of a man who is still mourned by many across the world.

CHE GUEVARA
A Revolutionary Life
JON LEE ANDERSON
'Absorbing and convincing...an indispensable work of contemporary history' Robin Blackburn, *Guardian*

JOHN LEE ANDERSON
1928 – 1967
Nationality: American
First Published: Bantam Press, 1997
Other Selected Titles:
Inside the League
(with Scott Anderson)
War Zones
(with Scott Anderson)

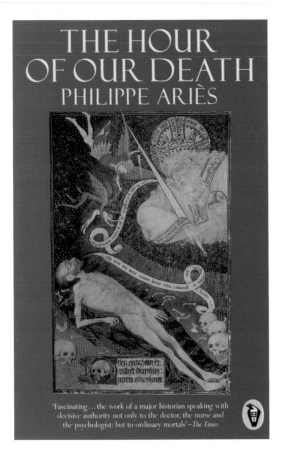

THE HOUR
OF OUR DEATH
PHILIPPE ARIÈS

'Fascinating...the work of a major historian speaking with
decisive authority not only to the doctor, the nurse and
the psychologist: but to ordinary mortals' – *The Times*

PHILIPPE ARIES
1914 – 1984
Nationality: French
First Published: Oxford University
Press, 1981 (first English translation)
Other Selected Titles:
Centuries of Childhood
Images of Man and Death
A History of Private Life

The Hour of Our Death

Death is a difficult topic for the historian, since
our understanding of it is forever deferred. We
either see it, alien and inexpressible, in others, or
face the impossibility of recording it as it
approaches us. Indeed, the writing of history is
often conceived of as a way of preserving past lives
for the profit of society, so a history of death might
seem to be going against the spirit of the discipline
itself. Philippe Ariès confronts these dilemmas in
his book *The Hour of Our Death* by telling a
superbly rich history of our attitudes towards
death, speculating on the changing perception of,
among other phenomena, illness, grief, burial,
memorial and afterlife.

Ranging from concepts of a 'welcome' or 'tame'
death within medieval knightly culture, to what
he sees as 20th-century embarrassment or 'denial'
in relation to death, Ariès is writing in a historical
genre with few precedents. Because of this, he
allows himself a double-method. He plays the
rigorous historian, tracing an astounding collection
of literary and material sources relating to death – theological
tracts, artistic figurations, contorted philosophies, orderly wills,
personal memorials and sacred shrines – each emanating
different nuances of fear, faith, loss and meditation in relation
to the cultural significance of death.

But Ariès is also the theorist of death as he sees it, an
autobiographical drive, employing intuition and experience,
guiding him as he writes. He empathizes with past cultures'
experiences of death, uses familial examples of his own and
rages against the loss of ritual, intellectual and social modes
of confronting death with honesty and dignity.

This ensures a welcome contrast of tone and subject,
where a meticulous interrogation of 16th-century tombstone
inscriptions might give way to impassioned calls for the
respectful treatment of the dying in our own society. This is
a powerful history that is at the same time cultural,
philosophical and intensely personal.

Berlin – The Downfall

It seemed both structurally and morally necessary for Antony Beevor to write *Berlin – The Downfall.* It provides perfect symmetry in relation to his opening World War Two epic, *Stalingrad*, published in 1998. An archival source had revealed to Beevor that a Russian colonel, surveying emaciated German prisoners amidst the rubble of his besieged city, had proclaimed 'That's how Berlin is going to look' in furious prophecy. And this is the story of that prophecy enacted a year later, with the Red Army descending on Berlin, 'exulting in their revenge'. Readers familiar with Beevor will be aware, however, that this story was never going to fall into the caricatures of justified vengeance or senseless retaliation: this is history told in kaleidoscopic detail with multiple perspectives.

Alongside the approach of the Russian forces, we hear the narrative of anticipation, siege and attrition from the claustrophobic sites of bunker and ruin, German diarists exposing the simultaneous impossibility of victory and of surrender as the SS forces sweep the city shooting 'deserters' on the spot. Textually and pictorially, this book imposes searing images of suffering on the reader – a German mother and daughters, for example, laid out neatly on a bedroom floor in choreographed suicide.

These portraits force a kind of adrenalin of despair as you read, a compulsion to stretch empathy and understanding further just at the point you feel like looking away. As well as providing emotive and dramatic narrative, Beevor masters the more clinical voice of the political and military historian as he describes international diplomacy, strategies of attack and resistance, Hitler's vanity and the Nazi elite's sacrifice of thousands – civilian and military – in their refusal to countenance the advance of history.

ANTONY BEEVOR
1946 –
Nationality: British
First Published: Viking, 2002
Other Selected Titles:
The Spanish Civil War
Stalingrad
Paris After the Liberation, 1944–1949

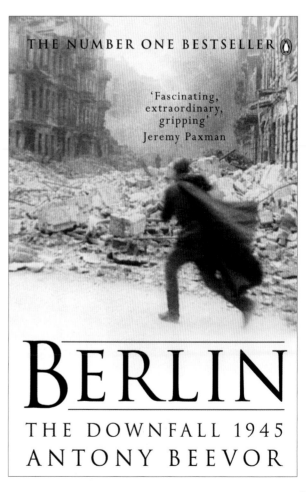

THE NUMBER ONE BESTSELLER

'Fascinating, extraordinary, gripping'
Jeremy Paxman

BERLIN

THE DOWNFALL 1945
ANTONY BEEVOR

The Mediterranean and the Mediterranean World in the Age of Philip II

FERNAND BRAUDEL
1902 – 1985
Nationality: French
First Published: Collins, 1972
(first English translation)
Other Selected Titles:
Civilization and Capitalism
Writings on History
A History of Civilizations

*French historian and writer
Fernand Braudel in his office,
Paris, 1984.*

Fernand Braudel wrote most of *The Mediterranean* during four years of captivity as a German prisoner of war, sending drafts to his intellectual ally in Paris, Lucien Febvre, co-founder in 1929 (with Marc Bloch) of the polemical journal *Annales*. This intellectual and political context informs not only the genesis but the very texture of Braudel's monumental work.

In a Europe that was engulfed in violent war for the second time in less than a generation, a Europe dominated by political systems which fetishized strong leaders and the mythical status of events, Braudel (and others of the *Annales* school) turned to a new method to enlarge the field of history and of historical understanding.

That method was defined and defended by Braudel in the style and structure of *The Mediterranean*. It was a method designed out of a rejection of history as a narrative of events, an *histoire événementielle*, which retold history as the doings of the few 'great' men in command of the few 'great' states. *The Mediterranean* takes instead a structural or analytical approach to history, using geographical and environmental time to enlarge our understanding of the civilizations, and their conflicts, which constituted the Mediterranean world between 1400 and 1600.

In the name of total history – a history which seeks historical understanding in the total play of structures and forces at work in any one historical moment – *The Mediterranean* relegates political history to its final section, Events, Politics and People. Section I, The Role of the Environment, is a brilliantly ambitious analysis of the material geography of the Mediterranean region; Section II, Collective Destinies and General Trends, provides a sustained exploration of the structures, the economies, trade patterns, empires and 'civilizations' of the early modern Mediterranean. The overall result is not a reduction of human history or agency but a stunning integration of the different levels of historical time which collectively make up the 'slow and powerful march of history'.

The Pleasures of the Imagination: English Culture in the Eighteenth Century

John Brewer's *The Pleasures of the Imagination* documents the 18th-century creation of 'high culture'. However, this creation is not reported as a formal aesthetic decision, supervised by an aloof elite of aristocrats and dilettantes. Instead what Brewer displays is the complex social and commercial interaction between artists and their patrons, amidst a turbulent world of engravers, printers, critics and pamphleteers, each exploiting new artistic techniques and subject matter for commercial or political gain.

Brewer unveils the intricate conventions of politeness and etiquette that flourished in 18th-century Britain, deconstructing the codes of dress, gesture and performance that orchestrated the behaviour of groups gathered in public gardens, galleries and theatres. He also invites the reader into the more rarefied sites of the English court and the country house. However, this history refuses to skate on the layers of high society, chaperoning the reader into the sub-cultures of satire, savage journalism and forgery that were the life-blood of 18th-century artistic markets. It is this artistic dialogue between the polite and the scandalous, the refined and the rakish, that Brewer's history records with relish.

Although this book carries a focused argument about the development of the century's aesthetic and artistic cultures, its thematic arrangement and liberal use of high quality images ensures that it is a history that can be dipped into pleasurably as well as read with scholarly intent. The reader can visit its pages in the manner of a curious tourist or obsessive collector, and obtain equal pleasure there.

JOHN BREWER
1810 – 1879
Nationality: British
First Published: Harper Collins, 1997
Other Selected Titles:
The Sinews of Power: War, Money and the English State, 1688–1783
Consumption and the World of Goods in the 17th and 18th Centuries

Frozen Desire: An Enquiry into The Meaning of Money

JAMES BUCHAN
1954 –
Nationality: British
First Published: Farrar, Straus & Giroux, 1997
Other Selected Titles:
The Authentic Adam Smith
Crowded with Genius: The Scottish Enlightenment
Capital of the Mind: How Edinburgh Changed the World

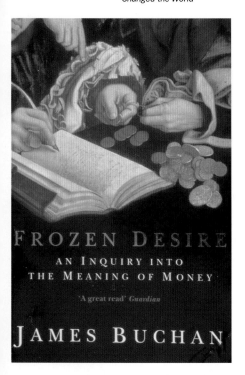

James Buchan's *Frozen Desire: The Meaning of Money* is an attempt to discern what he terms 'the psychological mystery' of money, beginning '…at the point at which economics leaves off.' Buchan, a former journalist for the *Financial Times*, contends that money is promiscuous – 'it will just as happily serve tyranny as guarantee liberty' – and, ultimately, immoral. He cites Timon of Athens in demonstrating the degenerative moral and social properties of money: 'This yellow slave will knit and break religions; bless the accursed;/Make the hoar leprosy ador'd;/ place thieves,/And give them title, knee, and approbation/With senators on the bench.'

Buchan maintains that it is only during the last two to three millennia that money has crept from the peripheries of human experience to claim dominion over relationships and, crucially, our most intimate sense of self. Even Jesus, perhaps the outstanding historical insurgent against the sovereignty of money, does not escape untarnished. Citing his advice to his followers to 'render therefore unto Caesar the things that are Caesar's', Buchan makes the questionable assertion that 'Jesus dug his own doctrinal grave'. Christopher Columbus, blinded by the corrupting power of money, is unable to acknowledge that he has found the 'new world'; rather, he is blinded by the prospect of finding gold.

Buchan's literary talent is evident in this elegantly written work. We are made tourists of the Italian town where double-entry bookkeeping was invented and terrified by his description of Rembrandt's *Judas Repentant, Returning the Pieces of Silver*. Commenting, later, on the 1980s and 1990s, his initial contention of the degenerative properties of money has intensified to the point that money has effectively banished all psychological goals: 'Duty, religion, public service, liberty, justice or aristocracy… only money, it seemed, was to be trusted.'

Though Buchan himself sometimes seems overly captivated, as well as horrified, by the tyranny of money, *Frozen Desire: The Meaning of Money* is a crucial historical exposé of the malign properties of capital.

Hitler and Stalin – Parallel Lives

'He pulled himself together, raising his voice as though addressing a large audience and shrieked "I shall build aeroplanes, build aeroplanes, aeroplanes, aeroplanes, and I shall annihilate my enemies".' This fragment, from the diaries of a businessman who overheard one of Hitler's private wartime rants, is the kind of historical source that Alan Bullock, author of *Hitler and Stalin – Parallel Lives* revels in. The double biography that Bullock constructs is a daring project, not just because the two figures never actually met but also because recent historians (such as Amis, 2003, and Thurston, 1999) have found even individual portraits of Hitler and Stalin both exhausting and elusive.

The logic behind the parallel history is, however, a clear one. Both leaders, sharing the extraordinary period between 1889 and 1945, can be read as agents of revolutionary political change, epitomes of tyranny, terror and charisma and dreamers of international empire. As 'perfect models of Machiavellian politics', Hitler and Stalin become the catalysts through which 20th-century world history can be told. The political philosophies and personal lives of the two men both mirror and refract each other, while never quite converging. Hitler envisions a totalitarian empire, Stalin achieves one. The two are forever in a dialogue of ambition, power and conflict as the Second World War unfolds, the 'ghost of Hitler' influencing Stalin's post-war policies.

Much of the narrative progresses through the rigour of detailed biography, political history and the meticulous restaging of the events the men shaped. However, Bullock also employs subtle philosophical and sociological theory throughout, drawing our attention to Hegel's concept of 'world historical individuals' and the structures of propaganda and terror that supported each man's popular power. In contrast to some texts and documentaries that almost fetishize the terror associated with these leaders, this is an admirably moral history, charting the horrors of the Final Solution and the Soviet Kulaks, the agencies of what Bullock calls the 'industrialization of mass murder'.

ALAN BULLOCK
1914 – 2004
Nationality: British
First Published: Harper Collins, 1991
Other Selected Titles:
Hitler: A Study in Tyranny
Past and the Future
The Norton Dictionary of Modern Thought (Ed. with Stephen Trombley)

The Civilization of the Renaissance in Italy

JACOB BURCKHARDT
1818 – 1897
Nationality: Swiss
First Published: 1860
The Age of Constantine
The Cicerone – an Art Guide of
Painting in Italy
The Greeks and Greek Civilization
Judgements on History and
Historians

For the contemporary reader, *The Civilization of the Renaissance in Italy*, published in 1860, feels almost too familiar. Michelangelo, Dante, Leonardo da Vinci – names that signify so much – reappear here in heroic garb, sublime manifestations of the Italian spirit during the 14th and 15th centuries. Indeed, the idea of the Renaissance itself, an integral part of modern sensibility, is restated by Burckhardt with disarming conviction. He confidently dismisses the Middle Ages as a period in which '(m)an was conscious of himself only as a member of a race, people, party, family, or corporation,' before proclaiming: 'In Italy this veil first melted into air; an objective treatment and consideration of the State and of all things of this world became possible. The subjective side at the same time asserted itself with corresponding emphasis; man became a spiritual individual and recognized himself as such.'

Of course, the reason for the déjà vu is that it was Burckhardt's 'historicist' classic itself which shaped the idea of the Renaissance as the cradle of modernity. He showed how notions such as the autonomous individual, fostered in the bustling cosmopolis of the Italian city, or the modern secular state, a product not of providence but conscious 'reflection and calculation', had their source in the historical development of the Italian spirit. And its dramatis personae, be it the artistic genius or the brutal tyrant, were merely its most striking emanations.

But it is the tone that is most striking. As opposed to New Historicist treatments, or drier, diachronic analyses, separating the cultural level from the economic, Burckhardt's is impassioned. For if the spirit of modernity forged itself in the Italian city-states, indeed, if it reached peaks in 15th-century Florence, Burckhardt was convinced he wrote in the period of its decline. Like Nietzsche, who attended some of Burckhardt's lectures, he surveyed modern liberalism, particularly after 1848, with dismay. The confidence, indeed the flamboyance of emancipated subjectivity manifest in Burckhardt's history of the Renaissance, can also be viewed as a critique of its contemporary degeneration.

PENGUIN CLASSICS

JACOB BURCKHARDT
The Civilization of the Renaissance in Italy

Daily Life in Ancient Rome

Faced, in 1939, with the multi-faceted topic of the Roman Empire, Carcopino distinguished himself with a methodological turn that, even today, separates him from most classical scholars. His method, marked by sharp temporal focus, precision of detail and faithful reconstruction, is the kind that acts as a blessing to current film and documentary makers: the researchers for *Gladiator* (2000) and the recent BBC/HBO series *Rome* (2005) no doubt pay heavy debts to Carpocino's pioneering study of daily life in Rome from the middle of the first century AD up to the reign of Emperor Hadrian (117–138).

Carpocino argues that this period represents the height of empire, before the corrosive internal disruption of Christianity and the overstretching of colonial responsibility, and presents Rome as 'the hub and centre of the universe, proud and wealthy queen of a world she seemed to have pacified for ever'. He spends Part I of the study contextualizing Roman life thematically, surveying the structure of society, the institutions of marriage and family life and the forces of education and religion that shape political and legal power. Of notable interest here is the account of the wife and mother's developing power during this period, where the 'Roman Matron' is claimed to have 'enjoyed a dignity and independence at least equal if not superior to those claimed by contemporary feminists'.

Most distinctive, however, is Carcopino's second section, which chaperones the reader through the 'daily routine' of Roman life, remarking first on the sundials and water-clocks that signalled breakfast time and the elaborate ornamentation of dressing, before detailing the diverse occupations, spectacles and social rituals that textured the rest of the day. It is this sense of intimacy and privileged access, backed up by tremendous archaeological, linguistic and cultural scholarship, that ensures Carpocino's study a lasting legacy.

JEROME CARCOPINO
1881 – 1970
Nationality: Italian
First Published: Routledge, 1941
(first English translation)
Other Selected Titles:
Cicero: The Secrets of his Correspondence

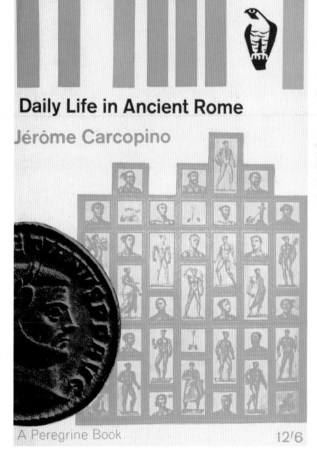

Daily Life in Ancient Rome

Jérôme Carcopino

A Peregrine Book   12/6

The Accursed Kings

French author Maurice Druon at home in France, 2001.

MAURICE DRUON
1918 –
Nationality: French
First Published: Hart-Davis, 1959
(first English translation)

Maurice Druon is the kind of scholar you might associate with the 18th rather than 20th century, achieving equal prominence in the disciplines of academia, fiction and politics. He wrote the lyrics for the Chant des Partisans, the French resistance anthem, in 1943; became a member of the Academie Française in 1966 and served as the Minister for Cultural affairs from 1973–4. A 2004 *Le Figaro* aricle reveals Druon in healthy form at 86, expressing disdain for nations without historical sensibility, arguing that, for the USA, 'history is far too short for them to really know and understand cultures with millennia under their feet'. For someone so entwined with French national identity and its layered history, it is no surprise that his historical work evinces the same passion, and his *Accursed Kings*, a seven-volume epic tracing elite French society in the 14th century, is the perfect example.

Druon's historical novel, reminiscent in grandeur and scale of Walter Scott and model to modern examples such as Stella Tillyard's *Aristocrats*, traces the reigns of severn monarchs from Philip the Fair to John II, a succession cursed by the discordance of murder, famine, rebellion and religious schism and climaxing at the time of the 100 years' war. Meticulously researched, Druon's text veils this rigour with an intimate, accessible style relaying not only the activity and dialogue, but the interior world, of the principal characters. In volume IV, Royal Succession, we hear that Mahaut, Countess of Artois, 'had a man's intelligence and strength of will' and 'suppressed a slight feeling of legitimate vanity'. Such expansive psychologizing might push readers to ponder the blurred line between historical storytelling and fictional fancy, but Druon is the type of writer who prefers to energize history this way, rather than consign it to the silence of archival repose.

The Age of the Cathedrals

Georges Duby follows the leading example of French historian, Marc Bloch, in constructing a form of history broad enough to extend beyond a lineage of 'great men' and transformative events, and rigorous enough to 'discover the living people behind the dust of the archives'. Duby's subject matter in *The Age of the Cathedrals* is the development of feudal society in Northern Europe between 980 and 1420, and to refine such an ambitious project, his method locates the interplay between medieval art (sculpture, architecture and painting) and social and religious forces.

The work is structured architecturally, with its textual tectonics shifting from 'Monastery' to 'Cathedral' to 'Palace' as the chronology unfolds, and there is a particular logic behind this spatial organization. What Duby is concerned with, essentially, is the changing encounter between the human and the divine during this era. While attention is given to the forces of medieval theology, philosophy and logic as catalysts of divine understanding, the study focuses on location, monument and image, the material power of art and architecture, as the privileged site of this encounter.

A succulent piece of freestyle description opens the book, musing on the austerity and wilderness of the early medieval peasant's world, where eyes are cast downwards towards the furrow and the presence of the divine seems hidden, inscrutable.

One of Duby's central themes is how this peasant population, tightly controlled and exploited as resource and congregation, was 'weighed upon' by religious and noble feudalism so that sacred architectural art, from Romanesque through to Gothic forms, could emerge as a lasting, visible sacrifice to the power of the divine. Glimpsing the presence of God in the cloistered statues of monasteries and in the sublime cascade of light through cathedral arches, Duby takes us through a time when the religious was communicated through the magical and aesthetic powers of the visual.

GEORGES DUBY
1919 – 1996
Nationality: French
First Published: Levieux & Thompson, 1981 (first English translation)
Other Selected Titles:
Art and Society in the Middle Ages
The Chivalrous Society
Foundations of a New Humanism, 1280–1440
A History of French Civilization

French historian Georges Duby in 1982.

The Stripping of the Altars

EAMON DUFFY
1947 –
Nationality: British
First Published: Yale University Press, 1992
Other Selected Titles:
Faith of Our Fathers
The Voices of Morebath: Reformation and Rebellion in an English Village
Saints and Sinners: A History of the Popes

In this groundbreaking, revisionist study of the English Reformation, Eamon Duffy is keen to halt what he sees as two dangerous tendencies in the scholarship of religious history. One is the temptation to present the 15th and 16th centuries as a melodrama of extreme practices, where witches and devils make pacts on secluded forest paths and where villagers congregate and commune in a mist of obscure local worship and residual paganism. The other is the historian's habit of registering a gulf between elite and popular religion in the period, a divide between Latin and vernacular cultures, between rarefied theological dispute and local superstition.

Duffy's mode of attacking such crude and polarized explanations is to tell an intricate history of the effective relationship between the parishioner and the church during the late medieval and reformation period, charting the interaction between worshippers and the clergy, saints, relics, pictures and scriptures that mediated their relationship with God. Assembling case-studies and accounts from parishes across England, Duffy's account carries such novelty and rigorous polemic that no serious account of the English Reformation over the last 14 years has been anything other than a form of response to it. The first section unveils the local significance and machinations of Catholicism, focusing on the power of mass, saints, prayer and purgatory as agencies of divine power. The second section details the often brutal transformation of public worship as the reformed religion, Protestantism, is superimposed on traditional religion between 1530–1580, describing the iconoclastic purification of worship – the 'stripping of the altars' – with powerful detail.

Sidestepping stereotype and myth about the corruption and decadence of the pre-Reformation Catholic church, Duffy makes it clear that religion in 15th- and 16th-century England was not merely an aspect of popular culture, but the catalyst for everyday life in its totality. His account is an essential introduction to arguably the most profound period of intellectual and cultural change in English history.

Rites of Spring

Military and aesthetic history are two genres usually kept well apart in 20th-century scholarship, with the presumption that high culture and aesthetic discourse are divorced from the brutal strategies and consequences of warfare. Modris Eksteins' challenge to this separation comes in the form of his groundbreaking work, *The Rites of Spring*, which takes its title from a Stravinsky ballet performed in 1913 on the eve of the First World War. Eksteins tries to make sense of the fact that, between 1890 and 1940, European society produced cultural and artistic movements striving for fresh, liberating forms of expression at the same time as 'acquiring the power of ultimate destruction, the dance of death, with its orgiastic-nihilistic irony'. Strains of modernism, the avant garde, cubism and primitivism are all discussed in detail and their challenge to societal values is seen to resonate through the whole of European society, not merely the cultural elite. Placing art, politics and warfare into a startling nexus of mutual influence, Eksteins tells the stories of political revolution, the transformation of culture and the horrors of trench warfare simultaneously.

Sometimes, with his scattergun references and disciplinary shifts, Eksteins makes it hard for the reader to travel comfortably from dance-hall to art gallery and then to rat-infested trenches where 'working parties digging or repairing trenches repeatedly uncovered corpses in all stages of decay or mutilation', but this displays the bravery of the work.

Flitting from one cultural capital or artistic institution to another, Eksteins is always proving the relevance of artistic technique and imagination to the reality of political and social life. Examining new forms of choreography, prose style, composition and fashion he argues that these do not merely act as mirrors to the social and political discordance of the age, but actually shape the cultural context in which war, revolution and mass destruction occur. A Europe of artistic discordance and continental conflict are placed in a fascinating harmony.

MODRIS EKSTEINS
1911 –
Nationality: Latvian
First Published: Houghton Mifflin, 1989
Other Selected Titles:
The Limits of Reason: the German democratic Press and the Collapse of Weimar Democracy
Walking since Daybreak: a Story of Eastern Europe, World War II, and the Heart of Our Century

THE GREAT WAR AND THE BIRTH OF THE MODERN AGE

RITES OF SPRING

"A bold and unforgettable journey into the heart of our daemonic century." — Alfred Kazin

MODRIS EKSTEINS

FRANZ FANON
1925 – 1961
Nationality: French
First Published: McGibbon & Kee,
1965 (first English translation)
Other Selected Titles:
A Dying Colonialism
Black Skin, White Mask

The Wretched of the Earth

This book should be read by those who suspect that history is merely a discipline concerned with distanced reflection or playful dialogues with past curiosities. The text is about the use of history to transform thinking and action in the present and immediate future. History, for Franz Fanon, is a force for change.

Fanon's text, written during the Algerian War of Independence in 1960, addresses the history of colonization and the contemporary crisis of decolonization. He reflects on the psychology of the European settlers, relaying the way they entered into a process of 'domination, exploitation and pillage', while disguising these actions with the affect of 'making history' and 'shaping civilization'. Fanon's critique quickly moves away from the European colonist, however, and addresses the indigenous population of colonies either fighting for independence or existing in the limbo of early decolonization. He isolates the educated and politically powerful classes of these nations for devastating attack, calling them 'the spoilt children of yesterday's colonialism' and calls on the 'Wretched' of the title – the poor rural classes of these countries – to redeem themselves and their nations through revolution.

For Fanon, who had served in the French army before becoming a psychotherapist, the only effective way of wrenching territory, national identity and, most strikingly, personal sanity back from the control of the colonizers is by violence. Properly directed, violence has a cleansing effect on history and on the perpetrator. His text thereby becomes a justification for violence in the name of liberation and refreshes Marxist theories of revolutionary action against the immediate backdrop of freedom-fighting in the mid-20th century. Facing new forms of political imperialism and resistance today, we should be encouraged to read and test these justifications ourselves, in relation to the current uses and abuses of violence in world politics.

Colossus: The Rise and Fall of the American Empire

NIALL FERGUSON
1964 –
Nationality: Scottish
First Published: Penguin, 2000
Other Selected Titles:
Empire: How Britain Made the Modern World
The Cash Nexus: Money and Power in the Modern World

Niall Ferguson, operating simultaneously through text and television, has become one of the most interventionist historians of our time, reshaping current controversies by placing them in dialogue with history. He does this well enough with his book *Empire: How Britain Made the Modern World*, which attacks what he sees as a false consensus of shame and embarrassment regarding past imperial power. Even more urgent and controversial is his book *Colossus*, which speculates on the history and future of American global power, precisely at a time when debate rages about the ethics of international intervention.

So sullied is the popular concept of empire, Ferguson suggests, that American politicians and military strategists compete with each other to deny links with such ambition. This, says Ferguson, is clearly a matter of protesting too much – American power politics is obsessed with a kind of imperialism, substituting compromised language with that of a 'new world order', the 'spread of democracy', the provision of 'economic stability' and 'Christian, civilized values'. Such rhetoric invites Ferguson's most daring historical move, the equation of these American policies with the criteria of the British Imperialists who also, he points out, sought to impose models of trade, government and morality across the world.

At some points, Ferguson may seem to be playing into the hands of those who see history as a lamentable pattern of imperial domination. It is precisely these readers, however, that Ferguson wants to discombobulate, suggesting instead that American intervention should be more vigorous. No crude celebration of American power, this is instead an attempt at imagining a benign form of empire, drawing up criteria by which America's economic and political influence might go hand-in-hand with genuine provision of humanitarian aid, economic growth and political co-operation. Though readers might balk at this conflation of international dominance and liberal progress, Ferguson's polemic is a courageous attempt at revivifying a positive concept of Empire, and should be taken seriously in relation to current affairs.

'Brilliant ... revealing ... something challenging, amusing or fresh on almost every page'
Daily Telegraph

NIALL FERGUSON
COLOSSUS
THE RISE AND FALL OF THE AMERICAN EMPIRE
THE NEW BESTSELLER FROM THE AUTHOR OF *EMPIRE*

Millennium

FELIPE FERNÁNDEZ-ARMESTO
1950 –
Nationality: British
First Published: Bantam Press, 1995
Other Selected Titles:
The Americas
Civilizations
Columbus

The past 30 years of academic history has seen a succession of challenges to 'grand narrative' styles of historical storytelling, tending to eschew the study of epochs and empires in favour of close contextual studies of communities, ideas and events. The confident sweep of historical survey is sometimes, as a consequence, replaced by blinkered study. Step forward Felipe Fernández-Armesto, author of the extraordinarily ambitious *Millennium* and a man seemingly determined to revivify the hubris of 18th and 19th writers such as Edward Gibbon and Thomas Macaulay: 'I set out consciously to create a work of art, and to me that's as important as conveying information.'

This 830-page history of our last millennium takes as its subject 'the fate of civilizations' and leaps from continent to continent as well as across centuries to tell the story of discovery, conflict and co-existence between successive cultures. It aims to set history beyond Eurocentric preoccupations. Christianity, empire, scientific development and industrialization are all covered here, but with a particular interest in the ideas and experiences that have radiated from Eastern, African and South American civilizations.

Instead of re-analysing familiar historical figures and events, we see a democratic fascination with the punctilious detail of world history enlarged into a magnificent portrait: 'I climb the rigging of the cosmic crow's nest and try to share with my reader the perspective of the galactic museum keeper of the future, seeing a planet entire.' This is the paradoxical tone of the book, offering readers mere glimpses of exotic and curious sights, yet irresistibly drawn to the panoramic presentation of a thousand years of world history. Some readers may find it absurd that the writer can describe the French Revolution as 'parochial' and that Descartes and Michelangelo are absent from this history, but the same readers will also be surprised and delighted by a kaleidescopic refiltering of world history.

Pagans and Christians

In terms of popular historical representation, it would be hard to find a belief-system more maligned than Paganism, since it suffers from the double denigration of historical redundancy (Christianity 'triumphed' over Paganism) and moral condemnation (derogatory links with superstition and the demonic). Writers of history cannot be held entirely responsible for constructing this popular conception, but the tendency to equate the emergence of Christianity as a sign of moral and cultural 'progress' has left its mark on our imagination. Robin Lane Fox's *Pagans and Christians* is the book to read to complicate such commonplace ideas.

Concentrating on the co-existence and conflict of Paganism and Christianity between the 2nd and 4th centuries, Fox presents a study of Paganism as a vibrant, popular polytheism that is eclipsed by Christianity not because of inherent flaws, but specific political and structural reasons. Early chapters trace what we should call a rich culture of Paganism, since the emphasis is on popular worship and the manifestation of the divine in everyday life, rather than on theology or doctrine. Fox's study of Pagan statues and sacred sites is a particularly strong one, since he later details the way Christian practice eclipses or appropriates these spaces for itself to consolidate its power.

Though Fox gives some space to the power of missionary activity, martyrdom and intellectual exclusivity to explain the rise of Christianity, his central thesis revolves around the conversion of the Roman Emperor Constantine in the year 312. His investment of Christianity with the grandeur of Imperial authority, and the subsequent infusion of political and social life with Christian morality are the prime reasons for its rise to orthodoxy, Fox claims. In redressing a historical imbalance, Fox may be accused of celebrating the diversity and accessibility of Paganism in contrast to the 'single-mindedness' of Christianity, but even if he sometimes falls into caricature himself, this is a prime example of sparkling, revisionist history.

ROBIN LANE FOX
1946 –
Nationality: British
First Published: Viking, 1986
Other Selected Titles:
The Classical World
Alexander the Great
The Unauthorized Version: Truth and Fiction in the Bible

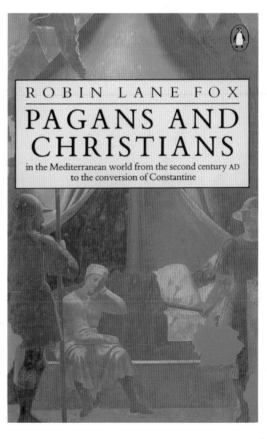

ROBIN LANE FOX

PAGANS AND CHRISTIANS

in the Mediterranean world from the second century AD to the conversion of Constantine

The End of History and the Last Man

FRANCIS FUKUYAMA
1952 –
Nationality: American
First Published: Free Press, 1992
Other Selected Titles:
Trust: the Social Virtues and the Creation of Prosperity
The Great Disruption: Human Nature and the Reconstitution of Social Order
Our Posthuman Future: Consequences of the Biotechnology Revolution
State-Building: Governance and World Order in the 21st Century

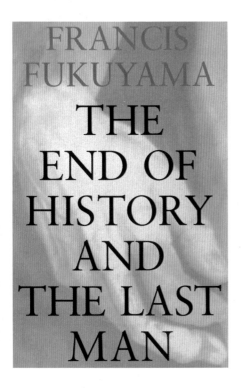

At the centre of Fukuyama's *The End of History and the Last Man* lies an intellectual knot comprised equally of a concept, a claim and a worry. The claim provided the grounds for Fukuyama's notoriety as a thinker allied to the Project for the New American Century. Fukuyama's text draws on the traditions of political economy and philosophy to elaborate his claim that history could be read as an evolutionary progression towards Western models of liberal capitalism.

In a language paradoxically modest in its simplicity and precision, Fukuyama argues that history's teleological pattern had reached its final form with liberal democracy and free markets. Time is on the side of liberalism: we may improve on the internal structures and processes of liberal capitalism but we cannot advance beyond it.

Underlying the ambition of the claim, there is an equally ambitious idea – the idea of a Universal History. The historiographic legitimacy and explanatory power of such 'meta-narratives' had been deflated in the 1970s and 1980s by post-structuralist and narrativist historians.

In *The End of History*, Fukuyama does not enter into a theoretical defence of the methods or project of universal history but instead reads the loss of faith in such grand narratives as part of a general profound post-war pessimism. His return to the grandest of all such narratives – Hegel's philosophy of history – is then, for Fukuyama, also a return to historical optimism.

It is the worry – set forth in the final section of the text – which complicates Fukuyama's thesis and prevents him from becoming fully a Reaganite triumphalist. Drawing on Nietzsche, Fukuyama speculates that liberal capitalism could well corrode from within in a welter of dissatisfaction. It is not then 'external' threats – religious fundamentalisms for example – which need to be guarded against but the will-to-superiority of the elite few who find their ambitions thwarted in a Western order which treats everyone as equals.

The Naked Heart

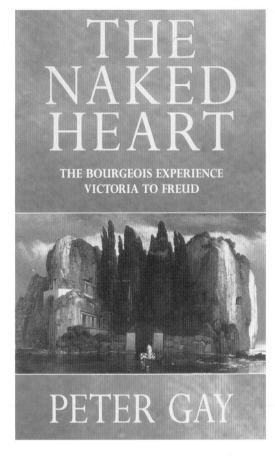

In *The Naked Heart*, Peter Gay frequently uses the term 'inwardness' to define his theme in the fourth volume of his magisterial series on the 19th-century 'bourgeois experience'.

It is not a misleading term: Gay does indeed go in search of expressions and reflections of the 19th-century bourgeoisie's fascination with and fear of the psyche, the 'inward' life of the self.

But the term 'inwardness' does signal something of the difficulty of Gay's project in *The Naked Heart*: how does a historian find and represent what is 'inward'; how can he or she engage with the concealed spaces of the self; how is it possible to explore past self-consciousnesses and the ways in which long-dead selves perceived and responded to other selves?

Gay responds to this methodological problem by turning to Freud. Using a psychoanalytic model of the self as a creature divided against itself, he traces the various manifestations of these inner conflicts in a rich array of cultural texts drawn from European and American traditions.

Using a multiplicity of case-studies, Gay demonstrates a 19th-century 'preoccupation with the self' which cuts across popular notions of the period's preoccupation with external landscapes and with ways of penetrating and conquering them.

Just as Gay's bourgeoisie is more concerned with the 'great voyage to the interior' than with Empire or profit, the bourgeois self he portrays is far from the figures beloved of popular dramatizations of the period – the legendary philistine and hypocritical patriarch trapped in a stuffy propriety.

Gay's refusal of theory, his rejection of any need for a theoretical rather than an instinctive understanding of what makes something or someone 'bourgeois', is of a piece with his joyful immersion in the cultural history of a century. He is a superb communicator of both this enthusiasm and of the learning it sustains and his effortless style and plethora of examples make *The Naked Heart* a really stimulating read.

PETER GAY
1923 –
Nationality: American
First Published: Harper Collins, 1995
Other Selected Titles:
The Enlightenment: an Interpretation
A Godless Jew: Freud, Atheism and the Making of Psychoanalysis
Pleasure Wars

An engraving of Edward Gibbon by William Holl after a portrait by Sir Joshua Reynolds.

The Decline and Fall of the Roman Empire

The continuing popularity of Gibbon's *Decline and Fall of the Roman Empire* is in part due to his subject matter. The Roman Empire presents the most intriguing of historical paradoxes: a golden age of civilization, learning and achievement and a symbol of decadence, cruelty and volatility. Two models of historical explanation, 'progress' and 'corruption', are enshrined in one subject.

The time scale of Gibbon's work is bewildering, covering about 1300 years from the 'Age of the Antonines' in 180 AD to the fall of Constantinople in 1453. However, the thematic diversity this generates is the most remarkable part of his project. The 'decline' of the Roman Empire becomes a catalyst for telling multiple, interconnected stories, such as the development of Christianity within Pagan culture, the competition of Islamic power and territory, the threat of Barbarian forces from Northern Europe and the evolution of political strategy in the face of massive colonial responsibility.

These broad narratives are told through detailed documentation of the practice of religion, politics, warfare and learning within the multiple sites of the Empire's domain. Gibbon's narrative therefore defies genre, at once a sweeping history of politics and belief and a minute sociology of public life.

Gibbon transforms our understanding of politics, religion and empire by writing this work, but most significantly he transforms our concept of history itself. Famous for meticulous accuracy and careful interrogation of sources, the text is one of the great products of Enlightenment study, displaying a commitment to encyclopaedic survey, rational analysis and religious critique. As they did on publication, Chapters 15 and 16 of his *Decline and Fall* continue to generate the most scholarly controversy, suggesting that Christianity disrupted a relatively tolerant Roman society with its missionary zeal. Gibbon's text should be revisited today to inform our reaction to current religious fanaticism and global politics.

EDWARD GIBBON
1737 – 1794
Nationality: British
First Published: Edward Gibbbon, 1776–8
Other Selected Titles:
Vindication (Essay defending *Decline and Fall*)
Memoirs of My Own Life
The English Essays of Edward Gibbon

The Holocaust: The Jewish Tragedy

The recent imprisonment of the historian David Irving, on charges of holocaust denial, is a timely reminder of the moral implications of writing history. The misrepresentation of the past, whether deliberately perverse or merely misguided, matters. Not just intellectually in this case, but politically and legally. Incarcerating a writer for questioning the veracity of the slaughter of six million Jews by Nazi-lead Germany is one way of dealing with this moral dimension to history. Reading other, manifestly superior accounts of the Holocaust is perhaps a more effective one. Martin Gilbert's *The Holocaust* provides a perfect opportunity to do this.

Gilbert faces the task, common to most historians of the Holocaust, of making the genocide of European Jewry between 1938 and 1945 comprehensible to the reader. The scale of orchestrated cruelty and killing by the perpetrators and the suffering and endurance of the Jews are, in different ways, elusive to rational historical logic and analysis – these are events and facts that refuse to fully 'make sense'.

Gilbert's primary method is to produce a record of the Jewish commentaries, primarily letters and diaries, that act as witness to the experience of humiliation, ghettoisation, deportation and annihilation that shaped their lives and deaths during this period. This means that the book is more a historical commemoration than a historical explanation – suffering and resistance are expressed in terms of bewilderment and anger and the localized, emotionally searing effect of the primary evidence (sometimes quoted for whole chapters) eclipses broader investigation of the cultural and political causes of the Holocaust.

Such distance, though, would be antithetical to Gilbert's project. While the history of anti-Semitism, Nazi policies, military murder squads and the dreadful complicity of the European 'bystander' are commented on, his text is produced so that we can listen to and respect the voices of the Jews themselves, who, in the great majority of cases, were silenced soon after they left their fragmented testimony.

MARTIN GILBERT
1936 –
Nationality: British
First Published: Collins, 1986
Other Selected Titles:
Atlas of the Arab-Israeli Conflict
Churchill: a Life
Auschwitz and the Allies

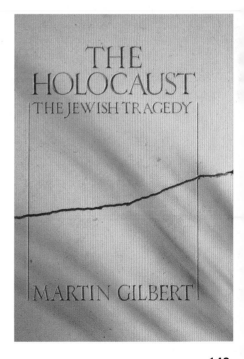

The Cheese and the Worms

CARLO GINZBURG
1939 –
Nationality: Italian
First Published: John Hopkins
University Press, 1980 (first English
translation)
Other Selected Titles:
*Ecstasies: Deciphering the Witches'
Sabbath
Myths, Emblems, Clues*

In his career as a historian, Carlo Ginzburg told histories so that the true voices and meanings of popular culture could be released from silence and stereotype. A later work *Ecstasies: Deciphering the Witches' Sabbath* (1990) offers a masterful study of the myths relating to fertility rites, werewolves, night time demon battles and witches over thousands of years and multiple continents, insisting that we look beyond the stereotyped accusations and forced confessions of the 16th and 17th centuries to discover the real significance of witchcraft.

In *The Cheese and the Worms*, Ginzburg does something similar, but on a completely different scale. He presents the reader with a meticulous reconstruction of one peasant's life and beliefs in a rural Italian village in the 16th century. The peasant in question is Menocchio, a poor miller and carpenter who fathered 11 children in a village called Friuli. Against the mundanity of his material existence, Ginzburg brilliantly sets the extraordinary novelty of Menocchio's mental world.

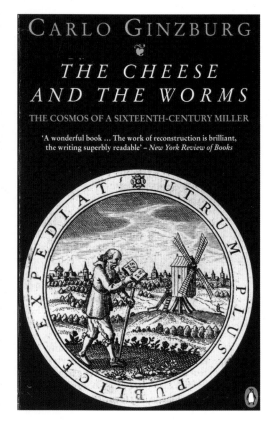

This is a man who, inventively combining a selection of classical and early modern texts on medicine, theology and philosophy with his own speculations, builds whole theologies and cosmological theories, challenging and often mocking the Roman Catholic faith that dominated (or seemed to dominate) Italian culture. Ginzburg tells the story of how his very public expressions of these ideas invite the attentions of the Inquisition – he was interrogated on multiple occasions and finally put to death with the encouragement of the current Pope, Clement VIII, himself.

Ginzburg takes some liberties himself in this reconstruction of a humble but exceptional life, sometimes bullying the reader into conclusions about what Menocchio said, believed or did next. However, he uses this case-study to speculate brilliantly on the diversity and subversive quality of popular and oral culture, arguing that vibrant and uncontrollable elements of lower class tradition, stimulated by the power of an exceptional mind, can always battle against the forces of convention, authority and oppression.

God's First Love

This is a book calculated in its anger and provocation, a form of history written as condemnation, warning and prophecy. Friedrich Heer's extraordinary survey of Christian anti-Semitism opens with a series of comments about the state of global society in 1967, when the planet seems, for Heer, on the edge of atomic obliteration and where the Christian church, 'in the process of decomposition... continues to infect succeeding generations'.

The text unfolds to detail what Heer regards as the malign morality of a Christian tradition responsible, he argues, not just for the ideological construction of anti-Semitism but for the abuses committed against humanity by the Western world: 'Auschwitz, Hiroshima and its successors rest on fifteen centuries of illustrious church tradition.'

It is the intellectual history of anti-Semitism that Heer wants us to understand most precisely, working initially from the Mosaic prophecies of Jewish suffering. In his chapters on the developing patterns of persecution within the Middle Ages and Early Modern society, Heer argues for a cultural consistency of hatred: 'at times of religious crisis in Europe the Jews were always the scapegoats, represented as incarnations of the Devil'.

At more intricate levels of analysis, Heer shows particular skill in explaining the theological and psychological motivations for the anti-Semitism of Martin Luther, whose ideas infused and authorized Nazi ideology 400 years later. This ideology, he argues in the most powerful chapter, Crushed between Cross and Swastika, develops not as a political aberration in German history, but as a shared logic of theological and racial hatred in which the Christian church is entirely complicit.

Readers will find Heer's survey brutally polemical at times and his conclusions are moulded by an insistent faith in the return to Jewish spiritual and scholarly primacy: 'Christianity will find the humanity it so urgently needs only by planting its roots in the piety and spirituality of His people, who were and are God's first love.' Beyond this confessional basis, however, the book unveils the persecutory logic within our Christian heritage and rightly demands our attention.

FRIEDRICH HEER
1916 – 1983
Nationality: German
First Published: Weidenfeld & Nicholson, 1970 (first English translation)
Other Selected Titles:
The Holy Roman Empire
Medieval World
The Intellectual History of Europe

Herodotus, the Greek historian reading his chronicals to his contemporaries.

HERODOTUS
circa 484 – 425BC
Nationality: Greek
First Published: circa 430BC

Histories

The inception of History as a discrete discipline, separate from adjacent forms of epic, drama and rhetoric, begins with Herodotus. His *Histories* emerge, magnificently diverse and digressive, from a series of recitations delivered to audiences in Greek cities during the middle of the 5th century BC. His work takes shape, therefore, within the hubris of the Greek Enlightenment, when power had shifted from Persian dominance to the focus of Athenian democracy, philosophy and artistic experimentation. In their cycles of injustice, violence and retribution, the *Histories* show thematic and formal links with Tragedy and it is likely Sophocles and Euripides (as well as the philosopher Socrates) were among his audience.

The essential subject matter of the *Histories* is the Persian Empire, detailing its expansion within a 'custom of conquest' from the reign of Cyrus in 557BC to its fall through the defeat of Xerxes by the Greeks in 479BC. This chronological thread is often only a structural prop, however, and Herodotus admits to a wilful revelry in digression as he uses Persian expansion and conflict in the Mediterranean and North Africa to create a polycentric narrative. Voices and stories emanate from multiple cultures, showcasing Herodotus' own layered knowledge of the world as he had experienced it through wide travel and dialogue with the storytellers of respective communities.

In this sense, the origin of History is bedevilled with the questions that still haunt it today concerning the relationship between truth and storytelling, subjective witnessing and objective record. Herodotus himself is sometimes a critic of the information he gathers, questioning the partisan accounts provided by rhetoricians, oracles and epic residues. On the other hand, he is happy himself to indulge in patterns of associative thinking, where stories of distant Arab and Indian cultures filter into his records of Mediterranean life, infusing the work with the value of thematic, as well as chronological, continuity. Careful how you go – the paths are sinuous – but enjoy this inaugural journey.

Hiroshima

John Hersey's text is an extraordinary piece of historical writing because of its immediacy and provenance. *Hiroshima* was originally published as an article in the *New Yorker* magazine on August 31st, 1946, a year after the nuclear attacks on Hiroshima and Nagasaki, prefaced by these words: 'few of us have yet comprehended the all but incredible destructive power of the atom bomb, and everyone might well take time to consider the terrible implications of its use.' The piece constituted the entire issue, which sold out within hours, and was soon translated to radio broadcasts in the USA and around the world, transforming a fragment of journalism into one of the most dynamic and accessible works of history the genre has seen.

Hersey's account follows the experience of six inhabitants of the infamous city – clerk, widow, priest, pastor, doctor and surgeon, detailing their activity on the day of the blast and their state after three months of survival. Each person's early morning routine is traced out, their respective reactions to the 'noiseless flash' are recorded meticulously before the text unfolds the stories of attempted rescue, recovery and care. The chronology is tightly disciplined as it moves across contexts of riverbank, factory, home and hospital in a city enveloped by fire and panic. The subject matter is so searingly emotive that Hersey deliberately eclipses his own authorial persona, writing in a cool, pragmatic and even flat style so that the reader encounters the six characters' voices and experience with as little mediation as possible.

Before Hersey's piece, numerous articles had been written on the military justification for the use of the atomic bomb and on the destruction it caused, but these were broadly political and even aesthetic pieces. For the first time, the effects of the bomb on the lives of specific people were presented to a global audience and the allied countries had to grapple with their consciences for inflicting such devastation on the lives of civilian innocents.

JOHN HERSEY
1917 – 1993
Nationality: American
First Published: Penguin, 1946
Other Selected Titles:
A Bell for Adano
Under the Eye of the Storm
Key West Tales

American writer John Hersey driving a jeep during the Second World War.

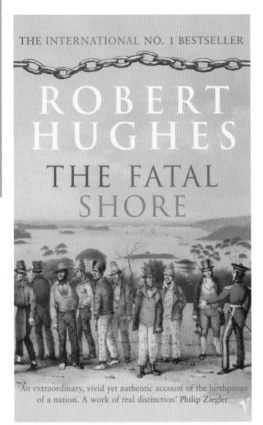

THE INTERNATIONAL NO. 1 BESTSELLER

ROBERT HUGHES

THE FATAL SHORE

'An extraordinary, vivid yet authentic account of the birthpangs of a nation. A work of real distinction' Philip Ziegler

ROBERT HUGHES
1938 –
Nationality: Australian
First Published: Collins, 1987
Other Selected Titles:
American Visions: the Epic History of Art in America
Culture of Complaint: the Fraying of America
Barcelona
The Art of Australia

The Fatal Shore

Famous for his art criticism and TV documentaries (including *The Shock of the New*, 1981, on modern art), Robert Hughes defined his reputation as a historian with *The Fatal Shore*, a pioneering study of transportation in the late 18th and 19th century. His motivation for writing was ignorance as well as interest, since the Australian education system of the 1950s and 1960s had failed to provide him with any information, viewing this population of convict settlers as 'statistics, absences and finally embarrassments'. Hughes' work rescues this community from the silence of academic myopia and international shame, charting the social circumstances that lead to transportation, the gruelling sea voyages (up to 40 per cent died on early voyages) and the evolution of the lives and status of the settlers in Australia.

Transportation emerged as a solution for a British criminal system which, by the 1780s, found capital punishment an overly brutal measure for thieves, poachers and vagabonds, but which also found jails filling to bursting point. Hughes' scholarly brilliance emerges from the way he revives not only the logic of the authorities that put transportation ('The System') in operation, but also the voices of the early convicts and settlers, who faced starvation, flogging, slave-like exploitation by landowners and conflict with Aboriginal tribesmen when they arrived. We hear notes of shame, bewilderment and fear in letters and diaries. One convict, John Ward, arriving in 1841, states that 'remorse for an instant filled my breast ... the many enemies there was to contend with all stood in dark array before my imagination'.

This history is not just one of suffering and exploitation, though. Hughes surveys the way settler convicts gradually achieve legal rights, marry with 'free' settlers, and, supported by pressure from emancipatory reform movements at home, develop communities that shape Australia's future. The tone of the quoted extracts increasingly takes on notes of pioneering discovery: 'we'll wonder over valleys and we'll gallop over plains And we'll scorn to live in slavery, bound down by chains'.

Pandaemonium

Pandaemonium is a survey of the British industrial revolution that progresses through a series of 'images' rather than a sustained historical argument. Published after the author's death, the text acts as the legacy of 14 years of research (1937–1950), during which Humphrey Jennings compiled a repository of observations concerning the 'coming of the machine', stretching from 1660 to 1886. The editors, Mary-Lou Jennings and Charles Madge, streamline material from a series of 'red books' that Jennings, film-maker and co-founder of the Mass Observation movement, had filled with the words of scientists, poets, novelists, philosophers and workers as they witnessed the evolution of industrial society.

The catalogue of entries is chronological and ostensibly 'objective' in that there is only occasional editorial intervention to guide the reader's thoughts. We are given some fragments that celebrate the progress of technology and industry, such as Thomas Sprat's 1667 observations on planetary ellipses and 'frozen beer' which typify the excitement and diversity of the early scientific revolution. The thrill of invention and aesthetic wonder is also evident in extracts recording the building of the 'perfect steam engine', the spread of electricity and the mechanical wonders produced by Brunel, 'a gentleman of the rarest genius'.

The selection is, however, dominated by an anxiety, sometimes a fatalism, about what the development of industry has done to human society. A scan of the entries reveals that the context of the industrial machine is imagined as bedlam, hell, apocalypse and, more prosaically, the workhouse, the stifling factory floor and the soot-encrusted northern town. There are beautiful writings and sublime images of power and production in this text, but its overriding moral message (Jennings compiled this material during the years of the 1930s Depression and the Second World War) is that 'the coming of the machine is destroying something in our life.'

HUMPHREY JENNINGS
1907 – 1950
Nationality: British
First Published: André Deutsch Limited, 1985
Other Selected Titles:
The Humphrey Jennings' Film Reader
May the Twelfth: Mass-Observation Day Surveys 1937
Fires Were Started

HUMPHREY JENNINGS

PANDÆMONIUM

The Coming of the Machine
As Seen by Contemporary Observers

'An extraordinary and wonderful book.' *Sunday Times*

A History of Warfare

JOHN KEEGAN
1934 –
Nationality: British
First Published: Hutchinson, 1995
Other Selected Titles:
Churchill
*The Mask of Command: a Study
of Generalship*
*The Battle for History: Re-fighting
World War Two*
World Armies

Some historians choose their subjects because their early lives have been pervaded by the events or places that they write about. Of those who appear in this selection, Ackroyd and Fanon are examples. John Keegan is very different. His introduction informs us that he 'was not fated to be a warrior', a childhood illness depriving him of the honour of a call-up, and that he spent his time at University jealously tuning in to the memories and bonhomie of those who had done military service and been touched by 'the dash, élan and vitality' of army officers.

The book Keegan writes emerges as a kind of textual surrogate for this missed experience and one in which he argues that there is a single 'warrior culture' that unites humanity and has been the shaping force in the development of civilization.

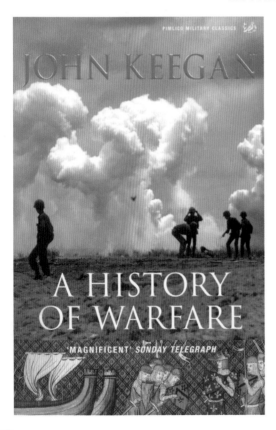

This claim alone, relegating the dynamics of artistic, intellectual and social development to the supreme historical will of warfare, makes this book a compelling, controversial read. Keegan's history of warfare is at once military and anthropological, studying cultural and genetic explanations for human aggression and competition (one chapter is entitled Why do Men Fight?) as he traces the evolution of the philosophy, strategy and practice of warfare.

The scale of Keegan's work is extraordinary, working from Stone Age scuffles and spear construction to the mass killings of the Second World War, commenting not only on developments in the tactics and fortifications of warfare, but on changing cultures of conflict. It is this latter aspect of Keegan's work that is most interesting, since it looks at the way Chinese, Greek and Egyptian military cultures attempted to ritualize, limit or defer warfare so that its effects could be focused and the destructive consequences contained. This ethical edge to the work investigates how warfare (something inevitable and continuous for Keegan) can be restricted in the light of the apocalyptic possibilities of modern conflict.

A Short Account of the Destruction of the Indies

The testimony of the witness is perhaps the most valuable currency history trades in, and Bartolomé De Las Casas enriches the genre uniquely. He published *A Short Account...* in 1552, presenting King Philip II of Spain with a catalogue of the atrocities performed by Spanish colonists of Mexico, South America and the Caribbean during the first half of the 16th century, appealing to the king to condemn 'the boldness and unreason of those who count it as nothing to drench the Americas in human blood'.

Las Casas' knowledge of the exploitation and devastation of indigenous culture during this period develops from 40 years of travel and work as a missionary priest, during which he witnessed the conquest of Cuba and Venezuela and the destruction of the Aztec and Inca empires at first hand.

His account is unrelenting and brutally explicit in its depiction of the slaughter and humiliation of the 'Indians' the Spanish encounter as they conquer and plunder lands 'granted' to them by papal authority in 1493. Writing of the conquest of Haiti, he describes the way soldiers 'grabbed suckling infants by the feet and, ripping them from their mother's breasts, dashed them headlong against the rocks'.

As well as being a vivid form of political and moral protest, the report is philosophically and theologically important, since it critiques the assumed superiority of European races and lays bare the greed and ambition underlying the missionary criteria of colonization, suggesting that Spain itself would receive divine retribution unless the destruction halted.

Indeed, Las Casas offers the reader a perfect inversion of the logic of colonization. It is the Spanish who are presented as savage and rapacious, whereas the indigenous, in an almost Utopian portrait, are deemed gentle, peace-loving and generous. Las Casas has been celebrated in Spain as the country's 'authentic conscience' and his work continues to inspire political protest against imperialism and against the erosion of indigenous culture across the world.

Illustration of the missionary Saint Bartolomé de las Casas.

BARTOLOMÉ DE LAS CASAS
1484 – 1576
Nationality: Spanish
First Published: Penguin, 1999 (first English translation)
Other Selected Titles:
The Apologetic History of the Indies

Seven Pillars of Wisdom

British archaeologist, soldier and writer T.E. Lawrence (Lawrence of Arabia) in 1927.

THOMAS EDWARD LAWRENCE
1888 – 1935
Nationality: Welsh
First Published: The Oxford Times, 1922
Other Selected Titles:
The Mint

As is compulsory for a legendary figure, there is still something enigmatic about T.E. Lawrence, Lawrence of Arabia, the Welsh-born Oxford-educated 'illegitimate' son of Sir Robert Chapman. His career led him early to the Middle East where he began work as an archaeologist in 1911. In the First World War, he worked for army intelligence in the Arab Bureau in North Africa. His exploits as British Liaison Officer to the Arab Revolt against the Turks – coupled with his appearance as an advisor to the Arab delegation at the Versailles Conference – forged him a name as a hero in post-war England.

Shyness, however, and dissatisfaction with Britain's post-war treatment of his Arab comrades, and not a little scorn for the public which needed heroes, pushed Lawrence to evade honours and enlist in the RAF under assumed names. His early death in 1935 (in a motorcycle accident) and David Lean's 1962 film, *Lawrence of Arabia*, cemented the myth of the English 'sheik': irreducibly 'English' in stoicism, commitment to 'fairness' and 'truth' yet irreducibly other in his capacity to be at one with this exotic 'Arab' world.

Seven Pillars of Wisdom, Lawrence's autobiographical portrayal of his experience of the Arab Revolt against the Ottoman Turks in 1916 and 1918, carries with it the enigmas of its author. For its critics, it is a piece of self-aggrandizing blindness, an episode of imperial charity too immersed in itself to recognize its limits. For its many admirers, it is both a beautifully written and sincerely felt defence of 'Arab' culture and history, a plea for the Western powers to cease using this dignified and ancient culture as a pawn in its own power games. As a history of the Arab Revolt, *Seven Pillars of Wisdom* is sometimes lacking in precision and perspective; as an intimate memoir, however, of the ways in which English post-war sensibilities towards other cultures were changing, the text is a classic.

Islam in History

'We live in a time when great energies are devoted to the falsification of history – to flatter, deceive or serve a variety of sectional interests.' So Bernard Lewis begins the concluding paragraph in this work, *Islam in History*, written in the early 1970s but more profoundly relevant as each day dawns to reveal commentators and politicians caricaturing the history of Islamic and Christian culture.

As Islamic politicians deny the holocaust and revive the violence of the Crusades at daily junctures while anticipating the destruction of Israel, we need history that reveals the roots of Islamic antagonism to Western influence. As Western leaders and commentators, no less problematically, caricature Islam as a domain of unreasoned tyranny and fanaticism, we need history that reveals the Islamic logic of religious duty, political revolution and popular freedom.

Lewis fulfils these demands elegantly, writing a book that simultaneously narrates relations between Muslims, Jews and Christians through history, while critiquing existing work on the subject. Rather like Maalouf's more populist reconstruction of Arab history (also featured in this section), Lewis feels it imperative to trace the scholarship of Muslim historians as they encounter and imagine the West.

A brilliant chapter on Islamic colonization turns our world upside down and tells the story of how the Muslim explorer encounters the Western barbarian in their 'age of discovery'. In another, Lewis complicates the historical antipathy between Arabs and Jews by unveiling a strong 19th-century Jewish admiration for Islam, extending beyond Orientalists and romance-writers to the writings of Disraeli himself.

There is no attempt by Lewis to hide the religious and cultural differences between Islam and the West that often harden into intractable antagonism in modern contexts. However, we are presented with a text that explains these antagonisms as the product of constructed as well as essential differences. It is argued that, as a prime builder of meaning in the modern world, history needs to be protected on both sides from distortions that promote the respective ubiquity of the infidel and the fanatic.

BERNARD LEWIS
1916 –
Nationality: British
First Published: Alcove Press, 1973
Other Selected Titles:
What Went Wrong?: Western Impact and Middle Eastern Response
The Middle East
The Arabs in History

Chinese Shadows

**SIMON LEYS
(PIERRE RYCKMANS)**
1935 –
Nationality: Belgian
First Published: Penguin, 1978 (first
English translation)
Other Selected Titles:
The Death of Napoleon
*The Chairman's New Clothes: Mao
and the Cultural Revolution*
*Broken Images: Essays on Chinese
Culture and Politics*

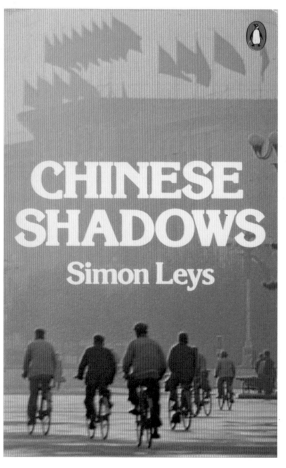

Current perception of Chinese society is dominated by focus on its economic revolution and the threats and possibilities it poses to American and European power. Fed stories about stock-piles of cheap imported clothes and premonitions of rival superpower status, the Western audience hears little about Chinese life itself. When Simon Leys wrote his book *Chinese Shadows* in the early 1970s, the situation was similar but more acute. In his Prologue, Leys speaks not only of the careful self-censorship of China's international image, but of a Western distortion of Chinese life, the Maoist Cultural Revolution ignored, effaced or blindly celebrated by commentators. Following 20 years of intimacy with Chinese culture, Leys himself (working under a pseudonym) reveals a dilemma. He wants to uncover the reality of Maoist China, but fears consequent banishment from the land he loves. This, he argues, is how the current regime has 'blackmailed into silence countless witnesses'.

Leys' work is not an ideological attack on Communism or even on the principles of the Cultural Revolution itself, but a journalistic demystification of the local effects of revolutionary change. A brilliantly observed and sometimes comical chapter on Bureaucracy reveals the way a class system has not been abolished but disguised and intensified, '30 layers' of administrative status defining the food you eat, the cafeterias you eat in and the mode of transport (only Mandarins drive cars) you use.

Relaying the foreigner's experience of China, he explains the way carefully orchestrated tours and lavish banquets, redolent of China's past, greet the official tourist, but how spontaneous visits to provincial capitals reveal levelled temples and cleared gardens, the iconoclasm of the Maoist imperative to 'Destroy the Old and Establish the New'.

Hovering in the space between insider and outsider, disciple and critic, Leys is a historian displaying empathy and indignant critique towards a nation transformed.

The Crusades through Arab Eyes

A central tenet of Edward Said's famous thesis, Orientalism, is that we, as European readers, necessarily understand other civilizations from a Western point of view, and that it is almost impossible to 'study other cultures and peoples from a nonrepressive and nonmanipulative perspective'. This seems true of our historical understanding of the Crusades, which typically ignores the Arab experience and concentrates on Western commentary, focusing on the inaugural recruitment by Pope Urban II in 1095, the recovery of holy Christian sites and the regression from initial victories to humiliating defeat. Maalouf, in a dynamic and accessible account, reverses this outlook and describes the 'Frankish Wars' through the testimony of Arab participants, chroniclers and historians.

His strategy for making the Arab perspective relevant to us is to create a sense of authenticity by providing a 'true-life novel' format, where Turkish emirs and Muslim warriors speak and act with compelling proximity to the reader. We hear, for example, that Aislan, a Turkish opponent of the first Crusade, 'stalked his prey', 'threw himself furiously into the fray' and 'laughed out loud' – the distant 'other' is made familiar to us by intimate witnessing. Maalouf presents us with the bewilderment and panic of initial Arab responses to the Crusades, repeating accounts of the Christian army catapulting the heads of its victims into besieged cities and cannibalizing Turkish messengers. Whether these details are authentic or mythical, Maalouf allows a legacy of Arab commentary to balance the historical orthodoxy of its Western counterpart.

This historical 'novel' progresses to explain the Muslim commitment to a retaliatory 'Jihad' against a Western invasion regarded as rapacious and barbaric, and dramatizes the re-conquest of Jerusalem, Antioch and Acre, up to the point where the Christian armies were repelled in 1291. Maalouf also provides a powerful epilogue which explains the modern resonance of these conflicts in Islamic culture, currently reacting once again to the impact of Western invasion: the historical legacies and symmetries are profound.

Amin Maalouf in 1993.

AMIN MAALOUF
1949 –
Nationality: Lebanese
First Published: Al Saqi Books, 1984
(first English translation)
Other Selected Titles:
*In the Name of Identity – Violence
and the Need to Belong
Rock of Tanios*

GARRETT MATTINGLY
1900 – 1962
Nationality: American
First Published: Houghton Mifflin &
Cape, 1959
Other Selected Titles:
Renaissance Diplomacy
Catherine of Aragon

The Defeat of the Spanish Armada

Garrett Mattingly belongs to a breed of humble, self-deprecating historians that are endangered today in a habitat often dominated by harsh academic competition and sniping media rivalry. In the preface to this book, he talks about himself as a 'sedentary middle-age historian' holding a 'nodding acquaintance' with naval history, offering 'no startling fresh interpretation'. Don't let his words fool you. To provide a near daily account of the confrontation between English and Spanish forces between February 1587 and New Year's Day, 1589, and also to embrace the broad political and religious tensions of late 16th century Europe, you have to be a brilliant historian.

The tightly chronological structure of the narrative is compelling, reading like a thriller as it tells the story of shadowy diplomatic intrigue between the courts of Elizabeth and Phillip II of Spain, the anticipatory raids on Cadiz by Francis Drake and the defensive construction of the coastal beacons that flared in warning as the Armada approached.

The plot unfurls to dramatize the actual Armada conflict, the lengthy retreat and pursuit and the final rout and destruction of the Spanish fleet off the Irish and Scottish coasts. In this sense, Mattingly is the consummate popular historian, supporting lead actors such as Drake and Duke Don Pedro (commander of one Spanish ship) with a cast of numerous extras; captains, sailors and fishermen whose voices shriek over the waves to record the events for posterity.

Most impressive, perhaps, is the way Mattingly undermines historical myths along the way. He scoffs at the idea that a tempest (thought to be divinely inspired in support of the Protestant cause) had any real influence on the battle, and undermines the suggestion that the victory immediately inaugurated England's global naval supremacy. In remarkable parallel to the focused account of the Armada, Mattingly also manages to narrate the events of the French Wars of Religion, thereby playing out another crucial scene in the conflict between Protestants and Catholics that dominates this period of European history.

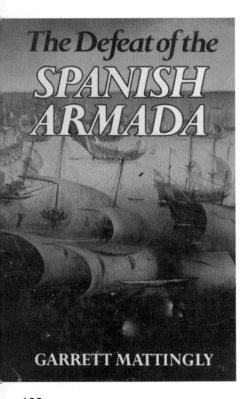

The Story of English

The historian who undertakes to trace the development and ordeals of a language is courageous indeed. To write the history of a language would be to write the history of the people who speak it, and of the country for which it provides both a medium of being and a self-image. The ambition of the task is tangible when its raw material is German say, or Polish, but its difficulty becomes an impossible idealism when faced with the travelling, shifting monster that is contemporary English. Robert McCrum's book, *The Story of English*, is then aptly titled for it does not aspire to be a history of English as much as a narrative description of its growth as a 'global language'.

ROBERT MCCRUM
1953 –
Nationality: British
WILLIAM CRAN
Nationality: Australian
ROBERT MACNEIL
1931 –
Nationality: American
First Published: Faber & Faber, 1986

Faced with the challenge of describing the nature and varieties, above all the spread of a language currently spoken by almost 2000 million people, McCrum and his associates, Robert MacNeil and William Cran, opt for a story form almost Dickensian in its array of plot-turns, digressions and its authors' cheerful way with statistics.

The story's primary actor, hero and anti-hero by turn, is the language once described by Daniel Defoe as 'your Roman-Saxon-Danish-Norman English'. Spoken by some 5 to 7 million English men and women by 1600, this hybrid language is today the 'mother tongue' of some 350 million speakers – the majority of them living outside of Engand. It is the 'second tongue' of some 350 million more and is taught to another 1000 million. The story of this language is one that develops by way of British Imperialism and American commercial and military hegemony. It cannot, therefore, be a story without violence, disgrace and tragedies. It is also, however, a story of resistance, invention, imagination and creativity. *The Story of English* pays due attention to both aspects.

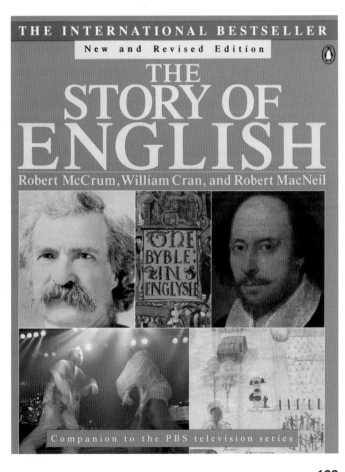

THE INTERNATIONAL BESTSELLER

New and Revised Edition

THE STORY OF ENGLISH

Robert McCrum, William Cran, and Robert MacNeil

ONE BYBLE IN ENGLYSE

Companion to the PBS television series

The Ornament of the World

MARIA ROSA MENOCAL
1953 –
Nationality: American
First Published: Little Brown & Co.,
2002
Other Selected Titles:
*The Arabic Role in Medieval Literary
History*
*Shards of Love: Exile and the Origins
of the Lyric*

Concepts of 'tolerance' and 'multiculturalism' are currently ubiquitous in political speechwriting, but their currency seems devalued or confusing. Are these positive modes of thinking, or bywords for the lazy accommodation of diversity, even for a damaging indifference to the moral conflicts of our time? Menocal's study of the interaction between Muslim, Christian and Jewish cultures in Medieval Spain is precisely the book to sharpen our debate around such issues. As she traces the dynamics of religious, artistic and social interaction between the 8th and 15th centuries, she applies a philosophy of toleration inspired, incongruously but effectively, by an F. Scott Fitzgerald definition of 'first-rate': 'the ability to hold two opposed ideas in the mind at the same time'.

It is this thought of the attrition of ideas as a force for stimulus rather than crisis that shapes Menocal's narrative. Her story takes us to the Umayyad empire that stretched from the Middle-East to northern Spain in the 8th century, and plots the way the Islamic dynasty adapted over 400 years, competing with the economic and religious rivalries posed by Jewish and Christian communities within its domain, but never collapsing entirely into social implosion. The 'ornament' of Menocal's story is Andalusia, and its gem Cordoba, a city lavishly landscaped and focus of the poetic and artistic competition Menocal sources as evidence of a 'golden age' of aesthetic and ethical interchange. The architectural evidence of religious 'syncretism' is particularly well displayed, evidence that conflicting beliefs and traditions can produce collective beauty rather than destruction.

Menocal's concluding chapters trace the collapse of toleration in the 14th and 15th centuries as the Black Death forces communities into scapegoating and destructive strategies of purification. A strict philosophy of religious and social 'harmony' develops, manifesting itself in the brutal slaughter and exclusion of Muslims and Jews by Christian Spain. Sometimes idealistic and often nostalgic, Menocal's portrait of medieval toleration is always revelatory, producing a logic of social diversity that escapes the clichés of modern rhetoric.

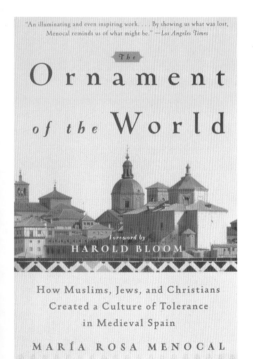

"An illuminating and even inspiring work. . . . By showing us what was lost, Menocal reminds us of what might be." —*Los Angeles Times*

The

Ornament

of the World

Foreword by
HAROLD BLOOM

How Muslims, Jews, and Christians
Created a Culture of Tolerance
in Medieval Spain

MARÍA ROSA MENOCAL

The Women's History of the World

History is made by men and 'History' is written by men. This is the destructive double bind that Rosalind Miles tries to untangle and falsify in her book, *The Women's History of the World* in which she aims to give voice to the silenced female participants in world history.

Writers have been trying to articulate the lost or muted voices of history for over a generation: we have seen a succession of books since the 1960s claiming to liberate the real identity and lives of the poverty-stricken, the heretical, the marginal and the oppressed, looking within and beneath the authoritative texts of powerful men to uncover hidden historical meanings. Rosalind Miles demands that we focus this process of historical recovery on the roles of women and the power of femininity (as identity, symbol and idea) through history, since 'women have been active, competent and important through all the ages of man and it is devastating for us if we don't understand this'.

This project is fraught with difficulties. One is the way Miles has to tell a story of oppression and a story of expression simultaneously: women have to be seen to have produced significant ideas, artistry, invention and cultural influence even as she reiterates the ways in which men have stifled that productivity through physical, mental and social domination. Another is that the author can be accused of a nostalgic presentation of a golden era of the 'great goddess' before 'the rise of the phallus' and of imagining a utopian future of perfect sexual equality. However, these are difficulties endemic to ambitious works which retell history and imagine the future, and Miles, refiguring the history of women, is in the very good company of Mary Wollstonecraft and Virginia Woolf in attempting this.

ROSALIND MILES
Nationality: British
First Published: Penguin, 1988
Other Selected Titles:
The Children we Deserve: Love and Hate in the Making of the Family
The Rites of Man: Love, Sex and Death in the Making of the Male
Ben Jonson: His Craft and Art

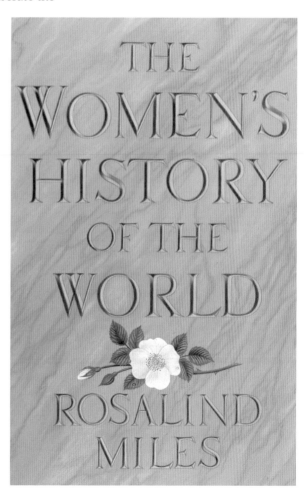

Pax Britannica: The Climax of an Empire

JAN (JAMES) MORRIS
1926 –
Nationality: British
First Published: Faber & Faber, 1968
Other Selected Titles:
Heaven's Command
Farewell the Trumpets
*The Matter of Wales: Epic Views of a
Small Country*
The Spectacle of Empire
Venice

Profiling Jan Morris, literary critics have anxiously discussed whether she should properly be labelled essayist, travel writer, novelist or historian. Reading *Pax Britannica*, the centrepiece of her trilogy about the British Empire, the generic diversity of her work resolves itself. This is a historical text, certainly, but one energized by the talents for travel journalism, storytelling and fictive nuances that can transform history into epic.

Her preface to the reader conjures some of this ambition, 'its pages are perfumed for me with saddle oil, joss-stick and railway steam', she says: 'I hope my readers will feel, as they close its pages, that they have spent a few hours looking through a big sash window at a scene of immense variety.' The text, using the Diamond Jubilee of Queen Victoria (1897) as its focal point and debating the criteria, ideology and experience of British empire-

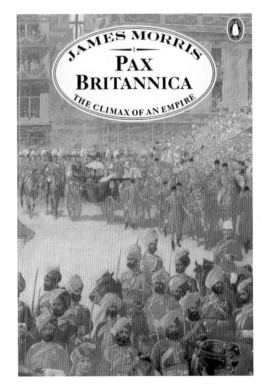

building in the late 19th and early 20th century, has more in common with the writing of Gibbon than of Las Casas, Fanon and Ferguson, the other historians concerned with empire in this section. The latter writers are essentially political, critiquing or justifying empire in ethical terms, whereas Morris' position is much more ambivalent.

Certainly, in the rigorous chapters 'The Profit' and 'Caste', she discusses the brutal economic criteria and racial ideologies that supported the 'cold superiority' of British imperialism. Equally, though, she is determined to record the empire as a rich, lived experience – a heterogeneous culture of dynamic trade, aesthetic diversity, architectural splendour and decadent recreation, and her central aim, if we can untangle one, is to trace the evolution of Britishness as it is superimposed upon, and suffused with, the indigenous cultures it encounters. Morris' portrait of the British Empire, written only a decade after its unravelling, is marked by awe as well as critique. The phrase 'imperialist' alternates, she argues, between 'the dubiously pejorative and the unarguably proper'.

Medieval Cities: Their Origins and the Revival of Trade

Henri Pirenne was a powerful, rambunctious academic, emanating intellectual charisma within 13 international academies, picking up 16 honorary degrees and reaching senior status within the Institute of France. In a career spanning from the 1880s to the1930s, Pirenne attempted to reconstitute the social history of medieval Europe just as modern Europe was fragmenting into territorial and political chaos. Along with his *History of Belgium*, a patriotic survey of Flemish social society, his greatest work is *Medieval Cities*, plotting the developments in civic organization, trade and politics that shaped Europe's most glorious urban centres.

His personality, as well as scholarship, explains why he was willing in this text to debunk entrenched historical explanations. Late 19th-century consensus decreed that the long interlude between Roman and Medieval progress was due to German Gothic invasions: a barbarian influence plunged Europe into the regressive 'dark ages'. Pirenne dismisses this, arguing instead that it was Islamic conquest in the southern Mediterranean during the 7th century, that cut-off trade routes with Africa and the East, emaciating cities and re-imposing a primitive feudalism. From this basis, Pirenne traces the revitalization of urban life in Europe, from the resilience of cathedral towns in France and the enduring civic traditions of Italy and Flanders, where social and commercial life revolved aroung Town and Guild Halls.

Pirenne's study carries almost audacious breadth, simultaneously a history of architecture, economics, public life and civic policy. Indeed, a whole genre speculating on the history of the European city, with modern British contributors such as Peter Ackroyd and Iain Sinclair, would be unrecognizable without Pirenne's grand intervention.

HENRI PIRENNE
1862 – 1935
Nationality: Belgian
First Published: Princeton University Press, 1925 (first English translation)
Other Selected Titles:
History of Belgium
Mohammed and Charlemagne
Economic and Social History of Medieval Europe

Parallel Lives

The Greek writer Plutarch.

The art of historical biography becomes more popular and profitable by the year, with novelists (Martin Amis on Stalin) and politicians (William Hague on William Pitt the Younger) as well as countless academics crossing over to a genre that rewards the drama of storytelling as much as historical accuracy. Plutarch, writing his *Parallel Lives* between 98 and 120AD, was perhaps the first to explicitly proclaim himself a biographer rather than a historian, so we can turn to him as a founding father of this ever popular discipline.

The daunting scale of his work – some 800,000 words on eminent Greek and Roman statesmen – forces the reader into selective perusal, and abridged translations often divide the original dialogue between 'parallel' Roman and Greek lives into separate editions, making it easier to trace the specific context of Greek and Roman society. This has its drawbacks, since Plutarch drew up the parallel structure so that a dialectic of life experience, morality and statemenship could emerge between the two dominant political and philosophical cultures of his time.

His project has profound significance for past and current definitions of history as a moral force, as suggested by the personal and universal claims in his work: 'I treat the narrative as a kind of mirror and try to find a way to arrange my life and assimilate it to the virtues of my subjects. Could one find a more effective means of moral improvement?'

Many first-time readers will be uncannily familiar with a number of Plutarch's lives, albeit through the ventriloquized words of Shakespeare, who plundered Plutarch for his dramatic portraits of Pericles, Pompey, Caesar and Anthony among others. Indeed, this extraordinary historical resource has filtered through centuries of classical scholarship and we should feel obliged to return to Plutarch's pages and meet the famous men that he 'welcomed in turn as a guest' and ushered into biographical immortality.

PLUTARCH
circa 46 – 120AD
Nationality: Greek
First Published: John Dryden, 1597
(first English translation)
Other Selected Titles:
Essays (Selection from Plutarch's Morals)

Flesh in the Age of Reason

Roy Porter's final book, published posthumously, attempts to fulfil an earlier promise to address the 'triangle of the moral, the material and the medical in the Enlightenment'. Quite a task, since Porter had been specializing in the history of psychiatry, medicine and Enlightenment philosophy during a 30-year publishing career, without quite being satisfied that he had woven these thematic strands together.

His histories of madness, medical progress and Enlightenment thinking have achieved the rare mix of academic respect and popular applause, simultaneously scholarly and accessible, energized by what Simon Schama calls, in the preface, 'a wickedly wonderful way with language'. *Flesh in the Age of Reason* can be seen as Porter's final flourish – ebulliantly written, with encyclopaedic knowledge enlevened by flashes of wit and the scale of the narrative oscillating, in typical style, between the panoramic and the intimate.

It is the subject matter, however, that allows Porter to free himself from generic constraints and produce a final, grand narrative. In Porter's text 'the body', passes from 17th-century Cartesian mistrust and religious debasement and through its 18th-century fetishization as the site of medical experiment, fashionable ornamentation, youthful beauty and moral decay. It ends up, in the concluding chapter, simultaneously celebrated and rejected in Byron's poetry, which revels in the sensuality of beautiful flesh, yet discovers immortality in the transcendental power of the mind. Porter's story, with its visceral focus, is also a history of the soul, the spirit and the imagination (the elements of the self consistently in attrition and dialogue with the body) as revealed in Enlightenment writing.

Porter apologizes for the 'elite' sources for his study – we hear about the body primarily from the perspective of male philosophers, poets, politicians and aristocrats – but case studies range so widely, from Swift's bloated caricatures to Blake's poetic liberation of the body from religious guilt, that this resource is sufficiently stimulating. The book acts as a dazzling epigraph to a brilliant historian's career.

ROY PORTER
1946 – 2002
Nationality: British
First Published: Penguin, 2003
Other Selected Titles:
Blood and Guts: a Short History of Medicine
The Faber Book of Madness
The Enlightenment
Edward Gibbon – Making History

'Masterly ... a great book' *Guardian*
ROY PORTER
WITH A FOREWORD BY SIMON SCHAMA

Flesh in the Age of Reason
How the Enlightenment Transformed the Way We See Our Bodies and Souls

Historian and TV presenter Simon Schama in 2000.

SIMON SCHAMA
1945 –
Nationality: British
First Published: Random House, 1989
Other Selected Titles:
*A History of Britain
Rembrandt's Eyes
Landscape and Memory
The Embarrassment of Riches*

Citizens – A Chronicle of the French Revolution

Simon Schama has become Britain's most familiar historian over the past decade, bellowing accounts of Viking invasions and Tudor decapitations over the whistling wind as TV cameras follow him lurching across hill-fort foundations and castle parapets. Before his *History of Britain* fame, though, Schama had established himself as a consummate historical storyteller. His work on the French Revolution, *Citizens – a Chronicle of the French Revolution*, fully defined his interdisciplinary, narrative approach to history. In the book's preface, he admits to it being a 'mischievously old-fashioned piece of storytelling', and distances himself from a school of scholarship on the French Revolution that prided itself on dispassionate commentary.

Narrating the events between 1778–1794, Schama chooses to avoid thematic surveys of the 'economy' or 'peasantry' and instead weaves the intimate stories of public and private individuals into the ruptured fabric of the French Revolution. Arguing two predominant factors, the power of family morality and the significance of terror as an agent of change, Schama chronicles personal protest, artistry and desire. Key royal, aristocratic and revolutionary figures, such as Louis XVI, Marie Antoinette, Robespierre and Georges Danton, receive detailed portraits, but only ever in relation to a careful history of the groups – labourers, printers and market women, for example – who acted as agencies of protest and reform.

Typical of Schama's interest in aesthetics, the book is punctuated by illustrations: royal portraits, caricatures, book-covers and even a teapot bearing revolutionary emblems. This rich texture of sources adds to the philosophies, manifestos and legal documents that trace revolutionary ideas, displaying the politicised objects and texts that circulated in French society. During his chapter on the role of terror, Schama suggests, in response to a caricature, that members of the revolutionary army 'lovingly cultivated their whiskers' to add to their fearsome presence. This is the kind of detail, integrated within a broader story, that makes Schama's account of the French Revolution so mesmerizing.

Leviathan and the Air-Pump

Shapin and Schaffer, co-authoring this text on the history of science, take us back to 1660s Britain. Shortly after the catastrophic civil war and regicide of Charles I, and still resonating with 150 years of religious and social discordance, this is a time when the restoration of order and the institution of sound knowledge are the priorities.

The pretext for the book is a controversy between Thomas Hobbes, philosopher, and Robert Boyle, founder member of the Royal Society and the institution's greatest experimenter. Hobbes' antagonism centres around the claims made by Boyle about experiments on the creation of vacuum by an air-pump.

So far, this may sound like highly specialized and intricate historical investigation, but the brilliance of Shapin and Schaffer is that they make this contretemps in 'natural philosophy' a symbol for the ruptures of the scientific revolution as a whole. Their interest lies in how experimental science was nurtured as a successor to knowledge distilled from classical learning and logic. They explain the way the propriety of experimental method is set up within the Royal Society, justified by elaborate procedures of witnessing, repetition and carefully orchestrated publicity. They also unveil the controversies that surrounded the production of experimental 'facts' as they clashed and mixed with religious, philosophical and logical 'truths', tracing the impulse towards a new definition of truth itself.

Much of the success of the book is down to a superb methodological structure. Boyle's (often leaky) air-pump becomes the emblem and metaphor for the site of experimental science itself; a space of attempted purity, framed by scholarly supervision and invested with daring patronage, in which new knowledge could emerge, protected from religious controversy and the corrupted textual residues of ancient scholarship. Shapin and Schaffer thereby invest a focused portrait of scientific controversy with the philosophical and social significance of the scientific revolution itself.

STEVEN SHAPIN
Nationality: American
Other Selected Titles:
The Scientific Revolution
A Social History of Truth: Civility and Science in 17th-Century England
SIMON SCHAFFER
1955 –
Nationality: British
Other Selected Titles:
The Uses of Experiment: Studies in the Natural Sciences (Ed. with David Gooding and Trevor Pinch)
First Published: Princeton University Press, 1985

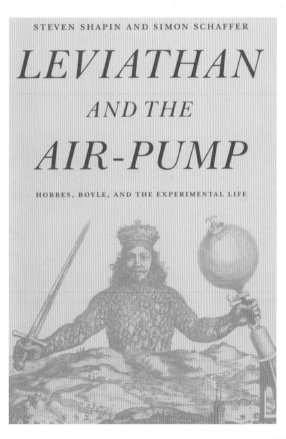

The Decline of the West

OSWALD SPENGLER
1880 – 1936
Nationality: German
First Published: Alfred A. Knopf,
1926 (first English translation)
Other Selected Titles:
The Hour of Decision
*Man and Technics: a Contribution to
the Philosophy of Life*

*German historian and educator
Oswald Spengler
in 1932.*

Oswald Spengler's *The Decline of the West* has suffered
something of a decline itself. Its importance now rests not so
much on its actual historical analyses but with its own status as a
historical artefact. Nowhere is this more apparent than in its
recourse to the rhetoric of 'blood and soil' – a counter point to
the purely economic social bonds of 'bourgeois civilization'.
If the topical affinities with Nazism are arresting, they are
also at times alienating.

Upon publication, however, its disquisition on the organic
decline of all cultures, from the Babylonian to the Western, found
a more than receptive audience in post-First World War
Europe, where the defeated nations mused on their
failed ambitions and where even the victorious surveyed
the rubble of civilization on their doorstep. 'Culture',
the creative form-giving moment of a people, is
destined, so Spengler argued, to ossify into 'civilization',
its functional but degraded form. Although he looks
individually at his eight 'high cultures' in turn, and
shows how this degenerative process manifests itself in
each, it is his diagnosis of the Western predicament that
proved resonant. For the West, once innervated by the
Faustian spirit, was now a slave to the very same reason
that had once been its liberation. Spengler effectively
provided a supra-history, charting a series of cultural
losses resulting from the emaciation of traditional forms
of living, the dominance of urban rationalism and the
pervasion of Western humanity by 'the money-spirit',
which allows forms of life to evolve while destroying the
spirit of cultural dynamism and belonging.

At times bombastic, at others melancholy,
Spengler's *The Decline of the West* should be grasped
in relation to the philosophical works on culture,
conscience and spirit that surrounded it, such as
Nietzsche's *Genealogy of Morals* and Heidegger's *Being
and Time*. Although the stories of each are different,
Spengler's work transfigures the abstract ambition of
philosophy into the more accessible and immediate
concerns of cultural history.

The Trial of Socrates

Isador Stone spent his journalistic career investigating political power, corruption and censorship, interrogating McCarthyism, exposing the futility of the Vietnam War and critiquing the racist policies of President Hoover. Retiring from this career, his study turned to Greek society and in particular the culture of Athenian democracy, which provided Stone with the historical foundation for the free speech and debate he treasured. The riddle Stone tries to work out in *The Trial of Socrates* is how, in a city where 'free speech was as much taken for granted as breathing', the philosopher Socrates could be tried and executed for his teachings.

Taking us back to Athens in 399BC, Stone recalls the encounter between Socrates and the Athenian court. Plato used the trial soon after in his *Apology* to make Socrates the 'secular martyr of the struggle against democracy', indicting the Athenian establishment for stupidity and reducing democratic politics to brutal mob-rule. Part of Stone's task is to reconstruct the case for the prosecution and see how Socrates appeared threatening to his fellow citizens. His projects are fraught with difficulty, since Stone's most proximal sources are the celebratory, evasive accounts of Plato and Xenophon, disciples to the trialist. The prosecution is also vague and flimsy in that Socrates allegedly 'refused reverence to the city's gods' and 'corrupted its youth'.

Crucially, Stone's historical investigation stretches further to documents, produced 50 years after the philosopher's death, which suggest Socrates was in fact giving philosophical support and training to an incipient dictatorship, moulded by his pupil Çritas, who was to become 'the bloodiest dictator Athens had ever known'. Re-appraising Socrates in this way, suggesting the totalitarian tendencies of his thought, Stone has received inevitable scholarly backlash, but this is precisely the value of his work. At a time when the values of free speech are being weighed against the destructive promotion of religious and political extremism, Stone's writing unveils pertinent moral and political dilemmas, and, true to form, allows debate to flourish.

Detail from The Death of Socrates by Jacques-Louis David.

ISADOR STONE
1907 – 1989
Nationality: American
First Published: Anchor, 1988
Other Selected Titles:
Underground to Palestine
The Killings at Kent State
The Hidden History of the Korean War

Annals of Imperial Rome

TACITUS
circa 55 – 117AD
Nationality: Roman
First Published: Penguin, 1956 (first English translation)

Bust of Roman historian Cornelius Tacitus.

Tacitus' *Annals* cover the period between 14 and 65AD, relating the turbulent reigns of Roman emperors Tiberius, Claudius and Nero. In one guise, the work is a supremely detailed commentary on the political and military development of the Roman Empire during the period, detailing imperial campaigns in Germany, Syria and Britain and tracing the political intrigue of succession and power within the Roman court and senate. Tacitus, rather like meticulous parliamentary historians today, revelled in his access to the minutes, acts and speeches that provided insight into the machinations of Roman rule, and his narrative elegantly distils power politics for the reader. This rhetorical lucidity, at that time unprecedented in its levels of precision and economy, perhaps emerges from Tacitus' education by Quintilian and a lifetime friendship and correspondence with Pliny, with whom he swopped theories of oratory and composition.

The power and perverse pleasure of Tacitus' *Annals*, despite a gesture of impartiality, comes from their impact as an indictment of political corruption. The vacuum following the reign of Augustus Caesar is taken up by three successive emperors whose names reach us gilded by infamy and sonorous with the strident abuse of power, and this is largely due to the implications of Tacitus' text. In Book VI, for example, Tiberius withdraws from political life and leaves rule in the hands of Sejanus, and Tacitus reports, with typical impassivity, that Rome was 'a scene of ceaseless bloodshed' and meticulously records a list of plots, murders, suicides and banishments. The effect of Tacitus' style – clean, dry and relentlessly explicit – is to present deception and cruelty as inevitable constituents of power. His work, written during a succeeding period of tyranny, comes down to us, sometimes fatalistic but always moral, as much a warning as a record.

The Origins of the Second World War

When *The Origins of the Second World War* was first published, its author was accused of offering an apologia for Hitler. Such accusations were generated by the enduring power of the explanatory narrative which Taylor's text sets out to debunk. For Taylor, the thesis that explains the origins of World War Two in terms of Hitler's demonic 'Great Plan' and the cowardice of a small bunch of 'appeasers', is not only wrong, it is malignly wrong as it vindicates all those other statesmen, policies and events without which war would not have been declared.

In this book, Taylor meticulously reconstructs the conditions and directions of international relations in the 1920s and 1930s. Drawing attention to the continuities between policies and decisions made then, and those dominant in the 19th century, Taylor asks his reader to radically rethink their knowledge of the 20th century.

Hitler's role, for example, is recreated by Taylor as that of an opportunistic inheritor of his predecessor's ambitions. Tracing the actions and rhetoric of France, Britain and the US at Versailles and in negotiations over reparations and disarmament, as well as their responses to German National Socialism, Taylor rereads 'appeasement' as an option that appeared powerfully practical to many, rather than as the escape clause of a cowardly few.

Wittily urbane, Taylor offers the reader a history that is indeed radical in its revision of received interpretations, but which is also a determinedly traditional history in its narrative approach to the order and meaning of events. In keeping with the philosophy of history expressed in his other works, statesmen are the movers and shakers, the definers of history. Politicians, bureaucrats, military men and diplomats are the often blind, frequently stupid and rarely noble creatures of systems of power they neither control nor understand. Taylor's method infuriates some but it makes his otherwise formidable text an exhilarating and accessible read.

English Historian and TV presenter A.J.P. Taylor in 1953.

A.J.P. TAYLOR
1906 – 1990
Nationality: British
First Published: Hamish Hamilton, 1961
Other Selected Titles:
The Trouble Makers
The First World War: an Illustrated History
Europe: Grandeur and Decline

A Distant Mirror: The Calamitous 14th Century

BARBARA M. TUCHMAN
1912 – 1989
Nationality: American
First Published: Macmillan, 1978
Other Selected Titles:
Practising History: Selected Essays
*Bible and Sword: How the British
Came to Palestine*
*The Proud Tower: a Portrait of the
World Before the War, 1890–1914*

The world of 14th-century Europe might seem particularly elusive and alien to us, lacking the political or philosophical structure of ancient civilizations and naked of the rich cultural attire of the Renaissance. Barbara Tuchman ushers us into this world, in which the population of Europe has been decimated by the Black Death and where people occupy 'a violent, tormented, bewildering, suffering and disintegrating age'.

The challenge Tuchman has, of course, is to make this baffling era understandable, even familiar, to us. She does this in two ways, first by telling the history through the life of Enguerrand de Coucy VII, a French Knight and nobleman, and secondly by drawing parallels between the crises of the 14th century and the ruptures and uncertainty of the 20th century.

The first strategy works particularly well, Coucy's well-connected, well-travelled existence lending focus and coherence to Tuchman's surveys of chivalric codes, conflict, disease and theological schism. This allows a personal perspective in stories that could, in clumsier hands, be moulded into amorphous monuments to communal suffering.

The second technique is more hit and miss: the 'distant mirroring' of 14th-century conflict in Flanders and Normandy with the slaughter of the First World War works well, because of the clear echoes of place names, senseless military strategies and mass killing.

Less successful, perhaps, are the parallels Tuchman attempts between the ideological schisms she traces in 14th-century Europe and the 1960s and 1970s as decades of 'collapsing assumptions' and 'similar disarray': this may be stretching historical symmetry a little too far.

Nevertheless, Tuchman tells a story of 14th-century Europe that captivates the reader and popularizes a complex period of medieval history, rescuing it from obscurity and stereotype and offering it visceral life in relation to our own world.

THE GREAT BESTSELLER
A DISTANT MIRROR
THE CALAMITOUS 14th CENTURY

BARBARA W. TUCHMAN

A People's History of the United States

In the opening pages of *A People's History of the United States*, Howard Zinn warns the reader that 'we must not accept the memory of states as our own. Nations are not communities and never have been.' This statement is particularly pertinent in the context of the United States where questions of national belonging have always been underpinned by questions of national allegiance. Acceptance of the dominant national narrative was key to the Americanization of diverse immigrant communities. America, as Eric Hobsbawn asserts, 'had to be made'. What of the history of those who rejected, interrupted, displaced or disturbed the official narrative of America's past? Zinn's epic history of the United States is an attempt to chronicle and venerate those who represented a different America.

This enthusiastically partisan book (now in its third edition) reinterprets American history from below. *A People's History* is a war against 'objectivity' which Zinn defines as a 'learned sense of moral proportion'. In its place we are presented with a history book which acknowledges and embraces its own politically radical motivations. From Columbus to the War on Terror, this book eschews the perceived objectivity of dominant narratives of American history and reconfigures that history from the standpoint of the marginalized, oppressed and resistant. The America which emerges from this book is one which is marked by internal conflict and struggle. Zinn's eloquent and passionate account of America's dissident historical subjects fighting slavery, racism, labour exploitation and corporate greed is also a call for the continuation of that struggle. Yet this is no political polemic garbed in historical dress. Rather we are given a meticulous and readable history which reanimates the familiarity of the nation's official history by carving a space for its disremembered voices.

HOWARD ZINN
1922 –
Nationality: American
First Published: Harper Collins, 1980
Other Selected Titles:
*Hijacking Catastrophe: 9/11
Fear And The Selling Of American
Empire
The Twentieth Century: A People's
History
Passionate Declarations: Essays on
War and Justice*

American writer Howard Zinn in Havana, Cuba, in 2004.

MEMOIRS

Isabel Allende is one of Latin America's leading novelists.

ISABEL ALLENDE
1942 –
Nationality: Chilean
First Published: HarperCollins, 1995
Other Selected Titles:
The House of the Spirits
Of Love and Shadows
Eva Luna
The Infinite Plan
Daughter of Fortune
Portrait in Sepia
My Invented Country
Zorro: A Novel

Paula

Isabel Allende began writing her first novel, *The House of the Spirits*, on 8 January, 1981, as a letter to her dying grandfather. Again on 8 January, 11 years later, she sat down to compose a letter to her daughter Paula, who had been in a coma for a month due to a rare genetic disease. Allende begins, 'Listen, Paula, I am going to tell you a story, so that when you wake up you will not feel so lost.'

Paula never did wake up – she died one year later, having never regained consciousness. Allende wrote this moving tribute to Paula while keeping vigil by her bedside at a Madrid hospital, and then in her home in California. The story moves back and forth from present to past and back again. Paula's illness inspired Allende to reflect on her own extraordinary life, and the lives of her ancestors. She tells of her childhood spent in Peru, Chile, Bolivia and Lebanon; marriage and motherhood; her career as a journalist and writer; her romantic love affairs. She also chronicles the coup of 1973, in which her uncle Salvador Allende, the President of Chile, was overthrown and killed, and her subsequent period of exile in Venezuela.

Continually, Allende draws the reader back to Paula's bedside, where we witness a mother's anguish as her child's life gradually ebbs away. What sustains her throughout the ordeal is her belief that the souls of our loved ones never leave us. She ends her story with a blessing: 'Godspeed, Paula, woman. Welcome, Paula, spirit.'

Paula is the masterwork of one of Latin America's leading storytellers. Allende brings all the passion and magic of her fiction into this spellbinding memoir, and leaves you feeling like you have spent time with a wonderful friend.

Journal Intime

Henri-Frédéric Amiel was a nineteenth-century Swiss poet, philosopher and professor, who published some poems in his lifetime but is best known for his *Journal Intime*, released a year after his death.

In his Introduction, Amiel's friend, critic M. Edmond Scherer explained that the journal 'was not a volume of memoirs, but the confidences of a solitary thinker, the meditations of a philosopher for whom the things of the soul were the sovereign realities of existence'. Amiel himself said that 'the chief utility of the *journal intime* is to restore the integrity of the mind…', and a substantial part of the diary is taken up with the state of the author's psychological condition. He gives himself spiritual directives, and at times lapses into melancholy and self-castigation, but though disheartened he is never despairing.

In his journal, Amiel discusses religion, philosophy and politics and comments on his reading material, which includes the works of Tocqueville, Joubert and Rousseau. But he becomes most alive when he gets out of his head and goes out of doors, observing people and nature. At times, he seems almost Wordsworthian in his recollections of childhood and natural beauty.

The *Journal Intime* is full of pithy sayings full of deep insight. For example: 'Life is short and we have never too much time for gladdening the hearts of those who are travelling the dark journey with us,' and 'Confusion is the enemy of all comfort, and confusion is born of procrastination.' Despite suffering great physical pain, Amiel kept his journal up until the end, as he faced death with courage and serenity. This classic book is a must-read as an example of a person's quest for relevance, inner peace and self-acceptance.

HENRI-FRÉDÉRIC AMIEL
1821 – 1881
Nationality: Swiss
First Published: Geneva, 1882
Other Selected Titles:
Grains de Mil
Il Penseroso
Part du Rêve
Les Etrangères
Charles le Téméraire
Romancero Historiquan
Jour à Jour

Amiel's Journal

HENRI-FREDERIC AMIEL and Mrs. Humphry Ward

The Echo Library

Aubrey's Brief Lives

JOHN AUBREY
1626 – 1697
Nationality: British
First Published: Secker and Warburg, 1949
Other Selected Titles:
Miscellanies
Architectonica Sacra
Life of Mr. Thomas Hobbes of Malmesbury

John Aubrey was a contemporary of Samuel Pepys, and although his collection of biographical sketches entitled *Brief Lives* is not as universally known as Pepys' *Diary*, it is nevertheless an original and illuminating work, and a great classic of the period.

John Aubrey was born to wealth and property, but on the death of his father he was left with debts and lawsuits. However, he continued to enjoy the good life due to the generosity of his well-off friends. Some people would classify Aubrey as a dilettante because he rarely completed a project and was disorganized and undisciplined. Kinder people would say he was a man of many talents and numerous enthusiasms.

Brief Lives came into being while Aubrey was working as a research assistant to Oxford don Anthony Wood. 'How these curiosities would be quite forgot, did not such idle fellowes as I am putt them down…' The book includes relatively brief sketches of many notable people of the time including William Shakespeare, John Milton, Francis Bacon, Sir Walter Raleigh, Elizabeth Broughton and Mary Herbert, Countess of Pembroke.

Aubrey has a real knack for storytelling. For example, he says of Shakespeare: 'His father was a Butcher, and I have been told heretofore by some of the neighbours, that when he was a boy he exercised his father's Trade, but when he kill'd a Calfe he would doe it in a high style, and make a Speech.' He doesn't hold back in revealing the more intimate details about his subjects, and in this respect, this book can be seen as a precursor to gossip magazines and the 'tell-all' biographies of today.

Brief Lives is a colourful account of important English people who lived between the Elizabethan period and the Restoration. There are several editions available.

Confessions

Augustine of Hippo is a Catholic saint and
one of the greatest of the Latin Church
fathers. His teachings have been enshrined
in the Church's canon, and have influenced
the philosophies of St. Thomas Aquinas
and Protestant theologians Martin Luther
and John Calvin. Augustine was a professor
of rhetoric and devotee of the Manichaean-
Gnostic sect until his conversion to
Christianity in 386. Five years later he was
ordained to the priesthood, and in 396
became Bishop of Hippo, in Algeria.

In his *Confessions*, which is considered
the first Western autobiography, he tells
the story of his conversion from paganism
to Christianity, from a wayward, self-
seeking life to a life dedicated to Jesus
Christ. It was not an easy conversion –
Augustine went through years of vacillation
and self-doubt before he surrendered to
what he believed was the will of God.

Confessions is composed of 13 books.
The first ten books contain the story of
Augustine's life. He tells of his mother,
Monica, a devoted Catholic who later
became a saint; his years of indulgence in
sensual pleasures; and his attraction to
magic and astrology. Apart from his
mother's prayers for his conversion, several other major
influences led him to Christianity, including his friendship with
Bishop Ambrose of Milan, and his reading of the life of St.
Anthony of the Desert.

Whatever your belief system, if you have an interest in the
genre of memoir or autobiography, Augustine's *Confessions*
(especially the first ten sections) is well worth reading. It lays
bare the soul of a man searching for truth and inner peace, and
gives an illuminating account of the early days of Christianity as
told by one of its most revered teachers.

Saint Augustine in His Study *by*
Sandro Botticelli

AUGUSTINE
354 – 430AD
First Published: 397
Other Selected Titles:
On Christian Doctrine
The City of God
On the Trinity
Enchiridion
Retractions
The Literal Meaning of Genesis

Simone de Beauvoir, 1947.

SIMONE DE BEAUVOIR
1808 – 1986
Nationality: French
First Published: Librairie Gallimard,
1958
Other Selected Titles:
She Came to Stay
The Blood of Others
All Men are Mortal
The Ethics of Ambiguity
The Second Sex
The Mandarins
The Coming of Age
Adieux: A Farewell to Sartre

Memoirs of a Dutiful Daughter

Memoirs of a Dutiful Daughter (*Mémoirs d'une Jeune Fille Rangeé*) is the first of four volumes of autobiography by notable author, philosopher and feminist, Simone de Beauvoir. It is a detailed account of her childhood, youth and loss of innocence – starting at the moment of her birth and ending with the death of her dearest friend Zaza.

De Beauvoir's mother was a pious Catholic and her father was a lawyer who would rather have become an actor. As a young child, de Beauvoir was diligent and devout, but her religious fervour transformed itself into a rigorous drive toward scholastic achievement. She eventually grew to scorn the respectable bourgeois values of her family and was committed to the ideal of being true to one's self. To that end, she pursued an academic career which took her to the Sorbonne, where she first met her life partner, Jean-Paul Sartre. This is where Volume I ends.

In her memoir, de Beauvoir tells of her decision, at the age of 15, to become a writer, because 'the most celebrated women had distinguished themselves in literature'. Early influences were Louisa May Alcott and George Eliot.

Memoirs of a Dutiful Daughter is a rich tapestry of thoughts, emotions, character sketches and details, written with the elegance of a novelist and the insight of a philosopher, a woman in the fullness of maturity looking back on her youth. Having read it, you will probably want also to read the books that document the next stages of her amazing life: *The Prime of Life*, *Forces of Circumstance* and *All Said and Done*.

My Left Foot

Published when the author was only 22 years old, *My Left Foot* is the story of an extraordinary person. Christy Brown was an imaginative, sensitive soul trapped in a body twisted and crippled by cerebral palsy. Barely able to talk, at the age of five he picked up a piece of chalk with his left foot, the only part of his body with any flexibility, and thus began to communicate.

Brown has the Irish gift of storytelling, and writes simply and lyrically about his life. At times, when he tells of his feelings of loneliness, entrapment and suffocation, it is heartbreakingly painful. But through painting and writing – with his left foot – he is able to express his pent-up feelings and experience moments of transcendence. One of the most moving scenes is of the candlelight procession at Lourdes, which Brown describes as 'the most beautiful moment of my life'.

The book is not without humour, however. Particularly funny are the author's descriptions of his large brood of siblings, who take him on adventures through working-class Dublin in a battered little go-cart named Henry.

Throughout his autobiography, Brown acknowledges the friends and guides who have helped him along the way: social worker Katriona Delahunt, doctor and writer Robert Collis, teacher Mr. Guthrie, and especially his mother, who from the time he was born, vehemently denied that he was mentally defective and refused to let him be placed in an institution.

My Left Foot, without lapsing into sentimentality, helps us to empathize with severely disabled people and see them as complete human beings. Jim Sheridan adapted the text into an equally fine film starring Daniel Day Lewis and Brenda Fricker, both of whom received Academy Awards for their fine performances.

CHRISTY BROWN
1932 – 1981
Nationality: Irish
First Published: Martin, Secker & Warburg Ltd, 1954
Other Selected Titles:
Down All the Days
Come Softly to My Wake
Background Music
A Shadow on Summer
Wild Grow the Lilies
Of Snails and Skylarks

my left foot

CHRISTY BROWN

'One of the literary greats of the modern age'
Irish Times

The Autobiography of Benvenuto Cellini

BENVENUTO CELLINI
1500 – 1571
Nationality: Italian
First Published: 1728
Other Selected Titles:
The Treatise on Goldsmithing and Sculpture

Benvenuto Cellini begins his memoir: 'All men who have accomplished anything worthwhile should set down the story of their own lives with their own hands. But they should wait before undertaking so delicate an enterprise until they have passed the age of forty.' Cellini was 58 when he began writing his autobiography, which ranks along with Samuel Pepys' *Diary* and Jean-Jacques Rousseau's *Confessions* as one of the finest examples of the genre.

Cellini was born and lived most of his life in Florence, at that time the epicentre of European culture. The son of a musician, he chose not to follow in his father's footsteps, but rather pursued a career as a goldsmith. He was also a sculptor, although his only sculpture of note is the bronze statue *Perseus Holding the Head of Medusa*.

However, Cellini's autobiography is his best-known achievement. It reads like a veritable who's who of the Renaissance art world, including such personages as Michelangelo, Leonardo da Vinci, and members of the powerful Medici family, who patronized his work. It is written in a lively, readable style, although Cellini is rather prone to hyperbole and self-aggrandizement; he even confesses to a murder or two. Paradoxically, he is also very religious, and the description of his supernatural experience while he was imprisoned in the Castle of St. Angelo in Rome is highly evocative.

The Autobiography of Benvenuto Cellini provides a wonderful eyewitness account of Europe as it was during the Renaissance, and a picture of the life of one of the period's most flamboyant figures.

Francis I visiting the studio of Benvenuto Cellini in Rome.

The Unquiet Grave: A Word Cycle by Palinurus

In *The Unquiet Grave*, Cyril Connolly adopted the pseudonym of Palinurus, the pilot of Æneas who 'is the core of melancholy and guilt that works destruction on us from within'. Connolly wrote this memoir of sorts between the autumn of 1942 and the autumn of 1943, when London was at its darkest. He describes *The Unquiet Grave* as a 'word cycle', which is about the best way to categorize a book that defies categorization.

In Connolly's introduction, he says that Palinurus wished to 'proclaim his faith in the unity and continuity of Western culture in its moment of crisis'. At first glance, it seems that one needs a Classical education, as well as fluency in French, to understand this book. They would help. But the willing reader can also pick up *The Unquiet Grave* at random and sample its reflections, musings, epigrams and quotes from famous men as diverse as Pascal, Flaubert, Sir Walter Raleigh, Buddha and Yeats.

Some of Connolly's insights on religion, relationships and art are as relevant now as they were 60 years ago, although many people would disagree with his strong opinions.

He goes into great detail about the causes of angst, and postulates that in his 'past incarnations he lived in the Augustan age in Rome, in Paris and London from 1660 to 1740, and lastly from 1770 to 1850'.

In 1945, Nancy Mitford sent *The Unquiet Grave* to her friend Evelyn Waugh, believing it to be a must-read book. Because of its originality, honesty and beauty of language, many others think so too.

CYRIL CONNOLLY
1903 – 1974
Nationality: British
First Published: *Horizon* magazine, 1944
Other Selected Titles:
The Rock Pool
The Enemies of Promise
The Condemned Playground
Les Pavilions
Previous Convictions
The Modern Movement: 100 Key Books from England, France and America
The Evening Collonade

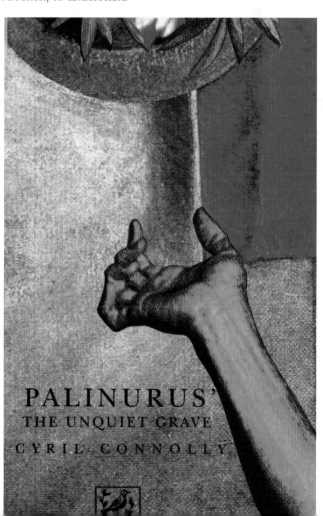

PALINURUS'
THE UNQUIET GRAVE
CYRIL CONNOLLY

Boy: Tales of Childhood

ROALD DAHL
1916 – 1990
Nationality: Norwegian-British
First Published: Jonathan Cape,
1984
Other Selected Titles:
James and the Giant Peach
Charlie and the Chocolate Factory
Danny the Champion of the World
The BFG
Revolting Rhymes
My Uncle Oswald
Someone Like You
Tales of the Unexpected

*Roald Dahl is one of the world's
greatest children's authors.*

Boy: Tales of Childhood is the first volume of memoirs by novelist, poet, short story writer, screenwriter and one of the most popular children's authors of all time, Roald Dahl. It covers the period from Dahl's birth in Wales in 1916 to the age of 20, when he was sent to Africa with the Shell Oil Company.

Dahl says of his childhood experiences, 'Some are funny. Some are painful. Some are unpleasant. I suppose that is why I have always remembered them so vividly. All are true.' He tells of his Norwegian parents, the premature and tragic deaths of his sister and father, his first ride in a motor car, his experiences at English boarding schools, and summer holidays in Norway, all in the engaging, conversational style that has made him such a favourite with young readers.

Dahl's funny memories are very funny indeed, particularly the chapters 'The Great Mouse Plot' and 'Goat's Tobacco'. Some of his recollections are extremely uncomfortable to read, such as the school canings, and his adenoidectomy, which was performed without anaesthetic. Dahl devotees will recognize familiar settings, characters and themes. His Norwegian holidays were recreated in *The Witches*; his sadistic schoolmasters (one who later became the Archbishop of Canterbury) were amalgamated into the character of Trunchbull in *Matilda*; and his childhood fantasies about being a chocolate inventor ended up enchanting us in *Charlie and the Chocolate Factory*.

Boy and the second volume of memoirs, *Flying Solo*, appear in both the adult and children's sections of libraries and bookshops. Like many of Dahl's children's stories, *Boy* includes the whimsical illustrations of Quentin Blake, as well as photographs and handwritten letters. It is an enchanting read for Roald Dahl fans of all ages.

My Family and Other Animals

When naturalist Gerald Durrell was ten years old, his family left England to live on the Greek island of Corfu for five years. *My Family and Other Animals* is a rollicking account of those years as told from the point of view of young Gerald. Durrell prefaces his memoir by telling us that 'it was originally intended to be a mildly nostalgic account of the natural history of the island, but I made a grave mistake by introducing my family into the book in the first few pages.'

Naturalist and author Gerald Durrell.

The book is divided into three parts, each taking place in one of the different homes the Durrells inhabited during their stay on Corfu: 'the strawberry-pink villa', 'the daffodil-yellow villa' and the 'snow-white villa'. It contains a wonderful cast of characters, starting with Gerald's genial widowed mother and older siblings Margo, Leslie and Larry (acclaimed novelist Lawrence Durrell). Other friends and local identities include the irrepressible Spiro, Dr. Theodore Stephanides (a mentor to the budding young zoologist), and Gerald's eccentric English tutor called George.

When the Durrells arrived on Corfu they had brought with them their dog Roger, who accompanied Gerald on his adventures. Along the way, they acquired a menagerie which included Achilles the tortoise, Quasimodo the pigeon, Geronimo the gecko, and puppies Widdle and Puke.

My Family and Other Animals is engaging for its humour, its gorgeous descriptions of the wonders of Corfu, and a look at the unusual childhood of one of Britain's leading naturalists. It was made into a BBC series in 1989 and again in 2005, starring Imelda Staunton as Mother. If you want to read more of the Durrell family, the sequels *Birds, Beasts and Relatives* and *The Garden of the Gods* are also great fun.

GERALD DURRELL
1925 – 1995
Nationality: British
First Published: Rupert Hart-Davis, 1956
Other Selected Titles:
The Overloaded Ark
The Bafut Beagles
The New Noah
The Drunken Forest
A Zoo in My Luggage
A Whispering Land
How to Shoot an Amateur Naturalist
Rosie Is My Relative

An Angel at My Table

JANET FRAME
1924 – 2004
Nationality: New Zealand
First Published: Hutchinson, 1984
Other Selected Titles:
The Lagoon and Other Stories
Owls Do Cry
Faces in the Water
Scented Gardens for the Blind
A State of Siege
The Pocket Mirror
Intensive Care
Daughter Buffalo

This is the second volume of autobiography by acclaimed novelist, poet and short story writer, Janet Frame.

The first volume, *To the Is-land*, tells of her childhood in a large, impoverished family in New Zealand. In *An Angel at My Table*, Frame sensitively recounts her years as a college student, trainee teacher, and apprentice writer. What should have been the best time of her life was in fact a nightmare, marked by the death of a second of her sisters by drowning (the first had drowned ten years earlier), a crippling nervous breakdown and a suicide attempt.

Frame was painfully introverted and awkward, more comfortable in the world of fantasy. If she sought psychiatric help today she would probably be labelled 'social phobic' and prescribed Prozac. However, she was diagnosed with schizophrenia (wrongly, as it turned out) and spent most of her twenties in and out of mental institutions, enduring more than a hundred episodes of electroconvulsive therapy. Just as she was about to undergo a lobotomy, the doctors found out she had received the Hubert Church literary award for *The Lagoon and Other Stories*, thus sparing her such a terrible fate.

The last quarter of the book is much happier. Freed from family and institutional constraints, Frame is able to do the only thing she had ever wanted to do – write. She meets like-minded people, including writer Frank Sargeson, who encourages her to apply for a literary grant. As the memoir ends, Frame is sailing for Europe – her experiences there are described in the third volume, *The Envoy from Mirror City*.

An Angel at My Table is a tale of hardship, resilience and hope, a fascinating glimpse into the mind of an amazing writer. The 1990 film, directed by Jane Campion, is a faithful and beautiful adaptation.

The Diary of a Young Girl

Anne Frank is a Jewish schoolgirl living in Amsterdam when she commences her diary on her thirteenth birthday. Early in her journal she states, 'After May 1940 the good times were few and far between', and lists all the deprivations and restrictions that the Jews in Europe had to endure during Hitler's regime. It gets even worse when, a month after her diary begins, Anne, her family and four others go into hiding in the 'secret annexe' of her father's office, where they remain for two years.

In many ways Anne's diary is like that of any normal adolescent, in which she vents her anger toward her mother, her jealousy of her sister and her developing sexual feelings. We realize just how terribly abnormal her situation is when she describes the lack of privacy, the shortage of nourishing food, the lack of freedom, fresh air and sunlight, and most of all, the ever-present fear of getting caught. But however sad she sometimes becomes, she never loses joy or hope.

Anne begins each entry with 'Dear Kitty', as though she were writing to a close friend. When the book ends abruptly on 1 August, 1944, we feel we are on intimate terms with this spirited young girl, making it all the more tragic to learn that the Nazis discovered the Franks' hiding place and that Anne died of typhoid in Bergen-Belsen concentration camp less than a year later. Of the eight occupants of the annexe only one survived – Anne's father, Otto – who eventually arranged for the diary's publication.

Anne Frank's diary is one of the world's best-loved books, and rightly so. It is beautifully written, and gives an innocent human voice to the millions of anonymous Jews who suffered and died under the German occupation.

ANNE FRANK
1929 – 1945
Nationality: Dutch
First Published: Contact Publishers, 1947

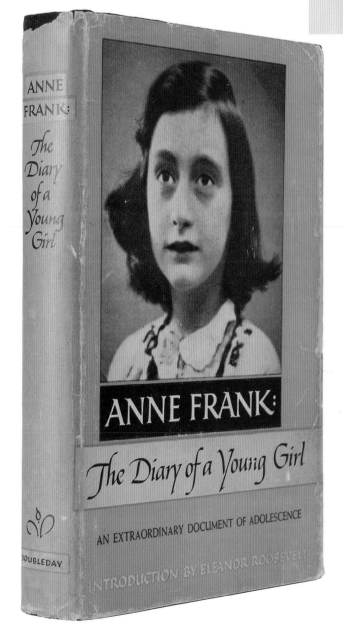

Journals 1889-1949

André Gide won the Nobel Prize for Literature in 1947.

ANDRE PAUL GUILLAUME GIDE
1869 – 1951
Nationality: French
First Published: Gallimard, 1939
Other Selected Titles:
*The Notebooks of André Walter
Fruits of the Earth
The Immoralist
The Prodigal's Return
Strait is the Gate
The Vatican Cellars
The Counterfeiters
Travels in the Congo*

André Gide is one of the greatest of French writers, who throughout his long and prolific career produced plays, novels, criticism, translations, travel journals, political commentary and autobiography. He was awarded the Nobel Prize for Literature in 1947, and in 1952, a year after his death, his works were placed on the Catholic Church's Index of Forbidden Books.

His *Journals* span 60 years from 1889 to 1949 – and are available either in a single volume or in four separate volumes. The journals are not so much a story of his life (although they sometimes relate personal details), but are more philosophical reflections, meditations on art and aesthetics, comments on his readings (and he was a voracious reader), and analysis of world events. Gide was a sensualist as well as a profoundly spiritual person, and his journals were a vehicle for him to integrate these seemingly contradictory sides to his nature.

Much of the content of the *Journals* is weighty and erudite, but Gide occasionally shows a lighter, down-to-earth side. For example, in an entry from 1906, he tells of how he took in a scruffy-looking stray poodle: 'And I who wanted a pedigreed dog. I've got what's coming to me! No matter; it is time to learn once more to prefer the events that choose me to those I should have chosen myself.'

Another must-read book is Gide's autobiography *If It Die*, published in 1926. Like his novels, it was considered very shocking at the time, and tells of his many and varied life experiences. One of the highlights is his meeting with Oscar Wilde and Lord Alfred Douglas in North Africa.

Poetry and Truth:
From My Own Life

Johann Wolfgang von Goethe is one of the leading figures in German literature, and indeed, in European culture. He is best known for his novel *The Sorrows of Young Werther* and his drama *Faust*. As well as being a novelist and playwright, Goethe excelled as a poet, philosopher, statesman, painter and scientist.

Goethe began writing his autobiography in 1811, but did not complete it until 1831. He was familiar with the genre – the mid 18th to the mid 19th century was the golden age of autobiography, and some years earlier Goethe translated Benvenuto Cellini's memoirs. He opens his story quite charmingly: 'On the twenty-eighth of August, 1749, at mid-day, as the clock struck twelve, I came into the world, at Frankfort on the Main. My horoscope was propitious: the sun stood in the sign of the Virgin, and had culminated for the day…' He tells of his early childhood, his relationships with his family, his education and some of his romantic interests, but as Ralph Waldo Emerson pointed out, he gives 'few dates, no correspondence, no details of offices or employments, no light on his marriage; and a period of ten years, that should be the most active in his life, after his settlement at Weimar, is sunk in silence.' A great deal of the text is taken up with his reflections on philosophy and art, including analysis of some of his own works.

Because Goethe was a scientist as well as a poet, and as much a product of the Age of Reason as the Romantic period, his work is poised between objectivity and emotionalism. *Poetry and Truth* ranks with Rousseau's *Confessions* as a major influence on the modern Western autobiography, and is a balanced account of a brilliant mind.

JOHANN WOLFGANG VON GOETHE
1749 – 1832
Nationality: German
First Published: Henry G. Bohn, 1848
Other Selected Titles:
Iron Hand
The Sorrows of Young Werther
Roman Elegies
Faust
Wilhelm Meister's Apprenticeship
Hermann and Dorothea
Elective Affinities
The Italian Journey

Johann Wolfgang von Goethe.

Father and Son: A Study of Two Temperaments

EDMUND GOSSE
1849 – 1928
Nationality: British
First Published: W.W. Norton, 1907
Other Selected Titles:
King Erik
Seventeenth Century Studies
Life of William Congreve
Life and Letters of Dr John Donne
Jeremy Taylor
Life of Sir Thomas Browne
A History of Eighteenth Century Literature

As well as being a poet, journalist and critic, Edmund Gosse served as Librarian of the House of Lords for many years. But as he explains in *Father and Son*, his parents had planned for him a very different future.

Edmund Gosse was the only child of Emily Bowes, an evangelist and writer of religious verse, and Philip Henry Gosse, a botanist, zoologist and lay preacher, who struggled to reconcile science and religion. Emily and Philip met each other at a service of the Plymouth Brethren, a harsh puritanical sect.

Gosse tells us that when he was born, 'The Great Scheme…had been…that I should be exclusively and consecutively dedicated through the whole of my life to the manifest and uninterrupted and uncompromised service of the Lord.' To that end, his parents set about preparing him for his future role, thus depriving him of a normal childhood. He had no friends, no outdoor amusements and no storybooks: 'I was told about missionaries, but never about pirates.' Young Edmund's life became even bleaker when his mother died of cancer when he was only seven.

Sir Edmund Gosse fought against his strict religious upbringing.

By the time he was in his teens, Gosse began to chafe at the restrictions placed on his imagination. He discovered the wonders of Shakespeare, Coleridge, Carlyle and Ruskin, and had grown sick of the Bible because it had become so familiar. Gosse ends his book by pronouncing that he and his father had 'walked in opposite hemispheres of the soul'. In reading *Father and Son*, one gets the impression that Edmund Gosse genuinely loved his father, who was essentially a good and caring man, albeit a misguided one.

Father and Son is a seminal Victorian autobiography. It was adapted by Dennis Potter as a 1976 television play, *Where Adam Stood*.

Ways of Escape

In the Preface to his second volume of memoirs, *Ways of Escape*, Graham Greene quotes W.H. Auden: 'Man needs escape as he needs food and deep sleep.' As someone who suffered from manic-depression, Greene needed escape perhaps more than most. He sought it through travel, danger, drugs, alcohol, women and religion, but most of all, through writing.

Greene was possibly one of the most popular story-tellers of the 20th century, and throughout his long career he wrote novels, short stories, plays, travel books, essays, biographies, screenplays, newspaper articles and book and film reviews. He was devoted to his craft, and it is not surprising that much of *Ways of Escape* is a discussion of the process of writing, and the circumstances surrounding many of his books. Greene also talks about his own favourite authors (including Henry James) and his friendships with other literary figures such as T.S. Eliot and Evelyn Waugh.

Throughout his life, Greene criss-crossed the globe in search of adventure and inspiration (not to mention escape), and his wanderings took him to such political hot-spots as Vietnam, Haiti, Cuba, Paraguay and Kenya. One of the most evocative sections of the book is a passage from his journal dated December 31, 1953, in which he describes an opium den in Saigon. Greene was also a scriptwriter during the golden years of Hollywood, and his anecdotes about Carol Reed, David Selznik, Alexander Korda and Shirley Temple prove to be most entertaining.

Whether you are familiar with his oeuvre, or are a newcomer to 'Greeneland', *Ways of Escape* (best read in conjunction with *A Sort of Life*) is a must-read for a candid portrayal of a complex and gifted writer.

Graham Greene, 1975.

GRAHAM GREENE
1904 – 1991
Nationality: British
First Published: The Bodley Head, 1980
Other Selected Titles:
Brighton Rock
The Power and the Glory
The Heart of the Matter
The End of the Affair
The Quiet American
Our Man in Havana
A Burnt-out Case
Travels with My Aunt

Black Like Me

John Howard Griffin in Austin, Texas, 1964.

JOHN HOWARD GRIFFIN
1920 – 1980
Nationality: American
First Published: Houghton Mifflin, 1961
Other Selected Titles:
The Devil Rides Outside
Nuni, Land of the High Sky
The Church and the Black Man
A Time to be Human
Jacques Maritain: Homage in Words and Pictures
A Hidden Wholeness
The Hermitage Journals

In 1959, American journalist John Howard Griffin decided to find out about racism first hand. He shaved his head, and through the use of ultraviolet sun lamps, skin dye and special drugs, Griffin turned himself into a black man. For six weeks he travelled as an itinerant through the southern states of Louisiana, Mississippi, Alabama and Georgia, and wrote about his experiences for *Sepia* magazine. These articles were then published as the groundbreaking book, *Black Like Me*.

Griffin has a keen ear for dialogue and sharp eye for detail, so the memoir reads like a gripping, well-written novel. He tells of the kindness and generosity he receives from other 'Negroes' (as African-Americans were known back then), and the humiliation, cruelty and prejudice inflicted by most of the white people he encounters. Because of segregation laws, Griffin learns what it is like to have to sit at the back of a bus or train, to be denied access to hotels, restaurants and toilets, and to be continually knocked back for jobs. He becomes disheartened at the picture of poverty and despair, and realizes that the only hope is for black people to take pride in themselves and to stand together.

Black Like Me caused such a furore when it came out that Griffin and his family had to leave their home in Texas and live in Mexico for a time. However, it soon became an extremely popular and influential book, and has since been translated into many languages.

This book is as relevant today as it was nearly 50 years ago, in a world still rife with bigotry and hatred.

84, Charing Cross Road

This little gem is a collection of letters between struggling New York writer Helene Hanff and Frank Doel of Marks & Co. booksellers at 84 Charing Cross Road, London.

Hanff first writes to Marks & Co. after she sees their ad in the *Saturday Review of Literature* in 1949, thus beginning a twenty-year 'pen friendship'. Their correspondence starts off in a businesslike manner, addressing each other as 'Gentlemen' and 'Dear Madam'. However, Hanff's brashness and informality soon has Doul writing to 'Dear Helene'.

As the book progresses, we learn about Hanff through her distinctive taste in English literature. At first her feistiness is somewhat intimidating, but she soon reveals a romantic, funny and very generous personality. When she discovers that the British are still on post-war rationing, Hanff sends gifts of food packages, not only to Doel but to his family and the rest of the staff. They in turn send her beautiful rare first editions.

Helene Hanff was immeasurably enriched by her friendship with Frank Doel. He became the personal link to the London of her beloved authors that she'd only ever dreamed about. And, in turn, her goodwill, humour and glimpses of New York life added sparkle to Frank's daily routine.

There is a bittersweet ending to this story. Frank dies and the shop is closed down by the time Hanff is finally able to visit England. Ironically, it is the publication of the letters (with his wife Sheila's approval) that enables Hanff to make the transatlantic trip, described in her next book, *The Duchess of Bloomsbury Street*.

84, Charing Cross Road is a tale of a very special relationship, and a must-read for anyone who cares about books. The 1987 film version, starring Anne Bancroft, Anthony Hopkins and Judi Dench, is a must-see.

HELENE HANFF
1916 – 1997
Nationality: American
First Published: André Deutsch Ltd., 1971
Other Selected Titles:
Underfoot in Showbusiness
Terrible Thomas
Movers and Shakers
Apple of My Eye
Q's Legacy
Letter from New York: BBC Woman's Hour Broadcasts

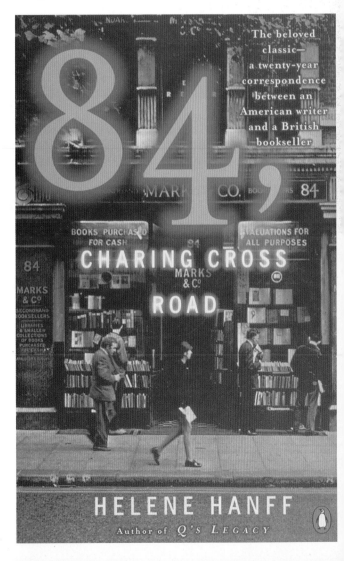

Pentimento

LILLIAN HELLMAN
1905 – 1984
Nationality: American
First Published: Little Brown & Co., 1974
Other Selected Titles:
The Children's Hour
Days to Come
The Little Foxes
Watch on the Rhine
The Searching Wind
Montserrat
Toys in the Attic

Lillian Hellman won the National Book Award in 1969 for her first volume of memoirs.

Pentimento is the second in a series of memoirs by American playwright and screenwriter, Lillian Hellman. The first volume, *An Unfinished Woman*, recounts her early life, as well as her relationship with crime writer Dashiell Hammett. It won the National Book Award in 1969. The third volume, *Scoundrel Time*, focuses on the Communist 'witch hunts' in the 1950s, during which many left-wing writers and artists, including Hellman and Hammett, were blacklisted.

Subtitled *A Book of Portraits*, *Pentimento* consists of seven self-contained chapters, each relating to an influential person or experience in her life. In her introduction she says, 'The paint has aged now and I wanted to see what was there for me once, and what is there for me now.'

In the first two chapters, 'Bethe' and 'Willy', Hellman returns to her New Orleans childhood. The dialogue is rich and the humour sometimes biting, and in these episodes, Hellman paddles in the sometimes murky waters of complex family relationships, as she does in some of her best plays. The chapter 'Julia' is based on her close, long-standing friendship with a woman who was a protégé of Sigmund Freud and was killed for her involvement in the anti-fascist resistance movement. Sometimes criticized for its fictitiousness, 'Julia' is nevertheless an excellent and moving story, which was adapted into an award-winning film starring Jane Fonda as Hellman, Vanessa Redgrave as Julia and Jason Robards as Hammett. 'Theatre' gives a rare insight into the life and work of a dramatist and screenwriter, and is full of interesting anecdotes about people such as Samuel Goldwyn, Tallulah Bankhead, Dorothy Parker and Edmund Wilson.

Pentimento is a highly readable and unconventional look at an extraordinary woman who is considered one of the leading lights of American theatre.

Childhood, Youth and Exile

Alexander Herzen holds an important place in Russian history as an influential philosopher and writer. Although born into privilege, he advocated the abolition of serfdom and is considered a pioneer of the socialist movement. He left Russia in 1847 and lived the remainder of his life in various European cities, dying in Paris at the age of 58.

Childhood, Youth and Exile comprises Volumes I and II of Herzen's six-volume memoir, *My Past and Thoughts*. Part I is entitled 'Nursery and University' and Part II 'Prison and Exile'.

When Herzen was an infant, Napoleon invaded Moscow. The book opens with young Alexander begging, 'Oh, please, Nurse, tell me again how the French came to Moscow!', showing how even as a small child he was concerned with wider historical issues. As a youth he was lonely but not unhappy. He loved reading and nature, and was strongly influenced by his tutor Ivan Protopopov. At the age of 15, Herzen formed a strong friendship with Nikolay Ogarev, a man who shared his political idealism and beliefs.

Herzen studied mathematics and science at Moscow University. His description of 'The Chemist' is just one example of his narrative skill: '...here The Chemist was always to be found, wearing a stained dressing gown trimmed with squirrel fur, sitting behind a rampart of books...' At age 22, Herzen and Ogarev were arrested for their socialist beliefs. His years of imprisonment and exile are illustrated in Part II.

In his introduction to the English translation of *Childhood, Youth and Exile*, Isaiah Berlin states, 'His autobiography is one of the great monuments to Russian literary and psychological genius, worthy to stand beside the great novels of Turgenev and Tolstoy.' It is recommended reading for anyone interested in learning more about nineteenth-century Russian history from a unique personal perspective.

ALEXANDER HERZEN
1812 – 1870
Nationality: Russian
First Published: 1855
Other Selected Titles:
Letters on the Study of Nature
Whose Fault?
From Another Shore

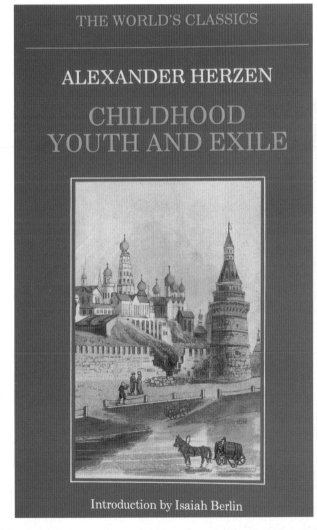

THE WORLD'S CLASSICS

ALEXANDER HERZEN

CHILDHOOD YOUTH AND EXILE

Introduction by Isaiah Berlin

The Diary of Alice James

ALICE JAMES
1848 – 1892
Nationality: American
First Published: Dodd, Mead & Co.,
1934

Alice James begins her diary on 31 May, 1889: 'I think that if I get into the habit of writing a bit about what happens, or rather doesn't happen, I may lose a little of the sense of loneliness and desolation which abides with me.' At that point in her life, James was 40 years old and had spent the best part of 20 years as an invalid, having been diagnosed with a wide variety of complaints ranging from 'hysteria' to 'neurasthenia' (an antiquated term for fatigue or lethargy).

The Penguin American Library

THE DIARY OF ALICE JAMES

EDITED WITH AN INTRODUCTION BY LEON EDEL

The journal starts off on a decidedly sombre note, but doesn't remain that way. James cultivated a rich inner life and her writing reflects her keen interest in current affairs. She was particularly sympathetic to Home Rule for Ireland and nationalist leader, Charles Stewart Parnell, finding in him a hero and kindred spirit. As would be expected of the sister of William and Henry James, Alice James was a bibliophile, and her diary is full of her opinions about various books. As well as reading, James drew great comfort from nature (although she rarely went out of doors) and her friendship with nurse-companion Katharine Peabody Loring.

When James was diagnosed with breast cancer, she rejoiced: 'Ever since I have been ill, I have longed and longed for some palpable disease…' She died ten months later. Feminist scholars have proposed that James's illnesses were symptomatic of Victorian patriarchy and sexual repression. If she had not lived under the shadow of illness and her two famous brothers, one wonders if she may have achieved the success of, say, Dickinson, Alcott, Eliot, Gaskell or the Brontës. Her diary nevertheless stands up in its own right as an intelligent chronicle of a privileged yet restricted life, and gives an interesting look at late-Victorian society.

Memories, Dreams, Reflections

Memories, Dreams, Reflections is an absorbing account of the life of eminent psychiatrist and one of the 20th century's most influential thinkers, Carl Gustav Jung. More accurately, it is an account of Jung's inner life, because 'In the end, the only events in my life worth telling are those when the imperishable world irrupted into this transitory one.'

In spite of many requests over many years, Jung did not begin to 'tell his personal myth' until he was 82. Most of it is original material, recorded and edited by his assistant Aniela Jaffé. A substantial part of the content is gleaned from his journals – the 'red book' and the 'black book' – that he kept during his tumultuous middle years.

Jung's memoirs proceed chronologically, from his early childhood in a Swiss parsonage, his school and university years in Basel, and his time as a fledgling psychiatrist. He devotes a whole chapter to his mentor, Sigmund Freud, and their parting of the ways, after which Jung went through a period of disorientation. This he describes most vividly in the chapter 'Confrontations with the Unconscious', the mid-point of the book and the mid-point of his life. It chronicles the emotional and spiritual transformations that took place during this period, in which dreams, myths, and visions played an increasingly important part.

In the second half of the book, Jung recounts his travels, describes his mystical experiences after a heart attack and muses on life after death. He concludes, 'The more uncertain I have felt about myself, the more there has grown up in me a feeling of kinship with all things' – a remarkable achievement for someone who had always felt like an outsider.

Memories, Dreams, Reflections is an accessible introduction to Jung's ideas and theories, as filtered through his own personal experiences.

Carl Jung was an eminent psychiatrist and influential thinker.

CARL GUSTAV JUNG
1875 – 1961
Nationality: Swiss
First Published: Collins & Routledge & Kegan Paul, 1961
Other Selected Titles:
Psychology of the Unconscious
Psychological Types (or *The Psychology of Individuation*)
Modern Man in Search for a Soul
Synchronicity: An Acausal Connecting Principle
Man and His Symbols

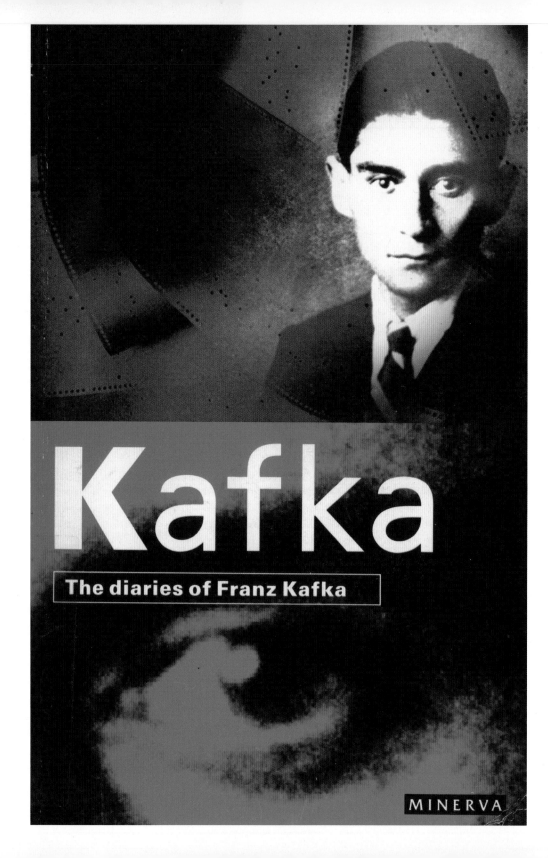

Kafka

The diaries of Franz Kafka

MINERVA

Diaries 1919–23

In the postscript to Kafka's diaries, Max Brod, Kafka's closest friend and literary executor explains, 'When you keep a diary, you usually put down only what is oppressive or irritating. By being put down on paper, painful impressions are got rid of.' Brod goes on to say, '…diaries resemble a kind of defective barometric curve that registers only the "lows", the hours of greatest depression, but not the "highs".'

Indeed, Franz Kafka's journal often reads like an endless litany of woes: writer's block, insomnia, headaches, lethargy, melancholy, loneliness and anxiety. But it is much more than that. It is also rich in the minutiae of daily life, occasionally peppered with joy and wry humour. He discusses the authors he is reading at the time (Goethe, Dostoyevsky and Dickens, to name but a few), and his attendance at the theatre and lectures. One of the most interesting passages is entitled 'My Visit to Dr. (Rudolf) Steiner'.

Kafka's diaries lack the flow and cohesiveness of those of, say, Anne Frank or Samuel Pepys. His entries are often disjointed, and at times it is impossible to discern whether he is describing a dream or an incident from real life, or a work in progress. This is not surprising, because as Kafka writes, 'My talent for portraying my dreamlike inner life has thrust all other matters into the background…' But it is worth persevering for his sharp observations of people and places, and the frequent flashes of wisdom.

Read in conjunction with the moving and powerful *Letter to his Father*, Kafka's diaries give us an intriguing look into the soul of one of the most innovative modern European novelists.

FRANZ KAFKA
1883 – 1924
Nationality: Czech
First Published: Schoken Books Inc.,
1948 (first English translation)
Other Selected Titles:
The Metamorphosis
The Trial
The Castle
Amerika

The Story of My Life

HELEN KELLER
1880 – 1968
Nationality: American
First Published: Doubleday, Page & Co., 1902
Other Selected Titles:
Optimism
The World I Live In
The Song of the Stone Wall
Out of the Dark
My Religion
Peace at Eventide
Teacher: Anne Sullivan Macy
The Open Door

Helen Keller (left) reads with her teacher, Anne Sullivan.

Helen Keller wrote this, her first autobiography, when she was a student at Radcliffe College. An illness at the age of 19 months had left her permanently deaf, dumb and blind. A bright child trapped in darkness and silence, Helen would become angry and frustrated in her unsuccessful attempts to communicate with the world.

She marks the third of March, 1887 as 'The most important day in all my life is the one on which my teacher, Anne Mansfield Sullivan, came to me.' In teaching Helen the manual alphabet, Anne connected the missing link of memory for Helen, opening the door to a world of words.

Helen continued her education at the Perkins School for the Blind in Boston and the Wright-Humason School for the Deaf in New York, learning Braille and the Tadoma method, and even how to speak. She enjoyed school and was a voracious reader: 'No barrier of the senses shuts me out from the sweet, gracious discourse of my book-friends'. Helen also loved her 'dog friends' (who understood her limitations) and her 'tree friends'. Indeed, the most enjoyable passages in the book are the ones in which Helen describes her connectedness with the natural world, especially her first encounter with the ocean and her visit to Niagara Falls.

The second part of the book contains Helen's letters from 1887 to 1901. Not only do they chart her linguistic development, they show her altruistic nature which she later channelled into social activism.

The Story of My Life is an inspirational narrative written by an exceptionally intelligent and perceptive young woman who has since become an American legend. Patty Duke and Anne Bancroft deservedly won Academy Awards for their portrayals of Helen Keller and Anne Sullivan in the film *The Miracle Worker*.

The Book of Margery Kempe

Margery Kempe's memoir is a most unusual one. Extracts of the work first appeared in 1501 as a seven-page devotional pamphlet. The manuscript then languished in obscurity until 1934, when it was discovered in a home in Lancashire. Many believe it to be the first autobiography written in English, and the first by a woman. Because she was illiterate (unusual for a girl of her class), her narrative was transcribed by monks.

MARGERY KEMPE
circa 1373 – 1438
Nationality: British
First Published: Jonathan Cape, 1936

Kempe was the daughter of John Brunham, a prominent merchant in Norfolk. At the age of 20 she married John Kempe. Her story begins as she is giving birth to her first child. After the birth she suffered horrendous physical and spiritual torments, including visions of demons. She was cured by an apparition of Christ, who said, 'Daughter, why have you forsaken me, and I never forsook you?' This would be the first of many 'confabulations' she would have with the Lord.

After 20 years of marriage and 14 children, Kempe made a bargain with her husband. She would pay his debts (she had recently inherited a sum of money from her father) if he would move out of the marriage bed and allow her to travel. He agreed. A substantial part of the book is taken up with her pilgrimages to the Holy Land, Rome, and Santiago de Compostela in Spain, and visits to notable pious people such as Dame Julian of Norwich.

In her lifetime, Margery Kempe was branded as a heretic and madwoman. She was especially prone to crying fits, which often accompanied ecstatic visions. It doesn't matter if we believe that she was a fanatical madwoman, a mystic or both, or something between the two extremes. Her book is a unique account of medieval life as told by a unique and spirited woman.

I Will Bear Witness

VICTOR KLEMPERER
1881 – 1960
Nationality: German
First Published: Aufbau-Verlag
GmbH, 1995
Other Selected Titles:
To the Bitter End: Diaries Volume II
(1942–45)
The Lesser Evil: Diaries Volume III
(1945–59)
Language of the Third Reich

I Will Bear Witness: The Diaries of Victor Klemperer 1933–41 is an immediate, intimate and subjective account of one Jewish man's experience in Germany during Nazi rule. This, the first volume of diaries, starts when Hitler first comes to power, and ends just as the Holocaust begins.

Although Klemperer was a rabbi's son, he had converted to Christianity, was married to an 'Aryan', fought for Germany during World War I, and identified culturally as German rather than Jewish. Nevertheless, the Third Reich recognized him as a Jew, and over the next eight years Klemperer was forced to endure a slow and steady process of dehumanization.

When the book opens, he is employed as a Professor of Romance Languages and Literature at Dresden Technical University. In 1935 he lost his job, in 1940 he lost his home and was exiled to a 'Jew's House', and in 1941 he was made to wear the 'yellow star', and was imprisoned for disobeying blackout regulations. In between these 'turning points', Klemperer chronicles the difficulties of living day to day, recording the gradual losses of life's simple pleasures and privileges such as coffee, cigarettes, pets, flowers, telephones and typewriters, and visiting the library and cinema. Even worse is the gradual loss of friends – many of his non-Jewish friends disowned him, and the Jewish ones either escaped or disappeared.

Writing a diary – an act of risk and defiance – somehow gave order and meaning to his life and saved his sanity. It is not pleasant reading. The second volume (*To the Bitter End*), in which Klemperer and others like him struggle to just stay alive, is even more difficult. But as a historical record and a testament to human endurance, *I Will Bear Witness* is a significant and edifying work.

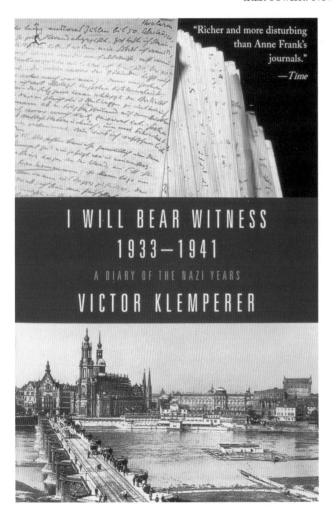

"Richer and more disturbing than Anne Frank's journals."
—*Time*

I WILL BEAR WITNESS
1933–1941
A DIARY OF THE NAZI YEARS
VICTOR KLEMPERER

In the Castle of My Skin

George Lamming is a highly respected West Indian novelist, recipient of the Somerset Maugham Award for Literature, and a Fellow of the Institute of Jamaica. He was born and raised in Carrington Village, Barbados, the setting of his first and best-known book, *In the Castle of My Skin*. This autobiographical novel is considered a seminal work in post-colonial fiction – the title is taken from a poem by Derek Walcott: 'You in the castle of your skin, I among the swineherd.'

In the Castle of My Skin is a personal story that 'came out of the gut'. It also deals with the broader issues of imperialism, class, racism, economics and education. The novel is set during the riots of the 1930s, and is cleverly told from three perspectives: the young first-person narrator known only as G. (the mouthpiece for Lamming himself); the third-person voices of Ma and Pa, and an omniscient third-person narrator.

Lamming has a rhythmic, musical style, and a firm grasp of the local dialect. His writing was influenced by Thomas Hardy, Joseph Conrad, Jane Austen and the King James Bible.

Just as Lamming himself had to travel to England for educational and employment prospects, so G. also had to separate from his family and peer group and try for a better life in the 'mother country'. The book ends on a sad note, as G. is bidding farewell to Pa.

In the Castle of My Skin gives a powerful, clear and sometimes disturbing picture of Barbadian life in the 1930s, a must-read for anyone interested in the history of this fascinating part of the world.

George Lamming at home in Barbados, 1986.

GEORGE LAMMING
1927 –
Nationality: West Indian
First Published: Michael Joseph, 1953
Other Selected Titles:
The Emigrants
Of Age and Innocence
Season of Adventure
Water with Berries
Natives of My Person

C.S. Lewis died just a few years after his beloved wife Joy.

C.S. LEWIS
1898 – 1963
Nationality: British
First Published: Faber and Faber Ltd, 1961
Other Selected Titles:
Beyond Personality
Miracles: A Preliminary Study
Surprised by Joy: The Shape of My Early Life
The Pilgrim's Regress
Space Trilogy
The Screwtape Letters
The Chronicles of Narnia

A Grief Observed

C.S. Lewis began writing *A Grief Observed* a month after his wife died of bone cancer. It is a poignant, angry journal in which he attempts to come to terms, not only with the loss of his wife, but also with the temporary loss of his conscious contact with God.

An Oxford Don and confirmed bachelor, Lewis found love in late middle-age when he met American writer and single mother, Joy Davidman Gresham. A fascinating account of their romance is told in the book *Joy and C.S. Lewis: The Story of an Extraordinary Marriage* by Lyle W. Dorset (1988), and fictionally in the touching 1993 film *Shadowlands* starring Anthony Hopkins and Debra Winger.

Anyone who has suffered the death of a loved one will identify with the emotions that Lewis so viscerally describes: the 'fluttering in the stomach', the feeling of 'being mildly drunk or concussed', the lethargy and the fury. One of the most heart-wrenching passages in the book is when he rails, 'Oh God, God, why did you take such trouble to force this creature out of its shell if it is now doomed to crawl back – to be sucked back – into it?' But somehow, he comes out the other side of his dark night, and reaches a state of acceptance and peace. C.S. Lewis died just a few years after this book was published.

A Grief Observed is arguably one of the finest meditations on death and mourning written in modern English literature. Written in the elegant, balanced prose style of a master, it supports the sentiment expressed in *Shadowlands*: 'We read to know we're not alone.'

The Towers of Trebizond

In a career that spanned nearly half a century, Rose Macaulay wrote a total of 35 books, including novels, poetry, travel stories, essays and journalism. Being an intensely private person, she never wrote her memoirs, although her life had its share of drama and excitement. Her last novel (and widely said to be her best), *The Towers of Trebizond* is the most autobiographical of all her works and has therefore been included in this chapter. It was awarded the James Tait Black Memorial Prize, and Anthony Burgess pronounced it 'among the 20 best novels of the century.'

The Towers of Trebizond begins on a light, whimsical note and ends in melancholy and grief. The opening passage is often quoted: '"Take my camel, dear," said my aunt Dot, as she climbed down from this animal on her return from High Mass.' In between the happy beginning and the sorrowful ending, the book tells the story of four characters as they travel through Turkey: the aforementioned slightly dotty Aunt Dot; Laurie, the narrator and Macaulay's emotional twin; the priggish Anglo-Catholic priest Rev. the Hon. Father Hugh Chantry-Prigg; and their guide, Dr. Halide, a feminist Anglican Turkish doctor. As in most 'picaresque' novels, the group meets with a variety of zany characters and situations along the way. The book is also a vehicle for Macaulay to explore her ambivalent feelings about the Anglican Church and her long-term relationship with a married man. (In real life, Macaulay was involved for many years with writer and former Catholic priest, Gerald O'Donovan, who was married with three children.)

After a long period of obscurity, *The Towers of Trebizond* has recently experienced a revival of sorts. It is an amusing travel story, but also a profound exploration of faith and doubt, love and loss.

ROSE MACAULAY
1881 – 1958
Nationality: British
First Published: William Collins Sons & Co. Ltd, 1956
Other Selected Titles:
About Verney
Views and Vagabonds
The Lee Shore
Orphan Island
They Were Defeated
I Would Be Private
No Man's Wit
The World My Wildnerness

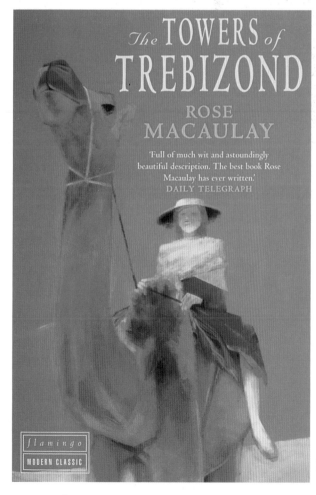

The TOWERS of TREBIZOND

ROSE MACAULAY

'Full of much wit and astoundingly beautiful description. The best book Rose Macaulay has ever written.'
DAILY TELEGRAPH

flamingo
MODERN CLASSIC

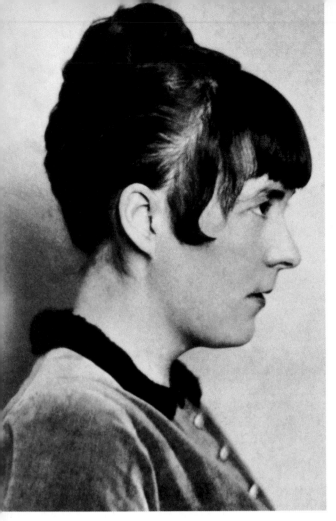

*Katherine Mansfield suffered
from tuberculosis for some time
before her death in 1923.*

KATHERINE MANSFIELD
1888 – 1923
Nationality: New Zealand
First Published: Constable & Co.,
1927
Other Selected Titles:
*In a German Pension
Prelude
Bliss and Other Stories
Garden Party and Other Stories
Poems
The Dove's Nest and Other Stories
The Aloe
Novels and Novelists*

Journal of Katherine Mansfield

Just months before Katherine Mansfield died at the age of 34, she bequeathed 'all manuscripts, notebooks, papers and letters' to her husband, John Middleton Murry. The will also stipulated, 'I should like him to publish as little as possible and tear up and burn as much as possible…'

Murry did not heed his wife's instructions. Although many people have accused him of profiting from poor Katherine's early demise, our literature is all the richer because he has published her journals. The journals are – at times – as poetic as her poems, as engaging as her short stories, and as sharp as her criticism. They were first published in 1927, the 'Definitive Edition' in 1954.

Born in New Zealand, Katherine Mansfield was educated in England, and after a brief sojourn in New Zealand during her young adulthood, she returned to Europe, never to see her homeland again. She had dramatic love affairs (before and during her marriage to Murry), and spent the rest of her life travelling between England and the Continent in search of health.

No matter whether she is describing Maori fishermen, her longing for a baby (which remained unfulfilled), D.H. and Frieda Lawrence, the 'full, transparent, glittering' moon, coughing up blood, or her imminent death from tuberculosis, Mansfield's journals exude a passion and intensity that are unparalleled, as well as a strong visual sense and joy in the commonplace.

Katherine Mansfield was also a prolific correspondent, to people such as Virginia Woolf, Lady Ottoline Morrell, Dorothy Brett, and especially J.M. Murry. These letters are also worth reading to see another side – or sides – of this fascinating writer. The Penguin Modern Classics edition of *The Letters and Journals of Katherine Mansfield (A Selection)* edited by C.K. Stead is highly recommended.

The Seven Storey Mountain

When *The Seven Storey Mountain* was first published in 1948, it was highly praised by notable Catholics Graham Greene, Evelyn Waugh, Clare Boothe Luce and Bishop Fulton J. Sheen (who compared it to St. Augustine's *Confessions*). Like *Confessions*, it has become one of the most widely read spiritual classics of all time.

In this beautifully written book, Merton chronicles the first half of his most remarkable life. His parents were artists, and as children, he and his brother led a rather nomadic existence, living in France, England, Bermuda and the United States. By the age of 16, Merton had lost both his parents – he describes their deaths with eloquence and pathos.

Educated at both Cambridge and Columbia University in New York, Merton set his sights on a literary career. But his restless, questing nature, combined with the death of his grandparents, eventually led him to the Catholic Church. He not only became a Catholic, but was called to a religious life in a strict contemplative order. The final chapters of the book tell of his early days as a monk in the Trappist Abbey of Gethsemani in Kentucky when he was 26 years old.

As it turned out, God also wanted Merton to become a writer. Not long after Merton's arrival at Gethsemani, his abbot encouraged him to compose his life story. *The Seven Storey Mountain* became the first of his many books which have inspired many people, Christian and non-Christian alike.

The Seven Storey Mountain is a must-read, but it would be a pity to stop there. Thomas Merton's spirituality grew and evolved over the next 20 years, and his later works show a greater depth of knowledge and understanding. The personal journals, released many years after his death, reveal a more human, vulnerable side to this devoted man of God.

THOMAS MERTON
1915 – 1968
Nationality: American
First Published: Harcourt, Brace & Co., 1948
Other Selected Titles:
Seeds of Contemplation
Bread in the Wilderness
No Man is an Island
Thoughts in Solitude
Mystics and Zen Masters
Entering the Silence
Dancing in the Water of Life
The Other Side of the Mountain

The Pursuit of Love

NANCY MITFORD
1904 – 1973
Nationality: British
First Published: Hamish Hamilton, 1945
Other Selected Titles:
Highland Fling
Christmas Pudding
Love in a Cold Climate
The Blessing
Madame de Pompadour
Voltaire in Love
Don't Tell Alfred
The Sun King

The Pursuit of Love and its sequel, *Love in a Cold Climate*, are thinly disguised autobiographical novels based on the life of Nancy Mitford and her outlandish upper-class family. The narrator is sensible, realistic Fanny – who watches with bemused detachment at the antics of her seven Radlett cousins, dominated by the horrifying and often hilarious Uncle Matthew (modelled on Mitford's father, Lord Redesdale).

Mitford used actual people and events as fodder for her books. Like the Radletts, the real-life Redesdale children had their own secret language and wacky sense of humour. They called themselves 'Hons', and held meetings in the 'Hons Cupboard'. Jessica (fictionalized as Jassy) saved money to run away, Lord Redesdale had an 'entrenching tool' that he'd used in World War I to kill the Hun, and like Lady Redesdale, Aunt Sadie held eccentric beliefs about diet and health. Mitford's alter-ego is the lovely Linda, whose tragic affair with Fabrice parallels her own ill-fated romance with French colonel Gaston Palewski (to whom the book is dedicated).

Nancy Mitford's autobiographical novels have stood the test of time, entertaining several generations of readers. Their continued popularity is due, in part, to two excellent television adaptations. The first, in 1980, starred Judi Dench as Aunt Sadie; it was revived twenty years later with Alan Bates in the role of Uncle Matthew.

The Pursuit of Love is a gently satirical look at a most unusual set of people, and at the lifestyle of the privileged classes between the two world wars. If it leaves you wanting to experience more of the Mitford family, the sequel *Love in a Cold Climate* is equally enjoyable, as is the memoir of younger sister Jessica Mitford entitled *Hons and Rebels*.

Unity, Diana and Nancy Mitford in 1932.

Borrowed Time

In 1985, Paul Monette had it all: intelligence, good looks, an Ivy League education, a successful writing career, frequent holidays abroad, and a smart house in West Hollywood, which he shared with his partner, Roger Horwitz.

But their perfect world fell apart when Roger discovered that he had AIDS. Paul Monette sites March 12, 1985 – the day of Roger's diagnosis – as 'the day we began to live on the moon'. By the time Paul began to write *Borrowed Time* – the story of his final years with Roger, he, too, had contracted the wretched disease. He begins the book with the simple sentence: 'I don't know if I will live to finish this.' Fortunately for us, he did live to finish it, as well as several more excellent books, before his death in 1995.

Borrowed Time is important because it is the first memoir of its kind to be written about the AIDS virus. It perfectly captures the mood of the early-to-mid-eighties when members of the gay community began falling prey to this strange illness. Monette doesn't skirt around the painful issues and emotions associated with AIDS – the denial, ignorance, fear, guilt and shame. Not to mention the physical horrors. But in telling his story, he also shows how much courage, tenacity, and optimism he and Roger somehow summoned to battle the medical system, battle the symptoms and battle the prejudice. Paul tenderly cared for Roger as his condition gradually descended into blindness, and finally death, on October 22, 1986.

More than anything, *Borrowed Time* is a story about love: sexual love, familial love, and friendship. It highlights the importance of enjoying life's simple pleasures when one can, and making the most of every day.

PAUL MONETTE
1945 – 1995
Nationality: American
First Published: Harcourt Brace
Jovanovich, 1988
Other Selected Titles:
Taking Care of Mrs.Carroll
The Long Shot
Love Alone: Eighteen Elegies for Rog
Afterlife
Halfway Home
Becoming a Man: Half a Life Story
Last Watch of the Night
West of Yesterday

BORROWED TIME

PAUL MONETTE

'To create a book as beautiful and honest as *Borrowed Time* requires literary and moral faculties almost beyond our imagination'
Mail on Sunday

My Place

SALLY MORGAN
1951 –
Nationality: Australian
First Published: Fremantle Arts Centre Press, 1987
Other Selected Titles:
Dan's Grandpa
In Your Dreams
Wanamurraganya
The Art of Sally Morgan
The Flying Emu and Other Australian Stories

Sally Morgan is a much respected artist, writer, and Professor at the Centre for Indigenous History and the Arts at the University of Western Australia.

When she was nine years old her father committed suicide as a result of alcoholism and post-war trauma. When Sally's schoolmates remarked that she and her siblings looked 'different', her mother Gladys explained that they had an Indian background. It wasn't until Sally was in her teens that her grandmother Daisy confessed that she was Aboriginal. Daisy and Gladys withheld the truth for so many years because they were terrified that as the children of an Aboriginal mother and European father, Sally and her brothers and sisters would be sent away to an institution, just as they themselves had been.

My Place is the result of Morgan's quest to unravel her true heritage. The first part of the book is about Sally's own life, and the remainder is devoted to the fascinating stories of her mother, grandmother, and great-uncle, Arthur Corunna. The high point of her memoir is when she and her family travelled to her grandmother's country and connected with the Palku people of the Pilbara region. Morgan explains, '...all of a sudden we had a context ... we weren't just this small isolated family in the non-Aboriginal community, we were part of this huge family and that really gave us a sense of belonging, that was very important.'

Sally Morgan was one of the first people to give a voice to the Stolen Generations, the 35,000 Aboriginal children who between approximately 1900 and 1970 were taken from their parents and placed in government or religious facilities. Her story is simple, honest and moving, enjoyable for everyone, especially those who have longed to find their place in the world.

An Australian Classic

My Place

SALLY MORGAN

Speak, Memory: An Autobiography Revisited

Speak, Memory is the 1966 revision of Nabokov's 1951 memoir entitled *Conclusive Evidence*, and has been hailed as 'the finest autobiography written in our time'. The book covers the author's life between 1903 and 1940, but in the main it is comprised of childhood impressions. Nabokov was the eldest of five children. He led a privileged life – his father was a politician – and the family lived in a grand home in St. Petersburg, enjoying holidays in France and on their Russian country estates. The last quarter of the book includes recollections of his years in Cambridge, Berlin and Paris before leaving for America, where he would find success and notoriety.

However, *Speak, Memory* is not totally linear, which isn't surprising because Nabokov continually plays with the notion of time and memory. His biography of his father is completely out of sequence and throws the reader right off balance: 'Vladimir Dmitrievich Nabokov, jurist, publicist and statesman, was born on July 20, 1870 at Tsarskoe Selo near St. Petersburg, and was killed by an assassin's bullet on March 28, 1922 in Berlin.' In another evocative and almost mystical passage, Nabokov describes the joys of butterfly hunting: 'And the highest enjoyment of timelessness – in a landscape selected at random – is when I stand among rare butterflies and their food plants. This is ecstasy, and behind the ecstasy is something else, which is hard to explain. It is like a momentary vacuum into which rushes all that I love.'

Speak, Memory is a sophisticated, adroit and highly entertaining read, employing the well-recognized stylistic skills that have earned Nabokov a prominent place in both European and American literature.

Vladimir Nabokov led a privileged life in Russia.

VLADIMIR NABOKOV
1899 – 1977
Nationality: Russian
First Published: Harper & Bros., 1951
Other Selected Titles:
The Defense
Laughter in the Dark
Invitation to a Beheading
Bend Sinister
Lolita
Pale Fire
Strong Opinions

Reading Lolita in Tehran: A Memoir in Books

AZAR NAFISI
1955 –
Nationality: Iranian
First Published: Random House, 2004
Other Selected Titles:
Eye of the Storm: Women in Post-Revolutionary Iran
Anti-Terra: A Critical Study of Vladimir Nabokov's Novels
Muslim Women and Politics of Participation
Religious Fundamentalism and the Human Rights of Women

Reading Lolita in Tehran is a multi-layered memoir written by an Iranian professor of English and American Literature. The author, Azar Nafisi, was educated in the United States, and taught in Iran from 1979 until 1995.

The first strand of the narrative tells of how, after resigning from her teaching position due to its many restrictions, Nafisi conducted a clandestine literature seminar in her home each week, attended by seven of her best and brightest female students. Through their discussions of such classic Western novels as *Lolita, The Great Gatsby, Daisy Miller* and *Pride and Prejudice* (all of which had to be photocopied because the books were outlawed), the young women learn about each other and themselves, and most importantly, how to exercise some degree of freedom in a totalitarian state.

In addition, Nafisi weaves her own life story around the history of Iran during the tumultuous period of the revolution, the rise of the Ayatollah Khomeini and the war with Iraq. Nafisi also reveals how her life could be inextricably linked with the books she is reading. For example, she wonders if the nineteenth-century novels she read during her pregnancy could have affected her daughter's personality.

Nafisi left Iran in 1997 to pursue an academic and literary career in America. In her Epilogue, she lets the reader know what had transpired in the lives of her students between 1997 and the time of publication.

Reading Lolita in Tehran is an original, intelligent and eye-opening book. Not only does it show how 'a great novel heightens your senses and sensitivity to the complexities of life and of individuals', it paints a vivid and often disturbing portrait of the repressive regime that is the Islamic Republic of Iran.

Memoirs

The full title of Pablo Neruda's Memoirs is *Confieso Que He Vivido: Memorias* (*I Confess That I Have Lived*), appropriate for a man who led such a rich and varied life as a poet, diplomat, adventurer and senator. Through his poetry and politics, Neruda was a catalyst for great change in Chile and beyond but for all that, he comes across as a modest and humble human being.

Neruda's memoirs progress in a fairly linear fashion, but he sometimes inserts anecdotes or episodes as memory dictates. In his gentle, melodic style, Neruda tells of his childhood in rural Chile, his university years in Santiago, his diplomatic postings in Asia, his involvement in the Spanish Civil War, and his Communist activities, which temporarily halted his political career and forced him from his native Chile.

Pablo Neruda reads from his poetry during a radio interview.

The book is an absolute delight to read. Neruda the poet is evident throughout, but especially in his depictions of nature. The first time he saw the ocean, he says, 'It wasn't just the immense snow-crested swells, rising many metres above our heads, but the loud pounding of a gigantic heart, the heartbeat of the universe.' When he tells about his sexual encounters he uses the type of luscious language that has made his love poems so popular: 'I was able to fondle and explore all that fruit of fiery snow.' Neruda can also be quite funny – for example, when he received the Nobel Prize, he compared the ceremony to the 'handing out of school prizes in any small country town'.

Pablo Neruda's *Memoirs* allow a close encounter with one of South America's leading literary and political figures.

PABLO NERUDA
1904 – 1973
Nationality: Chilean
First Published: Debolsillo, 1974
Other Selected Titles:
Twenty Love Poems and a Desperate Song
Residence on the Earth
Third Residence
General Song
Elemental Odes
Plenary Powers
The Book of Vagaries
One Hundred Love Sonnets

Portrait of a Marriage

Vita Sackville-West and Harold Nicolson at Sissinghurst.

Portrait of a Marriage is a unique sort of memoir. Although the credited author is Nigel Nicolson, nearly half of it is actually written by his mother, author Vita Sackville-West. Not long after Vita's death in 1962, Nicolson found a journal inside a Gladstone bag. 'It was,' he explains, 'an autobiography written when she was aged 28, a confession, an attempt to purge her mind and heart of a love which had possessed her, a love for another woman, Violet Trefusis.'

Nicolson has done a superb job in juxtaposing Vita's story with his own detached yet sympathetic commentary. The dramatic centre of the book is the passionate affair between Vita Sackville-West and Violet Trefusis, both married women, which took place when Nicolson was himself only three years old. However, much is also written (both by Nicolson and Vita) about Vita's aristocratic childhood, her travels, and her other friends and lovers including Virginia Woolf (whose novel *Orlando* is a tribute to their lesbian friendship).

But as the title indicates, *Portrait of a Marriage* is just that – a portrait of the unconventional yet enduring marriage between Vita Sackville-West and Harold Nicolson. Despite their mutual infidelities – both hetero- and homosexual – somehow their relationship grew and deepened as time passed. Nigel Nicolson tells us at the end of the book that his father never recovered from Vita's death.

Portrait of a Marriage is a fascinating read for many reasons: its romantic and exotic locations, its descriptions of 'Bloomsbury' life, but most importantly for its sensitive exploration of the human heart. In 1990, the BBC produced a television series based on the book, co-written by Nigel Nicolson and Penelope Mortimer.

NIGEL NICOLSON
1917 – 2004
Nationality: British
First Published: Weidenfeld & Nicolson, 1973
Other Selected Titles:
Sissinghurst Castle, Great House of Britain
The Himalayas
Mary Curzon
The World of Jane Austen
Virginia Woolf
Fanny Burney: The Mother of English Fiction

Running in the Family

'Exotic', 'otherworldly', 'shimmering', 'luscious', 'voluptuous', 'dreamlike': these are just a few of the praises that reviewers have bestowed upon Michael Ondaatje's eccentric memoir about his eccentric Ceylonese (Sri Lankan) family.

Ondaatje is of Ceylonese and Dutch extraction, and grew up in Ceylon and England. For many years he has been a resident of Canada. *Running in the Family* is the product of two visits Ondaatje made to Sri Lanka in 1978 and 1980 to learn more about his family of origin. He was particularly interested in exploring the life of his deceased father, Mervyn Ondaatje. Mervyn was a profligate youth; he took the money his parents gave him for Cambridge and led a dissolute life there for over two years without ever setting foot in a lecture. He ended up a melancholy alcoholic.

Ondaatje's anecdotes about his maternal grandmother Lalla are often hilarious. Lalla held the distinction of being the first woman in Ceylon to have a mastectomy. There is a very funny scene on a bus when a man puts his arm around her and gropes her breast. The onlookers are horrified, but Lalla can't feel a thing because the man is fondling her prosthesis. Eventually, Ondaatje tells us, 'My Grandmother died in the blue arms of a jacaranda tree. She could read thunder'. The book overflows with such poetic turns of phrase.

Running in the Family is non-linear and impressionistic, jumping from dream, to poem, to episode, and set against the backdrop of the colourful Sri Lankan landscape. The best way to approach this book is to just let it wash over you like a tropical shower. It provides an insight into the background of this award-winning poet and novelist.

MICHAEL ONDAATJE
1943 –
Nationality: Sri Lankan
First Published: W.W. Norton, 1982
Other Selected Titles:
The Dainty Monsters
Leonard Cohen
The Broken Ark: A Book of Beasts
The Cinnamon Peeler: Selected Poems
Coming through Slaughter
In the Skin of a Lion
The English Patient

By the author of *ANIL'S GHOST*

MICHAEL ONDAATJE

RUNNING IN THE FAMILY

Down and Out in Paris and London

GEORGE ORWELL
1903 – 1950
Nationality: British
First Published: Victor Gollancz
Limited, 1933
Other Selected Titles:
Burmese Days
A Clergyman's Daughter
Keep the Aspidistra Flying
The Road to Wigan Pier
Homage to Catalonia
Coming Up for Air
Animal Farm
Nineteen Eighty-four

George Orwell lived on the streets in Paris and London in his youth.

Down and Out in Paris and London straddles the genres of memoir, fiction and essay. It is Orwell's first book, and draws on his period of poverty and vagrancy in Paris, then London, while in his late twenties. The story is told by a nameless, first-person narrator (ostensibly Orwell). When it begins, he is unemployed and living in a bug-infested hotel in a Paris slum. He experiences days of hunger, often reduced to pawning his clothes to pay the rent and buy a crust of bread. His insights into the impoverished state are interesting. For example, 'the less money you have, the less you worry'.

Through his friend Boris, a Russian refugee, 'Orwell' finds work as a *plongeur* (dishwasher) in the restaurant of Hotel X. Here he has a roof over his head and enough to eat, but is forced to work exhausting 70-hour weeks in a stifling, putrid kitchen. He moves to another restaurant where the work is even harder, and concludes that the *plongeur* is the slave of the modern world.

The narrator returns to England where he lives as a vagrant in and around London. After Paris, London is 'cleaner, quieter, drearier', yet no less difficult. He meets various characters along the way: Paddy the Irishman, and Bozo, the lame 'screever' (pavement artist), who is a mouthpiece for Orwell's socialist philosophies. They move from one miserable place to another: dank, stuffy tramp shelters known as 'spikes', and Salvation Army hostels.

Down and Out in Paris and London is important as the debut work of one of the leading twentieth-century British writers, and a precursor to his later political novels. Using sharp imagery and colourful dialogue, Orwell cleverly paints an unforgettable picture of a side of life that most people, then and now, have chosen to ignore.

Autobiography of a Yogi

PARAMAHANSA YOGANANDA
1893 – 1952
Nationality: Indian
First Published: Self-Realization
Fellowship, 1946
Other Selected Titles:
The Divine Romance
Where There is Light
Man's Eternal Quest
The Science of Religion
Whispers from Eternity
Songs of the Soul
Scientific Healing Affirmations

Autobiography of a Yogi is a spiritual classic written by one of the first teachers to bring yoga and meditation to the West, a man who many regard as a saint. Since the book was first published in 1946, it has never been out of print.

Yogananda tells his story with fluency, liveliness and humility. Born Mukunda Lal Ghosh in Gorakhpur, India, he was a spiritually precocious child. At the age of 17 he met his guru, Swami Sri Yukteswar. As well as attending Calcutta University, Mukunda spent many years under the tutelage of Yukteswar. He was initiated as a swami and given the name 'Yogananda', meaning 'divine union through yoga'.

After establishing a school for boys, in 1920 Yogananda travelled to Boston, where he lectured on The Science of Religion at the International Congress of Religious Liberals. He was well received in the United States, and later founded the Self-Realization Fellowship in Los Angeles. Yogananda met many people throughout the course of his travels and teachings, including U.S. President Calvin Coolidge, Indian poet Rabindranath Tagore, American botanist Luther Burbank, and Mahatma Gandhi.

Three-quarters of the book is set in India, a land 'steeped in the centuried aura of saints'. In reading the yogi's autobiography, we learn much about his country's religious traditions: the deities, the sacred texts, the rituals and ceremonies and the guru-disciple relationship. Yogananda's descriptions of his mystical experiences – for example, his visions of the Divine Mother, Jesus Christ and Krishna – are truly awe-inspiring.

Autobiography of a Yogi gives us a rare insight into the life of a man who, probably more than anyone else, has bridged the spiritual gap between East and West. It is interesting both for those seeking truth and knowledge, or for anyone who wants to broaden their cultural horizons.

Diary

Pepys' *Diary* is probably the most famous and comprehensive memoir ever written in English. In the nine years that Pepys kept his diary, 1660–1669, he chronicled his life and times in extraordinary, vibrant detail.

Samuel Pepys lived through a fascinating period in European history. At the age of 16 he watched the execution of Charles I, and in the second year of his diary – 1661 – he records his impressions of the coronation of Charles II. The 'Restoration' meant a relaxation of Oliver Cromwell's puritan rigidity. Organs could now be played in churches, and not only were the theatres opened again after prohibition, but as Pepys notes on January 3, 1661, 'and here the first time that ever I saw Women come upon the stage'. Pepys as historian also writes at length about many other important events, including the Great Plague of 1665 and the Fire of London in September, 1666.

No less engaging are Pepys' descriptions of his personal life. He enjoyed meeting friends in coffee houses and taverns, going to the theatre, and especially playing and listening to music. He also had a weakness for women: 'Music and women I cannot but give way to, whatever my business is.' But Pepys was not a hedonist. He was meticulous and thorough in everything he did – from his work as a naval administrator to his pursuit of scientific knowledge and book collecting.

Pepys' journal entries end in 1669 when he begins to suffer with eye trouble, just before the death of his wife. The diaries were first published in 1825. For those who would find the full 11 volumes a somewhat daunting prospect, *The Shorter Pepys*, selected and edited by Robert Latham (1985), is a perfect introduction to this wonderful classic memoir.

SAMUEL PEPYS
1633 – 1703
Nationality: British
First Published: 1825
Other Selected Titles:
Memories Relating to the State of the Royal Navy 1679–1688

Samuel Pepys worked as a naval administrator.

Letters

PLINY THE YOUNGER
circa 63 – 113
Nationality: Roman
First Published: William Heinemann,
1746
Other Selected Titles:
Panegyricus Trajani

Pliny the Younger (Gaius Plinius Caecilius Secundus) was a poet, orator, lawyer, public servant and statesman. He was born at Novum Comum (Como, Italy) into the provincial nobility. When his father died, his appointed guardians were Verginius Rufus and his uncle Pliny the Elder, a naturalist.

Pliny studied rhetoric under Quintilian, and at the age of 18 was admitted to the bar. He steadily rose in the ranks of the civil service. He was in the military treasury, served as 'curator of the bed and banks of the Tiber and city sewers', and when he was a senator in 111, the Emperor Trajan appointed him Governor of Bithynia-Pontus (now Turkey).

For all his accomplishments, Pliny the Younger is most remembered for his letters, which were intended for publication from the start. They deal with all manner of public and social events, literature, leisure and architecture. One of Pliny's most famous letters was written to his friend Tacitus in 79, telling of the eruption of Mount Vesuvius which killed his uncle and destroyed the city of Pompeii.

The last book of letters contains correspondence between Pliny and Emperor Trajan (whose reign marks the high point of the Roman Empire). In one famous epistle, Pliny told the Emperor that he had executed a group of Christians, but was unsure if his course of action was correct. Trajan replied, 'these people are not to be sought for; but if they be accused and convicted, they are to be punished…'

Pliny the Younger's *Letters* are highly valued in modern times because they offer an interesting and informative picture of ancient Roman society.

Confessions

Jean-Jacques Rousseau is best known as a philosopher, but was also a political commentator, novelist, poet and musician. Positioned as he was on the cusp of Enlightenment and Romanticism, his theories had a bearing on both the French and American Revolutions and the environmental movement, and influenced writers and thinkers such as Goethe, Stendhal, Baudelaire, Rimbaud, Gide, Proust and Tolstoy.

Confessions is considered the prototype of the modern autobiography. Rousseau was a complex, contradictory and controversial human being, and these traits come through very strongly in his work, which covers his life up to the age of 53. The first volume tells of his childhood in Geneva, his short-lived apprenticeship as an engraver, and his relationship with the Baroness de Warens, who was a mother-figure, mentor and mistress.

At the beginning of the second volume, Rousseau relates an incident which marks a turning point in his career, when he decides to enter an essay contest. 'I did so,' he says, 'and from that moment I was lost. The misfortunes of the remainder of my life were the inevitable result of this moment of madness.'

Rousseau made many friends as well as enemies, and had a variety of lovers. With his de facto wife Therese he had five children, all of whom were left at the foundling home (ironically, one of his best known works, Emile, is a treatise on education and child-rearing). Rousseau regretted the abandonment of his children, but says he did what he believed was best for them.

Like the Romantics he preceded, Rousseau loved spending time out of doors, and the passages in which he describes the natural world are truly magical.

Confessions is a highly readable story of the life of an adventurous and exceptional man whose impact on Western thought cannot be overestimated.

JEAN-JACQUES ROUSSEAU
1712 – 1778
Nationality: French
First Published: 1782
Other Selected Titles:
Discourse on the Arts and Sciences
Discourse on Political Economy
Julie or The New Heloise
Emile: or On Education
The Social Contract, or Principles of Political Right
Reveries of a Solitary Walker

A portrait of Jean-Jacques Rousseau.

Words

Jean-Paul Satre sits with an Egyptian artifact at Luxor in 1967.

JEAN-PAUL SARTRE
1905 – 1980
Nationality: French
First Published: Gallimard, 1964
Other Selected Titles:
Imagination: A Psychological Critique
Sketch for a Theory of the Emotions
The Flies
No Exit
Beaudelaire
Situations
Critique of Dialectical Reason

Words is a memoir of the first ten years of the life of writer and philosopher, Jean-Paul Sartre. It is divided into two parts – 'Reading' and 'Writing', and as the book title and section titles indicate, Sartre lived in a world of words, more real and more important to him than anything or anyone else around him.

Sartre never knew his father, who died when he was 15 months old. His mother Anne-Marie took him to live with her parents, Karl and Louise Schweitzer, relations of Albert Schweitzer. Karl was Professor of German at the Sorbonne, a formidable Jehovah figure whom Sartre was never able to please. His mother doted on him, and their relationship became more like that of brother and sister. Familiar with Freudian analysis, Sartre commented, 'My father's hasty retreat had conferred on me a very incomplete Oedipus complex: no Super-Ego, I agree, but no aggression either.'

A somewhat frail, solitary child, Sartre took refuge in the world of books and the imagination. His childhood favourites were Flaubert, Hugo and the Larousse encyclopaedia. He explained, 'I had found my religion: nothing seemed more important to me than a book. I saw the library as a temple.' Similarly, he enjoyed the cinema – his description of going to the theatre is highly evocative.

In the second half of the book, Sartre tells about when he began to write, and how he knew before he was ten years old that he wanted to write professionally.

Colourful and detailed, *Words* is one of Sartre's more accessible books, and an absorbing introduction to the life of one of the most prominent thinkers of the 20th century.

Journal of a Solitude

Belgian-born American writer May Sarton is the author of over 50 books, encompassing poetry, fiction and no less than 11 personal journals. *Journal of a Solitude* is her third volume of memoirs, written over the course of a year during her late fifties. After a period of depression, she had made a conscious decision to go inward and to live a simple, balanced life, focusing on writing poetry and tending the garden of her rural New Hampshire home.

Sarton was not a hermit, by any means. The journal is full of accounts of visits to friends, and her reciprocal hospitality. However, she sought to rid her life of clutter – emotional, mental and physical – and resented unnecessary intrusions into her time and space.

As well as detailed accounts of her daily activities and emotional states, Sarton reflects on notable incidents from her earlier life, including her friendships with Elizabeth Bowen, Virginia Woolf and S.S. Koteliansky ('Kot'). The book was written during the height of the women's lib movement in America, and Sarton makes some incisive comments about marriage and gender relations. She also remarks on contemporary politics: 'What a cramped little soul comes through from Nixon!'

But the real strength of the journal lies in Sarton's ability to engage with the natural world, where she finds sacredness and solace. Some passages are breathtaking in their beauty: 'If one looks long enough at almost anything, looks with absolute attention at a flower, a stone, the bark of a tree, grass, snow, a cloud, something like revelation takes place...'

Feminist scholar Carolyn Heilbrun praised *Journal of a Solitude* as a 'turning point in women's autobiography'. It is certainly a fine record of the midpoint of the life and career of this highly underrated author.

May Sarton in 1946.

MAY SARTON
1912 – 1995
Nationality: American
First Published: W.W. Norton Inc., 1973
Other Selected Titles:
Coming into Eighty
Halfway to Silence
A Grain of Mustard Seed
I Knew a Phoenix
Plant Dreaming Deep
As We Are Now
The Poet and the Donkey
Mrs. Stevens Hears the Mermaids Singing

Walden

Henry David Thoreau is one of the most esteemed American writers and thinkers of the 19th century. His ideas were shaped by his mentor, Ralph Waldo Emerson, and by the ancient texts of Taoism, Hinduism and Buddhism. In turn, he has influenced a host of modern writers as varied as May Sarton, Barbara Kingsolver and Rachel Carson.

Walden is the product of a two-year period when Thoreau lived in semi-isolation by Walden Pond near Concord, Massachusetts. He built himself a little cabin and was almost totally self-sufficient, growing his own vegetables and doing the odd job or two. It was his intention at Walden Pond to live simply, to have time to contemplate, walk in the woods, write, and commune with nature. He stated, 'I went to the woods because I wished to live deliberately, to front only the essential facts of life…'

The book is a series of essays, or meditations, with titles such as 'Economy', 'Sounds', 'Solitude', 'Visitors', 'Higher Laws', 'Brute Neighbours', 'Winter Animals', and 'Spring'. Thoreau's style is somewhat ponderous, but it is well worth persisting with *Walden* for the pearls of wisdom contained therein, which are often quoted: 'The mass of men lead lives of quiet desperation', 'Beware of all enterprises that require new clothes', and 'If a man does not keep pace with his companions, perhaps it is because he hears a different drummer'.

In our fast-paced, quick-fix society marked by excess, materialism and superficiality, *Walden*'s message is more relevant and necessary now than when it was written a hundred and fifty years ago. Read it – you will be inspired.

Henry D. Thoreau in 1850.

HENRY DAVID THOREAU
1817 – 1862
Nationality: American
First Published: Ticknor and Field, 1854
Other Selected Titles:
A Week on the Concord and Merrimack Rivers
Excursions
The Maine Woods
Cape Cod
A Yankee in Canada
Civil Disobedience

De Profundis

De Profundis ('from the depths') is as sorrowful a lament as you are ever likely to read. Playwright and novelist Oscar Wilde wrote it as a letter to his companion, Lord Alfred Douglas, while he was serving a two-year prison sentence in Reading Gaol for acts of 'gross indecency'.

Wilde's biographer, Richard Ellman, says that as a love letter it 'must rank – with its love and hate, solicitude, vanity and philosophic musings – as one of the greatest, and the longest, ever written.' Over time, however, *De Profundis* has become more than a piece of personal correspondence and can be read as a reflection on the universality of human suffering.

When Wilde was arrested in 1895 (thanks to Douglas' father, the Marquis of Queensberry), he was at the peak of his creative powers, the darling of society, the master of the bon mot. In prison, he was stripped of all vestiges of human dignity – for a long time he was not even allowed to write. When he was finally given pen and paper he wrote to Douglas, 'not to put bitterness into your heart, but to pluck it out of mine.' The poignant phrases of *De Profundis* are a far cry from the witty and often barbed epigrams of his earlier writings, for example: 'A day in prison on which one does not weep is a day on which one's heart is hard, not a day on which one's heart is happy.'

De Profundis is important because it is one of the last pieces that Oscar Wilde ever wrote (his final work was *The Ballad of Reading Gaol*). It will strike a chord with anyone who has ever been obsessed, betrayed or humiliated, and shows a sadder and wiser side to one of the most fascinating literary figures of the 19th century.

OSCAR WILDE
1854 – 1900
Nationality: Irish
First Published: Methuen & Co., 1905
Other Selected Titles:
The Duchess of Padua
Salomé
An Ideal Husband
The Importance of Being Earnest
Lady Windermere's Fan
The Canterville Ghost
The Happy Prince and Other Stories
The Picture of Dorian Gray

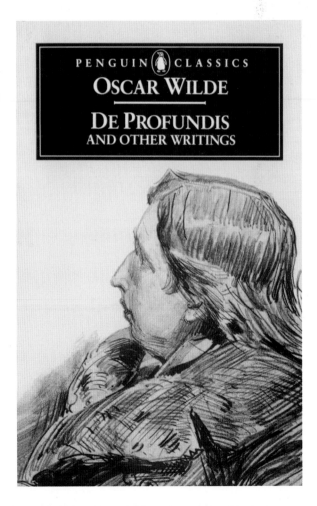

Oranges Are Not the Only Fruit

JEANETTE WINTERSON
1959 –
Nationality: British
First Published: Pandora, 1985
Other Selected Titles:
Boating for Beginners
Fit for the Future
The Passion
Sexing the Cherry
Written on the Body
Art Objects
Lighthousekeeping
Tanglewreck

In her introduction to *Oranges Are Not the Only Fruit*, Jeanette Winterson asks, as do many of her readers, 'Is *Oranges* an autobiographical novel?' She answers, 'No not at all and yes of course.' On another occasion she said, 'I wanted to invent myself as a fictional character. And I did.' In whatever way one chooses to classify this book – autobiographical novel, 'meta-fiction' or memoir – it is an unsettling and unforgettable story written by a 24-year-old author.

The life of the main character (whose name is also Jeanette) parallels Winterson's own. She is adopted and lives in a council house in Lancashire. Her father is all but invisible, her mother is a fanatical member of a Pentecostal Christian sect. Jeanette's life is a lonely one – her only friends are her dog and an elderly church member named 'Testifying Elsie'. Her mother has kept her out of school for years because it is a 'Breeding Ground', and when Jeanette finally does get to school, both teachers and students regard her as strange. At 16, Jeanette falls in love with a girl named Melanie. She is exorcized and ostracized, and eventually she leaves home to begin a new life.

Winterson's grasp of language and form is imaginative and facile. The book is divided into chapters named after books of the Bible, and the fairy tales that are woven into the story give it a magical and surreal energy. In 1989, Winterson herself wrote the screenplay for the BBC mini-series based on the novel, which won the BAFTA award for Best TV Drama.

Oranges Are Not the Only Fruit is the first (and in the opinion of some, the best) book by one of Britain's most inventive contemporary writers.

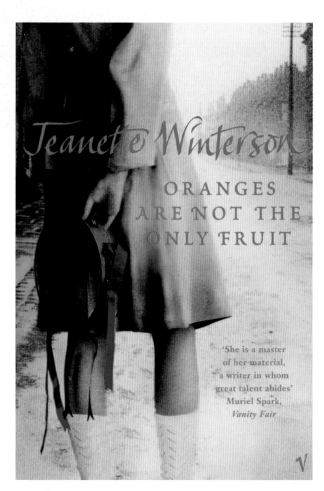

'She is a master of her material, a writer in whom great talent abides'
Muriel Spark,
Vanity Fair

Autobiographies

W.B. Yeats is arguably Ireland's greatest literary figure. He was one of the co-founders of the Abbey Theatre and was a leading light in the Irish literary revival, also known as the 'Celtic Twilight.' He also served in the Irish Senate from 1922 to 1928.

Autobiographies covers Yeats' life from childhood until 1923, when he won the Nobel Prize for Literature. It is divided into six sections: 'Reveries over Childhood and Youth', 'The Trembling of the Veil', 'Dramatis Personae', 'Estrangement', 'The Death of Synge' and 'The Bounty of Sweden', which are available in his *Collected Works Volume Three*.

Throughout his life, Yeats moved between London, Dublin, and the west of Ireland, and he had a special affinity with the landscape of Sligo, where he would return again and again. As well as Sligo, Yeats had other passions – poetry, drama, politics and mysticism – and in *Autobiographies* we meet people from the different facets of his life. For many years his muse and unrequited love was Maude Gonne – the first time he saw her, he says, 'her complexion was luminous, like that of apple-blossom through which the light falls…' He tells of his meetings with Oscar Wilde, and his associations with artist and visionary George Russell (who wrote under the pseudonym Æ) and Theosophist and occultist Madame Blavatsky (describing her as 'a sort of female Dr. Johnson'). Probably the most important influences in Yeats' life were his friendships with Lady Augusta Gregory and playwright John Millington Synge, and he speaks of them with great fondness and gratitude.

Yeats' *Autobiographies* are worth reading not just for a picture of the man and the writer, but for an awareness of the creative and political awakening of a nation to which he is inextricably linked.

William Butler Yeats arrives in New York in 1926.

WILLIAM BUTLER YEATS
1865 – 1939
Nationality: Irish
First Published: Macmillan & Co. Ltd, 1955
Other Selected Titles:
The Wanderings of Oisin and Other Poems
The Celtic Twilight
The Land of Heart's Desire
The Secret Rose
Cathleen ni Houlihan
A Vision
The Tower
The Winding Stair and Other Poems

MODERN FICTION

Things Fall Apart

CHINUA ACHEBE
1930 –
Nationality: Nigerian
First Published: Heinemann, 1958
Other Selected Titles:
No Longer at Ease
Arrow of God
A Man of the People
Anthills of the Savannah

Chinua Achebe at the Frankfurt Book Fair in 2002.

When, in 1958, Chinua Achebe wrote this seminal work in African and World literature, the novels of Africa, notably Conrad's *Heart of Darkness* and Joyce Cary's *Mister Johnson*, presented African culture and tradition as amorphous and valueless. Achebe's masterly riposte also served to remind his fellow Africans of their irreplaceable heritage.

Things Fall Apart maps the clash between the complex Ibo society of Umuofia, a group of nine villages in Nigeria, and colonialism and Christianity in the late 1800s. This conflict is vested in the story and character of Okokwo, a great man, who is forced to commit the ultimate sin against the very values he is trying to defend. The distinctive diction and use of Ibo proverb and idiom in Achebe's elegant English prose, together with the rich plot and characterization, carry his message in perfect balance.

Dona Flor and Her Two Husbands

Amado's vibrant, Modernist novel is a sensual celebration of his beloved Bahia, and the marvellous, passionate widow Dona Flor. Now remarried to upright pharmacist Teodoro, she is gloriously haunted by the love-biting ghost of her roguish first husband and our guide, the hedonistic Vadinho, who died as he lived, dancing the samba in drag. Has Dona Flor got the best of both worlds as Vadinho reminds her that life is not just for the living?

The spirited Vadinho can travel anywhere and in his company, Amado introduces us to many of his own favourite places, as we take a virtual tour of the pleasures of Bahia mingling with every strata of Brazilian society.

Dona Flor and Her Two Husbands is a masterclass in joi de vivre, joi de cooking and eating, making love, gambling, talking, laughing and dancing to the grave and far, far beyond, and all to the seductive rhythm of the samba.

JORGE AMADO
1912 – 2001
Nationality: Brazilian
First Published: Livraria Martins Editoria, 1966
Other Selected Titles:
Gabriela, Clove and Cinnamon
Shepherds of the Night
Tent of Miracles
Tereza Batista: Home from the Wars
Tieta, the Goat Girl
Showdown
The War of the Saints
How the Turks Discovered America

Le Grand Meaulnes

**ALAIN-FOURNIER
(HENRI ALBAN FOURNIER)**
1887 – 1914
Nationality: French
First Published: La Nouvelle Revue
Francaise, 1913

If the past is another country, adolescence, with its heightened emotions, missed opportunities and lost innocence, seems with hindsight to be another world. It is this quality of intense, melancholic nostalgia which is so strikingly present in this haunting novel.

The restless youth, Augustin Meaulnes, escapes school in a handcart, only to stray into a semi-magical domain, and a dreamlike masquerade. An elaborate wedding is in progress and Meaulnes meets very briefly, and falls instantly in love with, the beautiful Yvonne, and spends the rest of the novel trying to return to be with her in the 'domain'.

He is assisted in his quest by the narrator, his schoolfellow Francois, who hero-worships the charismatic Meaulnes. Both boys' lives are, of course, changed irrevocably and forever by the events of their adolescence.

Le Grand Meaulnes has often been compared with J.D Salinger's *Catcher in the Rye*, and could be compared with Herman Hesse's *Demian*, as a masterly evocation of the singularity of vanished youth.

Take a Girl Like You

'The Virgin's progress of attractive little Jenny Bunn, come south to teach … ' as the jacket blurb would have it. *Take a Girl Like You* is a comic satire on complacent, middle-class conventions, and the social and sexual mores of an England on the cusp of the Age of Aquarius.

Jenny, the infant school teacher who embodies the common sense and traditional naivety of the 1950s, is pitted against the arrogant cynicism of Patrick Standish, the public school Latin master whose predatory promiscuity presages the decade ahead.

In this unsentimental love story, Amis depicts genuinely deep feeling while exploring one of his favourite themes, the self-imposed difficulties caused by the selfish pursuit of pleasure. He perfectly captures the rhythm and tone of 1960 with his customary sharp ear for the way real people speak and mimic's talent for the *argot* of time and place.

KINGSLEY AMIS
1922 – 1995
Nationality: British
First Published: Gollancz, 1960
Other Selected Titles:
Lucky Jim
That Uncertain Feeling
One Fat Englishman
I Want It Now
The Green Man
Jake's Thing
Stanley and His Women
The Old Devils

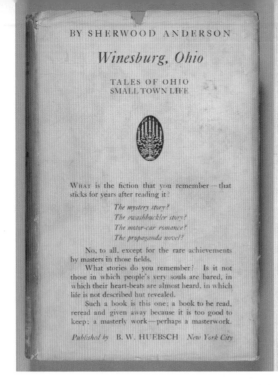

BY SHERWOOD ANDERSON

Winesburg, Ohio

TALES OF OHIO
SMALL TOWN LIFE

WHAT is the fiction that you remember—that
sticks for years after reading it?

The mystery story?
The swashbuckler story?
The motor-car romance?
The propaganda novel?

No, to all, except for the rare achievements
by masters in those fields.

What stories do you remember? Is it not
those in which people's very souls are bared, in
which their heart-beats are almost heard, in which
life is not described but revealed.

Such a book is this one; a book to be read,
reread and given away because it is too good to
keep; a masterly work—perhaps a masterwork.

Published by B. W. HUEBSCH *New York City*

*First Edition, First Issue,
inscibed by Anderson:
"To Henry J. Smith,
With Regards,
Sherwood Anderson."
The Chicago-based journalist
and author, Henry Justin
Smith, was an early friend and
supporter of Anderson.*

SHERWOOD ANDERSON
1876 – 1941
Nationality: American
First Published: B.W. Huebsch, 1919
Other Selected Titles:
*Windy McPherson's Son
Marching Men*

Winesburg, Ohio

Like *The Canterbury Tales*, Anderson's masterpiece is a collection of interlocking short stories in a circular narrative. A kind of literary precursor to the TV soap opera, *Winesburg, Ohio* tells the story of the lives of the inhabitants of a small town community.

Each story, like each life, is complete in itself, but is an essential part of the whole and exposes the unresolved complexities, conflicts and loneliness of each character, and of the human condition.

Winesburg, Ohio is pinpointed on the literary and historical map by simple direct speech and use of metaphors from nature, and the landscape of early 20th-century Ohio, yet the book remains completely pertinent in the early 21st century. Published to great acclaim, critics were nonetheless concerned by his treatment of subjects like homosexuality.

Winesburg, Ohio established Anderson as a literary master of the American short story. His work was a major influence on that of both William Faulkner and Ernest Hemingway, and it is said he used his personal influence to help both get their first novels published.

Surfacing

A young Canadian woman artist, her estranged lover, and a young married couple, return to the wilderness of Northern Quebec and her childhood, in search of her lost father.

While the wilderness is colonized by holidaymakers and her own companions, she comes to realize that she too has been colonized by all she has been taught about herself and her potential, both as an artist and a woman.

Increasingly convinced that her father has drowned in the fathomless lake, she dives in and undergoes an extraordinary metamorphosis. She strips herself, layer by layer, of her femininity, her beliefs, her personal history, its truths and lies, and ultimately even of language, to find the bare truth and her primeval self.

Surfacing is a compulsive read, an utterly compelling narrative, part detective story, part mystical quest, and a metaphor for the search in the fragmented woman for the wholeness of self. Some 30 years after its publication, the book now also seems to represent the post-colonial human condition as well as that of women.

MARGARET ATWOOD
1939 –
Nationality: Canadian
First Published: McClelland & Stewart, 1972
Other Selected Titles:
The Edible Woman
Life Before Man
Bodily Harm
The Handmaid's Tale
Cat's Eye
Alias Grace
The Blind Assassin
Oryx and Crake

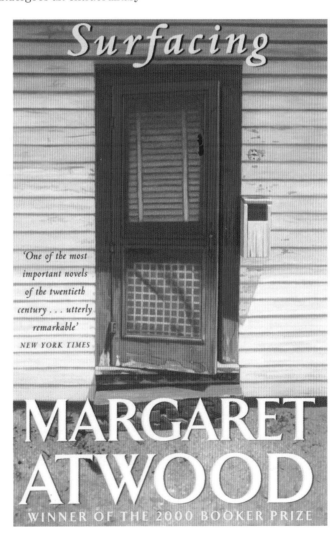

'One of the most important novels of the twentieth century . . . utterly remarkable'
NEW YORK TIMES

MARGARET ATWOOD

WINNER OF THE 2000 BOOKER PRIZE

Paul Auster in Paris, 1990.

PAUL AUSTER
1947 –
Nationality: American
First Published: Faber & Faber, 1985
Other Selected Titles:
In the Country of Last Things
Moon Palace
The Music of Chance
Leviathan
The Red Notebook
Mr. Vertigo
The Book of Illusions
Oracle Night

The New York Trilogy

Paul Auster's most accomplished work consists of three interlocking novels: *City of Glass* (1985), *Ghosts* (1986), and *The Locked Room* (1986), all haunting, pacy 'anti-mystery' detective stories exploring identity and the search for self. The streets of New York provide the hyper-real setting for the surreal lives of the characters.

Daniel Quinn, the hero of the first novel, is a tragically widowed writer of private eye stories, mistaken for a private eye named Paul Auster. *Ghosts*' protagonist is a wannabe detective called Blue, a student of Brown, hired by White to spy on a spy named Black who lives on Orange Street. The nameless Fanshawe's friend who takes up the life, wife and work of the late Fanshawe, a renowned author, narrates the third novel as he obsessively investigates the latter's death.

The combined edition is something of a compendium of literary games, featuring multiple identity confusion and sprinkled with literary references, straining at the bounds of Postmodernist fiction.

Tales of Odessa

Picture a 1920s Jewish ghetto on the outskirts of Odessa. This is a vibrant and carnivalesque underworld, bursting with life and peopled by whores and gangsters, merchants and inn-keepers, hustlers and rabbis, brokers and shop keepers, middle-men, fixers and entrepreneurs. At the centre reigns Benia Kirk, the gangster king. Run a sound track in the everyday Russian-Jewish dialect of the day and you will experience the flavour of Isaak Babel's masterly *Tales of Odessa*.

The author-narrator provides a blueprint for future writers as the other at the centre of his culture. Painted in broad brush strokes, with humour and affection, the four novellas, *The King* (1921), *The Way It Used To Be Done In Odessa* (1923), *The Father* (1924), and *Liubka the Cossack* (1924) first appeared in book form in 1931.

Babel won justifiable acclaim for his genius as one of the greatest short story writers of all time. In the late 1930s his work was deemed incompatible with the state's literary politics; he died in a Siberian prison camp in 1940.

ISAAK BABEL
1894 – 1940
Nationality: Russian
First Published: The Left, 1916
Other Selected Titles:
Red Cavalry
Collected Stories
You Must Know Everything: Stories

Giovanni's Room

JAMES BALDWIN
1924 – 1987
Nationality: American
First Published: Dial Press,
1956
Other Selected Titles:
*Go Tell It On the Mountain
Another Country
The Fire Next Time
Tell Me How Long the Train's
Been Gone
If Beale Street Could Talk
The Devil Finds Work
Just Above My Head
The Evidence of Things Not Seen*

In 1956, black American writer James Baldwin featured a white American, middle-class homosexual as the hero in his brilliantly written evocation of identity and desire, *Giovanni's Room*. Groundbreaking indeed.

The leitmotif of David's life is escape – from his father and the mid 20th-century masculine world he represents, from his shame at his first erotic encounter with a teenage friend Joey, and from his own world, his culture and his country.

In Paris, in the bohemian world of homosexuals and drag queens, whom he despises and ridicules, David attempts the ultimate escape, from himself. When the heady atmosphere of danger and violence threatens the conventional future that he has imagined for himself, he meets and proposes to Hella. While Hella goes away to consider the depth of her own love, he falls passionately in love with Italian barman Giovanni. They begin an affair and Giovanni faces execution for murder.

James Baldwin gets comfortable. New York, 1963.

The Sweet Hereafter

Tragedy strikes the upstate New York town of Sam Dent, one winter's day, when a bus carrying the town's children crashes into a quarry, leaving only two survivors, the driver, Dolores Driscoll, and 14-year-old Nicola Burnell, left paraplegic by the accident.

The Sweet Hereafter explores how the tragedy is suffered and endured by the townspeople. The powerful narrative of unimaginable loss, guilt, rage and despair unfolds in the stories of the two survivors and those of Billy Ansel, a widower who loses his twins and with them everything he loves in the crash, and Mitchell Stephens, a lawyer employed to represent the townspeople in a class action. He brings with him to Sam Dent his own tragedy, as his own daughter is lost to drugs.

Banks has described this complex novel as an exploration of the myth and stories – not lies – that people invent in order to survive and make sense of the chaos of inexplicable tragedy in an immoral universe.

Russell Banks at his New York home in 2005.

RUSSELL BANKS
1940 –
Nationality: American
First Published: Harper Collins, 1991
Other Selected Titles:
Hamilton Stark
The Book of Jamaica
Trailerpark
Continental Drift
Affliction
Rule of the Bone
Cloudsplitter

The Regeneration Trilogy

PAT BARKER
1943 –
Nationality: British
First Published: Viking, 1991
Other Selected Titles:
Union Street
Blow Your House Down
The Century's Daughter
The Man Who Wasn't There
Another World
Border Crossing
Double Vision
A Mind to Kill

This compelling First World War trilogy explores the imagined relationships between the military psychoanalyst W.H.R. Rivers, the poets Siegfried Sassoon, Wilfred Owen and Robert Graves, and the fictional Billy Prior, during the time each of them spent at Craiglockhart War Hospital, Edinburgh, in 1917.

Regeneration features Sassoon, decorated for bravery, yet protesting against the war, being sent to Craiglockhart to be 'cured' and sent back to the trenches. Barker reveals interesting comparisons between Sassoon's homosexuality and the comradeship of soldiers, so vital to their survival of the horrors of war.

The Eye in the Door describes the atmosphere of mistrust in Britain and deals chiefly with the predatory bisexual Billy Prior and the blurred edges of morality, wherein the sane become mad, and prejudice grows, as millions die for freedom. *The Ghost Road* further explores the relationship between Rivers and Prior, before Prior too, as must Owen, return to the front and death.

Herzog

SAUL BELLOW
1915 – 2005
Nationality: Canadian
First Published: Viking Press, 1964
Other Selected Titles:
Seize the Day
Henderson the Rain King
Humboldt's Gift
The Dean's December
More Die of Heartbreak
A Theft
The Bellarosa Connection
Ravelstein

Moses Herzog, a failed academic and serial divorcee, retires to his decaying country home in the Berkshire mountains in the wake of his present wife's departure with his best friend.

Here, sharing his bread with the mice, he embarks on an extraordinary spiritual journey (or is it a nervous breakdown?). Through it, his ultimate redemption is revealed to be also that of America itself. For this reason, as well as the precise style and sheer erudition of the prose, *Herzog* is seen by many to be one of the greatest literary expressions of post-war America.

By the ruthless interrogation of all his friends and frantic letter-writing, though many of the letters are never sent, Herzog's inner life is revealed. In a world out of control, he enters a dialogue with long dead philosophers to attempt to understand and bring together the fragments of his personality.

Saul Bellow brings his unique literary gifts and razor sharp intelligence to this story, told with both compassion and an especially dry sense of humour.

RIGHT: Saul Bellow in 1958.

Ficciones ✓

Imagine a world without science fiction, fantasy, comic books, or computer games. Perhaps without *Ficciones* (*Fictions*), Borges' masterwork, these contemporary genres would not have existed. Considered to be a cornerstone of Postmodern fiction contained in 17 short stories, *Ficciones* is a towering exploration of the relationship between language and metaphysics, philosophy, theology and literature.

The Garden of Forking Paths (eight stories), ranges from a spy story about an impossible book and a magical labyrinth, to a mystical visionary trying to dream a human into being, and a review of a detective story about a search for an unreal person.

Artifices (nine stories) features the tale of an expatriate Irishman and the scar on his face, a writer's last days under a Nazi death sentence and the story of a 19-year-old invalid's discovery that language is an inadequate tool for those who can forget nothing. Fiction and reality become indistinguishable in this glorious collection.

JORGE LUIS BORGES
1899 – 1986
Nationality: Argentinian
First Published: Sur, 1944

Jorge Luis Borges.

Nadja

Nadja is a girl, but as you turn the pages of this Surrealist romance, you begin to wonder whether she really exists. She was inspired, it is said, by a strange girl whom Breton had met, who seemed to be experiencing what he was considering, a state of super-reality where dreams and reality merge. Sadly, for her the reality of the theory led to the asylum.

The Nadja of fiction is part muse, part agent provocateur, and it is the way that she makes the protagonist feel about the surreal things, objects, events, places and people in his everyday life that define them both. She inspires both him and the reader to meditate upon and consider the nature of reality.

Published in 1928, in French, this novel includes 44 photographs which illustrate and are integral to the first person narrative of the text.

Breton was considered, and still is, the founder of Surrealist literature. In 1924 he published the first Surrealist Manifesto.

ANDRÉ BRETON
1896 – 1966
Nationality: French
First Published: Gallimard, 1928
Other Selected Titles:
Surrealist Manifesto
L'Amour Fou

Surrealist poets André Breton, Paul Eluard, Tristan Tzara and Benjamin Peret in 1932.

VINTAGE CLASSICS

Mikhail Bulgakov
The Master and Margarita

The Master and Margarita ✓E

The original publication of the culmination of Bulgakov's life's work, in the journal *Moskva* in 1966–7, was as a rare, fresh breeze of freedom blowing through Soviet spiritual and artistic values. The courage of its themes (Jesus Christ, Pontius Pilate, Satan and The Great Terror of the 1930s), and its style (a combination of satire, clowning and intense honesty), combine in this devastating satire of Soviet life in general, and Soviet literary life in particular, to stun its readers.

The multi-layered plot pivots on a dialogue between the people's poet and a critic on the best way to portray Christ as an exploiter of the proletariat. Interrupted by a stranger (Satan in the guise of Woland), they unknowingly allow him and his chaos-bringing retinue of vampires, witches and even a giant cat, into their world.

For the modern reader, even without the historical and political context that saw Bulgakov's work banned by Stalin, this is a hugely enjoyable work of genius, terrifyingly brilliant, but at the same time darkly disturbing.

MIKHAIL BULGAKOV
1891 – 1940
Nationality: Russian
First Published: *Moskva* journal, 1966
Other Selected Titles:
Great Soviet Short Stories
Black Snow: Theatrical Novel
A Country Doctor's Notebook
Diaboliad and Other Stories
Notes on the Cuff and Other Stories
The Fatal Eggs and Other Soviet Satire

The Naked Lunch ✓

Icon of the Beat generation and heroin addict William Burroughs gleaned his most famous and acclaimed work from *The Word Hoard*, a collection of his random thoughts in Europe and Tangiers. Edited by Alan Ginsburg and Jack Kerouac, under the influence of some heavy dope, *The Naked Lunch* earned cult status by being banned in many countries as obscene.

William Lee, a junkie on the run, provides the fine narrative thread running through a non-linear collection of satirical essays. His revelations under the influence or absence of various drugs have been described as both a Dante's inferno of sex and degradation and a masterpiece of Postmodern literature.

Experimenting with the 'cut-up technique' used by his friend the painter Brion Gysin, Burroughs offers a paranoid's eye view of society's conspiracy to manipulate the individual, from the mass media to police surveillance. Visionary and terrifying, *The Naked Lunch* inspired a generation of artists, singers and writers.

WILLIAM BURROUGHS
1914 – 1997
Nationality: American
First Published: Olympia Press, 1959
Other Selected Titles:
Junky: Confessions of an Unredeemed Drug Addict (as William Lee until 1964)
The Soft Machine
The Ticket That Exploded
Nova Express
Roosevelt After Inauguration (as William Lee)
Queer

William S. Burroughs in Allen Ginsberg's apartment, New York, 1953.

Possession

A.S. BYATT
1936 –
Nationality: British
First Published: Chatto & Windus, 1990
Other Selected Titles:
The Virgin in the Garden
Still Life
Angels and Insects
The Matisse Stories
The Djinn in the Nightingale's Eye
Babel Tower
Elementals: Stories of Fire and Ice
The Biographer's Tale

In the fiercely competitive world of academia, two young researchers, Roland Michell and Maud Bailey, are each researching individually into the lives and works of two previously unconnected Victorian poets, Randolph Henry Ash and Christabel LaMotte.

As their fascination deepens, their research throws up hitherto unsuspected clues, which lead them from London to North Yorkshire and the magical west of Brittany, pursued by jealous colleagues and in pursuit of a mystery.

This extraordinarily ambitious novel is manifestly a great work of depth and scholarship, of ideas and analysis. But it is also a multi-layered love story, a Victorian novel and a very modern one, blending academia with spiritualism, passion with poetry, much of it original to the book.

A.S. Byatt's breadth of knowledge allows her to mix myth with modern university life, and romance with a detective story that is richly satisfying on many levels and so generous that it leaves the reader believing that they share Byatt's erudition.

Italo Calvino in a Parisian café, 1981.

If On a Winter's Night a Traveller

If On a Winter's Night a Traveller is an ingenious metafiction, which reaches gloriously dizzying heights in experimental writing.

A reader opens the novel; yes this novel, *If On a Winter's Night a Traveller*, to find that it has been misbound. He meets the lovely Ludmilla, who also has a misbound copy. As both try to track down the original novel they find that it has been replaced by the work of a Polish writer. This too is defective, containing part of the novel, and the beginnings of ten different novels, each a pastiche of a genre – detective, Japanese erotica, ghost story, mystery and so on. Each of them ends prematurely on a cliffhanger, and each contains an echo of the original book and clues to the overall mystery. Is this the work of a mischievous translator?

As Ludmilla and you, for the book is written in the second person, fall in love, you also have time to read Calvino's treatise on the difficulties of writing, the experience of reading, and his sardonic sniping at the publishing industry.

ITALO CALVINO
1923 – 1985
Nationality: Italian
First Published: G. Einaudi, 1979
Other Selected Titles:
The Cloven Viscount
The Baron in the Trees
The Nonexistent Knight
Our Ancestors
T Zero
Invisible Cities
The Castle of Crossed Destines
Six Memos for the Next Millennium

The Outsider

Widely considered to be an Absurdist rather than an Existentialist novel, Camus' brilliant *The Outsider* is, in essence, an attempt to describe his belief in man's alienation from his fellow man except as part of an uncaring, amoral, godless universe.

Meursault, a *pied-noir* (like Camus, a French inhabitant of Algeria), fails to cry at his mother's funeral. He is alienated from the proceedings, able only to experience relative truths by his physical senses. He befriends Raymond and helps him to dispose of a mistress, whose brother confronts the pair, and Raymond is injured in a knife fight.

Meursault returns to the beach and shoots the brother dead, in an act not of revenge, but induced by the sun's glare. He is tried for murder where his dedication to truth leads to his conviction. He is convicted for his inability to express emotion, especially remorse. As an atheist he is outraged by the chaplain's attempt to convert him and thus subvert the earthly justice in which he believes so passionately.

Albert Camus in 1959.

ALBERT CAMUS
1913 – 1960
Nationality: French
First Published: Gallimard, 1942
Other Selected Titles:
The Plague
The Fall
A Happy Death
The First Man
Exile and the Kingdom
The Guest
La Femme Adultère

ALBERT CAMUS
The Outsider

Auto da Fé

On October 15th 1981, Elias Canetti, Bulgarian novelist and playwright, was awarded the Nobel Prize for Literature, for, among his other works, his novel known in English as *Auto da Fé*.

It has been described as 'a great novel carrying a sense of the fantastic and the demonic like that of the 19th-century Russian masters Gogol and Dostoyevsky', but the academy also recognized the power of the writing itself and his great talent for aphorism, wit and satirical bite.

Auto da Fé is set in the decaying, cosmopolitan splendour of pre-war Vienna, where Canetti himself studied in the 1920s, before fleeing the Nazis to live in France and England. His protagonist, Peter Kien, is an expert on China, living in perfect isolation among 25,000 books. He succumbs to the brutality of the city's underworld and descends into depravity, when he is forced to rejoin it by the actions of his wife.

This towering and richly satisfying work reflects Canetti's preoccupation with the psychopathology of power, and the position of the individual at odds with society around him.

ELIAS CANETTI
1905 – 1994
Nationality: Bulgarian
First Published: Herbert Reichner Verlag, 1935
Other Selected Titles:
*Crowds and Power
The Memoirs of Elias Canetti: The Tongue Set Free, The Torch in My Ear, The Play of the Eyes
The Voices of Marrakesh
Kafka'a Other Trial: The Letters to Felice*

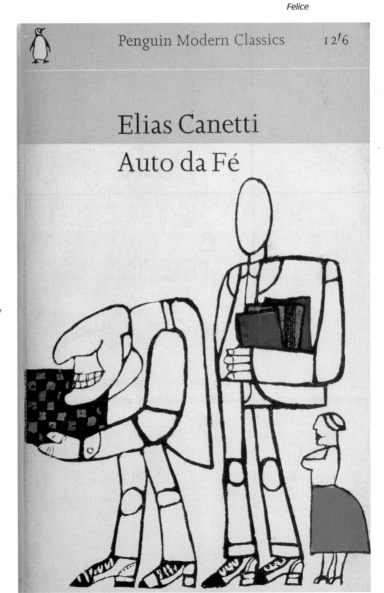

Penguin Modern Classics   12'6

Elias Canetti
Auto da Fé

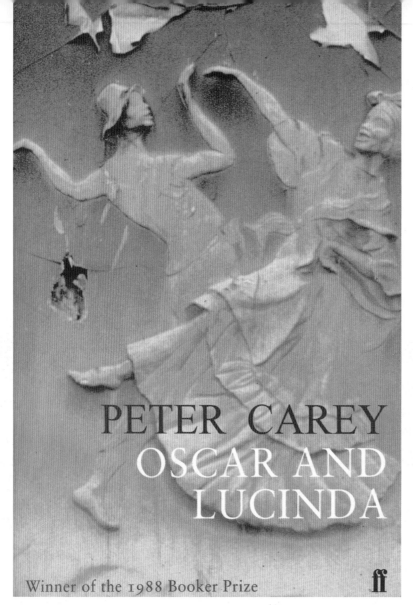

PETER CAREY
OSCAR AND
LUCINDA

Winner of the 1988 Booker Prize

ff

PETER CAREY
1943 –
Nationality: Australian
First Published: University of
Queenstown Press, 1988
Other Selected Titles:
Bliss
Illywhacker
The Tax Inspector
The Unusual Life of Tristan Smith
Jack Maggs
True History of the Kelly Gang
My Life as a Fake

Oscar and Lucinda

This all-encompassing Postmodernist pastiche is irrepressibly inventive. It is a 19th-century romance and an exploration of the precarious basis on which individuals and nations construct their lives, through the juxtaposition of the highly unlikely characters of Oscar and Lucinda.

Oscar Hopkins, the recalcitrant clergyman son of a rigidly uncompromising preacher, meets Lucinda Leplastrier, a teenage heiress who has just bought a glass factory, on a voyage to Australia, a New World paradise where a new future can be built. They fall in love and discover a mutual passion for gambling – a passion that leads them to transport a glass church across the virgin Australian outback.

Oscar and Lucinda won the Booker Prize in 1988, and is typical of Carey's highly creative fiction, which routinely mixes fact and fiction, time and history and improbable ideas with fantastic themes. The result is a truly rewarding read which says much about the fragile hopes of humanity in a world born out of chaos.

The Kingdom of This World

This dazzling fictional account of Haiti's glorious revolution captures the very essence and colour of both the country and its momentous history.

Alejo Carpentier was greatly influenced by Anontin Arnaud, Jacques Prevert and the surrealist movement, and *The Kingdom of This World*, like his other novels explores the Latin American world in all its rich diversity of cultures and his belief in the possibility of magical transformation.

The Kingdom of This World does not depend, in its 100 pages, upon a strong narrative thread to capture and keep our attention, but rather upon the startling beauty of the language and imagery. Divided into four parts, each deals with a different theme – Macandal, Boukman, the fall of Christophe and the endurance of the peasant. The only common element is the appearance in each of Ti Noel whom we follow from youth to old age as his life and livelihood are influenced by the social and political changes of his country.

This book is like listening to music or reading poetry, a sensual and aesthetic experience as well as an educative one.

ALEJO CARPENTIER
1904 – 1980
Nationality: Cuban
First Published: Publicaciones Iberoamericana, 1949
Other Selected Titles:
The Lost Steps
The Chase
The War of Time
Reasons of State
The Harp and the Shadow

Alejo Carpentier, writer, essayist and musicologist.

The Bloody Chamber

This unique reinterpretation of the fairy tales of Western Europe carries all the hallmarks of Angela Carter's brilliance, both as storyteller and a feminist social commentator.

The Bloody Chamber of the title is a reworking of Bluebeard's gory tale; other titles include *The Courtship of Mr. Lyon*, *The Tiger's Bride*, *Puss-in-Boots*, *The Snow Child*, *The Werewolf*, *The Company of Wolves* and *Wolf-Alice*. Carter has not so much retold the tales as used archetypes to recreate the spirit of the original, from an oral tradition.

Each is told in dense, sparkling prose, exploring the Jungian psychology and latent warnings of the sexual predation of men, present in the originals, but with subtlety and understated endings, some of which are less than happy. Beauty may be more self-reliant and knowing than we are used to, but her happy ending comes from her understanding of the nature of man… and woman. Magical, realistic, erotic, gothic and surreal, this collection should be coming soon to a fireside near you.

ANGELA CARTER
1940 – 1992
Nationality: British
First Published: Victor Gollancz, 1979
Other Selected Titles:
Shadow Dance (U.S. *Honeybuzzard*)
Heroes and Villains
The Infernal Desire Machines of Doctor Hoffman (U.S. *The War of Dreams*)
The Passion of New Eve
Nights at the Circus
Wise Children
Burning Your Boats

What We Talk about When We Talk about Love

RAYMOND CARVER
1938 – 1998
Nationality: American
First Published: Vintage, 1981
Other Selected Titles:
Carnations
Put Yourself in My Shoes
Will You Please Be Quiet, Please?
The Stories of Raymond Carver
Elephant and Other Stories
Where I'm Calling From
Carnations
Short Cuts

What We Talk about When We Talk about Love is both the title of this anthology of 17 short stories, and the first in the collection.

Published in 1981, it secured Carver's reputation as the leading contemporary proponent of the minimalist, hyper-realistic style of short story writing. Set in the poor, blue-collar, suburban America in which he grew up, the stories create a world which, though it may be foreign to many of us, is nonetheless inhabited by men and women in whose lives and loves we see our own reflected.

Carver's art has been described as creating stories of effect rather than cause; his characters are always caught at a moment of truth in their lives, their work, their relationships or their very identities and his spare and subtle prose carries with it a sense of unfulfilled mystery.

His own struggles with poverty and alcohol inform his work and the stories depict both real violence and the violence of alienation.

This collection should be read and re-read by anyone interested in the universality of the human condition.

RAYMOND CARVER

What We Talk about When We Talk about Love

HARVILL PANTHER

"One of America's most original, truest voices"
SALMAN RUSHDIE

The Horse's Mouth

Arthur Joyce Carey.

JOYCE CAREY
1888 – 1957
Nationality: British
First Published: Penguin, 1944
Other Selected Titles:
An American Visitor
Charley is My Darling
A House of Children
The Moonlight
A Fearful Joy
Prisoner of Grace
Not Honour More
The Captive and the Free

Through this dark comedy, Joyce Carey portrays the ability of the human spirit to accommodate great contradiction; in this case to be streetwise while retaining a naivety of spirit that transcends all of life's experiences.

It was written in 1944, the last book of a trilogy that includes *Herself Surprised* (1941) and *To Be a Pilgrim* (1942). Nevertheless, it stands alone both as a novel and a film. The trilogy is set contemporaneously at the end of the Second World War and, perhaps uniquely, epitomizes a society that bravely battled against the odds, fighting for freedom, while creating a sub-culture of corruption and black markets. The central character is Gully Jimson, a painter in the autumn of his career and years. As this wonderfully written story unfolds with black humour, Gulley is revealed as an ex-con petty criminal operating in London, dealing and stealing a livelihood. Ironically, he is also portrayed as a visionary artist with enormous energy to create new works through deprivation and illness. You are left to decide if Gulley is truly a great painter or just a wheeler-dealer with delusions of artistic grandeur.

Journey to the End of Night

Céline's critically acclaimed work *Journey to the End of Night* is not for the faint-hearted or those subject to bouts of depression.

The story of a tormented man's (Ferdinand Bardamu) quest for meaning in a bleak world without beauty or morality, it led to its author being lauded as a great innovator in French literature when it was published in 1934. In part, this was because of the disconnected and fervid style in which Céline's prose is written, reflecting the nihilistic thesis of the novel.

Journey to the End of Night takes place in the shadow cast by the war to end all wars and opens with Bardamu, a doctor, whose patients mostly fail to thrive – indeed most die. He is seized by a recruiting officer as he discusses politics with a friend, and Bardamu's desolate personal journey begins.

Céline was later charged with misanthropy and many found his pre-war anti-Semitism distasteful. Although his work lost favour during the 1930s this book remains a vividly intense work of the imagination.

LOUIS-FERDINAND CELINE
1894 – 1961
Nationality: French
First Published: Denoël & Steele, 1932
Other Selected Titles:
Death on Credit
Mea Culpa
Guignol's Band
Castle to Castle
North

Original draft of Journey to the End of Night.

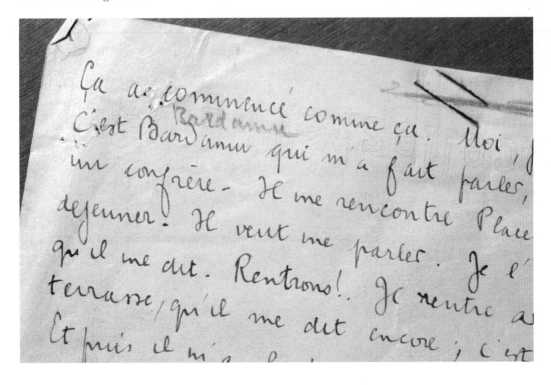

Soldiers of Salamis

JAVIER CERCAS
1962 –
Nationality: Spanish
First Published: Plot Ediciones, 2003
Other Selected Titles:
The Motive and the Tenant
The Speed of Light

Soldiers of Salamis is an extraordinary, contemporary epic novel and a search for truth and identity, through the life of a 'hero' of the Spanish Civil War, Rafael Sánchez Mazas. The identity sought by the book's narrator (a journalist, also called Javier Cercas) is that of Spain and the Spanish in the 21st century. In Spain's transition between Franco's rule and a modern democracy, Cercas realizes that the government and the people have colluded benevolently to forget their past.

Mazas, a founder of the fascist Falange, is captured by Republicans and faces execution in the woods. He escapes only to be faced with a soldier of the other side, who miraculously turns away. Mazas lives on, among the 'forest friends' and later rises to be a minister in Franco's post-war government.

Soldiers of Salamis is beautifully written and loses none of its power to move, its moral authenticity and honest humour in translation.

This is a book not just about Spain and her history, but about every nation's need to recognize its past and its part in the collective and individual identity of the present.

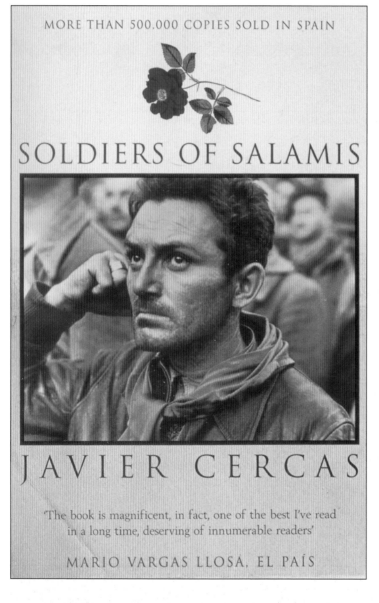

MORE THAN 500.000 COPIES SOLD IN SPAIN

SOLDIERS OF SALAMIS

JAVIER CERCAS

'The book is magnificent, in fact, one of the best I've read in a long time, deserving of innumerable readers'

MARIO VARGAS LLOSA, EL PAÍS

The Stories of John Cheever

American short story writer John Cheever was dubbed
'the Chekhov of the suburbs' and specialized in exploring the
vacuous pointlessness, both spiritually and emotionally, of
middle-class American suburban life. Many of his stories were
originally published in magazines, notably the *New Yorker*, and
his essentially bleak look on life was often tempered with
irony and sardonic humour.

The Stories of John Cheever won the Pulitzer Prize for
Fiction and included such well-known tales as *The Swimmer*
(which was made into a movie starring Burt Lancaster in 1968).
This is a blending of the real and surreal, the story of a man
whose physical and emotional decline is tracked, as he attempts
to swim his way home through the pools of his suburban set and
public pools, only to find that he has repressed the knowledge
that he has already lost everything and his home is empty
when he reaches it.

It was later revealed that Cheever had struggled to come to
terms with his own bisexuality and it has been suggested that
the duality of much of his work reflects, in part, his own search
for wholeness in his identity.

JOHN CHEEVER
1912 – 1982
Nationality: American
First Published: Knopf, 1978
Other Selected Titles:
*The Way Some People Live: A Book
of Short Stories*
*The Enormous Radio and Other
Stories*
The Day the Pig Fell Into the Well
The Wapshot Chronicle
*The Housebreaker at Shady Hill
and Other Stories*
The Wapshot Scandal
Bullet Park
The Leaves, the Lionfish and the Bear

*John Cheever in his study,
New York, 1977.*

Disgrace

J.M. COETZEE
1940 –
Nationality: South African
First Published: Secker & Warburg, 1999
Other Selected Titles:
Dusklands
In the Heart of the Country
Life & Times of Michael K
Age of Iron
The Master of Petersburg
The Lives of Animals
Elizabeth Costello
Slow Man

South African writer J.M. Coetzee is both winner of the Nobel Prize for Literature (2003) and twice-winner of the Booker Prize, the second for his novel *Disgrace*. Coetzee's work, and *Disgrace* is no exception, is driven by the responsibility he feels to address the effects of Western political and economic colonialism, post-colonialism and its bitter consequences.

David Lurie, a professor of Romantic fiction at the University of Cape Town, is disgraced by an affair with a student and takes refuge on the subsistence farm of his daughter Lucy, with whom relations are strained. Here, Lucy is raped and he is horribly injured in a brutal attack engineered by black farmer Petrus, in a successful bid to control the land they work together. Lucy does not report the rape and both she and Lurie submit to the new order and come to terms with a new morality, no longer informed by the colonial and post-colonial romanticism of the very works he teaches.

As a Postmodern writer, Coetzee is enormously versatile, attacking his theme from every platform, in a variety of styles. *Disgrace* is written in a bleak, spare style and though immensely truthful it could not be called an optimistic book.

WINNER OF THE 1999 BOOKER PRIZE

J.M.Coetzee

DISGRACE

'Exhilarating...One of the best novelists alive'
SUNDAY TIMES

Chéri

Colette (right) with film star Edwige Feuillere.

**COLETTE
(SIDONIE-GABRIELLE COLETTE)**
1873 – 1954
Nationality: French
First Published: Fayard, 1920
Other Selected Titles:
*La Vagabonde
La Paix Chez les Bêtes
Mitsou
La Fin de Chéri
Le Pur et L'Impur
La Chatte
Gigi
Le Fanal Bleu*

Chéri is the story of the end of a six-year affair between the exquisite middle-aged Léa, a wealthy courtesan reaching the end of her career, and Chéri, a 26-year-old man, the illegitimate son of her friend Charlotte. The story is set in Paris just before the First World War, and in many ways, Léa and her life of sensual, civilized pleasure, at the epicentre of intellectual life, society and fashion, can be seen as a metaphor for pre-war Paris itself.

In this beautifully crafted novel, we see the end of the affair from both Chéri and Léa's perspectives, as Chéri enters an arranged marriage with his 18-year-old bride. Both, Chéri and Léa knew that the change was inevitable and had built strong emotional defences against its coming, of which the sensual pleasure of their relationship is an integral part. However, the barriers that they have erected make it impossible for them to recognize the real emotions of love and loss when they appear.

Chéri is partly autobiographical, and Colette calls on her own eventful life in the theatre and elsewhere to inform both the relationship, and the changing times in which the novel is set. The language is a delight and deeply evocative of the period.

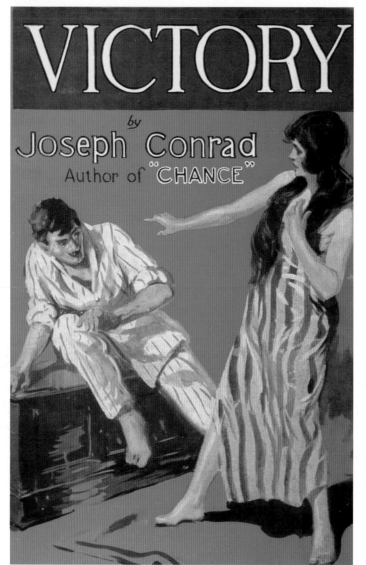

Victory

The remote, largely unpopulated island of Samburan in the East Indies is the setting for *Victory*, arguably Conrad's last great novel. His familiar passionate, dense prose is deftly used to explore his abiding themes of good versus evil, and innocence versus corruption, set against an exotic background in which East and West may skirmish, and around which his love of the sea, as ever, flows.

When Heyst's boss dies, he is actually and emotionally marooned, with only the seldom seen and rarely heard Wang and his Chinese wife. His occasional forays to a nearby island and the company of hotelkeeper Schomberg lead him to meet Lena, a young performer in the ladies' orchestra. The predatory Schomberg loathes Heyst and lustfully pursues Lena, until Heyst whisks her away to Samburan. Here, they live together in love and innocence until Schomberg wreaks his revenge, directing a desperate trio – Mr Jones, 'gentleman', Martin Ricardo, aggressive Latino, and Pedro his Neanderthal sidekick – to the island to relieve Heyst of a treasure Schomberg has invented.

Often considered to be the literary bridge between 19th-century Realism and early Modernism, Conrad tells a moving and compelling story of the ambiguities of human relationships.

JOSEPH CONRAD
1857 – 1924
Nationality: Polish
First Published: Methuen and Co., 1915
Other Selected Titles:
Almayer's Folly
Heart of Darkness
Lord Jim
Nostromo
The Secret Agent
The Shadow Line
The Rescue
The Rover

A House and Its Head

First published in 1935, *A House and Its Head*, like all Ivy Compton-Burnett's novels, expresses almost everything in terms of plot and characterization within the apparently boundless, yet narrow confines of conventional conversation. Every clue as to the interlocked fates of the characters is there for the discerning reader to see from the outset.

The eponymous head of the house, Duncan Edgeworth, is revealed from his first words or lack of them, to be a despotic, self-satisfied, arrogant, domestic tyrant to his first wife Ellen, his two daughters Nance and Sybil, and his nephew Grant. The characters of these five, and others, are seen through the everyday exchanges of a family in the airless, civilized domesticity of a Victorian household, in which death and duplicity await.

Ivy Compton-Burnett's manifest skill lies not only in her unusual and merciless ear for dialogue, but also in its pace and nuance, its crossings out and overwriting and for the spaces and silences in between the words. This facility would seem more appropriate to the cinema than to the written word, and yet it works perfectly.

Hugely entertaining, frighteningly chilling, brilliant in its observation, this book is a masterly study in the alliances, battles and mortal blows of family life.

IVY COMPTON-BURNETT
1884 – 1967
Nationality: English
First Published: William Heinemann, 1935
Other Selected Titles:
Pastors and Masters
Men and Wives
A Family and a Fortune
Elders and Betters
Manservant and Maidservant
The Present and the Past
The Mighty and Their Fall
The Last and the First

Dame Ivy Compton-Burnett sitting at her desk.

"Davies' trilogy is one of the splendid literary enterprises of the decade." - NEWSWEEK

WILLIAM ROBERTSON DAVIES
1913 – 1995
Nationality: Canadian
First Published: Macmillan, 1970
Other Selected Titles:
The Salterton Trilogy
The Deptford Trilogy
The Cornish Trilogy
The Toronto Trilogy
High Spirits

Fifth Business

'...those roles which, being neither those of Hero or Heroine, Confidante or Villain, but which were nonetheless essential to bring about the recognition or the denouement, were called the Fifth Business in drama...'

'...opera companies organized according to the old style; the player who acted these parts was often referred to as Fifth Business.'

These quotes from Robertson Davies' brilliant and best-known novel, the first in the Deptford Trilogy, describe its premise. Dunstable 'Dunny' Ramsey begins his life story as he ducks to avoid a snowball thrown by his boyhood friend Percy Boy Staunton. It hits a young woman and precipitates the premature birth of Paul Dempsey. At once, both Dunny and the event are established as 'Fifth Business'.

Dunny's guilt-induced relationship with the singular Mrs Dempsey sees her apparent decline into madness... or sainthood. Robertson Davies then explores how a saint would be received in a small town in Ontario in the early years of the 20th century. Paul, Percy and Dunny's lives remain intricately intertwined, leading Dunny to Europe, Percy to wealth and status, and Paul to run away with a travelling circus. Jungian archetypes, faultless, wryly humourous prose, erudition, magic and mythology characterize this Canadian masterpiece.

Captain Corelli's Mandolin

This beautiful love story is set on the Greek island of Cephalonia during the Second World War and the detested Italian occupation. *Captain Corelli's Mandolin* was published in 1994, and was awarded the Commonwealth Writer's Prize for Best Book. De Bernières skillfully juxtaposes tender passion and the hope of future dreams with the reality of the horrors and pain inflicted by the war on the civilian population.

The story is centred around Pelagia, the daughter of the local doctor, who is engaged to a handsome local fisherman, Mandras. The couple are inevitably separated when the war breaks out and Mandras enlists. Subsequently, Pelagia is thrown together with the sensitive, music-loving Captain Corelli, an Italian artillery officer.

Amidst a cast of beautifully drawn characters, their romance blossoms slowly, as Corelli attempts to win Pelagia's trust for him as a man, even as she must despise him as the enemy. In part, the book is an exploration of how individuals share a common humanity, which draws them together even as bloody war and national allegiances tear them apart.

LOUIS DE BERNIERES
1954 –
Nationality: British
First Published: Secker & Warburg, 1994
Other Selected Titles:
The War of Don Emmanuel's Nether Parts
Señor Vivo and the Coca Lord
The Troublesome Offspring of Cardinal Guzman
Labels
Red Dog
Sunday Morning at the Centre of the World
Birds Without Wings

LOUIS DE BERNIÈRES

Captain Corelli's Mandolin

Underworld

DON DELILLO
1936 –
Nationality: American
First Published: Scribner, 1997
Other Selected Titles:
Americana
End Zone
Ratner's Star
Running Dog
White Noise
Libra
The Body Artist
Cosmopolis

This author is respected as a leading proponent of American Postmodernism. *Underworld* is a monumental epic work, weighing in at over 800 pages.

The story takes place over 40 years, travelling through the Cold War years when Americans felt under threat of nuclear attack. The earliest scene is set in 1951, in New York City at a baseball game, where a famous home run has been hit. Simultaneously, the Russians are testing the atomic bomb. The story then jumps forward to 1992 when the reader is introduced to the protagonist Nick Shay, a middle-aged businessman who has bought the very same baseball.

The plot weaves back and forth between these two dates, introducing characters and vignettes along the way, that together describe, reflect and ultimately epitomize America during these decades.

DeLillo's descriptive and fragmented style requires concentration and its messages about the post-Cold War world are disturbing. This is not designed to be a comfortable read but it is truly a great one.

Don DeLillo in Paris, 1992.

Seven Gothic Tales

Countess Karen Blixen in Copenhagen, 1959.

This magical collection of short stories was written on Karen's return from Africa to her home in Denmark. Karen threw herself into writing, and it is thought she deliberately chose to write under a male nom de plume to make her work more acceptable. This was proved so. *Seven Gothic Tales* was published in 1934 amid much literary acclaim. Indeed it is said to have inspired Angela Carter's later magical realistic gothic style.

This medley of tales is set in the early 1800s lending a mood of authenticity to its gothic and mystical style. The very names themselves are reminiscent of folklore: *The Deluge at Norderney*, *The Roads Round Pisa*, *The Supper at Elsinore*, *The Poet*, *The Dreamers*, *The Monkey*, and *The Old Chevalier*. However, these are not pure whimsy, each is making a very real statement about feminism, sexuality and dreams.

Written in an enchanting and lyrical style these tales are made to be read and re-read.

ISAK DINESEN
also known as
KAREN BLIXEN
1885 – 1962
Nationality: Danish
First Published: Harrison Smith and
Robert Haas, 1934
Other Selected Titles:
Out of Africa
Winter's Tales
The Angelic Avengers
Last Tales
Shadows of the Grass

Berlin Alexanderplatz

In his early work, Döblin was known for his expressionism, particularly in his short stories. In the 1920s he moved on to adopt and develop a narrative style using colloquial language as a vehicle to develop his characters. This is often referred to as the 'James Joyce' style with characters representing a number of different viewpoints. *Berlin Alexanderplatz* was the first German novel of this genre, and was an immediate and sustained success.

The story is contemporaneously set in a working class part of Berlin. The main protagonist Franz Biberkopf has just been released from prison for manslaughter. He is determined to stay clean and lead a decent life. This story follows his journey into a world of unemployment and vice. Franz falls into bad company and events conspire against him.

A masterpiece of German literature and a towering achievement of its era!

ALFRED DOBLIN
1878 – 1957
Nationality: German
First Published: S. Fischer Verlag,
1929
Other Selected Titles:
Die Ermordung Einer Butterblume
Das Land Ohne Tod
November
Hamlet, Oder Die Lange Nacht Nimmt
Ein Ende

Once Were Warriors

This is a powerful tale of a Maori family struggling to make their way in life. But it is only when they re-establish their cultural roots that they can move forward. This theme resounds with a universal truth for everyone, the need for a sense of belonging and self respect.

The story centres on the Heke family. Beth, the mother, comes from the old warrior stock, and labours to hold the family together. Jack, the father, is a descendent of the freed slaves, and a violent alcoholic. They have five children, and as the story unfolds we learn of their individual problems and their vulnerabilities. The story reaches a climax in tragedy, which is the catalyst for Beth to find an inner strength and commitment to herself and to her people.

Duff's creative use of dialect and language makes this a truly compelling read.

ALAN DUFF
1950 –
Nationality: New Zealand
First Published: Tandem, 1990
Other Selected Titles:
One Night out Stealing
Books in Homes
What Becomes of the Broken Hearted
Two Sides of the Moon
Jakes Long Shadow

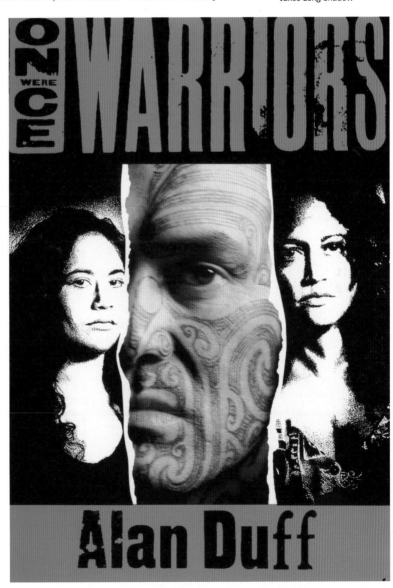

Rebecca

DAPHNE DU MAURIER
1907 – 1989
Nationality: British
First Published: V. Gollancz, 1938
Other Selected Titles:
Jamaica Inn
Frenchman's Creek
Hungry Hill
The Birds
Don't Look Now

Du Maurier's favourite authors were the Brontë sisters, and the plot and pace of *Rebecca* are reminiscent of *Jane Eyre*. Often considered a mid-brow, romantic gothic novel, this compelling read surprises us by its depth of understanding of the psychology of the mind, and its ability to haunt itself.

It is set evocatively in the wilds of Cornwall, in a large country house called Manderly. One of Du Maurier's devices that so intrigue us is her tantalizing refusal to name her heroine who recounts the story in the first person. The second Mrs De Winter has a timid nature, allowing her to be dominated by her older husband, Maxim, the terrifying Mrs Danvers and the manifest perfection of the late first Mrs De Winter… Rebecca.

The suspense builds as events lead to her increasing obsession with the beautiful Rebecca, and the circumstances surrounding her death. As a terrible truth is revealed, the heroine, rather than collapsing, discovers an inner strength and confidence. This leads to a shift in power between De Winter and his young wife.

This is an enjoyable romantic suspense thriller for all book lovers.

The Lover

Duras was a contemporary artist acclaimed not just as a writer, but also as a filmmaker. In the 1950s she embraced the *Nouveau Roman* literary genre and from this period her work was increasingly recognized and successful. Over time, her style developed, using less dialogue and becoming increasingly minimalist. What is not said is as important as what is.

Her early life had an enormous impact on her work and writings. Born in Saigon to a French ex-patriot family, her father died when she was a young child and her mother struggled to raise Marguerite and her two siblings.

The Lover is believed to be an autobiographical account of her unhappy adolescence. It is a bitter-sweet love story set in Indochina during the 1930s and focuses on two protagonists, a young French girl in her mid teens and a wealthy Chinese businessman. The novel is about innocence lost, and the cultural taboos faced by the couple.

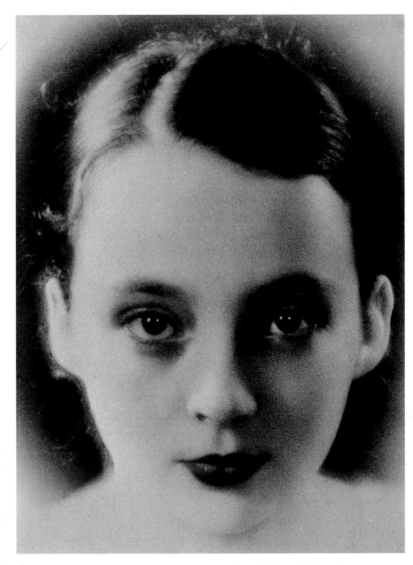

Writer and filmmaker Marguerite Duras.

MARGUERITE DURAS
also known as
MARGUERITE DONNADIEU
1914 – 1996
Nationality: French
First Published: Editions de Minuit, 1984
Other Selected Titles:
Un Barrage Contre le Pacifique
Le Marin de Gibraltar
Le Square
Moderato Cantabtle,
La Viacus de la Seine et Oise
Hiroshima Mon Amour

The Alexandria Quartet

This much acclaimed tetralogy published between 1957 and 1960 consists of *Justine* (1957), *Balthazar* (1958) *Mountolive* (1958) and *Clea* (1960). In these four vivid novels, Durrell uses an innovative Postmodernist style, recounting a set of events experienced by the same protagonists but from different perspectives. Each book reveals a little more of the whole truth of the matter, and ends in a death.

The overarching themes centre on love, lust and politics. The novels are set just before the Second World War in the exotic city of Alexandria, with its ancient Egyptian and Hellenic overtones.

The main characters include Darley (the narrator and a poet), his mistress Melissa, Justine (a free-loving Jewess) married to Nessim, Clea, Pursewarden (the brilliant novelist) and Mountolive (the British Ambassador). Together and individually they express the full range of passions, emotions and in some cases perversions.

Durrell's use of rich, exotic and even extravagant descriptions make this read a sumptuous banquet.

LAWRENCE GEORGE DURRELL
1912 – 1980
Nationality: British
First Published: Faber & Faber, 1957–60
Other Selected Titles:
Pied Piper of Lovers
Panic Spring (penned as Charles Norden)
The Black Book
The Dark Labyrinth
White Eagles Over Serbia
The Revolt of Aphrodite
The Avignon Quintet

The Name of the Rose

This novel is a multi-layered labyrinth of a book which, in the Postmodern tradition, mixes a number of genres to great effect. At its most fundamental level it is a gripping murder mystery, reminiscent curiously of Conan Doyle's Sherlock Holmes. Eco makes imaginative use of stories within stories, intertwining fact with fiction and planting clues to weave this haunting gothic tapestry of intrigue.

UMBERTO ECO
1932 –
Nationality: Italian
First Published: Bompiani, 1980
Other Selected Titles:
Foucault's Pendulum
The Island of the Day Before
Baudolino
The Mysterious Flame of
Queen Loana

The events take place during the early 14th century in northern Italy. This is a period of particular unrest for the Roman Catholic Church.

The plot centres on William of Baskerville, an English Franciscan monk, who travels with his apprentice Adso to an unnamed Benedictine monastery famous for its library.

The Abbot and librarian seek to control and keep secret the contents of many of the books held within the hidden maze of chambers. Is this to protect the monks' forbidden heresies? Or is it that knowledge is power?

A murder has already taken place at the monastery when William arrives and it is by no means the last. The monks believe that they are experiencing the second coming of Christ. William alone is convinced that there must be a logical and physical explanation for the happenings, rather than a demonic one.

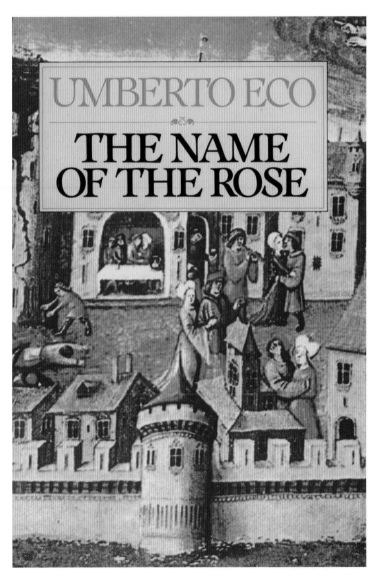

THE CAPTIVATING INTERNATIONAL BESTSELLER

THE NEVERENDING STORY

MICHAEL ENDE

TRANSLATED FROM THE GERMAN BY RALPH MANHEIM

MICHAEL ENDE
1929 – 1995
Nationality: German
First Published: Amereon, 1979
Other Selected Titles:
*Jim Button and Luke the Engine
Driver
Jim Button and the Wild 13
The Grey Gentlemen
Mirror in the Mirror
Ophelia's Shadow Theatre
The Night of Wishes*

The Neverending Story

Classic literature of the fantasy genre, this book explores the role of escapism in coming to terms with reality. The most famous of Michael Ende's books, it was originally published in German. Ende was renowned for writing fantasy novels and children's books.

The Neverending Story has been made into a popular children's film. However, the book with its fully detailed plot line and descriptive nuances also appeals to adults.

The main protagonist is Bastian, a young boy who loves to read. Bastian is lonely and isolated, finding it difficult to make friends and to socialize. One day he steals a book from an antique bookshop; returning to the attic of his old school he begins to read it. Through the book he travels to the magical world of Fantasia, where initially he is a voyeur.

However, through his own imagination Bastian eventually becomes a participant in the world he has discovered and has a role in saving the doomed Fantasia. Through these adventures, Bastian learns more about himself and how to live in the real world. This is a wonderfully satisfying and uplifting novel for readers of all ages.

The Sound and the Fury

'Life is a tale, told by an idiot, full of sound and fury, signifying nothing.' This quotation, from Shakespeare's *Macbeth*, forms the very basis of this, William Faulkner's acknowledged masterpiece.

This deeply haunting tale is told in four parts, each in the voice of its own narrator, with its own nuance and idiom. Benjy, the 33-year-old idiot son, Quentin the weak Harvard scholar, Jason, the selfish, greedy youngest boy, and their black servant Dilsey, each give their perspective on the decline of the southern aristocratic Compson family.

The first part is told in flashback through Benjy's disjointed memories, with the vocabulary and distractions of a retarded child, the second by Quentin and the third by Jason. Their absent sister Caddy's voice remains unheard though she is vital to the story. Instead, Dilsey's view is the last we read.

The Sound and the Fury is a tale told by a genius, reaching unforgettable and almost unbearably moving heights and depths of expression.

WILLIAM FAULKNER
1897 – 1962
Nationality: American
First Published: J. Cape & Harrison Smith, 1929
Other Selected Titles:
Sartoris
As I Lay Dying
Absalom, Absalom!
The Unvanquished
The Wild Palms
Go Down Moses
Knight's Gambit
The Reivers

William Faulkner's Underwood typewriter at his home in Mississippi.

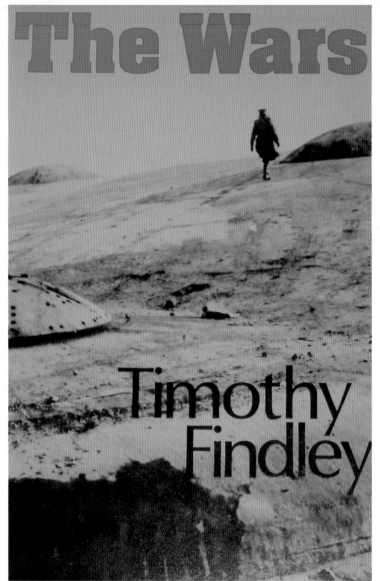

The Wars

Perhaps Findley's most widely known work, *The Wars* was published in 1977. This apocalyptic masterpiece explores the horror of war, and the depths of man's ability to inflict destruction and trauma on himself and other living creatures. All for no apparent purpose.

The book begins in the 1970s and is narrated by an objective researcher who is putting together the history of a Canadian officer, Robert Ross, and his participation in a significant event during the First World War.

As Ross' story unfolds we meet a sensitive and naive 19-year-old who is sent off across the sea to fight a war in Europe. The situations and events that Ross is faced with are increasingly shocking, random and violent. The world appears to have gone mad. Ross does all he can to save the lives of men and beasts, but even that is futile.

Findley's masterly description brings alive the poignancy of the Edwardian era and the indefensible horror of all wars.

TIMOTHY FINDLEY
1930 – 2002
Nationality: Canadian
First Published: Clarke and Irwin, 1977
Other Selected Titles:
The Butterfly Plague
Famous Last Words
Not Wanted on the Voyage
The Telling of Lies
Headhunter
The Piano Man's Daughter
Pilgrim
Spadework

The Good Soldier

Ford Maddox Ford's innovative novel, written in 1915, pioneered the use of flashbacks and somewhat disjointed plot lines that portend the Postmodern novel.

The plot centres around two apparently idyllic marriages. However, as it unfolds, both relationships are found to have unhappy secrets at their hearts. The main characters are John and Florence Dowell and Edward and Leonora Ashburnham. The couples know each other through their stays at a health spa. Florence and Edward are receiving treatment for heart conditions. Ford uses these ailments as an allegory, as their illnesses are not so much physical as emotional and spiritual. John Dowell, the book's narrator, reveals through non-chronological vignettes, a series of infidelities and the subsequent and tragic consequence.

This masterpiece of psychological drama portrays the damage caused by dysfunctional relationships, affecting all that come into emotional contact with them.

FORD MADDOX FORD
1873 – 1939
Nationality: British
First Published: The Bodley Head, 1915
Other Selected Titles:
The Cinque Ports
The Heart of the Country
Ladies Whose Bright Eyes
The Young Lovell
Between St Dennis and St George
Women and Men .
A Little Less Than Gods
Great Trade Route

Ford Maddox Ford, who served in the First World War.

Wildlife

RICHARD FORD
1944 –
Nationality: American
First Published: Atlantic Monthly Press, 1990
Other Selected Titles:
A Piece of My Heart
The Ultimate Good Luck
The Sportswriter
Independence Day

This is Richard Ford's fourth novel, written in 1990. He is perhaps better known for *Independence Day*, which won the Pulitzer Prize and Penn Prizes. Ford is often compared to Faulkner or Hemingway in that he holds a mirror up to American society and we see reflected in it and in the lives of the characters he creates, both the universal human condition and that of America's ordinary people. *Wildlife* is characterized by clear, tight, poetic, if a somewhat distant, narrative style. This reflects the overarching theme of the futility and sterility of unfulfilled lives.

The story is set in 1960, and is told in the first person, by Joe Brinson, a young man living with his parents. Like many of Ford's creations, he is caught at a moment of transience, having recently moved to Great Falls and not having made many friends. His father Jerry has recently lost his job, and becomes a fire fighter. He is sent off to fight a raging forest fire. In the few days he is gone, Joe's mother has an affair. The natural disaster serves as metaphor, too, for the explosive passions that the family must share.

'Every sentence Ford writes, illuminates...His prose is strong, clear and satisfying, resonant with the bleak rhythms of unrewarded lives' *Sunday Times*

RICHARD FORD

A Passage to India

Published in 1924 this was Forster's fifth and last novel published in his lifetime. The novel gestated between Forster's first and second visits to India in 1912 and 1921 respectively. This period also included the First World War, the start of Gandhi's Civil Disobedience campaign and the massacre at Amritsar. Although he claimed not, it is difficult to see how Forster's work could not have been informed by these events. Without doubt it is his most successful serious work, representing his view of the misunderstanding and conflict between classes and racial groups in the early 20th century.

Set in India during the days of the Raj, the key protagonists are the homely English woman, Adela Quested, and the idealistic Indian, Dr Aziz. Adela has come to India to marry her fiancé, a British officer. Dr Aziz has friends in the English community. The story consists of a series of hospitable events arranged to introduce Adela to the Indian community in which she will live. These progress with varying degrees of success, until Dr Aziz graciously offers to take the British visitors on a tour of the local caves.

While they are in the Marabar Caves, an incident takes place that forms the basis of the rest of the plot. Adela accuses Dr Aziz of assaulting her in the darkness. Dr Aziz is then brought to trial determined to clear his name. Although Adela realizes her mistake and withdraws her allegations, this incident heightens the tensions and deepens the misunderstandings between the British and the Indian communities.

E.M. Forster boards a plane for Italy in 1959.

E.M. FORSTER
1879 – 1970
Nationality: British
First Published: E. Arnold & Co., 1924
Other Selected Titles:
Where Angels Fear to Tread
The Longest Journey
A Room with a View
Howards End
The Celestial Omnibus
The Story of the Siren
Alexandria
Pharaos and Pharillon

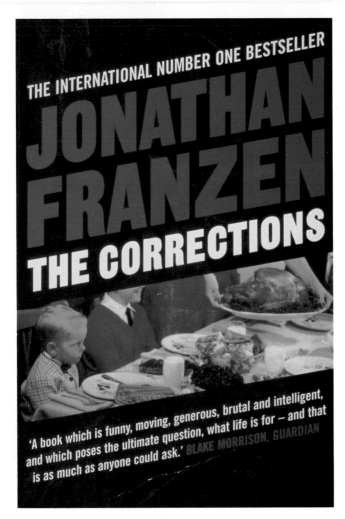

JONATHAN FRANZEN
1959 –
Nationality: American
First Published: Farrar, Straus &
Giroux, 2001
Other Selected Titles:
Strong Motion
How to Be Alone

The Corrections

Franzen's immense work of 21st-century American social criticism has been variously hailed as 'the Bleak House of the digital age' and 'hysterical realism', a sub-genre of Postmodern fiction, defined by 'chronic length, frenzied action, manic characters and a tendency to digress into other topics not central to the story'.

The Corrections does show these characteristics, but Franzen's appealing, intellectual style brings warmth and humanity to the epic tale of the dysfunctional Lambert family, and their attempt to meet for one last family Christmas; while simultaneously exploring the dark corners of globalization, the pharmaceutical industry, economic colonization and its effects on Central Europe and 21st-century university life.

Alfred and Enid Lambert and their three adult offspring, Gary, Chip and Denise, bear a heavy burden. Gary is navigating the straits of depression while trying to secure a happy family life; Chip is squaring his university tenure with his attraction to young girls and the inevitable consequences, and Denise is balancing her success as a chef with her undiscriminating sexual tastes and her mother's wish for her to settle down and marry. Enid has Alfred to bear, and he has Parkinson's disease.

This is a great work of modern literature, rightly popular with critics and the general public, but it is also a warm, funny, empathetic and courageous and hugely ambitious critique of modern times.

Birdsong

Sebastian Faulks' powerful novel, set in France before and during the First World War, received huge acclaim and achieved both literary and popular international success when it was published in 1993. It was deemed extraordinary for a writer as young as Faulks to treat both the period and the subject with such understanding, depth, scholarship and sensitivity.

In 1910, Stephen Wraysford arrives in Amiens as a guest of Monsieur Azaire and his family. He is there to study the French textile business, but he and his host's wife, Isabelle, fall passionately in love and begin an extraordinarily sensual and highly charged love affair, set against the stifling social mores of the time.

He returns six years later to Picardy, where as a young British officer he faces the profound horror of trench warfare and the matchless ferocity of the battles of the Marne, Verdun and the Somme. The wartime narrative centres on Wraysford, his friend Michael Weir, and a former miner Jack Firebrace, employed to blast the hellish labyrinth of tunnels in which mines are laid. Threaded through the narrative is the near present-day story of Wraysford's granddaughter, Elizabeth, who has discovered his coded diaries and is attempting to understand both her grandfather and the effects of the terrible and mindless war that shaped Europe.

Exquisitely written, devastatingly moving and disturbing, *Birdsong* is one of the best contemporary literary novels of the 20th century. Faulks explores the personal and the public human experiences of love, death and redemption for both men and women and the boundless endurance of the human spirit, amid the carnage and meaninglessness of war.

SEBASTIAN FAULKS
1953 –
Nationality: British
First Published: Hutchinson, 1993
Other Selected Titles:
A Trick of the Light
The Girl at the Lion D'Or
A Fool's Alphabet
Charlotte Gray
On Green Dolphin Street
Human Traces

Sebastian Faulks.

The Blue Flower

PENELOPE FITZGERALD
1916 – 2000
Nationality: British
First Published: Flamingo, 1995
Other Selected Titles:
The Golden Child
The Bookshop
Offshore
Human Voices
At Freddie's
Innocence
The Beginning of Spring
The Gate of Angels

The Blue Flower was probably Penelope Fitzgerald's masterpiece. A spare, yet perfect short novel, it won the Booker Prize in 1995 and helped to introduce one of the greatest British contemporary fiction authors to a wider American audience.

The novel is set in the age of Goethe, and is a fictional account of the 18th-century life of the Romantic poet, Novalis, and his love for a child.

Through the elegant, distinctive prose, at once surreal, ironic, comedic and morally sensitive that is characteristic of Fitzgerald, we learn of the mundane detail as well as the mercantile life of the late 1700s.

Fritz von Hardenberg, Novalis, is portrayed as a rather hapless innocent, whose inability to see anything but the object of his interest causes, albeit unknowingly, endless trouble to those around him. This is an abiding theme of Penelope Fitzgerald's. In the second half of the novel, she shifts the focus from Fritz to his 14-year-old fiancé, a TB sufferer who is otherwise rather dull. The subtlety of this transference is typical of Fitzgerald's consummate skill.

A beautiful book, beautifully written, in the highest tradition of English literature.

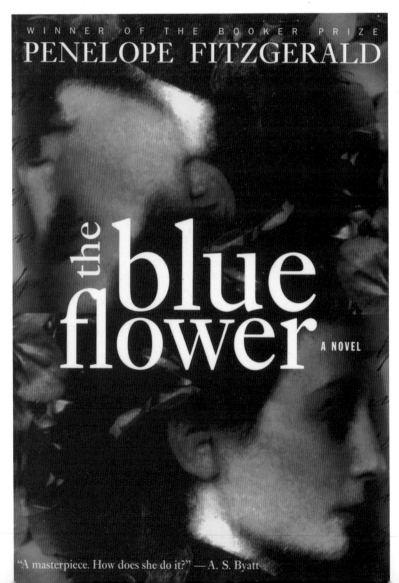

WINNER OF THE BOOKER PRIZE
PENELOPE FITZGERALD
the blue flower
A NOVEL

"A masterpiece. How does she do it?" — A. S. Byatt

From the Fifteenth District

From the Fifteenth District is a gem-like collection of short stories from this consummate storyteller. Canadian by birth, Gallant has lived in Europe since the 1950s and many of her stories feature ex-patriates. It is as if people, for all their bravado and concealed vulnerability, are even more themselves when taken out of their natural milieu. Always exquisitely observed and wryly humourous, this collection is a joy to read.

Set in Europe in the lasting shadow cast by the end of the Second World War, the nine stories contain and reflect on all manner of human relationships. An actor, once a soldier in Algeria, struggles with his new vocation in Paris; a family escape the poverty and rationing of England for the sake of their father's health in the South of France; a group of English ex-patriots cannot imagine how their life on the Italian Riviera should be affected by Mussolini or Hitler.

It is the wealth of detail and texture that make Gallant's writing so unique. Her characters are never set adrift without a context both immediate and in the wider world and yet every word is selected with great care and not one is wasted.

MAVIS GALLANT
1922 –
Nationality: Canadian
First Published: Macmillan, 1978
Other Selected Titles:
The Other Paris
My Heart Is Broken
The End of the World and Other Stories
In Transit
Across the Bridge

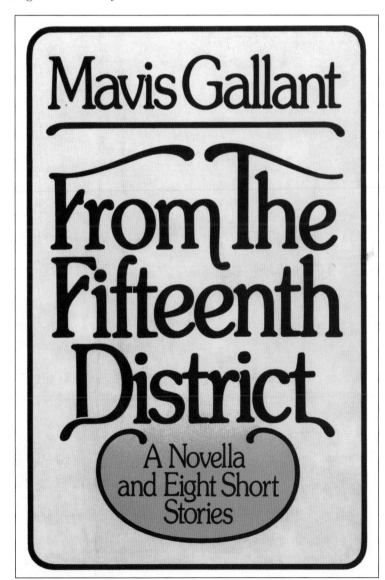

Mavis Gallant

From The Fifteenth District

A Novella and Eight Short Stories

285

One Hundred Years of Solitude

GABRIEL GARCÍA MÁRQUEZ
1928 –
Nationality: Colombian
First Published: Sudamericana, 1967
Other Selected Titles:
In Evil Hour
The Autumn of the Patriarch
Chronicle of a Death Foretold
Love in the Time of Cholera
The General in his Labyrinth
Of Love and Other Demons

This masterpiece of Postmodern fiction brought the extraordinary contemporary writing of this Colombian Nobel Laureate in literature to the wider world. It is an intensely personal work, drawing upon the politics, history, culture, myth, magic and ghosts that formed the background to Márquez's life growing up in Colombia.

One Hundred Years of Solitude is the history of Macondo, a fictional small town in an unspecified area of South America, from its beginnings, to its ultimate obliteration, when the last member of the seventh generation of the founding Buendía family finally translates the parchment that predicted the town's circular history. One of the features of the narrative is the way time changes, speeding up and slowing down, and moving in circles. The names of the protagonists are also repeated in each generation in variations of those of the founders. José Arcadio Buendía, a strong man with a passion for science (fired by Melquíades, the leader of a gypsy band, who recurs throughout) eventually goes mad and must be tied to a tree, while his wife Úrsula Iguarán lives to be over 130, having slowly shrunk to the size of a foetus. Their distinct physical and intellectual characteristics are also varied and repeated in each generation.

One Hundred Years of Solitude is known for its use of magical realism as well as the immense power, humour and beauty of its writing.

One hundred
years of
solitude

Gabriel
García
Márquez

Controversial writer and activist Jean Genet.

Our Lady of the Flowers

Our Lady of the Flowers was the debut novel of French existentialist, political activist, novelist, filmmaker, playwright and thief Jean Genet. Most of Genet's writing, and this brilliant first work is no exception, deals with the struggle and search for personal identity.

As an open and vociferous homosexual and a chronicler of outcasts and those who are marginalized, Genet challenged the notion of 'stable identities'. *Our Lady of the Flower*s was written while Genet was in prison, and the manuscript was confiscated more than once.

Narrated by Genet it is the explicit story of a homosexual prostitute Louis Culafroy on the streets of Paris and his erotic adventures with Gabriel, the soldier, the thief and pimp, Darling Daintyfoot, and the murderer, the eponymous Our Lady of the Flowers.

Genet's writing was a deliberate challenge to the sensibilities of the establishment, expressed in an explicit and unexpurgated sexual and erotic vocabulary. It can also be seen as Genet's imaginative triumph over the pain of his incarceration.

JEAN GENET
1910 – 1986
Nationality: French
First Published: L'Arbalete 1943
Other Selected Titles:
Miracle de la Rose
Pompes Funèbres
Querelle de Brest
Un Captif Amoureux

287

Lord of the Flies

WILLIAM GOLDING
1911 – 1993
Nationality: British
First Published: Faber & Faber, 1954
Other Selected Titles:
The Inheritors
The Brass Butterfly
Free Fall
The Spire
Darkness Visible
A Moving Target
The Paper Men
To the Ends of the Earth (a trilogy)

Although written in 1954 at the start of the Cold War, the significance of this book was not acknowledged until 1983, when Golding won a Pulitzer Prize. The book depicts Golding's view that man's inhumanity to man can only be controlled through imposed social order. In his allegorical world, he uses children, before maturity and experience and the bounds of convention can dictate their behaviour, to represent the true nature of man.

The story centres on a group of schoolboys (5–12 years of age), marooned on an island after their plane crashes. They were being evacuated from Britain during an atomic war. The only adult, the pilot, has died. In the beginning, the boys establish order through election of leaders and allocation of roles and responsibilities as they have seen adults do, and in imitation of the society from which they have come.

Soon their behaviour degenerates into competitive aggression between leaders and the bullying of the weak and different. The boys create a religion based on fear, symbolized by the beastie (a dead parachutist). This leads to a nightmare world of 'packing' behaviour, ritual murder and anarchy. It is only when a ship arrives, symbolizing society, that the boys revert to civilized behaviour and order is re-established.

July's People

Nadine Gordimer was born in 1923 in the Transvaal, and campaigned tirelessly as a prominent anti-apartheid campaigner in South Africa. She has received many honours including the Nobel Prize for Literature (1991).

July's People was written in 1981 and is one of Gordimer's finest novels dealing with the politics and morality of apartheid. The story is set in a fictional future when the whites have given up South Africa and Johannesburg has become a place of extreme violence. A liberal white family, the Smales, are forced to flee the city for the sanctuary of the countryside. They are led to safety and given refuge by their black servant, July.

July's People is a rich descriptive narrative in which Gordimer characteristically also explores the search for identity, and the varied experience of love, in the dynamics of the change in relationship between the Smales and July. She also turns the searchlight of fiction on the politics of real life. This is revealed from every perspective as the power is seen to shift from white to black African.

This is a wonderful novel, speaking for both the white and the black South Africans who could not speak for themselves, and capturing the atmosphere, fears and impact of apartheid in South Africa.

Nelson Mandela and Nadine Gordimer sing the National Liberation Anthem at Ghandi Memorial, 1993.

NADINE GORDIMER
1923 –
Nationality: South African
First Published: Jonathan Cape, 1981
Other Selected Titles:
The Lying Days
Occasion for Loving
A Guest of Honour
The Conservationist
My Son's Story
The House Gun
The Pickup
Get a Life

FerdyDurke

WITOLD GOMBROWICZ
1904 – 1969
Nationality: Polish
First Published: Towarzystwo
Wydawnicze Roj, 1937
Other Selected Titles:
Trans-Atlantyk
Pornografia
Kosmos

*Witold Gombrowicz in
Paris, 1967.*

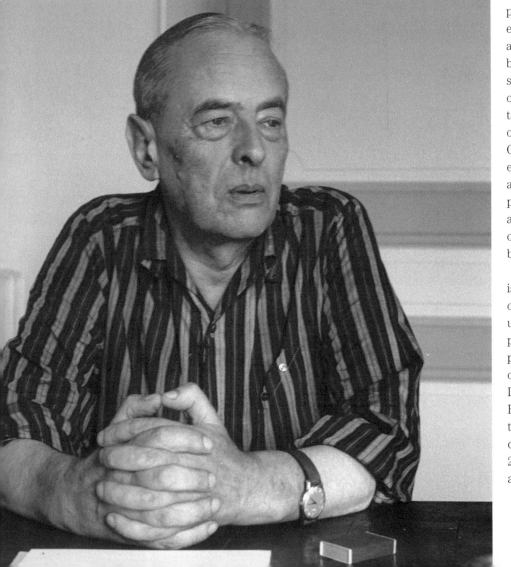

Witold Gombrowicz now enjoys a large cult following, yet for much of his career his work was relatively unrecognized. His work was banned by the Polish authorities and he spent many years in exile in Argentina and France. FerdyDurke is a darkly satirical comedy which is considered to be a triumph of European Modernism

Joey Kawalski, a 30-year-old writer, is the narrator of this story told in the first person. Under the hypnotism of an evil professor, regression takes him back to his teenage years and school. As the plot unfolds, he experiences again all the angst, bullying and sexual awakening of adolescence. In telling the story of Joey's life, Gombrowicz explores identity and cultural and political mores and the shaping of people's lives by form.

Gombrowicz is known for his original and unique use of playful prose and pastiche in the original Polish. Danuta Borchardt's translation, completed in 2002, is highly acclaimed.

The Tin Drum

Günter Grass is often lauded as the spokesman for a generation of Germans who grew up during the Nazi era. In 1999, he received the Nobel Prize for Literature, but it was his explosive debut novel *The Tin Drum* which took the literary world by storm.

This is the autobiography of Oskar Matzerath, and is, we are told, written in a sanatorium in the early 1950s, but it begins in Poland in the 1900s when Oskar's mother marries Alfred, a shopkeeper. Oskar, however, may be the child of an affair with her cousin Jan. At the age of three, Oskar decides as an act of will and of protest at the stupidity and wickedness of adults that he will not grow, and communicates largely through his tin drum, from which he is inseparable.

The Tin Drum is a marvellously memorable novel, both for the treatment of its subject, and for the richness of the images, the ironic humour and wit of the text, the power of the writing and the towering, enlightened imagination of its author.

GÜNTER GRASS
1927 –
Nationality: German
First Published: Luchterhand, 1959
Other Selected Titles:
Cat and Mouse
Dog Years
From the Diary of a Snail
The Flounder
Show Your Tongue
The Call of the Toad
Crabwalk

Hunger

KNUT HAMSUN
1859 – 1952
Nationality: Norwegian
First Published: Philipsen, 1890
Other Selected Titles:
Mysteries
Shallow Soil
The Game of Life
Dreamers
Under the Autumn Star
Wayfarers
The Ring is Closed
On Overgrown Paths

Hamsun is one of the foremost Norwegian authors, known for his creative and beautiful use of his native language. This is readily discernible too, in the English translation of *Hunger*, with its poignant descriptions and dry comic wit. Written in 1890, this is not his first novel, but was his first successful work.

The story is semi-autobiographical, centring on a young impoverished writer who goes to Oslo (then Christiania) to earn a living. As winter approaches, he struggles to establish himself both as a writer and in the metropolis. Through an introspective dialogue, we experience his physical deprivations without food or shelter, and how this affects him mentally and psychologically, leaving him isolated in a world that seems to him, not to care whether he lives or dies, and even less about his sanity.

Divided into four sections, which Hamsun described as analyses, this novel also reflects his impatience and disapproval of the alienation of the modern industrial city. Hamsun is sometimes seen as the forerunner of Kafka and was influenced by both Dostoyevsky and Emile Zola.

This 19th-century journey with its early Modernist concentration on the individual's psychology being representative of the society as a whole, is great literature and well worth reading in the 21st century.

Norwegian Knut Hamsun had many jobs in the United States before becoming a writer.

The Blind Owl √E

This extraordinarily powerful, beautifully written, poetic and haunting story is considered to be both a masterpiece of Iranian and World literature, and the consummate work of its author Hedayat who tragically committed suicide in 1951. *The Blind Owl* was the first work of fiction written in Farsi to be translated and available internationally. Originally published in Bombay (Mumbai), it was not published in Iran until 1941.

A nameless young painter of miniatures feels compelled to relate the nightmare that his life has become to his shadow on the wall, which looks like an owl. He is haunted by visions of the subjects of his paintings, a beautiful young woman, an old man and a cypress tree, who become inextricably intertwined with his feverish, opium-fuelled, nightmare of death ever present and constantly calling.

Hedayat's work was unique in Iranian literature between the wars because it was not informed by romanticism and ideology but was a Modernist search for truth within a secular critique of contemporary life in Iran.

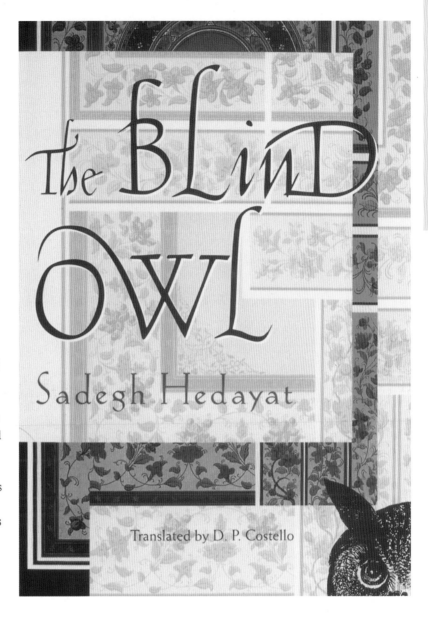

SADEGH HEDAYAT
1903 – 1951
Nationality: Iranian
First Published: 1937
Other Selected Titles:
Chiaroscuro
Mongol Shadow
Three Drops of Blood
The Stray Dog
The Elixir of Life
Tomorrow
The Pearl Cannon

The Old Man and the Sea

The Old Man and the Sea received mixed critical reviews when it was published in 1952, after a difficult ten-year period for Hemingway's work.

One critic claimed that he had raised his thesis of manhood to a religion; others hailed it as a work of genius. But the public loved the novella, and it certainly contributed to Hemingway receiving the Nobel Prize for Literature in 1954.

Santiago, an aging Cuban fisherman, has not caught a fish for 84 days, and even the family of his apprentice Manolin has encouraged the boy to leave the old fisherman, though Manolin continues to support him with food and bait. Santiago, convinced that his luck must change, takes his skiff far out into the Gulf Stream, where the water is very deep, and hooks a giant marlin. With all his great experience and strength, he struggles with the fish for two days and two nights...

Hemingway's trademark minimalist and spare writing with a stoical protagonist at the heart of the narrative, which saw him lauded as a great writer and major influence in 20th-century literature, is evident in this the last work of fiction he ever wrote.

Ernest Hemingway (left) with Fidel Castro in Cuba, 1960.

ERNEST HEMINGWAY
1899 – 1961
Nationality: American
First Published: C. Scribner's Sons, 1952
Other Selected Titles:
*The Sun Also Rises
A Farewell to Arms
To Have and Have Not
For Whom the Bell Tolls
Adventures of a Young Man
Islands in the Stream
The Garden of Eden*

The Glass Bead Game

The Glass Bead Game was Nobel Prize-winning German author Hermann Hesse's magnus opus, taking him over ten years to write. It is an extraordinarily complex novel, and although this is a great simplification, its central thesis asks whether those who specialize in the pursuit and perfection of knowledge for its own sake have a right to isolate themselves from the real world and its very real concerns. This was an extremely pertinent question in Germany between 1931 and 1943.

HERMANN HESSE
1877 – 1962
Nationality: German
First Published: Fretz & Wasmuth, 1943
Other Selected Titles:
Knulp
Demian
Strange News from Another Star
Klingsor's Last Summer
Siddhartha
Steppenwolf
Narcissus and Goldmund
One Hour After Midnight

In the imaginary province of Castalia, an order of monastic academics and intellectuals has perfected an ancient and complicated game which tests the synthesis of all knowledge. The players are required to make connections between unconnected abstract ideas as diverse as music and mathematics, and although the game might once have been played with glass tokens resembling an abacus it is now played with a series of formulae.

The book takes place in a distant future and is related by a future historian. In the course of the book, the relationships between abstract scholarship and useful labour, East and West, are explored in the relationships between individuals.

Of itself, *The Glass Bead Game* is a work of great breadth, scholarship and erudition.

A new translation of **Magister Ludi** by Richard and Clara Winston

Lost Horizon

JAMES HILTON
1900 – 1954
Nationality: English
First Published: Morrow, 1933
Other Selected Titles:
Catherine Herself
Goodbye, Mr. Chips
Random Harvest

This book has been hugely popular since it was written in 1933; indeed it has its place in the Hall of Fame as the first paperback to be published (1939). Even before its softcover debut, Frank Capra had made it into a film. President Roosevelt also named his retreat 'Shangri-la' after the utopian world described in the novel. (This is the same retreat now known as Camp David). *Lost Horizon* is an enchanting, fantasy adventure that can also be seen as a meditation as the gathering clouds of the Second World War loomed.

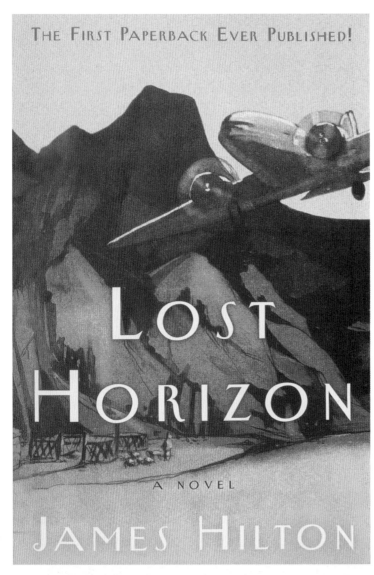

THE FIRST PAPERBACK EVER PUBLISHED!

LOST HORIZON

A NOVEL

JAMES HILTON

Lost Horizon is set in the Tibetan mountains where a plane crashes, leaving the four survivors stranded. They are Hugh Conway, a long-serving British diplomat, his assistant Mallinson, the evangelical Miss Brinklow and Barnard, an American. They are found by natives and taken to a green idyllic lamasery high in the mountains called Shangri-la, where the inhabitants live to a great old age.

The story as it unfolds recounts the spiritual journeys of these four, but particularly that of Conway. Here he discovers tranquillity, love and a sense of purpose that his life has lacked. Slowly, each sees and learns more of the Eastern philosophy epitomized by everything in moderation; and the value of contemplation – achieved by doing nothing.

This is also a tale of paradise lost, or perhaps it was always just an illusion? A magical read!

A High Wind in Jamaica ✓

Entitled *The Voyage of the Innocent* for the US market, this is the most famous of Hughes' four novels. On the surface, it is a sardonic fantasy adventure about seven English schoolchildren accidentally kidnapped by pirates during the 18th century. However, Hughes uses this vehicle to make a more serious allusion to the amorality and assumed innocence of children.

The story is told from the children's perspective as they spend weeks on the pirate ship. They slowly adjust to their new environment and freedom, even becoming attached to Captain Jonsen. Not only are the children no longer under parental control, but the adults are themselves children at heart.

Interestingly, Hughes extends this to freeing them from sexual stereotypes; the girls are able to cut their hair and play as the boys do. Then a tragic event occurs and there are misunderstandings over who is responsible that in turn lead to a miscarriage of justice.

A beautifully written masterpiece that explores the concept of the true innocence of children.

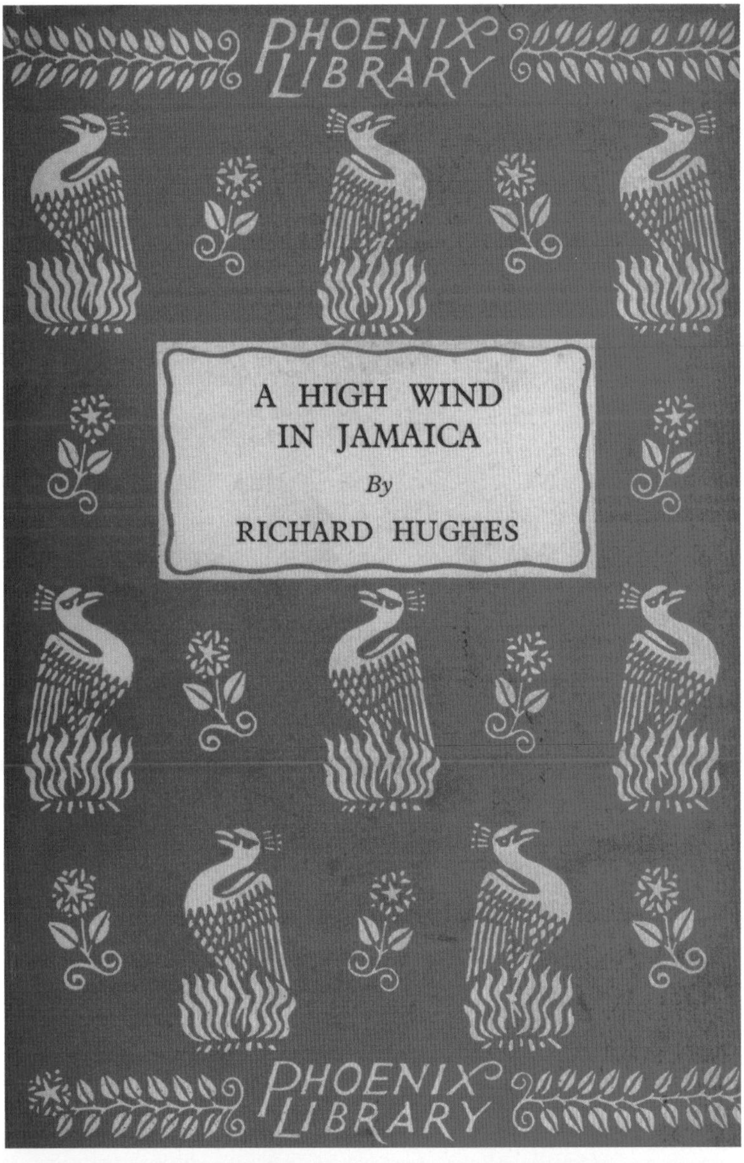

RICHARD HUGHES
1900 – 1976
Nationality: British
First Published: Harper and Brothers, 1929
Other Selected Titles:
The Fox in the Attic
The Wooden Shepherdess

The World According to Garp

JOHN IRVING
1942 –
Nationality: American
First Published: E.F. Dutton, 1978
Other Selected Titles:
The Cider House Rules
A Prayer for Owen Meany
A Son of the Circus
A Widow for One Year
The Fourth Hand
The Imaginary Girlfriend
Until I Find You

John Irving in 1980.

This is the fourth novel written by John Irving, and the one that launched his career in the United States. It is a book that is both funny and tragic. Irving makes us laugh, sometimes ruefully and often 'politically incorrectly' as the events unfold.

The main character is T.S. Garp, an author who was born the bastard son of Jenny Fields. She is a feminist who engineers his conception by seducing a wounded, brain-impaired soldier she is tending in a hospital. Her affluent shoe manufacturing family reject her as a result. From this propitious start, the book follows Garp's life, career and relationships, much of it as bizarre as his conception.

Irving cleverly uses the meta-fiction of Garp's writing to provide a clue to one of the underlying themes. Life is tough and full of tragedy; laughter is one way of enduring it.

20th ANNIVERSARY EDITION
with a new Afterword from the author

JOHN IRVING

Author of
A WIDOW FOR ONE YEAR

The World According to Garp

"A wonderful novel, full of energy and art, at once funny and horrifying and heartbreaking.... You know THE WORLD ACCORDING TO GARP is true. It is also terrific."
—*The Washington Post*

Berlin Stories ✓

This work is actually a loose confederation of two small novels, *Mr Norris Changes Trains* and *Goodbye to Berlin*, both written in the 1930s. *Goodbye to Berlin* formed the basis for John Van Druten's play, *I Am a Camera* which then morphed into the well-known musical *Cabaret* with the infamous Sally Bowles.

These stories were based on Isherwood's own experiences in Berlin between 1929–1933, the years leading up to the Second World War. As a homosexual, Isherwood found the city's reputation for sexual freedom alluring. The style is very much that of the camera, the non-participant, the observer, and although the characters are vividly painted there is a sense of alienation that permeates the whole.

The Berlin Stories seem to suggest that there is a difference between freedom and licence and these stories are a masterly depiction of the magic, decadence, vice and the lost souls in pre-war Germany – a world that was already in a downward spiral. In hindsight this fact seems obvious from these carefully drawn vignettes, and this is in part what makes this contemporaneous collection so compelling.

Christopher Isherwood and his friend W.H. Auden leaving London for China in 1938.

CHRISTOPHER ISHERWOOD
1904 – 1986
Nationality: British
First Published: Hogarth Press, 1939
Other Selected Titles:
All The Conspirators
The Memorial
The Dance Of Death (with W.H. Auden)
Mr. Norris Changes Trains
The Last Of Mr. Norris
Sally Bowles
Lions and Shadow

The Remains of the Day

KAZUO ISHIGURO
1954 –
Nationality: Japanese
First Published: Faber & Faber, 1989
Other Selected Titles:
A Pale View of Hills
An Artist of the Floating World
The Unconsoled
When We Were Orphans
Never Let Me Go

Kazuo Ishiguro in London, 2000.

The Remains of the Day is typical of Ishiguro's style: delicate, detailed and evocative prose which reveals the perceived flaws in a central character through that character's first person narrative. Events tend to unfold within the narrative and the character's discoveries about himself are revealed to the reader simultaneously, thus allowing us to empathize and identify strongly with him.

The main protagonist is Stevens, a traditional English butler, all reserve, discretion and decorum. The story is set in the 1950s towards the end of Stevens' career when he is looking back on his years of service, and forward to what is left of his life.

Stevens reveals his unquestioning loyalty and devotion to Lord Darlington, his long-term employer, who came under suspicion as a Nazi sympathizer during the war and suffered social ostracism. He also realizes his love for Miss Kenton, a love that is in conflict with his idea of life in service and which he struggles to acknowledge.

At the start of the book, Lord Darlington has been dead for several years, and the Hall now belongs to an American who wants a more informal relationship with his butler, in keeping with the times. Can the very traditional Stevens change the habits of a lifetime and rise to the challenge of the future?

This Booker Prize winner is brilliantly crafted and beautifully observed in every detail.

Ulysses

Joyce's towering masterpiece is a modern interpretation of Homer's *Odyssey*. The book was written over a number of years, then censored due to its sexual content, and was finally made legally available in 1933.

The story is set in Dublin and takes place over the course of one working day, though it represents Ulysses' protracted journey home over many years. The main characters are Leopold Bloom, a Jewish advertising salesman as Ulysses; his wife Molly as Penelope; and Stephen Dedalus, the protagonist of *Portrait of the Artist as a Young Man*, is Telemachus. The adventures include a funeral and several episodes of adultery. Each parallels an event from Homer's *Odyssey*.

The narrative of *Ulysses* uses a range of literary styles, including stream-of-consciousness, pun and parody and an extremely rich and varied vocabulary. The book is long and contains 18 chapters. It is acknowledged not to be the easiest read, but it certainly rewards the effort. Some scholars regard it as a masterwork of Modernism, while others as the pivotal point of Postmodernism.

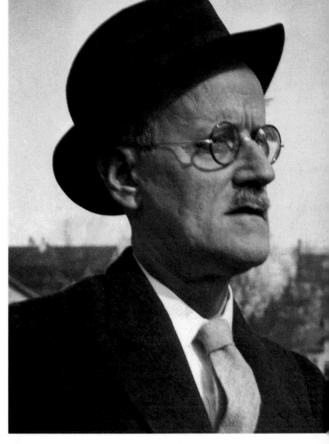

JAMES JOYCE
1882 – 1941
Nationality: Irish
First Published: Shakespeare & Co., 1922
Other Selected Titles:
Dubliners
A Portrait of the Artist as a Young Man
Finnegans Wake

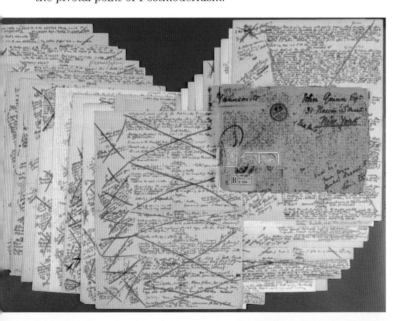

ABOVE: James Joyce in Paris in 1938.

LEFT: Original 27-page manuscript of the Circe chapter of Ulysses.

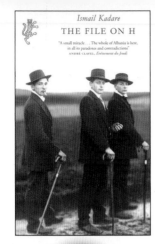

The File on H

Born in 1936, Ismail Kadare is an Albanian writer whose body of work won him the Man Booker International Award in 2005. He has been described by some as a dissident and sought political asylum in France in 1990. *The File on H* was translated into English from the French translation.

In the mid 1930s, two Homeric scholars, one Irish and one American, apply for visas to visit Albania to research the oral traditions still extant in the remote regions. Ostensibly, they want to understand the essence and variations of the Homeric traditions of creating and memorizing long epic poems. They bring with them the latest technology, a tape recorder. The local authorities however suspect the scholars of being spies and intend to use their visit and research for their own purposes. Ultimately the narrative is a metaphor for the slippery search for truth in myth, which, like all truth, is always open to individual interpretation, and thus is impossible to find.

Apart from the allegorical, metaphorical and literary significance of *The File on H,* it is also a cracking spy story.

ISMAIL KADARE
1936 –
Nationality: Albanian
First Published: Harvill Press, 1981
Other Selected Titles:
Why These Mountains Brood
The Castle
The Three-Arched Bridge
The Concert at the End of the Winter
The Palace of Dreams
Spring Flower, Spring Frost
The Life, Game and Death of Lul Mazreku
The Successor

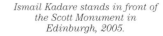

Ismail Kadare stands in front of the Scott Monument in Edinburgh, 2005.

The Trial

German novelist and short story writer Franz Kafka's canon of work, including this novel, was published posthumously against his express wishes. *The Trial* (unfinished at his death) is now iconic in Western literature. Kafka's work has been defined in terms of many of the genres of 20th-century fiction – Postmodern, Existentialist, Anarchic and so on, but *The Trial* is most often described as Surreal. The story of a young man who finds himself caught up in the mindless bureaucracy of the law, it has become synonymous with every man's struggle against an unreasoning and unreasonable authority.

FRANZ KAFKA
1883 – 1924
Nationality: Czech
First Published: Die Schmiede, 1925
Other Selected Titles:
The Metamorphosis
The Castle
Amerika

Josef K, a junior bank clerk, is arrested at his lodgings by two strangers on the morning of his 30th birthday. He has no notion of his crime and after waiting at his home is instructed to appear at a local court. He is not told the time of his trial and although he arrives early he is told that he is late and thus begins his nightmare struggle against the power and madness of the system…

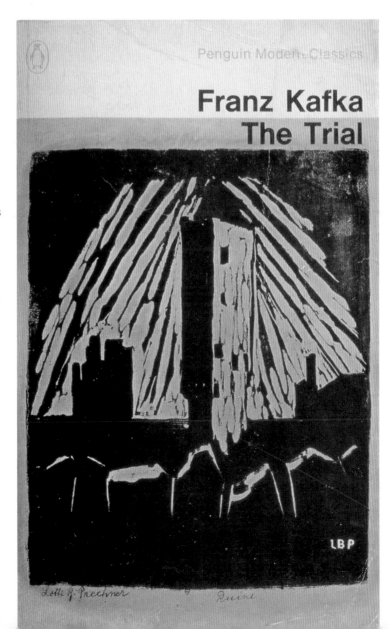

It

STEPHEN KING
1947 –
Nationality: American
First Published: Hodder and
Stoughton, 1986
Other Selected Titles:
Carrie
The Shining
Misery
Needful Things
Secret Window
From a Buick 8
The Colorado
Cell

This quintessential Stephen King horror story explores childhood terrors and trauma, and their enduring impact in the lives of their victims. The story is set in the fictional US town of Derry, Maine, initially in 1958 and later in 1985. The story begins when a band of seven 'uncool' 11-year-olds, led by Bill Denbrough, discovers and battles an evil, shape-changing monster named by the children as 'It'. It attacks every 27 years, taking on a variety of terrifying guises, but predominantly that of the clown Pennywise, and committing appalling acts. One of which is the killing of Bill's six-year-old brother George.

The children believe that they have destroyed It, but make a pact to come together again should It return. Lo and behold in 1985 the cycle of destruction begins again. The story continues as the now-adult gang once again set out to destroy It.

Written in King's characteristic conversational style, and set in an everyday world familiar to his readers, this powerful story has three threads. The first is the gang as children in 1958; the second as adults in 1985; and interleaved between the two are vignettes about the individuals and their life journeys. It marks King's transition into fantasy fiction but remains overt, no-holds-barred horror at its absolute best.

Horror writer Stephen King.

The Unbearable Lightness of Being ✓ E

Yet another example of a 20th-century masterpiece of European literature, Milan Kundera's 1984 novel remains remarkably undated in its elegant prose, memorable imagery, construct and exploration of Kundera's political and philosophical theses.

Ostensibly this is the story of four characters, Tomas, Tereza, Sabina and Franz. Their lives and loves cross and re-cross in the paradox of choice and irrevocable decisions, any of which will result in the same consequences with which they must live, whatever the weight or lightness of the morality informing them.

Kundera's characters spring fully formed from his imagination on to the pages of the book and he gives us no information about their origins or appearance, indeed he does not ask us to find them credible. He invites us to supply these details from our own imaginations. He, the author, constantly and overtly intrudes into the narrative and controls the lives of his protagonists in the same way that the totalitarian state in which he conceived the novel constantly intervened and controlled the lives of its citizens.

Bizarre but poignant images remain on the imagination's retina long after reading *The Unbearable Lightness of Being*; the lavatory seat like a floating lily, naked woman with bowler hat…

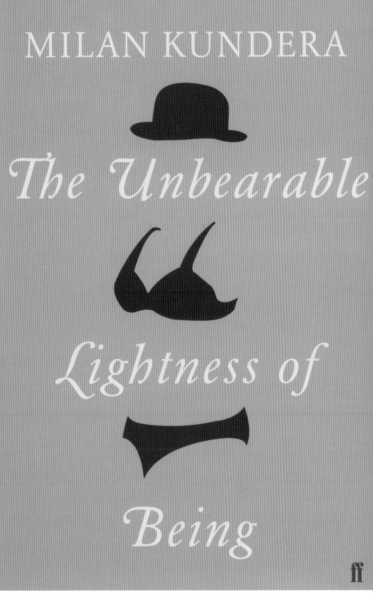

MILAN KUNDERA
1929 –
Nationality: Czech
First Published: Gallimard, 1984
Other Selected Titles:
The Joke
Life Is Elsewhere
The Farewell Waltz
The Book of Laughter and Forgetting
Immortality
Identity
Ignorance
The Curtain

GIUSEPPE DI LAMPEDUSA
1896 – 1957
Nationality: Italian
First Published: Feltrinelli, 1958
Other Selected Titles:
Lezioni Su Stendhal
Racconti
Invito Alle Lettere Trancesi Del
Cinquecento

The Leopard

Giuseppe di Lampedusa, Prince of Lampedusa and Duke of Palma, wrote his extraordinary novel of social change based on the years following Garibaldi's annexation of Sicily in 1860.

The novel centres on the declining political influence and literal decline of an aristocratic family and its head Don Fabrizio Corbera, Prince of Palma, who is prescient enough to foresee the fall of the aristocracy and the rise of the middle classes. His charming but irresponsible nephew, Tancredi, is promised to his cousin, Don Fabrizio's daughter, Concetta, an alliance which will, it is hoped, secure the line.

However, not only does Tancredi join the rebels but he falls for the charm and beauty of Angelica, a local girl of lower class. She is looking for upward mobility; Tancredi is searching for his place in the future, and Don Fabrizio looks to the family's history and feels that his life has been purposeless. The events of his own family are a metaphor for the transfer of power in Italy itself.

This powerful novel is a beautifully written contribution to Italian and European Literature and is also notable as the only major work of its author.

The Diviners

The Diviners is the third and final novel in Margaret Laurence's much acclaimed Manawaka cycle, the culmination of this epic work. Laurence is an outstanding Canadian writer, one of the best novelists of the 20th century, and this novel deservedly won her the Governor General's Award for Fiction in 1974.

Morag Gunn is a writer who lives alone in the fictional Canadian prairie of Manawaka. She is involved in an epic struggle to endure, embrace and understand both her solitude and her relationship with her lover, and with her daughter Pique, who seems lost in her loneliness.

Morag is a magnificent, honest and credible woman and a marvellous creation, who with integrity, humour and wit comes to understand that she really does need the love of her family, but not more than she needs her work, her independence and her solitude.

MARGARET LAURENCE
1926 – 1987
Nationality: Canadian
First Published: Knopf, 1974
Other Selected Titles:
A Tree for Poverty
The Tomorrow-Tamer
The Stone Angel
A Jest of God
The Fire-Dwellers
A Bird in the House
Heart of a Stranger
The Olden Days Coat

Women in Love

D.H. LAWRENCE
1885 – 1930
Nationality: British
First Published: M. Secker, 1921
Other Selected Titles:
Sons and Lovers
The Rainbow
The Plumed Serpent
The Escaped Cock
The Man who Died
Lady Chatterley's Lover
The Virgin and the Gypsy

One of Lawrence's finest works and written as a sequel to *The Rainbow*, *Women in Love* stands alone. At the time of publication it was censored as pornographic due to the explicit sexual content. In truth this is a reflection of the genre, Realism, in all aspects of life.

The story is set in a coal-mining town in England, and follows the love lives of two sisters, Ursula and Gudrun Brangwen. They meet Rupert Birkin and Gerald Cricht and the four become friends, sharing a passionate interest in world affairs and philosophical questions. The friends eventually pair off into lovers, Ursula with Rupert and Gudrun with Gerald. The novel explores the strains that class differences and social attitudes can place on relationships of kinship, friendship and love through the events and people who influence and shape these relationships.

Lawrence is relentless in exploring the fallacy around the quest for perfect love in the real world. Written in a lively descriptive style, rich in dialogue, you will find this enthralling book hard to put down.

David Herbert Lawrence around 1900.

The Golden Notebook

Doris Lessing in
Edinburgh, 2001.

The Golden Notebook was hailed on publication in 1962 as a
feminist novel and it is Lessing's most translated and successful
book. She did not believe that it formed part of the feminist
canon but said of the novel: 'This novel, then, is an attempt to
break a form; to break certain forms of consciousness and go
beyond them. While writing it, I found I did not believe some of
the things I thought I believed: or rather, that I hold in my mind
at the same time beliefs and ideas that are apparently
contradictory. Why not? We are, after all, living in the
middle of a whirlwind.'

Anna Wulf is a single mother, living with her daughter in a
flat, and a novelist whose debut novel is a success. Suffering
from writer's block she finds her life impossibly painful and feels
her personality to be fragmented.

To make sense of her predicament she decides to
compartmentalize her life and her experiences into four separate
coloured notebooks: black for her past life in Africa, red for her
current beliefs about politics, yellow for an imaginary version of
herself, and blue as a diary all framed within a conventional
novel. She hopes to meld her feelings – professional, political
and deeply emotional – into one golden notebook. This is a
powerful and uncomfortable but deeply touching reflection of
humanity and the search for self.

DORIS LESSING
1919 –
Nationality: British
First Published: Michael Joseph, 1962
Other Selected Titles:
The Grass Is Singing
Before The Deluge
A Proper Marriage
Mr Dollinger
A Man and Two Women
The Good Terrorist
The Sweetest Dream
The Grandmothers

Primo Levi at home in Rome, 1986.

PRIMO LEVI
1919 – 1987
Nationality: Italian
First Published: Schocken Books, 1975
Other Selected Titles:
If This is Man
The Truce
Moments of Reprieve
The Wrench
If Not Now, When?
The Drowned and Saved

The Periodic Table

This masterpiece does not need to associate with a genre, or to classify itself as fact or fiction, or define itself as anecdotal or semiotic. *The Periodic Table* has and is all these things but they are not relevant to its being truly great.

The author, an Italian Jew who trained as an industrial chemist, was captured as a member of the Italian resistance movement in the Second World War and survived Auschwitz. Levi started writing after his release, and all his works reflect these experiences, his faith, and the reconciliation of his guilt at being among the very few who survived.

The Periodic Table consists of 21 writings named after the chemical elements. This is an eclectic mixture of memories, essays and short stories. They are presented in chronological order of the author's life. Each elemental name has a physical or symbolic connection to the piece itself. For example, in 'Argon', Levi writes of his Jewish ancestry, while in 'Nickel' he muses about a mine and the value of the ore. Each is a jewel of literature and together they explore and teach eternal truths.

Changing Places

In this 1975 satire on academic life on both sides of the Atlantic, David Lodge begins his celebrated trilogy of novels of academia.

Philip Swallow is every inch the English academic, 40, conventional, and unprepared for the 'professional' life of a professor at Euphoria (read Berkeley) University, USA. Morris Zapp, an American top-flight career academic, driven only by his need to find alternative accommodation for six months to forestall his wife's divorce proceedings, agrees to an exchange with Philip and finds himself at Rummidge (read Birmingham) University in England. Initially, neither is convinced that this cross-Atlantic exchange will work for them either personally or professionally.

Lodge specializes in extremely witty, ironic and amusing work with a serious subtext, and *Changing Places* is no exception. This novel uses the plot to make serious observations about the similarities and differences in learning and teaching experiences and the perils of academic competition.

DAVID LODGE
1935 –
Nationality: British
First Published: Secker and Warburg, 1975
Other Selected Titles:
The Picturegoers
Ginger You're Barmy
The British Museum Is Falling Down
How Far Can You Go
Small World: An Academic Romance
Nice Work
Therapy
Thinks ...

David Lodge 🐧
Changing Places

'Not since *Lucky Jim* has such a funny book about academic life come my way' — *Sunday Times* (London)

The Posthumous Memoirs of Bras Cubas

J.M. MACHADO DE ASSIS
1839 – 1908
Nationality: Brazilian
First Published: 1881
Other Selected Titles:
The Hand and the Glove
Counselor Aires's Memorial

In his preface to *The Posthumous Memoirs of Bras Cubas* the author, Brazil's greatest novelist, acknowledges his debt to the 18th-century English novelist Lawrence Sterne. This novel marked a change in his work, which had always been experimental, and presaged the shape of avant-garde 20th-century literature that was to follow.

CLÁSSICOS DA LITERATURA BRASILEIRA

Memórias Póstumas de Brás Cubas

Machado de Assis

'At 2 o'clock on a Friday afternoon, in the month of August 1869' Bras Cubas died of pneumonia; an ironic end for one who had invented a placebo for melancholy hypochondriacs. His life as a bourgeois citizen is over, but from the vantage point of eternity he has limitless time to consider it and the manner of his passing. Through his rather quirky narration from the realms of the afterlife, we hear his life story and the philosophy by which he lived.

This technique of first person narration, the perspective of more than one person, and an awareness of self, was unknown in literature before Machado experimented with this new approach. But of course it is not unusual to the modern reader, so this entertaining and informative novel remains remarkably fresh and undated.

The Cairo Trilogy

In 1988, Egyptian author and social commentator Mahfouz won the Nobel Prize for Literature. In 1992, for the first time, a single volume translation of his magnificent epic, *The Cairo Trilogy* was published in English. This magisterial work (*Palace Walk*, *Palace of Desire* and *Sugar Street*) covers three generations of the lives of an Egyptian family between 1917 and 1944, encompassing two world wars and the British occupation.

NAGUIB MAHFOUZ
1911 –
Nationality: Egyptian
First Published: 1956–7
Other Selected Titles:
Whisper of Madness
Beginning and The End
Children of Gebelawi
The Thief and the Dogs
Love and the Veil
Arabian Nights and Days
Akhenaten, Dweller in Truth
Fountain and Tomb

LEFT: Egyptian novelist and commentator Naguib Mahfouz.

At the start, Al-Sayyid Ahmad, a shop-keeper and tyrannical patriarch, rules his obedient wife Amina and her two cloistered daughters, Aisha and Khadija, and his three sons, the idealistic Fahmy, the decadent Yasin and the intellectual Kamal, according to unchanging tradition. Outside the home, however, he leads a very different life. But Egypt is no longer isolated from the rapidly changing 20th-century world and neither is the family. By the time Mahfouz has woven his vibrant tapestry we see Al-Sayyid Ahmad's grandsons become a Muslim Fundamentalist, a Communist, and the lover of a politician.

This novel is replete with history and dialogue, both conversational and interior which may lose nuance in translation, but Mahfouz is consummately skilled in subtly increasing the pace, with the changing times and foreign influence. *The Cairo Trilogy* is both deeply satisfying as fiction and vitally informative as social commentary set in a fascinating period.

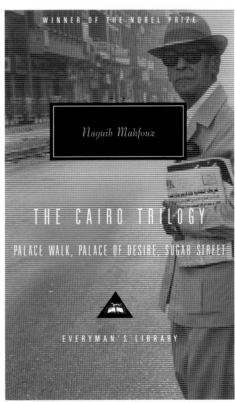

WINNER OF THE NOBEL PRIZE

Naguib Mahfouz

THE CAIRO TRILOGY

PALACE WALK, PALACE OF DESIRE, SUGAR STREET

EVERYMAN'S LIBRARY

The Executioner's Song

NORMAN MAILER
1923 –
Nationality: American
First Published: Hutchinson, 1979
Other Selected Titles:
The Naked and the Dead
An American Dream
Cannibals and Christians
The Prisoner of Sex
Of Women and Their Elegance
Tough Guys Don't Dance
The Gospel According to the Son
The Time of Our Time

Truman Capote's 1966 book *In Cold Blood* was said to be an innovation in modern fiction, by taking a true story and using both the skills of a journalist and those of a novelist to create a new genre. Norman Mailer is probably the greatest living proponent of this art form.

Interestingly, like *In Cold Blood*, *The Executioner's Song* has its roots in a brutal real-life crime. It is based on the life and death of convicted Utah killer, Gary Gilmore. Mailer interviewed Gilmore, his friends and family and those of his victims exhaustively. The book is divided into two parts: the events and relationships in Gilmore's life leading up to the crimes, and the crimes themselves, the lengthy trials, retrials and appeals, against Gilmore's wishes, and his final execution by firing squad in 1977.

Mailer's consummate skill as a writer made this not only a compelling book but also brought the national debate about the re-instatement of capital punishment in 1972 into the real public arena (Gilmore was the first to be executed after this date). No one who has read *The Executioner's Song* can fail to have re-examined his or her own conscience and beliefs about the taking of life.

RIGHT: Norman Mailer shouts out a joke to his audience at the University of Texas, 2005.

God's Grace

Pulitzer Prize-winner Bernard Malamud is most renowned for his brilliant, lyrical short stories, often set in Jewish ghettoes and written in a pastiche of Yiddish-English. *God's Grace* is a full-length novel, and like all Malamud's work deals with immense issues in microcosm.

Cohn, the lone survivor of a nuclear holocaust, wakes adrift in a boat with only a trained chimpanzee, Buz, for company. Cohn and Buz make their way to a deserted, uninhabited Eden-like island. Buz has been modified by his previous owner, a scientist, and fitted with a voice box. Cohn reconnects the dangling wires and the chimp begins to speak fluently, and fortuitously, in English. Soon other animals, all primates, begin to come to the island, and Cohn names them and tries to create a morally sustainable, peaceable society, but he is unable to control competition and jealousy. Eventually he mates with the female and she produces a half-ape-half human child. Ultimately Cohn is unable to maintain the moral basis in his private life and since his 'creations' have free will, they rebel against his authority.

God's Grace is a hugely imaginative, scholarly and thought-provoking meditation on a creator's relationship with his creation.

BERNARD MALAMUD
1914 – 1986
Nationality: American
First Published: Chatto and Windus, 1982
Other Selected Titles:
The Natural
The Assistant
The Magic Barrel
The Fixer
Pictures of Fidelman: An Exhibition
The Tenants
Rembrandt's Hat
Dubin's Lives

An Imaginary Life

An Imaginary Life has been described as 'an audacious and supremely moving work of fiction'. Its author takes as his starting point an event in the fictional life of the poet Ovid, exiled by Emperor Augustus in 8AD, to live among the barbarian Scythians on the Black Sea.

Through this event, Malouf explores how language is used as an expression of power, is the means by which groups share a sense of cultural identity and can also be used to convey a sense of cultural superiority. Ovid's sense of self is based in language and yet he is exiled among those with whom he cannot communicate, and with whom he does not share a common culture.

Malouf then introduces an *enfant sauvage*, a boy, brought up by wolves in the snow with no language at all, but whose sense of self comes from nature. Curiously and gradually these two outsiders build a relationship. Ovid is initially the protector, but then their roles are reversed and he becomes the protected.

From the boy and from nature, Ovid learns how language can separate us from ourselves; indeed it is the very means by which we come to understand the difference between self and other. But it is through the inner dialogue and the unspoken communication that we find our common humanity.

DAVID MALOUF
1934 –
Nationality: Australian
First Published: Chatto and Windus, 1978
Other Selected Titles:
Johnno
Prism
First Things Last
Antipodes
Harland's Half Acre
Baa Baa Black Sheep
Remembering Babylon
Dream Stuff

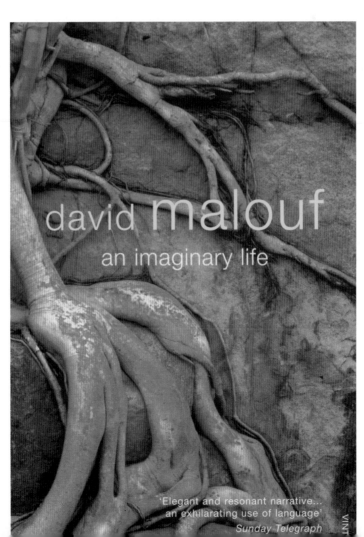

david malouf
an imaginary life

'Elegant and resonant narrative...
an exhilarating use of language'
Sunday Telegraph

Writer and exile from Nazi Germany, Thomas Mann (right), with Albert Einstein and Rabbi Stephen Wise in New York, 1938.

The Magic Mountain

Thomas Mann's enlightening and erudite work *The Magic Mountain* is no longer fashionable and in some ways defies categorization. It is a novel of ideas, allegory and allusion. Unlike more contemporary novels, the allegory is literal rather than magical, the allusion is to myth and knowledge which is often absent from our general 21st-century education. The ideas are philosophical and vitally centred in time and place: Europe in the build-up to the First World War.

The magic mountain itself provides a panoramic viewpoint from which the protagonist, young Hans Castorp, is able to consider the major conflicting European ideologies of the early 20th century – rationalism, idealism, totalitarianism and the inevitability of conflict.

Castorp, on the brink of his career as an engineer in Hamburg, takes a three-week break to visit his tubercular cousin at an elegant sanatorium in the Swiss Alps. He, too, is diagnosed with TB and stays for seven years to complete his recovery and, as it transpires, his education guided by the humanist Settembrini, Naptha, a totalitarian Jesuit, the pleasure-seeking Mynheer Peeperkorn, and Madame Chauchat with whom he falls instantly in love.

The Magic Mountain is a great and educative book which inspires its readers to serious contemplation and a more complete comprehension of the importance of our recent history.

THOMAS MANN
1875 – 1967
Nationality: German
First Published: S. Fischer Verlag, 1924
Other Selected Titles:
*The Clown
Buddenbrooks
Death in Venice
Disorder and Early Sorrow
Mario and the Magician
The Transposed Heads
Doctor Faustus
The Holy Sinner*

Embers

In recent years, Márai's 1942 masterpiece was rediscovered, published in English and became an instant bestseller in many countries. This extraordinarily powerful narrative replaces description, plot and characterization with tension, ambience and atmosphere. The protagonists reveal the story in the elegantly spare prose.

SÁNDOR MÁRAI
1900 – 1989
Nationality: Hungarian
First Published: 1942
Other Selected Titles:
Casanova in Bolzano
Memoir of Hungary, 1944–1948

One day in 1941, an elderly Hungarian aristocrat receives a letter informing him that a friend, who he has not seen since 1900, is arriving at his castle high in the Carpathian Mountains that very day. It would seem that this is an event for which he has long been waiting, and he makes preparations for greeting and entertaining the friend to an interesting dinner. During the long night that follows, the two discuss many matters: love, honour, friendship, fidelity, truth, lust, rage and revenge.

It becomes apparent that these subjects are personally relevant to the two men and not just the universally important conversation of civilized man.

When they last met at this same table following a stag hunt, the mistress of the house had been present, and it is in her absence, and in their silences and evasions, that the significance of this night rests.

Embers has been greeted as an exceptional and moving contribution to the canon of great European literature.

THE TOP-TEN BESTSELLER

Embers

Sándor Márai

TRANSLATED BY CAROL BROWN JANEWAY

'Magnificent. A spellbinding [story] driven by intense passion' THE TIMES

Life of Pi

A fantasy which won the Booker Prize in 2002, *Life of Pi* tells the magical story of a young Indian, who finds himself shipwrecked and lost at sea in a large lifeboat. His companions are four wild animals: an orangutan, a zebra, a hyena and most notably, Richard Parker, a 450lb tiger.

Soon there remains only Pi and the tiger, and his only purpose in the next 227 days is to survive the shipwreck and the hungry tiger, supported only by his own curious brand of religion, an eclectic mixture of Christianity, Islam and Buddhism.

The tale is told in retrospect by Pi, and the author to whom he tells it, and Martel interrupts the narrative with his commentary and observations. Through this highly descriptive and bizarre adventure, Martel depicts the rich cultural background of Pi's world and the lonely struggle of taming the savagery of nature 'red in tooth and claw' and surviving life. The role of spirituality in understanding and transcending the physical world is explored – and we also find out why the tiger is called Richard Parker!

Yann Martel in London, 2002.

YANN MARTEL
1963 –
Nationality: Canadian
First Published: Knopf Canada, 2001
Other Selected Titles:
*The Facts Behind the
Helsinki Roccamatios
Self
We Ate the Children Last*

Cakes and Ale

Somerset Maugham enjoyed a long and illustrious career, and although *Of Human Bondage*, his 1915 novel, is considered to be his masterpiece, both *Cakes and Ale* and its author enjoyed a resurgence in popularity in England when it was republished to celebrate Maugham's 80th birthday.

This was Maugham at his witty, ironic best in this wicked satire of the lives of the literati of London in the inter-war period. It seems that everyone recognized Maugham in his creation Ashenden, and Thomas Hardy in the character of Driffield. For Hugh Walpole was reserved the part of Kear, the hapless, social-climbing biographer chosen by Mrs Driffield to write an official life of her husband. In the process of research, and in pursuit of best-sellerdom, Kear discovers Driffield's true muse, his bubbly, lovable first wife Rosie. The respectable Driffields are not eager for Rosie's memory to damage Driffield's impeccably respectable image.

In *Cakes and Ale*, Maugham seems to have presaged the rise of the more salacious unauthorized biography of the late 20th century, but it is the economical writing and elegant, understated irony of this work that makes it so deeply satisfying.

W. SOMERSET MAUGHAM
1874 – 1965
Nationality: British
First Published: W. Heinemann, 1930
Other Selected Titles:
Liza of Lambeth
Of Human Bondage
The Moon and Sixpence
The Painted Veil
The Narrow Corner
The Razor's Edge
Then and Now
Creatures of Circumstance

Somerset Maugham poses with a bust of himself by Strobi, in 1948.

The Group

Mary McCarthy shown in a seductive pose.

MARY MCCARTHY
1912 – 1989
Nationality: American
First Published: Harvest/HBJ, 1962
Other Selected Titles:
The Company She Keeps
The Oasis
Cast a Cold Eye
The Groves Of Academe
Birds Of America
Cannibals and Missionaries

In 1963, Mary McCarthy's novel based on the lives of eight women Vassar students in the class of 1933 caused a ripple of protest in some circles. The alumnae of Vassar even requested that her degree be rescinded. It seems the more extraordinary that a book depicting the social, political and sexual mores of the previous generation of women should cause a stir, when at the time of publication the Western world was on the brink of the 'sexual revolution' and the 'women's movement'.

Perhaps it was the sophisticated McCarthy's reputation for disguising only thinly the autobiographical details of her own life, and that of her friends, in her work that offended the sensibilities of these matrons.

Each of the novel's eight chapters describes the life and loves of a different member of the group and follows them up to ten years after graduation. It is an examination not only of the social and sexual politics of the time, but of the way in which individuals from different backgrounds deal with the challenges of massive social change. The years between 1933 and 1945 offered plenty of those, including the Depression and the Second World War.

Frank, yes, talking openly about loss of virginity, contraception and orgasm, but *The Group* is also elegant, funny and witty and examines contemporaneous attitudes to marriage, careers and domestic duties as well as elite women's education.

The Heart is a Lonely Hunter

The Heart is a Lonely Hunter is a work of great literature, which depicts the loneliness, injustice and hunger in the soul of humanity. Carson McCullers was an ordinary girl from the deep south of America, who wrote with almost incomparable sensitivity, lyricism and profundity, and yet with a spareness and lack of sentimentality that is deeply moving.

McCullers was only 22 when she wrote *The Heart is a Lonely Hunter* and yet it speaks for characters of both sexes, and varying ages, both black and white, with the same unfailing comprehension and humanity. This is unusual in many more mature authors, in the politically correct 21st century, but in a young girl in 1940, it is beyond extraordinary.

Singer, a deaf-mute, works in a jeweller's store and is the recipient of the deepest thoughts and hopes of Mick, a 12-year-old girl, Biff Brannon, the owner of a café, Jake Blount, alcoholic and unionist, and Dr Copeland, a black physician. Singer is emotionally involved with another deaf-mute, who is taken away to an asylum, and dies, leading to Singer's suicide. These four seem to invest Singer with the qualities of priest in the confessional, but it is not simply because their secrets are safe with him.

All McCuller's work concerns the yearning for and finding of love of all kinds in the unlikeliest places, among the outcasts and marginalized, but that is to oversimplify the power of the universality of the simple truths in this genuine work of genius.

CARSON MCCULLERS
1917 – 1967
Nationality: American
First Published: Houghton Mifflin, 1940
Other Selected Titles:
Reflections in a Golden Eye
The Member of the Wedding
The Ballad of the Sad Cafe
Clock Without Hands

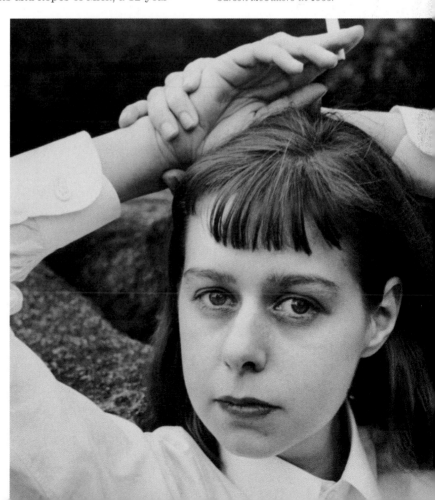

Carson McCullers in 1955.

Enduring Love

IAN MCEWAN
1948 –
Nationality: British
First Published: Jonathan Cape, 1997
Other Selected Titles:
The Comfort of Strangers
The Child in Time
The Innocent
Black Dogs
Atonement
Saturday

In this, Ian McEwan's fifth novel, he explores themes of altruism versus self-interest, obsessive love, communication and self-knowledge, and the stories that we create for ourselves in times of profound loss or shock.

On a sunny day, Joe Rose, a scientific writer, and his partner Clarissa, are celebrating their relationship after an absence, by picnicking in a field in the Chiltern Hills. A hot air balloon with a child in its basket breaks free of its moorings and floats dangerously away. One man is clinging to the rope. Joe and three others dash to help, each taking a rope. As the balloon hurtles towards a cliff edge, the men must decide whether to let go of the ropes or hold on. If they all hold on, the balloon will land safely, but if any lets go, the remaining men will be in great danger. Three let go and one holds on and is carried to his death. In the moment of decision, Joe exchanges a glance with one of the other men, Jed, who on the basis of their shared experience conceives an obsessive love for Joe, which he cannot accept Joe does not reciprocate. He stalks Joe, bringing him to the brink of losing everything, including his sanity.

Ultimately, *Enduring Love*, which carried a hoax case history of 'ertomania' or obsessive love in its appendices, concerns understanding between individuals and truth, and what we believe to be true in the constructs of self that we create.

ENDURING LOVE
IAN McEWAN

The Sea of Fertility

Yukio Mishima committed suicide in 1970 and the last volume in his tetralogy *The Sea of Fertility* is thought to reflect his own negative view of himself and his life's work. Mishima did not share the universally held belief that he is the greatest Japanese novelist of the 20th century. He wrote over 40 novels and other works and it is said that his work was informed by the pre-Modern literature of the West.

The Sea of Fertility is undoubtedly his masterwork, reflecting his view of 20th-century Japanese experience. Each book traces the reincarnation of the same character Kiyoaki Matsugae between 1912 and 1975, as tracked by his boyhood friend Shigekuni Honda, a student of law. Kiyoaki reincarnates in ever-increasingly self-destructive ways, first as a gentle aristocrat (in *Spring Snow*), then as Isao Iinuma, a violent extremist (in *Runaway Horses*), next as Ying Chan, a lazy Thai princess (in *The Temple of Dawn*), and finally as a sadistic orphan (in *The Decay of the Angel*). Honda's quest is to try to discover why his friend's karma is leading him to ultimate destruction and to try to save him. Yukio Mishima has left us the legacy of a brilliantly written and conceived complete picture of 20th-century Japan.

YUKIO MISHIMA
1925 – 1970
Nationality: Japanese
First Published: Shinchosha, 1965
Other Selected Titles:
Death in Midsummer
The Sound of Waves
The Boy Who Wrote Poetry
Patriotism
The Sailor Who Fell from Grace with the Sea
The Way of Samurai
My Friend Hitler

Yukio Mishima addresses the Japanese military at their headquarters and urges them to take action and save Japan. He then committed ritual disembowelment in the General's office.

A Fine Balance

Rohinton Mistry was born in Mumbai, but moved to Canada when he was 23. *A Fine Balance* is a finely crafted work of precise prose, which takes him back to an 'imaginary homeland' – Bombay in 1975, under the rule of Indhira Gandhi. A State of Emergency has been declared and Mistry explores a country on the brink of collapse and chaos.

In a small apartment, four diverse characters share their lives, their fears for their future and their fragile present and, in the case of the young student from the northern mountains, regret for a lost idyllic past.

The uncle and nephew, tailors by trade, are refugees from a far from idyllic past of vicious caste violence in their village. The fourth occupant is a widow in middle age who seeks only to maintain her independence.

Mistry weaves the dramatic events of his protagonists' lives into the vast tapestry that is India with breathtaking skill, compassion and understanding. Nominated for the Booker Prize, *A Fine Balance* should be read and thoroughly appreciated by everyone with an interest in the complex history of 20th-century India.

ROHINTON MISTRY
1952 –
Nationality: Indian
First Published: McClelland & Stewart, 1995
Other Selected Titles:
Such a Long Journey
Tales from Firozsha Baag
Family Matters

Cold Heaven

Brian Moore was an extraordinarily versatile writer of taut, carefully crafted novels in a variety of genres, often favouring the thriller to explore his anti-doctrinaire themes. Graham Greene once listed him as his favourite living novelist. He was also short-listed for the Booker Prize three times. In *Cold Heaven* he brings all the considerable power of his intelligence, empathy and skill to the subjects of loss and guilt.

BRIAN MOORE
1921 – 1999
Nationality: Irish
First Published: Cape, 1983
Other Selected Titles:
The Lonely Passion of Judith Hearne
The Luck of Ginger Coffey
The Emperor Of Ice-Cream
The Doctor's Wife
The Mangan Inheritance
Black Robe
The Magician's Wife

Marie's husband Alex is killed in a boating accident, and like many who suffer loss in a sudden and tragic way, she finds it difficult to believe that he is dead. Indeed he begins to appear in her life, it would seem very much alive. As Marie was contemplating leaving him for another man just before his death, she questions whether guilt and grief are causing her to see visions and, if so, what do they mean? Or is Alex in fact still alive? Rediscovering the Catholicism of her youth, Marie searches for the answers.

A tense, psychological, very literary thriller, *Cold Heaven* is also an examination of faith and love.

Beloved

TONI MORRISON
1931 –
Nationality: American
First Published: Knopf, 1987
Other Selected Titles:
The Bluest Eye
Sula
Song of Solomon
Tar Baby
Jazz
Paradise
Love

Toni Morrison's 1987 novel *Beloved* won the Pulitzer Prize for Fiction in 1988. It is one of the most powerfully evocative novels about slavery and its unthinkable legacy ever written. It is based on the true story of a black slave woman, Margaret Garner, who escaped from a Kentucky plantation with her husband Robert and sought refuge in Ohio. Recaptured, she killed her baby to save it from the slavery that she had escaped.

In the novel, Sethe is a passionately devoted mother and as an act of supreme love and sacrifice she tries to kill her children to prevent them becoming slaves. She succeeds only in killing her two-year-old daughter and since she cannot afford to write 'Dearly Beloved' on the gravestone, the child is known as Beloved. Sethe now lives with her teenage daughter Denver and the house is haunted and rocked by the rage of the dead baby. The hauntings are only alleviated by the occasional appearance of Paul D, a man so ravaged by his slave past that he keeps his feelings in a tobacco tin. One day a teenage girl turns up. Is she Beloved incarnate? She knows the song that only Sethe and Denver share. Sethe is obsessed with assuaging her guilt and the opportunity to love Beloved.

This intensely shocking and moving narrative is written in a variety of voices and lengthy, fragmentary monologues, which like Beloved herself are sometimes ambiguous. But this is also a novel about confronting unimaginable memories and becoming whole. Toni Morrison's beautiful language and intense imagery are impossible to forget.

Toni Morrison in New York, 1985.

The Progress of Love

Alice Munro is recognized and acknowledged as one of the greatest living short story writers. She has had many collections of short stories published and *The Progress of Love* deals, like much of her work, in the examination of human relationships in all their complexity through the minutiae of daily living in small, provincial and rural Canadian towns.

A young man examines his sense of responsibility for a younger sibling when he recalls the terrifying trauma of his childhood. A woman divorces and seeks sanctuary in her childhood home where she must confront her parent's ambiguous relationship. The trust between parents and their children is tested after the accidental near-drowning of a child. These are some of the themes of the stories in this collection, and through the lives of the protagonists we shine a light into the dark corners of our own humanity.

In this collection Alice Munro examines, in elegant witty prose, the constant paradoxes of our lives where responsibility vies with freedom, security with independence, and creativity with obligation.

ALICE MUNRO
1931 –
Nationality: Canadian
First Published: Knopf, 1986
Other Selected Titles:
Lives of Girls and Women
The Moons of Jupiter: Stories
Friend of My Youth
A Wilderness Station
The Love of a Good Woman
Queenie: A Story
Hateship, Friendship, Courtship,
Loveship, Marriage
Runaway

The Sea, the Sea

IRIS MURDOCH
1919 – 1999
Nationality: British
First Published: Chatto & Windus, 1978
Other Selected Titles:
The Bell
A Severed Head
The Nice and the Good
The Sacred and Profane Love Machine
The Philosopher's Pupil
The Good Apprentice
The Message to the Planet
Jackson's Dilemma

Author of over 40 novels, Iris Murdoch never offered her readers less than intellectual rigour, philosophical depth and her formidable intelligence. But she also brought symbolism, magical and mythical allusion and beautifully written sharp prose. *The Sea, the Sea* is generally regarded to be her masterwork; it won the Booker Prize in 1978.

An ageing and despotic director playwright, Charles Arrowby, is attempting his memoirs and this and his profound self-centred vanity brings him into contact with a childhood sweetheart whom he hasn't seen for 40 years. As is his character, he bullies her and then begins an affair with an 18-year-old girl.

This Murdoch reworking of *The Tempest* is set against a vivid magical landscape. She brings a surgical precision to uncovering the true emotions of jealousy, vanity and cruelty that her characters and we too attempt to hide behind the masks of civilized behaviour.

Iris Murdoch in 1977.

Lolita ✓

This ground-breaking work explores the relationship between a young pubescent girl and an older man. The plot focuses on the main character, Humbert Humbert's obsession with 12-year-old Lolita. His fixation is rationalized by the loss of his childhood love, 24 years before. Their idealistic puppy love was cut short by her tragic death, leaving him unable to move on. The story also studies Lolita's naive seductiveness and compliance in this relationship. In time, Lolita has other relationships and rejects Humbert; while he awakens from his obsession to discover a true love for the adult woman that Lolita has become.

The brilliance of *Lolita* is not just in the analysis and depiction of paedophilic desires, but how these have been expressed through Nabokov's beguiling use of the English language. He has rightly been acclaimed for his masterly alliterative style and use of word play. The story, told in a first person narrative through Humbert, is witty, tragic and compelling.

Customers at Foyles bookshop, London, browse through Lolita *on its first publication.*

VLADIMIR NABOKOV
1899 – 1977
Nationality: Russian
First Published: Olympia Press, 1955
Other Selected Titles:
The Real life of Sebastian Knight
Bend Sinister
Pnin
Pale Fire
Ada or Ardor: A Family Chronicle
Transparent Things
Look at the Harlequins!
The Original of Laura (unfinished)

V.S. Naipaul in 1968.

A House for Mr Biswas

V.S. NAIPAUL
1932 –
Nationality: Trinidadian
First Published: Andre Deutsch,
1961
Other Selected Titles:
The Mystic Masseur
The Suffrage of Elvira
Mr Stone and the Knight's
Companion
In a Free State
Guerillas
A Bend in the River
Half Life
Magic Seeds

Exquisitely penned, this novel is both moving and comic as it depicts one man's struggle for autonomy and dignity. The main protagonist in the novel is Mr Mohun Biswas, of Indian descent, born in Trinidad in the British-tinged post-colonial era. The story traces Mr Biswas' quest against many obstacles to own a house, a symbol of his independence and ability to control his own destiny. Born in humble circumstances, he is married very young to Shana Tulsi, the daughter of a wealthy and powerful family. The story line follows Mr Biswas' attempts at several careers (overseer of a sugar cane plantation, journalist and community worker) often thwarted by circumstance, and the belittling domination of the Tulsi family.

Naipaul won the Nobel Prize for Literature in 2001, and his writings have been likened to Joseph Conrad in confronting the issues of post-colonial societies and the impact that this has on the individuals.

The Third Policeman

Flann O'Brian's marvellous story *The Third Policeman*, it has been argued, is a proto-Postmodernist novel. O'Brian deploys many literary devices to move his plot along, or more properly around, as the end of the book echoes the beginning. *The Third Policeman* also features extensive fictional footnotes, perhaps a metafiction in themselves, in characterizing one of the protagonists de Selby, a mysterious scientist and philosopher who doesn't appear, but whom we learn cannot differentiate between the sexes. Surreal humour is Flann O'Brian's stock in trade.

The unnamed narrator is a student of de Selby, hoping to finance his major work on the scientist from the contents of a lost black box. At the start we are told he has already committed murder and robbery, and yet he attempts to enlist the help of the village policemen in his search. They are difficult to follow, as they speak in a variety of solecisms, spoonerisms and malapropisms.

This is a world familiar to many of us from our more colourful nightmares, though few of us possess the knowledge that O'Brian displays for our subconscious minds to distort.

The Third Policeman is vastly entertaining and, if you ride a bicycle, beware. According to one theory propounded here, you are exchanging atoms with your bike and may become half cyclist, half cycle!

FLANN O'BRIAN
1911 – 1966
Nationality: Irish
First Published: MacGibbon & Kee, 1967
Other Selected Titles:
The Dalkey Archive
The Hard Life: An Exegesis of Squalor
At Swim-Two-Birds
An Béal Bocht (*The Poor Mouth*)

Flann O'Brian, at the Palace Bar in Dublin, 1942.

FLANNERY O'CONNOR
A Good Man is Hard to Find
STORIES

'Once read, she cannot be forgotten' *The Financial Times*
'Ferocious and elegant' *The Guardian*

FLANNERY O'CONNOR
1925 – 1964
Nationality: American
First Published: Harcourt, 1955
Other Selected Titles:
Wise Blood
The Violent Bear It Away
A Memoir of Mary Ann
Three by Flannery O'Connor
Everything That Rises Must Converge
Mystery and Manners: Occasional Prose

A Good Man is Hard to Find

Mary Flannery O'Connor was born and lived all her life in Georgia and, like Carson McCullers, she seems to have been a born writer. She wrote in the Southern Gothic style and her work often featured odd and grotesque characters and was informed by her lifelong Catholicism. *A Good Man is Hard to Find* is a perfectly framed, tense and balanced narrative.

A Tennessee family is going on vacation. The grandmother does not want to go and she uses the news of an escaped convict, the Misfit, to try to persuade the family to choose a different holiday destination. None of them really believes that the Misfit presents a threat, and they set off by road, with two badly behaved children and a baby.

Grandma keeps up a constant stream of matriarchal chat, and when they stop for a meal she and the proprietor exchange pleasantries about the rise in anti-social behaviour and untrustworthiness in the country. Grandma causes a diversion in the next leg of the journey, recruiting the children to her cause and the cat escapes, causing an accident. Three sinister men appear and the family appeals to them for help.

A Good Man is Hard to Find is beautifully descriptive of the southern landscape, the character of the family and the social conditions in Tennessee and Georgia. All are contained within conversational exchanges. It is easy to see why this story is considered to be O'Connor's masterpiece.

The English Patient ✓

This haunting tale is presented to us in a tapestry of interwoven threads of past and present, spoken and interior dialogue. Ondaatje's Postmodernist style is visual and well suited to film and multi-media interpretation. *The English Patient* is a Booker Prize winner and the film won an academy award.

Set in Italy at the end of the Second World War, the narrative reveals the lives, characters and tragedies of four people. Hana, the Canadian nurse who stays behind to nurse an anonymous man; the terminally ill burns patient who is revealed to be German and not English; Carvaggio a thief turned spy for British Intelligence; and Kip the Indian Sikh who is a bomb disposal expert. Isolated in a rural villa these four develop a network of relationships and a 'family bond' that helps each to resolve their emotional and political pasts and move on.

The English Patient sensitively portrays the universal themes of unconditional love and the strength of national and cultural identity.

MICHAEL ONDAATJE
1943 –
Nationality: Sri Lankan
First Published: McClelland & Stewart, 1992
Other Selected Titles:
In the Skin of the Lion
Coming Through Slaughter
Anil's Ghost

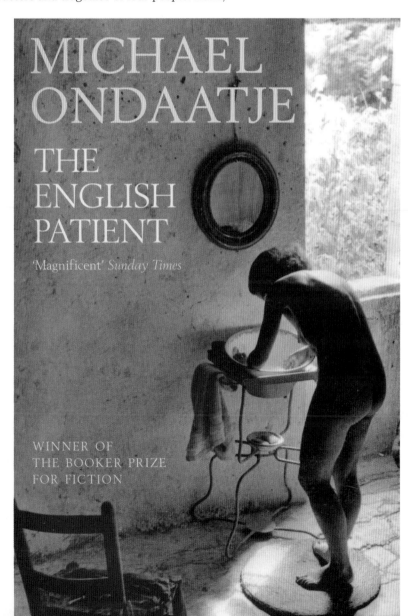

MICHAEL ONDAATJE

THE ENGLISH PATIENT

'Magnificent' *Sunday Times*

WINNER OF THE BOOKER PRIZE FOR FICTION

Where the Jackals Howl

AMOS OZ
1939 –
Nationality: Israeli
First Published: Massada, 1965
Other Selected Titles:
Black Box
The Hill of Evil Counsel
Touch the Water, Touch the Wind
My Michael
To Know a Woman
Under this Blazing Light
Don't Call It Night
Panther in the Basement

Amos Oz is one of Israel's finest writers, primarily of short stories, novels and essays. He writes in Hebrew, but his translated work is an acknowledged major contribution to World literature. Born in Israel in 1939, he moved to a kibbutz at 15 and lived there from the 1950s to the 1980s.

Oz's prose, both for adults and children, is drawn from the deep well of his homeland. It has been said that even Hebrew speakers sometimes fail to catch his geographical references and illusions. His passion for truth and a continuing open dialogue between individuals, nations and states is no less powerful for being couched, as it is, in simple elegant prose, informed by his honesty and sense of realism.

In this collection of stories, *Where the Jackals Howl*, he takes his text from the everyday life of ordinary Israeli people and, as ever, it is through his clear-sighted eloquent portrayal of these lives that we glimpse those aims towards which we should all strive – simple decency, humanity and the continued quest for peace.

Israeli-born Amos Oz.

The Messiah of Stockholm

Lars Andeming is a 40-something, twice married, middling reviewer for a middling Stockholm daily. He longs for a more illustrious life and history, and is convinced that he is the lost son of the great novelist Bruno Schulz, whose masterpiece *The Messiah*, is said to have disappeared just before his execution by the Nazis.

Lars would be redeemed in his own eyes if he could find the lost manuscript. Imagine his surprise then, when Schulz's putative daughter appears, with a manuscript she claims to be the masterwork. Lars' somewhat eccentric but none-the-less circumscribed life is changed irrevocably. Is the manuscript a forgery? Is the woman really Schulz's daughter?

Cynthia Ozick weaves a magical tale set against a backdrop of the Swedish/Jewish literary world. It has been said that in this book she has moved away from the Modernism of her earlier work towards a more Postmodern aesthetic. *The Messiah of Stockholm* is as lucidly and clearly written as her essays, but set within a magical imaginative landscape of ideas and philosophies.

The central theme explores familiar Ozick territory: the need for identity, the tension between the appreciation of art and literature, and obsession which can be seen as a kind of idolatry, which is at variance with Jewish teaching. Once again, Ozick keeps alive 'the Jewish sensibility' in this unusual and immensely readable book.

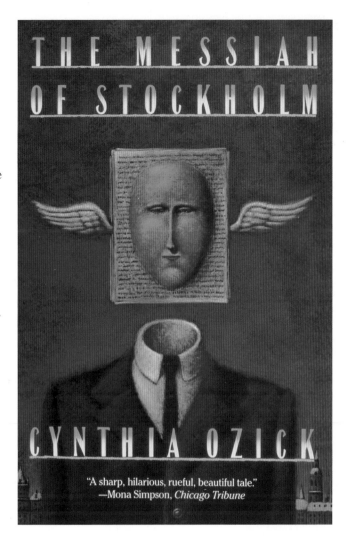

"A sharp, hilarious, rueful, beautiful tale."
—Mona Simpson, *Chicago Tribune*

CYNTHIA OZICK
1928 –
Nationality: American
First Published: Knopf, 1987
Other Selected Titles:
Trust
Levitation: Five Fictions
Art and Ardor
The Cannibal Galaxy
Metaphor and Memory
The Shawl
The Puttermesser Papers
The Bear Boy

Gormenghast

This, the second novel in Mervyn Peake's literally towering trilogy, is probably one of the greatest works in English fantasy literature.

In the first novel, *Titus Groan,* we visit the child heir Titus' intensely circumscribed world, and learn with him the purposeless rituals by which the Groans have lived and ruled for centuries. In the last, *Titus Alone*, we yearn with Titus the man, to break free of responsibilities that are bred in the bone. In *Gormenghast*, however, we are invited to explore the vast city/castle/state that is the crumbling edifice of the Groan family.

In this the longest of the three works, Peake peoples Titus' world with a vast cast of grotesques and curiosities with names as evocative as those of Charles Dickens. It is impossible not to be drawn into their world.

It is easy to become attached to even the most villainous and pitiful of Peake's people, and, if read at a particular time of one's life, the images evoked by Peake's prose remain indelible.

One critic said that trying to describe what the Gormenghast trilogy is about is like saying 'that Homer's Odyssey is about a man trying to get home to his wife'. But what should be said is that you will rarely read such a captivating, magical narrative which has been so beautifully written.

MERVYN PEAKE
1911 – 1968
Nationality: British
First Published: Eyre & Spottiswoode, 1950
Other Selected Titles:
Titus Groan
Titus Alone
Mr. Pye
Boy in Darkness (novella, appeared in *Sometime, Never* by Peake, William Golding and John Wyndham)

Mr. Weston's Good Wine

T.F. Powys was not much recognized in his own country, (England) nor in his own time for that matter. The younger and less successful brother of John Cowper Powys, he nevertheless produced a fascinating and idiosyncratic body of work of which *Mr. Weston's Good Wine* is the best known. Powys lived most of his hermit-like existence in rural Dorset and his work is centred on the savage, eccentric life of the country. His books were largely informed by an unconventional Christianity, love and death. *Mr Weston's Good Wine* defies literary categorization but has been described as allegorical fictional meditation.

T.F. POWYS
1875 – 1953
Nationality: British
First Published: Chatto and Windus, 1927
Other Selected Titles:
Black Bryony
Mockery Gap
Unclay
Mark Only
Mr Tasker's Gods

Mr. Weston, a wine merchant, and his assistant Michael arrive in the village of Folly Down in their Ford van, to sell 'good wine' to the villagers; the light wine of love and the dark wine of death. The good accept the wine, like the hermit and lover Luke Grobe, and the village postman philosopher who cannot accept his wife's death. The irredeemable, like the village Madam, Mrs. Vosper, decline and are punished by the lion kept in the van. In the end this van disappears with its occupants in heavenly smoke. Allegorically, Mr Weston is God visiting his creation and urging them to accept the twin illusions that make life bearable.

Overlooked in the razzamatazz of Modernism, *Mr. Weston's Good Wine* deserves to be read.

T. F. POWYS
Mr. Weston's Good Wine

The Nephew

JAMES PURDY
1923 –
Nationality: American
First Published: Secker and
Warburg, 1961
Other Selected Titles:
63: Dream Palace
Malcolm
Colour of Darkness
In a Shallow Grave
The House of the Solitary Maggot
Dream Palace: Selected Stories,
1956–87
Gertrude of Stoney Island Avenue
Moe's Villa and Other Stories

James Purdy's huge canon of work, though critically acclaimed, seems to have been neglected of late. He is an American writer whose books are difficult to classify. His characters often hail from a rural world, yet dwell in an urban one, which adds to their sense of isolation, loneliness and disassociation. It is these themes to which Purdy returns and explores in his work.

The Nephew is ostensibly the story of one middle-American woman's search for information about her nephew, who is reported missing in Korea. Alma Mason decides to compile a biographical scrapbook as a memorial to the boy she raised. In interviewing their friends and neighbours, she discovers more than the affectionate reminiscences she was expecting. She reveals the character of a boy she barely recognizes and who it seems is homosexual.

It has been said that a great part of Purdy's potency as a writer lies in his creation of a new form of narrative language; part vernacular, part pulpit, part hustings, to describe his bleak vision of the dysfunctional American dream.

Interview with the Vampire

The definitive Gothic masterpiece, *Interview with the Vampire* is not gratuitously scary, bloody and gory; it is literature that beautifully depicts the shared human experiences of guilt, love, sex and mortality through the eyes of the undead.

It is narrated in the first person by Louis, a vampire and the main protagonist, to a reporter Daniel Malloy in the 1970s. Louis recounts his history, beginning in 1791, when he was assaulted and initiated into the vampire brotherhood by Lestat. This victimization itself is presented as inevitable; Louis deliberately puts himself at risk as a response to his guilt for his brother's suicide. The experience of becoming a vampire and his relationships with Lestat and Claudia (child victim) are themselves erotic, homoerotic, and demonstrate nurturing love.

Throughout the book Louis exhibits a tremendous compulsion to justify his behaviour and to be seen as behaving morally. He does this by illustrating the immorality and savagery of the rest of his kind. The greatest irony is perhaps Daniel's reaction to Louis' narrative.

Rice's characterizations are peerless and her descriptions concise, compelling and subtle.

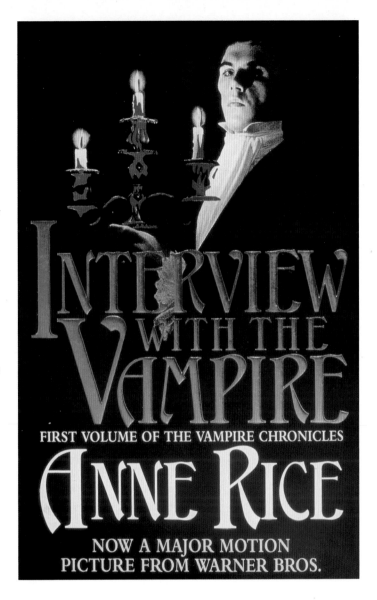

INTERVIEW WITH THE VAMPIRE

FIRST VOLUME OF THE VAMPIRE CHRONICLES

ANNE RICE

NOW A MAJOR MOTION PICTURE FROM WARNER BROS.

ANNE RICE
1941 –
Nationality: American
First Published: Knopf, 1976
Other Selected Titles:
The Vampire Lestat
The Queen of the Damned
The Tale of the Body Thief
Memnoch The Devil
The Vampire Armand
Merrick
Blackwood Farm
Blood Canticle

Mordecai Richler in 1992.

MORDECAI RICHLER
1931 – 2001
Nationality: Canadian
First Published: Knopf, 1997
Other Selected Titles:
The Acrobats
Son of a Smaller Hero
The Apprenticeship Of Duddy Kravitz
The Incomparable Atuk
Cocksure
St. Urbain's Horseman
Joshua Then and Now
Solomon Gursky Was Here

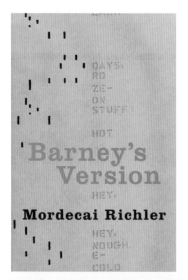

Barney's Version

Critics have wondered whether *Barney's Version* could in some degree be called 'Mordecai's version'. Not that anyone is implying that Richler has been accused of murdering his best friend, nor of most of Barney's other exploits, but Richler does use Barney's autobiography to explore aspects of 20th-century life dear to his heart: Quebec politics, and 20th-century literature, politics and film, to name but four.

Barney's version of events from his bohemian life in Paris, his two marriages, the mother of his children and third partner, his hard-drinking, hard smoking, career as a producer, is a rebuttal to that of a contemporary, and is self-serving and unscrupulous as his friends might expect, with pedantic footnotes by his son. But of one thing he is certain: he did not murder his best friend Boogie for dallying with his second wife – or is he? Barney is also aware of the onset of dementia, and the conflict between wanting to leave his story and defeat his failing memory.

Funny, acerbic, witty and with no punches pulled, *Barney's Version* bears all the hallmarks of Richler's best work; part social commentary, part apologia for the follies of youth and old age respectively.

Hadrian the Seventh

Frederick Rolfe, also known as Baron Corvo, was an English novelist, artist and eccentric, and *Hadrian the Seventh* is probably his best-known work. His prose style might seem out of date and of an earlier period; precious, erudite and rather baroque, it is nonetheless appealing. Much of his work was semi-autobiographical and *Hadrian the Seventh* is no exception.

Rejected by the Catholic Church, a failed vocation to the priesthood behind him, George Arthur Rose is living in squalor, penniless in London, when by the peculiarities of the electoral system he finds himself elected Pope. With masterly panache he confounds the Vatican bureaucracy and engages in international affairs, settling old scores along the way. The past however, like the poor, is always with us and George's past throws up some less-than-seemly confederates who intend to blackmail him.

Rose/Rolfe has plenty of scope for diatribes on politics and life in his defence, and the result is a strange but charming work.

FREDERICK ROLFE
1860 – 1913
Nationality: British
First Published: Chatto & Windus, 1904
Other Selected Titles:
*Stories Toto Told Me
Chronicles of the House of Borgia
Tarcissus the Boy Martyr of Rome
Nicholas Crabbe 1903–4
Don Tarquinio
Hubert's Arthur 1909–11
The Weird of the Wanderer
In His Own Image*

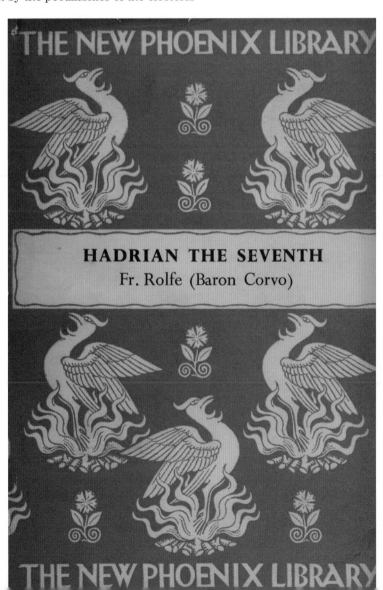

The Radetzky March

Joseph Roth started his distinguished career as a political journalist and is the acclaimed author of many novels, but his greatest work is acknowledged to be *The Radetzky March*. Here he follows the fortunes of three generations of the Trotta family, all loyal servants of the crown from the apogee of the Austro-Hungarian Empire under the Hapsburgs, to the cataclysm of the First World War. The rise and fall of the Trottas reflects that of the Empire itself.

Roth looked back nostalgically on a civilized, cosmopolitan and multi-ethnic society in which each nation had its own literature and language, and a right to its own ethnicity, as part of the whole and which was blown apart by an act of nationalist terrorism. This event began a cycle of European political history the effects of which are still felt today.

This is an extraordinary work of great breadth and authority which contains within it the events in history of which our society is the direct descendent. But it is also a gripping, sweeping story compellingly told. For students of literature Roth's style has been described as Viennese Impressionist.

JOSEPH ROTH
1894 – 1939
Nationality: Austrian
First Published: G. Kiepenheuer
Verlag, 1932
Other Selected Titles:
The Spider's Web
The Blind Mirror
The Wandering Jews
Zipper and His Father
Right and Left
Tarabas
The Legend of the Holy Drinker
The Leviathan

The Human Stain

Philip Roth is world renowned for shining his light onto the public and private morality of contemporary America with consummate wit and insight. *The Human Stain* is the final part of his trilogy exploring this theme. The first two books were *An American Pastoral* (1997) and *I Married a Communist* (1998).

Nathan Zuckerman, our narrator, has retired to the Elysian American Athena College to take up the position of writer in residence.

Against the backdrop of Bill Clinton's potential impeachment, political correctness seems to have replaced real integrity and Zuckerman meets Coleman Silk, a distinguished former classics professor, forced to resign over an alleged racial slur. Silk's life collapsed and the death of his wife followed, but he has now started a relationship with a janitor. The same student, who spearheaded the campaign for his dismissal, now begins to accuse him of exploitation. But Silk has a far more explosive secret that he has kept for 50 years.

As always, Philip Roth's writing is beautiful, incisive and ironic, but what is 'the human stain'? Roth would appear to believe that it is our resolve to be better that leads to fanaticism and essential untruthfulness.

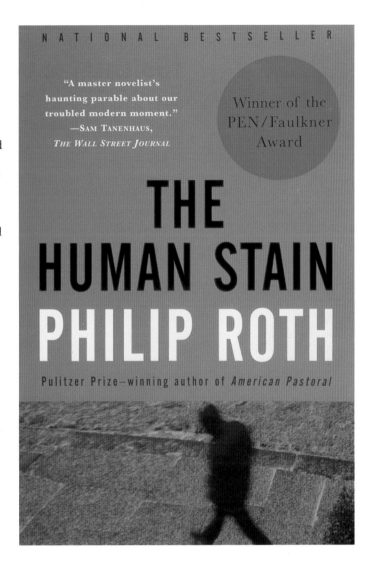

NATIONAL BESTSELLER

"A master novelist's haunting parable about our troubled modern moment."
—Sam Tanenhaus,
THE WALL STREET JOURNAL

Winner of the PEN/Faulkner Award

THE HUMAN STAIN
PHILIP ROTH

Pulitzer Prize—winning author of *American Pastoral*

PHILIP ROTH
1933 –
Nationality: American
First Published: Houghton Mifflin, 2000
Other Selected Titles:
Goodbye, Columbus
When She Was Good
Portnoy's Complaint
The Breast
My Life As a Man
The Ghost Writer
Zuckerman Unbound
The Anatomy Lesson

The Satanic Verses

SALMAN RUSHDIE
1947 –
Nationality: Indian
First Published: Viking, 1988
Other Selected Titles:
Shame
The Jaguar Smile: A Nicaraguan Journey
Haroun and the Sea of Stories
East, West
The Moor's Last Sigh
The Ground Beneath Her Feet
Fury
Shalimar the Clown

The most controversial book in recent time, Salman Rushdie's magical realist fiction is loosely based on the life of Muhammad. It was banned in many Muslim countries and led Ayatollah Ruhollah Khomeini, the Shi'a Muslim scholar who was also the Supreme Leader of Iran, to issue a fatwa which called for the death of Rushdie, an order which every Muslim had a duty to obey. Salman Rushdie is still under guard in 2006.

Gibreel Farishta and Saladin Chamcha are Indian expatriates living in England who have made a journey back to India. On their return journey, the plane in which they are travelling explodes over the English Channel.

By some miracle, the two protagonists survive but are transformed by the experience, literally as Gibreel finds that he now has a halo whilst Saladin has sprouted horns.

It is difficult to describe the full content of this novel in so few words. The dazzling literary brilliance, recognized when it was nominated for the Booker Prize in 1988, has been overshadowed by the Muslim world's reaction to its publication.

SALMAN RUSHDIE
THE SATANIC VERSES

'A STAGGERING ACHIEVEMENT, BRILLIANTLY ENJOYABLE'
NADINE GORDIMER

Pedro Páramo

The literary output of Juan Rulfo, the highly esteemed Mexican novelist, short story writer and photographer, adds up to just 300 pages and yet he has been a major influence on Spanish American writing and on the development of magical realism in fiction worldwide.

Gabriel Garcia Marquez cites *Pedro Páramo* as a masterpiece which influenced his novel *One Hundred Years of Solitude*. Rulfo's work was considered revolutionary in the Mexican canon, writing as he did with confused chronology, short sentences, a confection of fantasy and reality, and non-judgmental characterizations.

Juan Preciado returns to his mother's natal village Comala in search of the life story of his lost father the eponymous Pedro Páramo. He finds the village peopled only by ghosts, but they seem real to him. Through the people he meets he hears that his father ruined the village and through his actions killed it and all its inhabitants. Gradually, we come to understand that Juan is also a ghost.

Rulfo blends Mexican legend with his own experimental writing techniques, and adds a dash of dark humour to explore the difficulties of the father-son relationship and the importance of individual as well as national history. A fascinating work, in which the modern reader will feel very much at home.

'With the opening sentences ...we know we are in the hands of a master storyteller' - Susan Sontag ★★★★★

Juan Rulfo
PEDRO PÁRAMO

JUAN RULFO
1918 – 1986
Nationality: Mexican
First Published: 1955
Other Selected Titles:
The Burning Plain
Antología Personal (contains the two earlier books plus two new short stories)

Bonjour Tristesse

FRANCOISE SAGAN
1935 – 2004
Nationality: French
First Published: Julliard, 1954
Other Selected Titles:
A Certain Smile
Aimez-vous Brahams
Scars on the Soul
A Fleeting Sorrow

Françoise Sagan taking notes in a courthouse in Versailles, 1958.

'Hello Sadness' is the title's literal translation. Sagan's first novel, it was written when she was only 19. It was an immediate success and has had a cult following ever since. Indeed it is said to have been the inspiration for Simon and Garfunkel's *Sound of Silence*.

As with Salinger's *Catcher in the Rye*, it epitomizes teenage angst and the pain of and reluctance to assume adult responsibilities. The narrative is stream-of-conscience through the main protagonist, Cecile, who is 17 and spending the summer at the seaside with her widowed playboy father and two other women. The father Raymond is perhaps not the best role model, as his relationships are short-lived, usually with younger women. As the summer holiday unfolds Cecile has her own love affairs and has to come to terms with her father's engagement to Anne, who is a real adult.

This wonderfully descriptive 1950s classic portrays a rite of passage into the adult world.

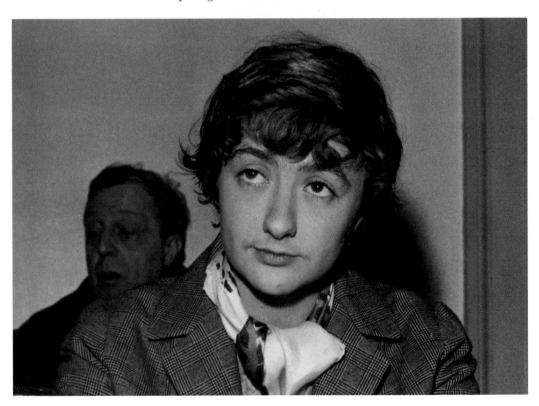

Bonjour Tristesse

Françoise Sagan

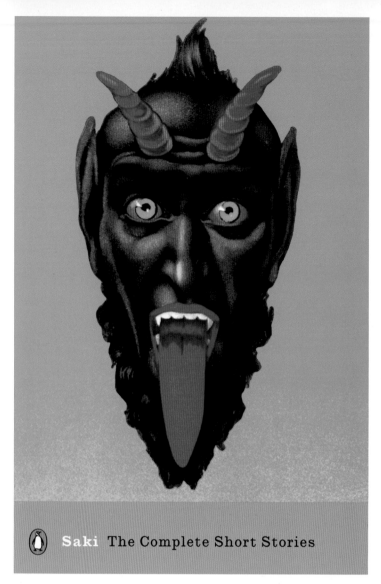

Saki The Complete Short Stories

Short Stories

This is an enchanting series of short stories that reflect the author's humourous, yet sardonic view of his Edwardian world. Saki is a master of the short story and is often compared to O Henry and Dorothy Parker. His leading character, Reginald, is very reminiscent of Wodehouse. Reginald lives in the world of the affluent upper classes. This character's tales depict his irreverent behaviour and his insightful and often amusing reflections on this society. Reginald's musings on how one should be trained in the science of buying presents will strike a chord even today. Saki's other famous protagonist is Clovis Sangrail, a clever young man who is also able to make fools of his fellow man. *The Unrest-Cure* is a not-to-be-missed story about curing the need for routine.

The author died in the First World War, enlisting as an ordinary soldier when over age. He perished on the battle field in 1916. Saki's light and elegant style overlays a more robust and enduring theme, that of the absurdity of fads and fashion against the horrors of the world.

**SAKI
(HECTOR HUGH MUNRO)**
1870 – 1916
Nationality: British
First Published: Oxford University
Press, 1993
Other Selected Titles:
*The Rise of the Russian Empire
Not-So-Stories
Reginald
The Chronicles of Clovis
The Unbearable Bassington
The Toys of Peace
The Square Egg and Other Sketches
The Works of Saki* (8 Volumes)

Catcher in the Rye

This Postmodernist novel concerns the relationships and escapades of an unstable teenage boy. It was published to much critical and popular acclaim, although its sexual and anti-social content did invoke criticism. It gained further notoriety by association. The murderer of John Lennon was said to be reading *Catcher in the Rye* at the time of the killing. John Hinckly Jr., who attempted to assassinate Ronald Reagan, is also believed to have been obsessed with the book.

Contemporaneously set, the narrator and protagonist, Holden Caulfield, tells his own tale through a stream-of-consciousness to his doctor while in a hospital. Holden is always isolated; he has moved from school to school. The book depicts his relationships with a large number of characters: school friends, teachers, girl friends, a prostitute, his siblings and parents. The recurrent themes are an obsession with and fear of sex, the feeling that adult or emerging adult behaviour is 'phoney', and identification with children. Holden speaks with his younger dead brother and he is best understood by his nine-year-old sister, Phoebe. His most positive fantasy is as a hero who saves children by catching them before they fall off a cliff while playing in a field of rye.

This book exposes the universal fear of growing up. It is a powerful, though at times unsettling, read.

J.D. SALINGER
1919 –
Nationality: American
First Published: Little Brown & Co., 1951
Other Selected Titles:
This Sandwich has No Mayonnaise
I'm Crazy
A Perfect Day for Bananafish
For Esme with Love and Squalor
Nine Stories
Franny and Zooey

The home of reclusive author J.D. Salinger in New Hampshire.

Staying On

PAUL SCOTT
1920 – 1978
Nationality: British
First Published: Heineman, 1977
Other Selected Titles:
Sahib and Memsahibs
The Jewel in the Crown
The Day of the Scorpion
Towers of Silence
A Division of Spoils

This is the sequel to the Raj Quartet which is best known for *The Jewel in the Crown*. With its wonderful characterizations, *Staying On* is a joy to read. One will never forget the retired ex-pat Colonel Tusker and the blue-rinsed Mrs Lucy Smalley, their landlords the robust bridge-playing Mrs Bhoolabhoy and the slim, mild Mr Bhoolabhoy. *Staying On* brings to life the post-Raj era of the 1940s and 1950s. Through the elderly Smalleys we gain an understanding of those that continued to cling to the faded remnants of the Empire. This in contrast to, and against the backdrop of an emerging India that is moving on, and asserting its own identity.

Scott's analysis of this period is both perceptive and unrelenting. It is not surprising that *Staying On* was immediately acclaimed and won a Booker Prize in 1977.

WINNER OF THE BOOKER PRIZE

PAUL SCOTT

Staying On

'A RICH AND JOYFUL BOOK'

SUNDAY TIMES

Austerlitz

The author of this book is one of the most significant German writers since the Second World War, whose untimely death is a great loss to the literary world. Brought up in the late 1940s and 1950s, Sebald reflects on the scars and trauma made by the horrors of the war on society.

W.G. SEBALD
1944 – 2001
Nationality: German
First Published: C. Hanser, 2001
Other Selected Titles:
Rings of Saturn
Vertigo
For Years Now: Poems
After Nature

This novel tells the story of Austerlitz, an infant boy sent from Czechoslovakia to Wales as a refugee in 1939. The book begins in the 1960s when Austerlitz has grown up and become a historian of architecture. The plot travels back through his childhood and forward to present day and from city to city (Brussels, Prague, Paris), slowly revealing Aulsterlitz' past and his origins. Also, it describes the death of his mother in a concentration camp while Austerlitz was safe in Britain.

Sebald's unique Postmodernist style heightens the mood of the book with use of photographic imagery and lack of paragraphs. A thought-provoking book that you will want to read from cover to cover.

W. G. SEBALD

'His tale of one man's odyssey through the dark ages of European history is one of the most moving and true fictions on the postwar

Last Exit to Brooklyn

HUBERT SELBY JR.
1920 – 1978
Nationality: American
First Published: Grove Press, 1964
Other Selected Titles:
The Room
The Demon
Requiem for a Dream
Song of the Silent Snow
The Willow Tree

Writer Hubert Selby, Jr.

This novel will be a profound awakening for anyone who still believes that the 1950s and 1960s in the US was all poodle skirts, prom dances, rock and roll and the burgeoning fast food industry.

In this hard-hitting look at the slums in New York City, Selby portrays a world of sexual deviants, street fighting, drug addiction, prostitution and gang rape. He also deals with taboo family issues, including domestic violence, pre-marital sex and pregnancy. Selby writes in Postmodernist style using little punctuation, creating his own dialect and spelling to enhance the characterization.

In 1966 when the book was first brought to Britain, it provoked a series of famous obscenity trials. However it was finally allowed to be published in 1968. In its time, *Last Exit to Brooklyn* was a shocking wake-up call to the social issues of the time. However, what makes it such a classic read is that his messages are equally relevant to us today.

Unless

This is an extraordinary book which explores profound social and gender issues through the genre of everyday life. It is not a book that shocks with language or creates new grammar to make an impact. The rage against social injustice and the questioning of why this must be, is done through conventional means and ordinary events (like dusting). And in doing so, it is all the more powerful.

The story centres on Reta Winters, a middle-aged woman with a happy and successful life. Reta is a mother of three, her partner Tom is a doctor, and she is an award-winning writer of light fiction and a translator of French feminist works.

Reta's sunny world is destabilized when her eldest daughter drops out of university and life, sits on the pavement with a sign around her neck saying 'Goodness', and mutely begs for money. Reta's bewilderment and grief spark her off on questioning the role of women and their disempowerment by men, often with their own compliance. In usual Shields style, this is done with humour and a finesse that are a delight to read.

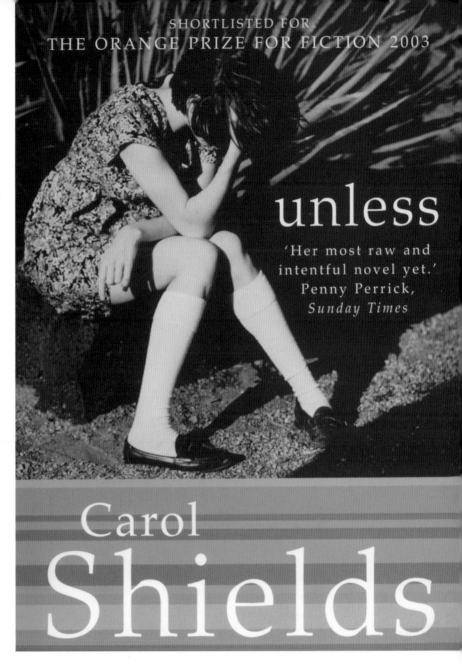

SHORTLISTED FOR THE ORANGE PRIZE FOR FICTION 2003

unless

'Her most raw and intentful novel yet.'
Penny Perrick,
Sunday Times

Carol Shields

CAROL SHIELDS
1935 – 2003
Nationality: Canadian
First Published: Fourth Estate, 2002
Other Selected Titles:
Happenstance
The Stone Diaries
Larry's Party
The Republic of Love

ISAAC BASHEVIS SINGER
The Magician Of Lublin

ISAAC BASHEVIS SINGER
1902 – 1991
Nationality: Polish
First Published: Secker and
Warburg, 1961
Other Selected Titles:
The Family Moskat
Elijah The Slave
Enemies, a Love Story
The Hasidim
Yentl the Yeshiva Boy
Scum
Meshugah
Shadows on the Hudson

The Magician of Lublin

The theme of this masterpiece is that of faith and conscience. The narrative of this book is beautifully lyrical, echoing Singer's native language Yiddish. It brings to life the atmosphere of late 19th-century Poland and the beguiling 'magician' Yasha Mazur.

Mazur, the main protagonist, is an acrobat, escape artist, fire eater and all-round entertainer. He is also a boyish rogue and womanizer. His patient loving wife Ester stays at home while Mazur tours and acquires a number of mistresses. To support his home, his women and his ambitions, Mazur needs money, and so his troubles begin. He decides to commit a robbery and one disaster follows another. His growing guilt and belief in God lead to a 'Road to Damascus' experience. Mazur renounces the world and lives the life of a hermit, no longer the Magician of Lublin, but a penitent. However, even then Mazur is still an attraction as pilgrims flock to see this holy man.

The Engineer of Human Souls

The title for this book comes from Stalin's vision of artists, and particularly writers, as those who engineer or re-engineer the human mind and soul. Although *The Engineer of Human Souls* certainly has political overtones, the book is better characterized by its subtitle: An Entertainment on the Old Themes of Life, Women, Fate, Dreams, the Working Class, Secret Agents, Love and Death.

JOSEF SKVORECKY
1924 –
Nationality: Czech
First Published: 1977
Other Selected Titles:
The Cowards
The Miracle Game
The Bass Saxophone
Dvorak in Love
The Bride of Texas

This witty and amusing tale is considered by many to be semi-autobiographical of Skvorecky's own life.

The story centres on Danny Smiricky, a Czech writer who escaped Communist rule in the late 1960s and lives in exile in Canada. He becomes a professor of literature at a university in Toronto. The book is full of episodes from his past when living in Prague under oppressive regimes, and of his new life full of college students and Czech secret police. Skvorecky's Postmodernist style has been described as labyrinthine or sprawling. This may be so but it only adds to the charm and mood of the book.

"MAGNIFICENT! A MAGNUM OPUS!"
MILAN KUNDERA

THE ENGINEER OF HUMAN SOULS

Josef Skvorecky

The Prime of Miss Jean Brodie ✓

MURIEL SPARK
1918 – 2006
Nationality: Scottish
First Published: Macmillan & Co.,
1961
Other Selected Titles:
The Girls of Slender Means
The Mandelbaum Gate
Not to Disturb
The Abbess of Crewe
Loitering with Intent
A Far Cry from Kensington
Symposium
Reality and Dreams

*Muriel Spark gets down
to work in 1960.*

This elegant yet sparse novel is written in the third person with wonderfully insightful characterizations, the signature of Murial Spark. The themes are the misuse of power and deception, including self-deception. It is also a moral tale, as in the end the evil is unmasked and punished.

The novel is primarily set in a private girls school in Scotland during the late 1930s; although at points the plot does traverse time, back in history and forward into the future. The main characters are Miss Jean Brodie, a spinster teacher, and Sandy Strange one of her students in the 'Brodie set'.

Miss Brodie is a charismatic and domineering woman who uses her position to influence her pupils, particularly the *crème de la crème* Brodie Set. Her anti-establishment teaching style and romantic notions win her popularity with the girls. They follow her unquestioningly, all except Sandy Strange who is her own person and begins to understand the true meaning of Miss Brodie's extreme fascist sympathies. A clever and enchanting book; Ms Spark will be sadly missed!

The Man Who Loved Children

A tale of the quintessentially dysfunctional family, this novel analyzes family dynamics and their impact on family members with insight and compassion. Said to be semi-autobiographical, it is set in the US, rather than Stead's native Australia. The book is wonderfully full of comic irony starting with its title. The Pollit family consists of dad, Sam, and the uncaring misogynist mother Henny (stepmother to Louisa). They have six children, with at the top of the heap Louisa (11 years of age), and ending with Charles Franklin, the baby. Sam sees himself as one of life's champions, but is in reality portrayed as a bully who abuses the very ones he should be taking care of. Henny sees herself as impoverished gentlefolk, but is 'no better than she should be', filching money, verbally berating Sam and having an affair. The children are placed in the centre of all this hate and despair.

Stead deals with the universal theme of the family in a hard-hitting and pragmatic style, with no morose self-indulgence. Written in the third person, her descriptions are transporting – one can see and smell R Street and Reservoir Road.

CHRISTINA STEAD
1902 – 1983
Nationality: Australian
First Published: Simon & Schuster, 1940
Other Selected Titles:
The Salzbury Tales
The Beauties and Furies
House of All Nations
For Love Alone
Modern Women in Love
A Little Tea. A Little Chat
Dark Places of the Heart
A Little Hotel: a Novel

John Steinbeck

The Grapes of Wrath

BK.

PENGUIN MODERN CLASSICS   5/-

The Grapes of Wrath

This Pulitzer Prize-winning epic confronts the themes of oppression and injustice. Steinbeck cleverly depicts the struggle to retain dignity and preserve the family in the face of disaster, natural and otherwise, while at the mercy of impersonal commercial influences.

Set in the Great Depression, the novel follows the Joad family's journey from the famine-hit Dust Bowl to the promised land of California. They are tenant farmers, forced by the famine to sell up and join the throngs that are heading west. Along the way there is great deprivation and some of the family die. The Joads and other travellers learn to create a sharing social network. Upon arrival in California, they find that their trials are not over, jobs are scarce and the pay poor. The Joads suffer abuse from the authorities and are exploited by organized business. This culminates in son Tom exploding with anger and killing a man.

This American classic is written in a narrative that uses colloquial dialogue to produce strong imagery.

JOHN STEINBECK
1902 – 1968
Nationality: American
First Published: Viking, 1939
Other Selected Titles:
Tortilla Flat
Of Mice and Men
Cannery Row
The Pearl
East of Eden
Sweet Thursday
Aiding and Abetting
The Finishing School

Sophie's Choice

This is a dark and disturbing tale which analyzes the theme of racial hatred and tyranny. Set in New York City in the late 1940s, the main characters are Stingo, a young writer from Virginia, Sophie, a beautiful Catholic Pole who survived Auschwitz, and her Jewish boyfriend Nathan. The story is reflectively narrated by Stingo, looking back on his youth and his friendship with Sophie and Nathan. He tells of his growing love for Sophie and her horrific story, as it had been gradually revealed to him layer on layer. Throughout his narrative, Nathan becomes increasingly mentally unstable, and bouts of violence are vividly portrayed. Slowly Stingo comes to realize that Nathan and Sophie's dysfunctional relationship is sustained by her overwhelming need to nurture, as well as to punish herself for surviving Auschwitz having made Sophie's Choice.

Styron is a master at confronting the big ticket social issues. He won a Pulitzer Prize for *The Confessions of Nat Turner*, a social commentary on slavery.

WILLIAM STYRON
1925 – 2006
Nationality: American
First Published: Random House, 1979
Other Selected Titles:
Lie Down in the Darkness
The Long March
Set This House on Fire
The Confessions of Nat Turner
Darkness Visible:
A Memoir of Madness
A Tidewater Morning:
Three Tales from Youth

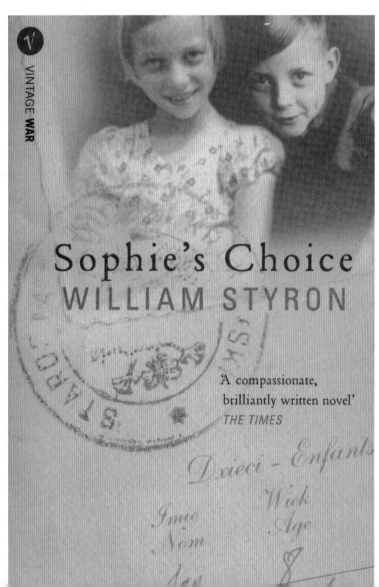

VINTAGE WAR

Sophie's Choice
WILLIAM STYRON

'A compassionate, brilliantly written novel'
THE TIMES

Perfume

PATRICK SUSKIND
1949 –
Nationality: German
First Published: Diogenes, 1985
Other Selected Titles:
The Story of Mr Sommer
The Pigeon
Double Bass
Three Stories and a Reflection

This is Gothic at its sensual best. The subtitle 'The Story of a Murder' does give a hint as to what it is about. Set in France during the 18th century, it is the tale of Jean-Baptiste Grenouille whose life's goal is to create the perfect fragrance. Jean-Baptiste is a unique individual, as he has no odour himself but has an extraordinary sense of smell. He becomes a perfumier's apprentice and identifies the most exquisite perfume in the world, that of virgin girls. The only way he can obtain it is to kill, and kill he does, many times.

Originally written in German, it has been faithfully translated into English. The descriptions of perfume production are wonderful. And those of scents and fragrances are evocative – truly a sensual experience of an olfactory nature. *Perfume* also addresses the age-old moral issue, can achieving perfection ever be justified at such cost to human life?

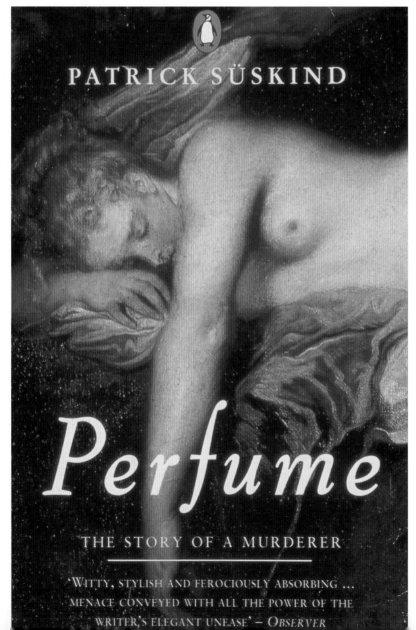

PATRICK SÜSKIND

Perfume

THE STORY OF A MURDERER

'WITTY, STYLISH AND FEROCIOUSLY ABSORBING ...
MENACE CONVEYED WITH ALL THE POWER OF THE
WRITER'S ELEGANT UNEASE' – *OBSERVER*

The Confessions of Zeno

The first book to attempt to answer the question, 'Why can't I give up smoking?', this is psychoanalytical work of the Modernist genre, said to be informed by the Sigmund Freud school. This clever, and at times humourous, novel is presented in the form of a diary written by Zeno Casino, the protagonist, used by his psychiatrist as part of his treatment.

The book follows Zeno's life of smoking from his early youth, and maps the number of times that he tries to give up, having the 'last cigarette'. The 'last cigarette' becomes a ritual that must be performed again, echoing the theme 'Today is the First Day of the Rest of Your Life'. Alas it also means that smoking must inevitably begin again. The diary follows key events in Zeno's life and the quest to be cured of his addiction.

Svevo published this masterpiece with his own money as it had been rejected by publishers. His work was discovered and championed by James Joyce whom he knew in Trieste.

ITALO SVEVO
1886 – 1928
Nationality: Italian
First Published: Cappelli, 1923
Other Selected Titles:
Translation
The Hoax
Generous Wine
*The Nice Old Man and the Pretty Girl
and Other Stories*
Inferiority
Further Confessions of Zeno

DECLARES PEREIRA

ANTONIO TABUCCHI

ANTONIO TABUCCHI
1943 –
Nationality: Italian
First Published: Feltrinelli, 1994
Other Selected Titles:
The Edge of the Horizon
The Missing Head of Damasceno Monteiro
Requiem: A Hallucination
It's Getting Later All the Time

Declares Pereira

This is a moving tale of growing political awareness and outrage set in Fascist Portugal in 1938 under Antonio Salazar.

The story's main protagonist is Dr Pereira, a middle-aged journalist writing the cultural page for a Lisbon paper. He is lost in the tranquil world of translating French classics, eating omelettes and generally keeping his head down.

Dr Pereira is a widower with no children, and talks regularly to his wife's photograph. His life changes when he hires a talented young student, Monteiro Rossi, who writes contentious articles and annoys the officials.

Rossi and his activist girlfriend make it impossible for Dr Pereira to continue in neutral anonymity. He is forced to make a moral choice. Tabbucchi uses an unusual third person style, portraying events from Periera's point of view and repeatedly using 'Pereira declares' in the narrative.

The White Hotel

This is a powerful psychological fantasy centred on a very mentally ill woman and set in the pre-World War Two era. The main protagonist is Elizabeth (or Lisa) Erdman, the daughter of a Russian Jewish father and Polish Catholic mother.

The book recounts her obsessions with sex and death. Her sexual fantasies are described in the first person in explicit and gripping detail. These may shock some readers, so be warned. Lisa is a patient of Freud and a section of the novel explores his analysis of her and the diagnosis of sexual hysteria. Freud describes her physical pain and pre-occupation with natural disasters and death. Thomas engineers a twist in the storyline with the holocaust and Lisa's own demise.

Thomas creates a Postmodern masterpiece; each section is presented from a different perspective, moving from first to third person narrative. His descriptions are powerful and his prose masterful. This is a compelling but rather disturbing read.

D.M. THOMAS
1935 –
Nationality: British
First Published: Gollancz, 1981
Other Selected Titles:
The Flute-Player
Birthstone
Russian Nights
Swallow
Sphinx
Lying Together
Flying into Love
Lady with a Laptop

THE
WHITE HOTEL
D. M. THOMAS
THE EXTRAORDINARY NOVEL WHICH
BECAME THE GREAT BESTSELLER

The Master

COLM TOIBIN
1955 –
Nationality: Irish
First Published: Picador, 2004
Other Selected Titles:
The South
The Heather Blazing
The Story of the Night
The Blackwater Lightship

This highly acclaimed novel won several awards and was nominated for a Booker Prize. This alone should signal that *The Master* is true literature and worth reading. It falls into a genre sometimes called biographical fiction, the elaboration and analysis of the life of a real person. In this case it is Henry James. *The Master* is beautifully written in elegant language evocative of the late 19th century.

Tóibín pulls us into the life of Henry James when he is in his 50s, and at a time when he is just about to undertake his theatrical production of Guy Domville. This turned out not to be one of his greatest triumphs, and leads him to become more isolated and introspective. Through James, Tóibín explores three distinct themes, that of latent homosexuality, that of being middle aged, and that of loss. The latter two are intertwined, as the impact of the past and of loss do not evaporate as one expects in youth.

Colm Tóibín in London, 2004.

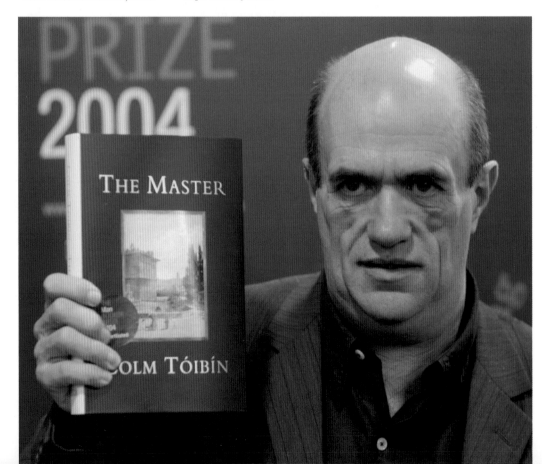

Felicia's Journey

A prolific author, Trevor won the Whitbread Prize (Best Novel) for this book in 1994. Subsequently it was made into an acclaimed film by Atom Egoyan starring Bob Hoskins. *Felicia's Journey* is the quintessential psychological thriller, and Felicia is an archetypal victim. After the death of her mother she is forced to take care of her family. Desperate and lonely, she meets Johnny, falls in love, is seduced, gets pregnant and unbeknownst to her is deceived and abandoned.

After the family rejects her, Felicia leaves her small town in Ireland to find Johnny in England. On her travels she falls into the clutches of Mr Hilditch, who initially seems like a nice man but who is really evil and has horrific plans for her. The tension mounts and the drama then plays out.

Wonderfully written by William Trevor, one lives Felicia's journey with her and even feels compassion for Mr Hilditch.

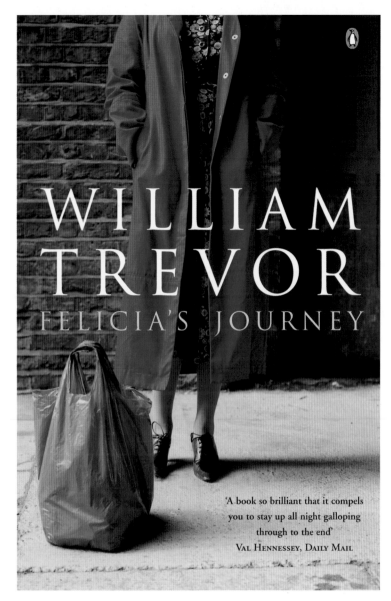

WILLIAM TREVOR

TREVOR

FELICIA'S JOURNEY

'A book so brilliant that it compels you to stay up all night galloping through to the end'
VAL HENNESSEY, DAILY MAIL

WILLIAM TREVOR
1928 –
Nationality: Irish
First Published: Viking, 1994
Other Selected Titles:
A Standard of Behaviour
The Old Boys
Mrs Eckdorf in O'Neill's Hotel
Miss Gomez and the Brethren
After Rain
Death in Summer
The Story of Lucy Gault
A Bit On the Side

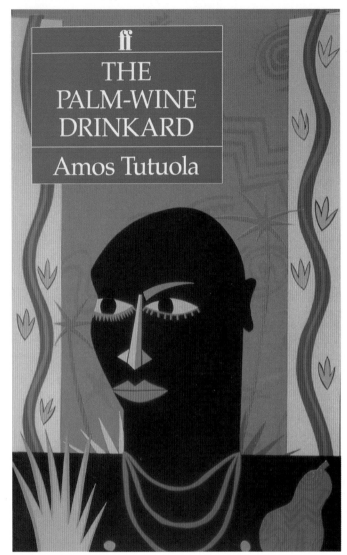

The Palm-Wine Drinkard

Based on Nigerian Yoruba folktales, this is the story of an 'expert' palm-wine drinkard who searches for his tapster in 'Deads Town'. The book is full of fantastic characters and images that transport the reader into a bizarre folktale world. The style and dialogue are reminiscent of oral traditions, using a form of pidgin English to reinforce the theme. Tutuola was a self-made man with only a limited education, and yet reportedly wrote this magical tale in only a few days.

When it was first published, *The Palm-Wine Drinkard* met with much critical acclaim in the United States and England. It came to the attention of Dylan Thomas who was an instant fan and actively promoted the book. Indeed this classic is now part of many educational curricula. However, it was not well received in Nigeria due to the use of broken English, primitive style and allusions to drunkenness. This is a must for all lovers of African fiction and folklorists.

AMOS TUTUOLA
1920 – 1997
Nationality: Nigerian
First Published: Faber and Faber, 1952
Other Selected Titles:
My Life in the Bush of Ghosts
Simbi and the Satyr of the Dark Jungle
The Brave African Huntress
The Feather Woman of the Jungle
Ajaiyi and his Inherited Poverty
Witch-Herbalist of the Remote Town
The Wild Hunter in the Bush of Ghosts
Pauper, Brawler and Slanderer

The Accidental Tourist

This is a beautifully written tale of bereavement and its impact on relationships. The main protagonist is Macon Leary, a middle-aged writer of travel books who does not like travel. He and his wife Sarah have lost their son in a shooting incident, and the story begins when they are still in the early stages of grief.

Sarah decides that Macon is not a comfort to her, and his idiosyncratic habits are getting on her nerves. The couple separate, leaving Macon with his writing and reorganizing the home. By happenstance, Macon takes on Murial to help train his dysfunctional dog. Murial is full of life and often described as eccentric. The story unfolds around Macon's relationships with Murial, Sarah and the rest of his family; and how he learns to move on.

This is a funny, sad book full of insight and a host of wonderful characters.

ANNE TYLER
1941 –
Nationality: American
First Published: The Ballantine Publishing Group, 1985
Other Selected Titles:
If Morning Ever Comes
Celestial Navigation
Earthly Possessions
Breathing Lessons
Saint Maybe
A Patchwork Planet
Back When We Were Grownups
The Amateur Marriage

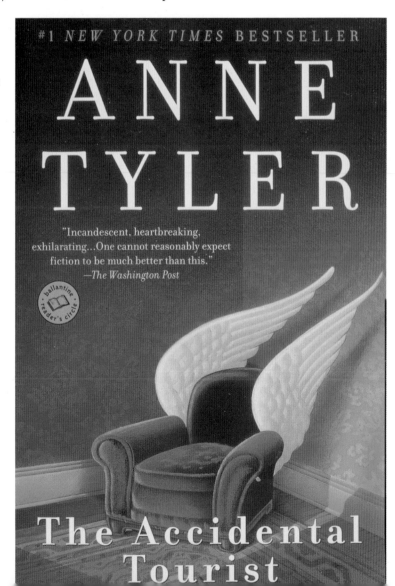

#1 *NEW YORK TIMES* BESTSELLER

ANNE TYLER

"Incandescent, heartbreaking, exhilarating...One cannot reasonably expect fiction to be much better than this."
—*The Washington Post*

The Accidental Tourist

Couples

When published, this book created a sensation in the United States along the lines of the author's *Rabbit Run*. Written in his signature style and in a genre of frank realism, Updike presents an explicit exposé of adulterous sex in middle-class America in the 1960s. The irony is that this was also the era when Hippies 'discovered' sex and free love, to the disapproval of their parents. And yet so much was already happening behind suburban net curtains. Set in a fictitious New England town, Tarbox, the novel details the adulterous exploits of the town's married

American novelist John Updike.

JOHN UPDIKE
1932 –
Nationality: American
First Published: Penguin, 1968
Other Selected Titles:
A Month of Sundays
Rabbit Run
The Witches of Eastwick
Roger's Version
Brazil
Gertrude and Claudius
Seek My Face
Villages

couples. The story centres on Piet, a builder, and his affairs, particularly with Foxy the new girl in town. Shockingly, Foxy is not just married to Ken but is also pregnant. Not that either of these are deterrents, though in a letter to Piet, Foxy notes that they may be obstacles to her sexual satisfaction. However, as the plot unfolds the course of true lust does not run smoothly.

Updike's artistry with language and mastery of characterization take this beyond just a saucy read and he really does delve into the psychology of adultery.

The Time of the Hero

This, the first novel of this highly acclaimed Peruvian and Latin American novelist, deals with the themes of justice and personal choice, and was influenced by his own experience as a student. The story is set in a military academy in Lima and follows the exploits of four cadets in a gang called The Circle. The boys steal an exam paper and eventually one of them informs on the others. In retaliation the informer is murdered. The crime is covered up by the authorities to preserve the reputation of the Academy and its 'honour'.

The Time of the Hero met with immediate international acclaim, not just for the contentious content, but also for Llosa's progressive Postmodernist style. Llosa uses structure not only to relate the events but also to evoke the emotion of the action and the feelings of the characters. The story moves from past to present, from third person to first person narrative, and simultaneously runs several plot threads, all to stunning effect.

MARIO VARGAS LLOSA
1936 –
Nationality: Peruvian
First Published: 1963
Other Selected Titles:
The Green House
Conversations in the Cathedral
Captain Pantoja and the Secret
Service
The War of the End of the World
In Praise of Stepmother
Notebooks of Don Rigoberto
The Feast of the Goat
The Way to Paradise

Peruvian writer Mario Vargas Llosa.

In Praise of Older Women

STEPHEN VIZINCZEY
1933 –
Nationality: Hungarian
First Published: Contemporary
Canada Press, 1965
Other Selected Titles:
An Innocent Millionaire
Truth and Lies in Literature

This author is a well-known Hungarian novelist, critic and translator. Vizinczey is also a social commentator and known for his quotes. 'Strange as it seems, no amount of learning can cure stupidity and higher education positively fortifies it.'
In Praise of Older Women, as the subtitle states, are 'The Amorous Recollections of Andras Vajda'. They are written in the first person from Andras' perspective. He recounts his early background as a Roman Catholic acolyte in post-war Hungary, who is contemplating becoming a priest. However, he has doubts about being celibate even then, because of his attraction to his mother's friends, and one particular aunt. This sensual novel then relates his first encounter with an older woman, and his continuing erotic adventures.

Beautifully written, this book gives an insight into the psychology of a young man during the period of sexual maturation. It is not viewed by all, however, as politically correct from a feminist's perspective.

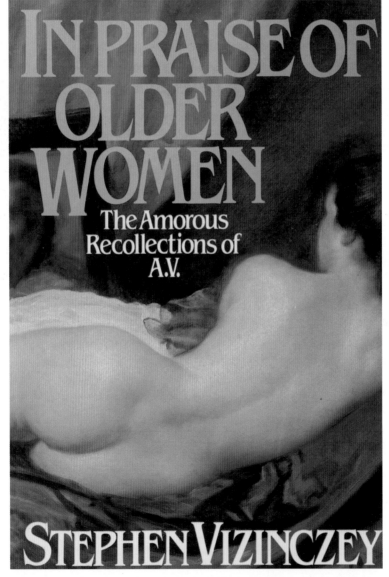

Brideshead Revisited ✓

His magnum opus, *Brideshead Revisited* is one of the best-loved novels by Evelyn Waugh. The television adaptation in 1981 gave *Brideshead Revisited* an enormous popular following and is still today considered one of the best British television productions. Waugh wrote this book as an expression of his Catholic faith and it deals with the themes of grace and forgiveness. The story is told about the aristocratic Flyte family, seen through the eyes of the protagonist, Charles Ryder. It is set in pre-War England, in the time of country houses and elegant weekend parties. The story follows the journey of redemption for members of the Flyte family, each reconciling with their faith and renouncing their quite considerable sins. Charles begins the novel as an agnostic, but in the end he is portrayed kneeling in the Brideshead Castle chapel as a symbol of his conversion.

Waugh's masterly and innovative use of prose makes *Brideshead Revisited* a delight to read and an inspirational classic.

Evelyn Waugh in 1943.

EVELYN WAUGH
1903 – 1966
Nationality: British
First Published: Chapman & Hall, 1945
Other Selected Titles:
Decline and Fall
Vile Bodies
Black Mischief
A Handful of Dust
Scoop
Love Among the Ruins
Officers and Gentlemen
Unconditional Surrender

Voss

PATRICK WHITE
1912 – 1990
Nationality: Australian
First Published: Eyre &
Spottiswoode, 1957
Other Selected Titles:
Happy Valley
The Living and the Dead
Riders in the Chariot
The Solid Mandala
The Vivisector
The Eye of the Storm
The Twyborn Affair
Flaws in the Glass

Published to much acclaim, this book won the Miles Franklin Literary award for best Australian novel in 1958. It is a superb epic adventure of a German explorer, Johann Voss, who sets out to cross the Australian continent in the mid 1800s. The expedition is doomed to failure; he becomes ill and never returns. This is said to be based on the true story of Ludwig Leichhardt, a Prussian explorer who disappeared in the Australian outback. *Voss* is a hard-hitting tale of one man's determination to triumph over the elements. It is also a poignant love story of a mystical connection between two people. Voss meets Laura Trevelyan, an orphaned spinster of character, before he starts his adventure. Even apart, their relationship and love deepens. They have a strong psychic connection which grows as he treks slowly through the desert.

This compelling novel depicting one man's quest is written in White's acclaimed Modernist style.

PENGUIN BOOKS

VOSS

Patrick White

Memoirs of Hadrian

Marguerite Yourcenar at a special dinner in her honour in Paris, 1981.

Written as a pseudo-autobiography, *Memoirs of Hadrian* was published to instant acclaim. This masterly work weaves fact and fiction together, bringing Hadrian and the Roman world to life. The historical detail of the life of this 2nd-century AD Roman Emperor has been superbly researched. Yourcenar wrote the book as a first person narrative in the form of a letter from Hadrian to his successor designate, Marcus Aurelius.

In it, Hadrian contemplates his past exploits, both personal and as a leader, his military triumphs, his love of the arts and his views on Rome. Yourcenar uses Hadrian to muse on the philosophy of life and love; the two universal imponderables. Of life, that first-hand experience is both the most valuable, and yet the most difficult; and of love, how one must throw oneself into love, regardless of the risk.

A book that one can get lost in, believing that it is truly Hadrian's voice, though this literary classic is so much more.

MARGUERITE YOURCENAR
1903 – 1987
Nationality: French
First Published: Librarie Plon, 1951
Other Selected Titles:
Oriental Tales
Mishima: A Vision of the Void

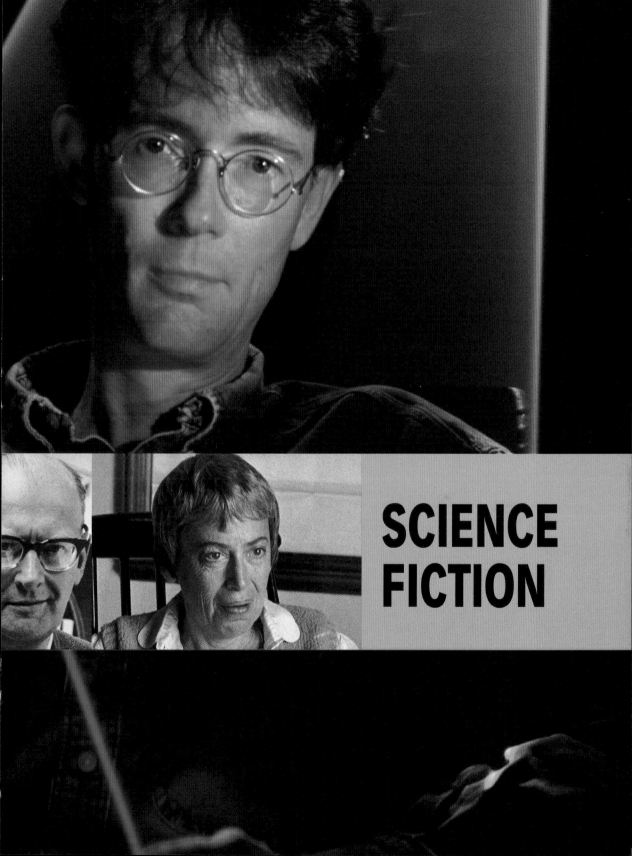

SCIENCE FICTION

The Hitch Hiker's Guide to the Galaxy

DOUGLAS NOEL ADAMS
1952 – 2001
Nationality: British
First Published: Pan, 1979
Other Selected Titles:
*The Restaurant at the End of
the Universe
Life, the Universe and Everything
So Long, and Thanks For All the Fish
Mostly Harmless
Pirate Planets
Dirk Gently's Holistic Detective
Agency
The Long Dark Tea Time of the Soul*

Douglas Adams in 1984.

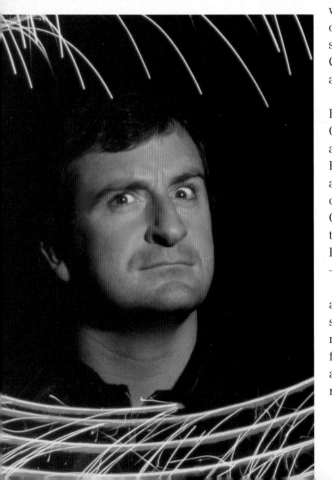

In the first book of his trilogy in five parts, adapted from his 1978 radio series, Douglas Adams unites comedy and science fiction in a way often imitated, but rarely matched, since. He introduces the completely hapless Arthur Dent, whose planet is about to be blown up to make way for a hyperspatial express route. Making his escape when his friend Ford Prefect hitches a lift from the Vogon destructor fleet, an increasingly bewildered Arthur discovers a galaxy as illogical and as full of maddening individuals as his own, now vaporized, planet.

Clad in his pyjamas and dressing gown, clutching his towel and the electronic guidebook that Ford has loaned him, and with a Babelfish stuck in his ear to translate what is going on, the typically reserved middle-class Englishman has to learn to cope with Vogon poetry, the vacuum of space, and the discovery that the Earth is in fact a giant supercomputer designed to provide the Ultimate Question to Life, the Universe and Everything, and all without a cup of tea.

Arthur's companions on his journey are Ford, who actually comes from Betelgeuse, not Guildford; Trillian, whom he once failed to pick up at a party in Islington; her pet mice Benjy and Frankie; Marvin the Paranoid Android; and Arthur's antithesis, Zaphod Beeblebrox, the supercool, self-obsessed and totally amoral President of the Galaxy who is quite willing to sell Arthur's brain to the pan-dimensional beings for whom the original Earth was built – Benjy mouse and Frankie mouse – so they can extract the Ultimate Question.

The Hitch Hiker's Guide to the Galaxy is a deeply funny account of the adventures of a slightly dull, originally reluctant space traveller, a man who has been wrenched away from everything familiar, who at times feels that life, the universe and everything are against him, and would really prefer to go home.

Hothouse

This science fiction classic is an
archetype of the 'dying Earth' genre.
The story is set tens of millions of years
in the future when the Sun has swollen to
a red giant. The Earth has stopped
rotating and one side of it swelters in the
heat of the Sun, while the other side
is in permanent darkness.

The descendants of humanity are
primitive, superstitious hunter-gatherers
who live in the branches of a vast banyan
tree that covers most of the hot side of
the planet, in a jungle where they
struggle against giant insects and
carnivorous plants that hunt.

Gren, a young man, rebels against
his tribe's beliefs and strikes out with a
companion on a dangerous journey
through the jungle where he encounters
terrifying monsters and sentient plant
forms, including a fungus that attaches
itself to him and begins to influence his
thoughts. Episode follows episode at a
fevered pace, all the time overlain with
Aldiss' fevered descriptions of the landscape and the fantastic
plants and creatures that inhabit it.

During his journey, which ends at the ocean, Gren meets
other people who have dreams of escaping the dying planet and
heading out into space. Having discovered much about their
world and about humanity's descent from its once-dominant
position, Gren and his companions must decide their own
futures. Do they head out into space or return to the jungle,
their curiosity satisfied?

Criticized at the time of publication for straying from
science fiction into the realms of fantasy, and ignoring the laws
of physics, Aldiss' novel addresses themes that are as relevant
today as when he wrote it, including the nature of religion and
the future of humanity and the planet on which we live.

*English writer Brian Aldiss in
Brittany, 2000.*

BRIAN ALDISS
1925 –
Nationality: British
First Published: Faber & Faber,
1962
Other Selected Titles:
Starship
Vanguard from Alpha
The Airs of Earth
The Dark Light Years
Greybeard
Brothers of the Head
Enemies of the System

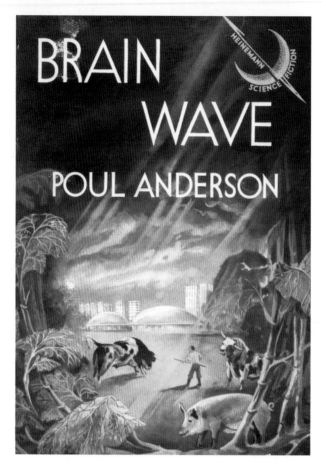

POUL ANDERSON
1926 – 2001
Nationality: American
First Published: Ballantine Books,
1954
Other Selected Titles:
Planet of No Return
War of the Wing-Men
War of Two Worlds
Virgin Planet
We Claim These Stars
Mayday Orbit
The Star Fox
The Rebel Worlds

Brain Wave

The basic premise of this the first of Anderson's novels is that there are areas in the galaxy where electromagnetic impulses and electrochemical reactions are inhibited, so slowing down nerve impulses and making humans, and animals, less intelligent than they would otherwise be. The narrative starts at the point when the Earth's movement through the galaxy suddenly takes it out of one of these regions, where it has been for millions of years, perhaps since before the dinosaurs died out.

People suddenly become more intelligent, cattle refuse to go to slaughter, horses will not be saddled and chimpanzees acquire basic speech. Many people find they have become more creative, and they begin to experience religious insights and unsettling dreams as their brains adjust. But technology and humanity's way of life in not geared up to a world where almost everyone has an IQ of over 400. No-one wants to do tedious or manual work any more, and they demand better.

Riots start in the streets and panic sets in. Revolutions are sparked off all over the planet, overthrowing oppressive regimes. Anderson tells this tale through its effects on a few individuals, including scientist Peter Corinth, who has become a genius, and Archie Brock, a peasant labourer who has changed from 'moron' to 'normal' overnight. The latter's story is particularly poignant; as the novel unfolds, it becomes clear that old prejudices die hard and Archie is as much of an outcast as before. 'Normal' is no longer good enough and people like him will be left behind with the animals as the superintelligent desert them for the stars. This thought-provoking story looks at how society is organized and at our skewed values, while stretching the reader's imagination.

I, Robot

I, Robot is a collection of short stories linked by an interview between a reporter and robopsychologist Susan Calvin about her work with dysfunctional robots and problems with human-robot interactions.

It is in these stories that Asimov took the fundamental step of treating robots as aware entities with their own set of programmed ethics – the Three Laws of Robotics – rather than Frankenstein's monster creations of mad scientists. The laws are: 1) A robot may not injure a human being, or, through inaction, allow a human being to come to harm. 2) A robot must obey the orders given to it by human beings except where such orders would conflict with the First Law. 3) A robot must protect its own existence as long as such protection does not conflict with the First or Second Laws of Robotics.

Asimov deliberately left loopholes in the laws, and each of the stories is a detective story in which Calvin or her colleagues at U.S. Robotics and Mechanical Men Inc., Martin and Donovan, discover which ambiguity or conflict between the laws is causing the robot to behave in an unexpected way.

The stories are arranged chronologically with the development of positronic robots. The first robot to appear is Robbie, the perfect playmate for a young girl, who because of him becomes isolated from other children. Other robots include Nestor 10, whose programming conflict can only be solved by adjusting the First Law for him so that he can allow his employers to put themselves at risk in order to do their work. Asimov's Three Laws have spread throughout science fiction and almost every robot in books or on screen is created with the assumption that these laws govern its behaviour.

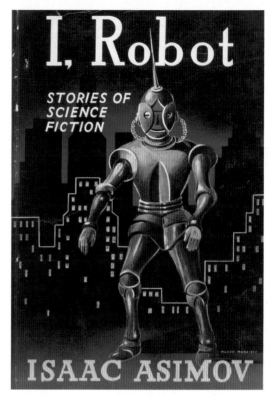

ISAAC ASIMOV
1920 – 1992
Nationality: Russian
First Published: Gnome Press, 1950
Other Selected Titles:
Pebble in the Sky
Foundation
The Stars, Like Dust
The Currents of Space
Foundation and Empire
David Starr, Space Ranger
Lucky Starr and the Pirates of the Asteroids
The Caves of Steel

Biochemist and science fiction novelist Isaac Asimov in 1970.

The Handmaid's Tale

MARGARET ATWOOD
1939 –
Nationality: Canadian
First Published: McClelland and Stewart, 1985
Other Selected Titles:
Oryx and Crake
The Edible Woman
Surfacing
Lady Oracle
Life Before Man
The Robber Bride
Alias Grace
The Blind Assassin

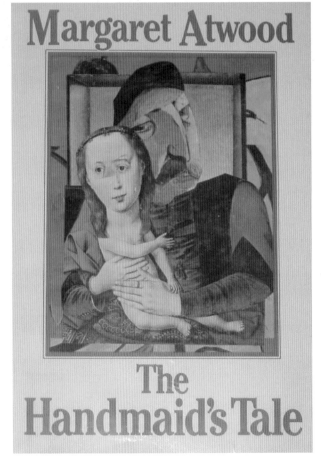

This novel is set in the Republic of Gilead, formerly the USA, a few years after a military coup that has installed a totalitarian sectarian regime under an elite group of men called Commanders. The population is kept in check through fear. Torture is commonplace, spying and denunciation are encouraged, and there are frequent public executions.

The society is strictly hierarchical; women are subservient and few have a role outside the home. Most people are infertile, so women who have had children outside a first marriage are, after a period of indoctrination, forced to bear children for childless high-status couples and are known as handmaids. The narrator is one of these, Offred. She is in her mid-30s, and is running out of time before being sent to the colonies to clear up hazardous waste. Her growing despair with her existence permeates the book.

Fred is Offred's second Commander. As a leader of the regime, Fred feels he can bend the rules: instead of confining his contact with Offred to the monthly insemination ceremony, he seeks out her company. His wife, Serena Joy, is desperate for a child, so arranges for Offred to have sex with the chauffeur, Nick, which would result in death for both of them if they were found out.

In snatched conversations, Offred learns from another handmaid, Ofglen, that there is an underground rebellion. When Ofglen is found out, she commits suicide rather than betray other members of the group, so buying precious time for Offred. Nick, another member of the underground, helps Offred to escape. As well as being a warning to women not to become complacent about the gains that previous generations of women have achieved, Atwood's novel provides a chilling glimpse at the horrors that can occur when religion and politics collide.

The Crystal World

The fourth of Ballard's end-of-the-world eco-disaster novels is set in late colonial West Africa. Dr Sanders runs a leper colony on the coast. He starts to receive disturbing letters from Suzanne Clair, an ex-lover who runs a jungle clinic inland with her husband Max. Sanders, who finds a peculiar crystal sculpture and sees a crystallized body in the river, decides to visit Suzanne and Max. Because the army is preventing anyone from going in by road, Sanders makes the arduous journey upriver. He takes with him a journalist called Louise, with whom he has a brief affair. They discover that something, presumed to be a virus, is rapidly turning the jungle, and every living thing in it, to crystal. It is Ballard's portrayal of the crystalline jungle that lingers in the memory.

Ballard was highly influenced by Surrealism, and his descriptions of snakes with blank crystal eyes, crocodiles with mirror-shiny skin and trees turned into colossal jewels have an acid-trip sense of detachment and dream-like quality. While most people fear the encroaching crystal, some are enthralled by it and decide to stay. These include Suzanne, who is going insane, has early leprosy and heads off to the centre of the jungle with a group of other lepers to find paradise, and Father Balthus, a Jesuit having a religious crisis. At the end of the book, Sanders has escaped back to the coast, but must then decide whether to remain in safety or to return to the jungle to embrace the same oblivion as Suzanne.

J.G. Ballard in Los Angeles, 1987.

J.G. BALLARD
1930 –
Nationality: British
First Published: Jonathan Cape, 1966
Other Selected Titles:
The Drowned World
The Wind from Nowhere
The Burning World
Concrete Island
High Rise
Empire of the Sun
Cocaine Nights
Millenium People

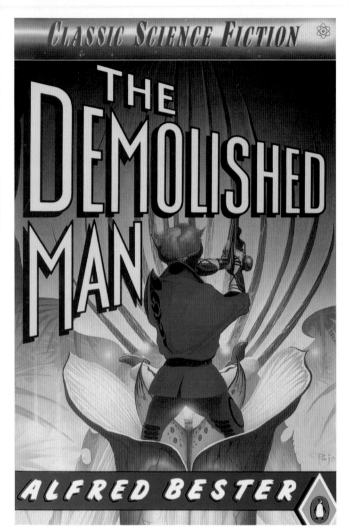

ALFRED BESTER
1913 – 1987
Nationality: American
First Published: Shasta Publishers,
1953
Other Selected Titles:
The Computer Connection
Tiger, Tiger
Golem 100
The Deceivers
The Dark Side of the Earth
The Light Fantastic
Star Light, Star Bright

The Demolished Man

Ben Reich is, up to now, the second most powerful businessman in the Solar System, but is becoming dangerously obsessed with his hatred of his even more successful rival Craye D'Courtney. He eventually comes to the conclusion that the only thing to do is to kill him. However, in the early 24th century, premeditated crimes have become impossible because law enforcement agencies employ telepaths who read your intentions and forestall you.

Reich, who is a borderline psychopath, however, employs a corrupt telepath to devise a method to screen his mind – a repetitive jingle – and carries out the murder. He is seen by the victim's daughter Barbara who is so traumatized that she loses the power of speech and flees. What follows is a dark cat and mouse chase across the Solar System between Reich and the telepathic police prefect Lincoln Powell, himself no paragon, with Reich trying to escape, Lincoln trying to find concrete proof of Reich's guilt and both of them trying to find Barbara.

Reich is a driven monster, continually plagued by nightmares of a man with no face. Lincoln is little better and when Barbara is found, despite her fragile mental state, he breaks every rule by digging for clues in her mind, almost losing her in the process.

This is one of the earliest books to introduce the idea of a world where telepaths are legitimized, rather than outcasts, and play positive roles in society. It prefigures similar set-ups, including *Minority Report* and *Babylon 5*.

Who Goes There

This is a collection of seven short stories originally published under the pseudonym Don A. Stuart in *Astounding Science Fiction* magazine, which Campbell later edited. A group of scientists at an Antarctic observation station find an alien spacecraft and, nearby, the alien, which has been frozen there for millions of years. They haul the alien back to their base in order to thaw and study it. As soon as it thaws, it escapes and attacks the dogs, killing one of them before it is itself killed, shape-shifting in an effort to defend itself.

One scientist, Blair, refuses to believe that it is dead and convinces the others that it may already have killed and assumed the appearance and behaviour of one or more of them. He destroys their ability to get away from the base in order to prevent the creature getting away, but is confined himself to prevent him attacking other team members, as is Connant, who was alone with the creature when it woke up.

The nightmare of not knowing who is human and who is not continues while the men wait for a serum to be developed and their ingenuity and mental strength are tested to the full as they try to come up with ways to identify the creatures and destroy them. This is a nightmare-inducing tale, at its darkest in the horrifying moment when the serum fails because it was already contaminated with alien blood, and they realize that their worst fears have come true. They descend into pack-animal behaviour, as they track down and slaughter the creatures. The other six stories in the collection are *Blindness*, *Frictional Losses*, *Dead Knowledge*, *Elimination*, *Twilight* and its sequel, *Night*.

JOHN W. CAMPBELL
1910 – 1971
Nationality: American
First Published: Shasta Publishers, 1948
Other Selected Titles:
The Black Star Passes
Islands of Space
Invaders From the Infinite
The Mightiest Machine
The Incredible Planet
The Planeteers

The Invention of Morel

ADOLFO BIOY CASARES
1914 – 1999
Nationality: Argentinian
First Published: University of Texas
Press, 1964 (first English translation)
Other Selected Titles:
The Dream of the Heroes
Asleep in the Sun
A Plan for Escape

Adolfo Bioy Casares in 1975.

While the title of this novella is obviously taken from H.G. Wells' *The Island of Dr Moreau* and there are many similarities in setting and plot, the inspiration comes from the author's love for the silent movie actress Louise Brooks. It is set on a mysterious, supposedly deserted and disease-ridden island, where a fugitive is hiding from justice, having committed a crime (which is never explained). Suddenly, a group of people appear, but they do not respond to his presence and ignore him. Is he imagining them in his growing paranoia, or is he imaginary? Despite this, he falls in love with one of the women, Faustine, and gradually this begins to turn to obsession. He notices that Faustine and her companions disappear periodically and repeat conversations. Even more strangely, there are two Suns and two Moons. Eventually it emerges that these people had visited the island years earlier, and the leader of the group, Morel, had set up a recording device that could project not just three-dimensional images, but sounds and smells as well. On a more esoteric level, and half a century before even the earliest forms of Virtual Reality, Bioy is writing about the boundaries between reality and unreality – like the picture of Dorian Gray in reverse, the image is linked to the original woman and takes some of her reality. This story looks at the nature of infatuation and is as relevant to today's celebrity-obsessed culture as it was in its own time.

Planet of the Apes

Far more thought-provoking than either of the films or the television series, Boulle's satirical novel opens with a space-faring couple finding a canister. The canister contains an account of the 300-light-year journey of three Frenchmen to a planet in orbit around Betelgeuse, which they call Soror. The men are caught by a pack of savage human-like beings, and as they plot their escape they are trapped by intelligent gorillas and caged in a zoo, where they are experimented on or killed if they are disobedient.

While the leader of the three men, Professor Antelle, retreats into imbecility because of his inability to deal with the situation, one of the younger men, Ulysse Merou, is forced gradually to abandon all his ideas of man's supremacy. Darkly comic moments include his realization that he is responding to Pavlovian conditioning, salivating when a whistle is blown and he receives a banana as a reward.

Drawing on his own experience as a prisoner-of-war, Boulle explores the nature of the relationship between prisoner and jailer, and Ulysse comes to identify more with his captors than he does with the humans. He is befriended by Zira, one of the chimp scientists, but even when he addresses a meeting of an important scientific institution in fluent ape, he is assumed by most to be a trained animal. The story is disturbing, questioning our assumptions about our position relative to animals, and ends with several ironic twists which serve to underline this message.

French author Pierre Boulle arrives in London in 1978.

PIERRE BOULLE
1912 – 1994
Nationality: French
First Published: Vanguard Press, 1963
Other Selected Titles:
Garden on the Moon
The Bridge on the River Kwai
Time Out of Mind

The Martian Chronicles

RAY BRADBURY
1920 –
Nationality: American
First Published: Doubleday, 1950
Other Selected Titles:
Fahrenheit 451
It Came From Outer Space
The Day It Rained Forever
The Small Assassin
R Is For Rocket
The Machineries of Joy
S Is For Space
Driving Blind

Ray Bradbury in 2000.

A classic of science fiction, *The Martian Chronicles* is a collection of short stories, some of which had previously been published, that relate the history of the colonization of Mars by humans. It is also an allegory of the arrival of Europeans in the Americas and explores many of the issues important to Americans in the 1940s and 1950s, such as nuclear war, fear of foreign invasion, censorship and racism.

The first expedition is launched in January 1999, but the crew members are killed as soon as they arrive the following month by a jealous Martian husband. The second crew is shot by a doctor who thinks the captain is merely an insane Martian. The third crew is greeted with a replica of a midwestern American town and long-lost members of their families. By the next morning, they are all dead. By the time the fourth expedition arrives in June 2001, every single Martian has died from chicken pox, brought by a member of the second crew, so now humanity can claim Mars for itself. Over the next year or so, more and more colonists arrive, spreading out across the planet, obliterating the remnants of Martian civilization and trying to create a copy of home. However, when nuclear war breaks out on Earth in 2005, most return home and the colony withers. By 2026, the only person there is one of the fourth expedition's crew, who dies before he can be taken back to Earth and all that is left are the robotic replicas of his family. The dreamy nature of the language Bradbury uses adds to the sense of loneliness and melancholy that runs throughout this story of two civilizations brought to destruction through humanity's greed.

The Sheep Look Up

Brunner's second eco-disaster novel serves as a grim warning that we must not ignore the consequences of what mankind is doing to the planet. It is set in an isolationist America, ruled by large corporations and a corrupt political system led by a half-wit. It invades third-world countries in order to acquire their natural resources because its own have been over-exploited. Pollution levels are sky-rocketing and everyone eats junk food and pops tranquillizers. The poor are getting poorer, the rich exploit the poor and the powerful are in denial, refusing to believe what is in front of their eyes as it does not suit their politics or their friends in big business. Wars are breaking out all over the planet and terrorist attacks are widespread.

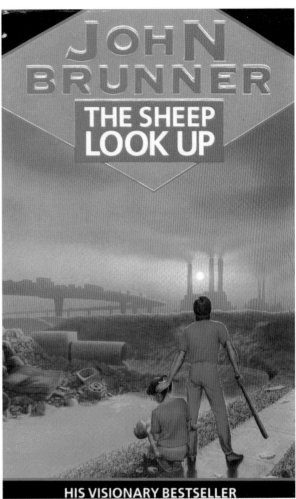

Into this depressing, and familiar, scenario come the Trainites, ecowarriors and devotees of the reclusive environmentalist and writer Austin Train. They are trying to raise public awareness that the ecological disasters with which the characters in the book are continually bombarded are the result of humanity's own actions. They want Train to come out of his self-imposed purdah and lead them, while the government brands them all as traitors to the nation and seeks to shut them, and Train, up.

This fast-paced tale is told through short sections of narrative, linked very effectively by news flashes, advertisements, speeches, extracts from newspapers and poems. In the early 21st century, with ecological catastrophes gaining in both severity and frequency, and – as ever – impacting more on the poor than the super-rich, Brunner's depressing portrayal of our near-future is as relevant today as it has ever been.

JOHN BRUNNER
1934 – 1995
Nationality: British
First Published: Harper & Row, 1972
Other Selected Titles:
The Hundredth Millennium
The Atlantic Abomination
Slavers of Space
The Rites of Ohe
Endless Shadow
The Whole Man
A Planet of Our Own
The Shockwave Rider

389

yarbles,
bolshy great
yarblockos to
thee and thine

ANTHONY BURGESS
1917 – 1993
Nationality: British
First Published: Heinemann, 1962
Other Selected Titles:
The Wanting Seed
The End of the World News
Inside Mr Enderby
The Eve of Saint Venus
Tremor of Intent
Enderby Outside
Earthly Powers
Any Old Iron

A Clockwork Orange

Burgess' chilling novel was partly inspired by the seaside fights of the mods and rockers of the early 1960s. It follows the exploits of a gang of particularly violent teenagers – the Droogs – through the eyes of one member, the Beethoven-loving 15-year-old Alex. Their drug-fuelled orgies of robbery, rape and torture are detailed with enjoyment in Burgess' made-up slang, Nadsat.

When an attempted robbery goes wrong and Alex commits murder, he is caught and sentenced to 14 years. Unable to cope with life in prison, Alex volunteers to undergo an experimental programme called the Ludovico Technique, unaware that it is a brutal form of aversion therapy that will brainwash him into being physically sick if he even thinks about committing a crime. Here lie the main ethical questions in the book: whether it better for a man to decide to be bad than to be forced to be good, and whether forcibly suppressing Alex's free will is acceptable. Does the state have the right to use violence against some individuals in order to protect the majority?

After his release from prison, Alex finds that a side-effect of the treatment means that he can no longer bear to listen to Beethoven, which, together with the deprivation of his free will, leads him to attempt suicide by throwing himself out of a window. He is unsuccessful, but his free will returns and he is free to revel in the idea of violence again. It is at this point that the version of the book published in the USA, on which Kubrick's film was based, stops. However, the final chapter of the UK edition holds out hope for Alex's redemption. More than 40 years after it was written, this book still has the power to shock, sicken and move the reader.

British writer Anthony Burgess in France, 1979.

Erewhon

Butler's highly satirical first book has two main themes: his alternative theory of evolution and his thinly disguised attack on the social mores and customs of contemporary Victorian Britain. Higgs and Chowbok, a sheep farmer and an old man, decide to journey to the forbidden lands on the other side of the mountains. When Chowbok takes fright and returns home, Higgs continues alone. After a journey fraught with danger, he wakes one morning surrounded by pretty shepherdesses, who relieve him of his possessions, give him a medical examination and throw him into prison. In this topsy-turvy land, the ill and the unhappy are imprisoned because it must be their own fault, while robbers and murderers are hospitalized and cared for.

Butler's was an era of great social and economic hypocrisy – women could be arrested, given medical examinations and locked away, and petty criminals hanged – and here he is adding his satirical note to the growing outcry from social reformers.

One of the most misunderstood sections of the book was the chapter on machines. These were banned from Erewhon after a philosopher proposed that they might be able to evolve and take over the world. Butler had his own theory of the evolution of species, which worked through a different mechanism to Darwin's, and here he is promoting it. Critics claimed that he was ridiculing Darwin, which he denied.

There are also passages describing the illogic of some Erewhonian philosophy, including the idea that people who die were never actually born, using eggs only three months after they could not possibly hatch live chicks, and eating only vegetables and fruit that were rotting on the ground or dead. The sheer absurdity of his contentions make this book an intriguing read.

SAMUEL BUTLER
1835 – 1902
Nationality: British
First Published: Trubner & Co., 1872
Other Selected Titles:
Erewhon Revisited
The Way of All Flesh

PENGUIN CLASSICS

SAMUEL BUTLER
Erewhon

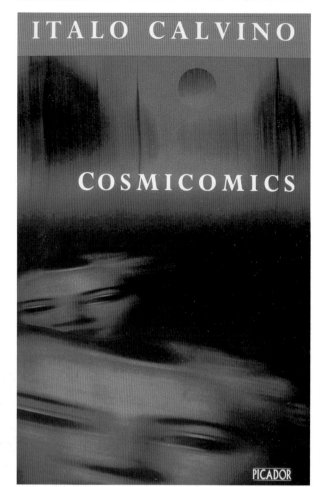

ITALO CALVINO

COSMICOMICS

PICADOR

ITALO CALVINO
1923 – 1985
Nationality: Italian
First Published: Harcourt Brace &
Ward, 1965 (first English translation)
Other Selected Titles:
The Path to the Nest of Spiders
The Cloven Viscount
Baron in the Trees
The Non-Existent Knight
Marcovaldo
If On a Winter's Night a Traveller
The Road to San Giovanni

Cosmicomics

This is an enchanting book which takes facts about the Universe and makes quirky short stories from them. Each story starts with a scientific fact, as you might find in a scientific text book, and then turns into a tale narrated by a being called Qfwfq, who has always existed, and always will. He has witnessed all of the events, and if he cannot remember them, he looks them up in his diary. He remembers what it was like before time and space came into being, when all matter existed in a single point. 'Naturally, we were all there,' old Qfwfq said, 'where else could we have been? Nobody knew then that there could be space. Or time either: what use did we have for time, packed in there like sardines?'

What was it like to be the last dinosaur on the planet, feared by all the mammals around you? What can a family that has evolved and moved from the water to the land do about an old uncle who is refusing to come out of the sea? Qfwfq and his friend Pfwfp chase around the developing universe, play marbles with hydrogen atoms, and watch light, matter and galaxies form. Although few of Calvino's characters are human, they all have very human personalities, with all our foibles. On one level, these are charming tales that are a delight to read, but Calvino's imagination has translated concepts that may be difficult to grasp into human terms, and given readers a glimpse into the wonder of the Universe, allowing them to gain an understanding, whether fleeting or longer lasting, of their own place in it.

2001: A Space Odyssey

Expanded from a short story, *The Sentinel*, published a few years earlier, *2001: A Space Odyssey* is a science fiction classic, containing many elements and technological ideas that have recurred in the genre ever since. The story begins 3,000,000 years ago when a large black monolith teaches a group of endangered hominids in Africa how to make tools, so that they can catch prey. It emerges that the monolith is a member of an advanced civilization that eons ago evolved from slime mould into carbon-based life forms, then into machines and then into pure energy forms that nudge other life forms into evolving.

The book then makes a giant leap forward to 1999 and the unearthing of a large black monolith on the Moon. As sunlight hits it for the first time in millions of years, it sends a piercing radio transmission in the direction of Saturn's moon Japetus (Iapetus). Whether the monoliths are a threat to humans is not known, so a decision is made to send a mission to Japetus. Clarke's account of Poole and Bowman's journey, accompanied by the malfunctioning murderous HAL 9000 AI computer, addresses the fear prevalent at the time of whether we should be creating technologies that we cannot control. This was only a few years after electronic computers had been invented and at a time of great worry about nuclear warfare.

The invention of AIs, and the last part of Bowman's journey as he is turned into the Star Child and returns to watch over the Earth, explores the idea that, like the monoliths, humans are not yet at the end of the evolutionary process. Even though the technology is somewhat dated after 50 years, the book is still an enthralling and thought-provoking read, crammed full of suspense.

ARTHUR C. CLARKE
1917 –
Nationality: British
First Published: Hutchinson, 1968
Other Selected Titles:
Prelude to Space
The Sands of Mars
A Fall of Moondust
The Lion of Camarre &
Against the Fall of Night
Imperial Earth
2010: Odyssey Two
2061: Odyssey Three
3001: The Final Odyssey

Arthur C. Clarke in 1976.

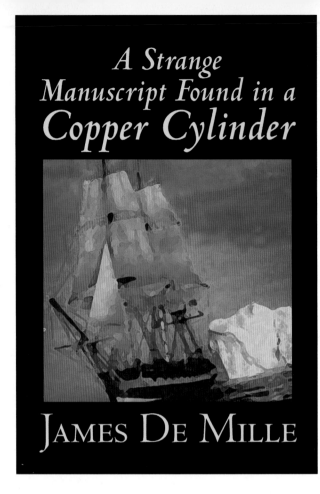

A Strange Manuscript Found in a Copper Cylinder

JAMES DE MILLE

JAMES DE MILLE
1833 – 1880
Nationality: British
First Published: *Harper's Weekly*, 1888
Other Selected Titles:
The Martyr in the Catacombs; a Tale of Ancient Rome
The Boys of Grand Pre School
Lost in the Fog
Among the Brigade
Fire in the Woods
Picked Up Adrift
The Treasure of the Seas
The Seven Hills

A Strange Manuscript Found in a Copper Cylinder

Much like the work of his near contemporary Jules Verne, De Mille's novel is set in far-off lands where few people have travelled. A group of wealthy yachtsmen find a copper cylinder bobbing on the ocean waves. Inside it they discover a manuscript giving the account of the extensive travels in the Antarctic of a sailor called Adam More. Adrift on the ocean, he and his companion Agnew had landed on an island, only to fall into the clutches of cannibals. More escaped, but Agnew did not. His boat was drawn to a distant land where it plunged into a vast tunnel and continued through caverns and chasms. There he encountered such hazards as sea monsters and active volcanoes. Eventually he met a lost race, the Kosekin, whose philosophy embraced darkness, poverty and death.

He fell in love with a beautiful young woman called Almah, and they tried to escape, but were caught by a rival for his affections and told that they would have the starring roles in a human sacrifice, the greatest honour possible in that society.

As in many books of the time, the adventures and the language are sensationalist, with danger piled upon danger. However, in the passages where the yachtsmen try to rationalize More's story as if dissecting a scientific paper, De Mille is poking fun at himself and his story. There is, however, a moral lurking in the background: the absurdity of the Kosekins' philosophy reflects late Victorian concerns about the declining role of God in society.

The Three Stigmata of Palmer Eldritch

Widely acknowledged as Dick's masterpiece, *The Three Stigmata of Palmer Eldritch* is a disorientating exploration of reality and perception, religion, mind-altering drugs and the nature of god. Barney Mayerson is a precog for P.P. Layouts, predicting what the next fashions will be. The front for the company, owned by Leo Bulero, is that it makes dolls and miniature layouts for them to live in, which the colonists on Mars love to collect. But in reality these are devices that, in conjunction with the narcotic Can-D, allow the users to inhabit an illusory world and participate in the adult game of Perky Pat. Bulero, of course, has the monopoly on the illegal Can-D.

Into this bleak scene comes Palmer Eldritch, a cyborg with an artifical hand, eyes and teeth – his stigmata. Eldritch has returned from a ten-year voyage to Prox, reputedly with supplies of Chew-Z, a mind-altering drug with even stronger and more long-lasting effects than Can-D. Is the cyborg just a business rival out to destroy P.P. Layouts (helped by a distinctly corrupt U.N.), or is he the advance guard of an invasion from Prox who is using Chew-Z to control whomever he wants?

Once Bulero and Mayerson have been slipped Chew-Z by Eldritch, neither they nor the reader is sure again whether they are seeing reality or are still under the influence of the drug. The fast-moving, highly amusing plot skips around the Solar System as Bulero plots against Eldritch, and Eldritch manipulates all those around him.

"Dick was one of the genuine visionaries....His best novels constitute as significant a body of work as that of any writer in this country in the last thirty years."
—Steve Erickson, L.A. Weekly

PHILIP K. DICK
1918 – 1982
Nationality: American
First Published: Doubleday, 1965
Other Selected Titles:
The Cosmic Puppets
Eye in the Sky
The Game-players of Titan
The Crack in Space
The Unteleported Man
A Maze of Death
Our Friends from Frolix 8
Do Androids Dream of Electronic Sheep?

To Your Scattered Bodies Go

In this book, the first part of his Riverworld series, Farmer introduces what is one of the most ambitious concepts in science fiction. All of mankind who live to adulthood find themselves resurrected, simultaneously, naked on the banks of an immense river. None of them knows why they are there or who has provided them with the devices that supply them with food and drink.

The incurably adventurous 19th-century explorer Sir Richard Francis Burton (who in real life searched for the source of the Nile, visited Mecca when it was forbidden for non-Muslims to do so and translated *The Arabian Nights*), catches a glimpse of something that leads him to decide to sail up the million-mile river to uncover the mystery of why they are there.

On his journey, he is accompanied by Alice Liddell Hargreaves (Alice in Wonderland) as a stereotypical love interest, a holocaust survivor, a wise alien, and a caveman who speaks English. Of course, it is not just the good humans who have been resurrected: there is a startling amount of violence, including graphic descriptions of rapes. Among the adventures the group encounters Hermann Goering and his band of ancient Romans. What are the motives of the beings who created the Riverworld – and are they good or bad? Burton is inspired to carry on up river by a being who claims to be a renegade from the creators and tells him that he and his group must carry on with their quest to prevent humanity suffering a terrible fate.

PHILIP JOSE FARMER
1918 –
Nationality: American
First Published: Putnam, 1971
Other Selected Titles:
The Green Odyssey
The Gate of Time
The Fabulous Riverboat
The Dark Design
Gods of the Riverworld
Dayworld
Hadon of Ancient Opar
Red Orc's Rage

Neuromancer

Neuromancer is known as the first book of the Cyberpunk genre, the book that introduced the concept of Cyberspace. In a technology-dominated, dystopian society, Case was a console cowboy – a hacker – who could link his brain directly into computer networks and steal the data. This was until he double-crossed the wrong people, who repaid him by burning out his talent a micron at a time. A year later, he has spent all his money in the search for a cure and is contemplating suicide, until a man called Armitage gives him the chance of a cure, as long as he agrees to do a job for him in return.

Gibson's book is, in fact, intended as a stark warning against letting ourselves become controlled by technology. Written a few years before the invention of the internet, it foresees a materialistic, hedonistic, dysfunctional age, where giant corporations control the world through computer networks, large parts of the population are addicted to computer gaming, and normal society has all but broken down. As Case, Armitage, Molly the half-woman-half-computer assassin, and Riviera a holographic performance artist, work towards their goal, it becomes increasingly obvious to Case that larger forces are in control.

The plot twists and thickens in a story interwoven with corruption and crime, until the final twist reveals just who has been behind everything. The concept of cyberspace as a habitable place, far preferable to reality, was so perfectly thought out and worked so well it inspired a whole new generation of sci-fi writers.

WILLIAM GIBSON
1948 –
Nationality: American
First Published: Ace Books, 1984
Other Selected Titles:
Count Zero
Mona Lisa Overdrive
Virtual Light
Idoru
Johnny Mnemonic
All Tomorrow's Parties
Pattern Recognition
Burning Chrome

Science fiction writer William Gibson.

Stranger in a Strange Land

ROBERT A. HEINLEIN
1907 – 1988
Nationality: American
First Published: Putnam, 1961
Other Selected Titles:
Rocket Ship Galileo
Beyond this Horizon
Space Cadet
Methuselah's Children
Star Ship Troopers
I Will Fear No Evil
Time Enough For Love
Destination Moon

Valentine Michael Smith (Mike) was born on Mars to two members of the first expedition from earth. He was also the only survivor and was brought up by members of an ancient Martian civilization. Twenty years later, he is found by the second expedition and brought back to an Earth that is to him a completely alien culture and often terrifying, with a telepathic link to the Martians so that they can study Earth and decide whether it is a threat or not.

Hidden by the government, partly for his own sake and partly because they are afraid of him, he is helped to escape by Jill Boardman, the first woman he has ever seen, and they end up taking refuge at the home of writer Jubal Harshaw. After learning enough about human culture to get by, Mike decides to form his own church based on his own brand of Martian philosophy, which involves nudity, copious free love, individual responsibility and a message of peace. There are long diatribes against ineffectual government, organized religion and many of America's contemporary values. These are, in effect, Heinlein's own views and at the beginning of the 1960s were so shocking that the publisher cut the book by about 60,000 words. The unexpurgated version was published by his widow some years after his death.

The book is of its era, and was very influential in some hippie circles over the following years. But bearing that in mind, many of the questions it raises about society, politics and belief are relevant today. Heinlein's attitude towards women, and some of the slang, have dated, but this book is still an enthralling story from the discovery of the young man to the inevitable conclusion.

Robert Heinlein in 1986.

Dune

Set on the desert planet Arrakis, known by its indigenous inhabitants as Dune, Herbert's epic story remains a bestseller more than forty years after it was first published. Dune is the only source of the near priceless spice (Melange), which is vital for space-travel and confers longevity and mental powers on its users. The plot centres around Paul, son of Duke Leto Atreides to whom the Emperor has given Arrakis at the expense of their bitter rivals the House Harkonnen.

After the latter, as the Emperor had planned, assassinate Leto, Paul and his mother Jessica escape into the desert, where they join the nomadic tribesmen known as the Fremen. In the background, the mysterious sisterhood of the Bene Gesseret has been conducting a breeding programme to create a superhuman, the Kwisatz Haderach.

They have nearly reached their goal, but Jessica had Paul, not the girl she was told, and his unexpected mental powers, which are enhanced by increased contact with spice in the desert, have upset their plans for galactic domination. To become fully accepted as one of the Fremen and lead them in taking back his planet, Paul must learn to ride the huge sandworms. The description of his first ride is one of the most exhilarating passages in science fiction.

Paul's acceptance by, and leadership of, the desert-dwelling Fremen have been likened to T.E. Lawrence's role with the Arabs in their revolt during the First World War, and *Dune* is on a similarly epic scale as the story of Lawrence of Arabia. Herbert's vision of this strange world and his exploration of belief, evolution, politics and ecology remain believable and engrossing to this day.

FRANK HERBERT
1920 – 1986
Nationality: American
First Published: Chilton Books, 1965
Other Selected Titles:
Dune Messiah
Children of Dune
God Emperor of Dune
Heretics of Dune
Chapterhouse Dune
Whipping Star
The Dragon in the Sea
The Eyes of Heisenberg

Brave New World ✓

ALDOUS HUXLEY
1894 – 1963
Nationality: British
First Published: Chatto & Windus,
1932
Other Selected Titles:
After Many a Summer Dies the Swan
Ape and Essence
Chrome Yellow
Antic Hay
Those Barren Leaves
Point Counter Point
Eyeless In Gaza
Music at Night

In the 26th century, the world has become a united state, without war, conflict or poverty. Humans are not born, but grown in a hatchery with up to 15,000 clones grown from each embryo. They mature rapidly until they appear to be about 20 years old, then stay the same until they die at about 50. From the start children are conditioned, with chemicals and recordings played to them while they sleep, into happiness, conformity and conspicuous consumption, according to tenets loosely based around those of Henry Ford. Their status and roles are determined long before they are 'decanted' from the flasks in which they hatch. From an early age, they are encouraged in erotic play, and promiscuous sex is the norm. There is no religion, love or philosophy, most books are banned and thinking is discouraged. What would happen if someone from a different society were introduced?

John the Savage, ironically the son of the Director of the main hatchery, is brought with his mother from the Malpais Savage Reservation to London. Brought up as an outsider in a society where marriage and love are the norm, he finds the way of life in the World State disgusting and it is through his reactions and behaviour that Huxley satirizes both his own society and utopian novels such as H.G. Wells' *Men Like Gods*. Written in

an age of increasing mechanization, the frightening vision Huxley created in *Brave New World* is a call to recognize that a society in which everyone is controlled for the benefit of all would result in a complete loss of individuality and freedom.

Aldous Huxley in 1946.

Two Planets

KURD LASSWITZ
1848 – 1910
Nationality: German
First Published: Southern Illinois
University Press, 1971 (first English
translation)

Although it was highly influential on German-language science fiction, this book only reached an English-language audience as an abridged version in 1971. The plot is based on the premise that Martians will have evolved more quickly than humans and will be more technologically and ethically advanced. The action starts as three German and Austrian scientists fly towards the North Pole in a balloon. There they discover a Martian base.

The Martians want to help mankind to develop, in return for solar power and air, in which Mars is lacking. However, the English interfere and this leads to a war followed by a Martian protectorate of Europe. After a rebellion, the Martians withdraw. Only when humans have reached an equal state of ethical, sociological and technological development as the Martians can relationships between the two planets be fully re-established.

Lasswitz was a scientist, and his description of Mars relates closely to the ideas published in the US by Percival Lowell in 1895, which detailed vast stretches of irrigation canals criss-crossing the planet's surface. In its turn, the book was highly influential on a number of future German scientists, including Wernher von Braun, the developer of the V1 and V2 flying bombs, and architect of the Apollo missions to the moon. His story also reflects both the political situation in Europe at that time, when Britain and Germany were struggling for supremacy.

His Kantian philosophy about equality and benign beings living in harmony led to the book being banned by the Nazis in 1930 for being too democratic. Although dated, it merits reading today and makes an interesting comparison with H.G. Wells' treatment of the subject written the following year.

Left Hand of Darkness

Genly Ai is an ethnologist from the federation of planets called the Ekumen, who is observing the people of the planet Gethen (also known as Winter) with a view to asking if they wish to ally themselves to the federation for intellectual and technological exchange. The Gethenians were genetically modified millennia

American writer Ursula K. Le Guin in San Francisco, 1985.

ago to be androgynes, with each becoming either male or female for one week a month. There are no gender-specific roles and the planet is largely peaceful.

In the kingdom of Karhide, there is a complex system for determining social standing, based largely on honour, protocol and back-stabbing, which Ai completely fails to understand. He gets caught on the edge of court politics and when his mentor, the Prime Minister Estraven, is banished, his mission seems over.

In another kingdom, Orgoreyn, he fares even worse and has to be rescued by Estraven. Their only hope is to appeal to the honour of the king of Karhide, which forces them to make an 80-day journey across the barren glaciers of Gethren. This ground-breaking story proceeds at a fluid pace. It is as much about subtleties of plot and character as it is about narrative.

In her writing, Le Guin is asking questions about what it is to be human, whether a race without gender would be better or worse than our own and whether cultural prejudices can be overcome. Written at a time when, in science fiction, men were all-action and women were there to fill gaps in the scenery, this beautiful story broke away from such stereotypes and has allowed other writers to do the same. It is inventive and intelligent and is deservedly regarded as a classic.

URSULA K. LE GUIN
1929 –
Nationality: American
First Published: Walker, 1969
Other Selected Titles:
Rocannon's World
City of Illusions
The Lathe of Heaven
Always Coming Home
The Telling
The Adventures of Cobbler's Rune
The Eye of the Heron
The Waylord

Solaris

STANISLAW LEM
1921 – 2006
Nationality: Polish
First Published: Faber & Faber, 1970
(first English translation)
Other Selected Titles:
The Invincible
The Star Diaries
Tales of Pirx the Pilot
Return from the Stars
Memoirs of a Space Traveller
Peace on Earth
Memoirs Found in a Bathtub
Fiasco

Stanislaw Lem.

For more than 100 years, humans have been studying the ocean of Solaris. It is, in fact, a vast organism covering the surface of the planet. In all this time, they have been unable to do more than describe and classify its actions and creations, without any breakthrough in understanding, because it is alien and incomprehensible. The scientists on the space station orbiting Solaris believe that the organism may be trying to make contact, so they try to communicate with it.

At this point Kris Kelvin, a psychologist, arrives on the station. He discovers that one of the scientists has killed himself, the second has locked himself in his cabin and the third is behaving oddly. He also encounters people (or phantoms) who should not be there, including his own wife Rheya who committed suicide years before. In terror, he launches the phantom into space, only for another to appear.

It emerges that the organism is dredging through the men's memories and sending phantoms of people associated with guilt in the past. Why is it doing this? Is it studying the men or is it trying to drive them away? That aliens are not humanoid and that they cannot accurately be understood in human concepts or described in human language is central to Lem's writing.

Unlike so many writers, he creates a completely new type of world, rather than one that is a mirror of some aspect of our own, moulded to fit in with our own preconceptions. In the sub-plot, where Kelvin falls in love with the fake Rheya, Lem explores what it means to be human. This is an intelligent, thought-provoking story.

Shikasta

The Canopeans are an ancient benevolent civilization on the planet Canopus in Argos who have for millennia been watching over and promoting the evolution of the inhabitants of the planet they call Shikasta (the Earth). At one point in the past they colonized Shikasta, and in fact the full title of the book is *Canopus in Argos: Archives; Re: Colonised Planet 5, Shikasta; Personal Psychological Historical Documents Relating to Visit by Johor (George Sherban): Emissary (Grade 9), 87th of the Last Period of the Last Days.*

Harmony and development were encouraged through the flow of an energy called Substance-of-we-feeling (SOWF) from Canopus to Shikasta, but a cosmological accident disrupted the flow and humanity began to turn away from harmony, assisted by the machinations of the evil inhabitants of the planet Shammat.

The first part of the book is a revision of human history, exposing our frailties and documenting our descent into what the Canopeans see as barbarism. In the second part, the Canopean agent Johor has returned to Earth in a human incarnation as George Sherban, after thousands of years, in order to head off World War Three and the destruction of the human race. A deep sense of spirituality runs through the book, with elements of Sufism, Old Testament mysticism and Gnosticism. Lessing uses the medium of science fiction, and the perspective of an alien viewpoint, to present some unpleasant truths about 20th-century society, which is particularly hard-hitting in the show trial of the white races (or the north-western fringes as the Canopeans know them) for the thousands of years of repression they have inflicted on the rest of the planet's population. It is a challenging book, which looks at the nature of good and evil, life and death, and asks if humanity can ever be saved from itself.

CANOPUS EM ARGOS: ARQUIVOS

SHIKASTA

DORIS LESSING

3ª EDIÇÃO

EDITORA NOVA FRONTEIRA

DORIS LESSING
1919 –
Nationality: British
First Published: Jonathan Cape, 1973
Other Selected Titles:
The Marriage Between Zones 3, 4 and 5
The Sirian Experiments
The Making of the Representative for Planet 8
The Sentimental Agents in the Volyen Empire
This Was the Old Chief's Country
A Man and Two Women
The Golden Notebook

Stepford Wives

NOW A MAJOR
MOTION PICTURE
STARRING
**NICOLE
KIDMAN**

IRA LEVIN

'Every novel Ira Levin has ever written
has been a marvel of plotting. He is the Swiss
watchmaker of the suspense novel' Stephen King

IRA LEVIN
1929 –
Nationality: American
First Published: Random House
New York, 1972
Other Selected Titles:
*This Perfect Day
The Boys from Brazil
A Kiss Before Dying
Rosemary's Baby
Sliver
Son of Rosemary*

Stepford Wives

Photographer Joanne Eberhart and her husband
Walter have just moved to Stepford in
Connecticut with their two children. It's a lovely
little town, with picture-postcard houses, neat
gardens and happy children. While Walter
commutes to work, Joanne tries to make friends
with other women, but they are all housework-
obsessed, perfectly dressed, manicured and
made-up domestic slaves, and seemingly happy
that way. Joanne makes friends with two
women, Bobbie and Charmaine, who are also
new arrivals. They, and Walter, agree that there
is something odd going on, which appears to be
centred on the Men's Club. Walter agrees to join
the club to investigate.

Shortly after feisty feminist Charmaine tries
to organize a consciousness-raising meeting for
the women, she goes on a second honeymoon
with her husband, and comes back as a perfect
Stepford Wife. Now seriously spooked, Bobbie
and Joanne try to find out what is going on. Are
the women being brainwashed or is something
even more sinister taking place? What is
happening to Walter at the Men's Club that
makes him come home shaking? The chilling horror of the novel
switches into overdrive when he brings friends from the club to
the house. While one sketches Joanne's face, the others poke
around in the bedroom.

Her fears seem justified when Bobbie returns from a weekend
away as yet another obedient bimbo. Is Joanne next on the list?
In her paranoia, she consults an out-of-town psychiatrist who
warns her to get herself and the children away as quickly as
possible. Whether Joanne escapes, whether the women are being
replaced by robot replicas and who is behind everything are not
explained in the book, but left to the reader's imagination.
Written at the height of radical 1970s bra-burning feminism, this
book offers a deeply satirical view of America's consumerism-
driven society and a chilling foretaste of the post-feminist backlash.

Out of the Silent Planet

Dr Elwin Ransom, a Cambridge philologist, is on a walking tour of England when by chance he knocks on the door of an old (and unpopular) ex-schoolfellow's cottage. He is drugged and kidnapped by the man, Devine, and his accomplice, Professor Weston, who has discovered the secret of space flight.

They set off for Mars in Weston's rocket, and during the journey Ransom wakes to hear that he is to be offered to the inhabitants, the sorns, as a sacrifice. He manages to escape and encounters Hyoi, one of the otterlike hrossa, who take him in. He learns that they are one of three intelligent species on the planet, which they call Malacandra: the hrossa, the pfifltriggi and the seroni (sorns), who cooperate peacefully under the guidance of the ethereal Oyarsa.

After Hyoi is killed by Weston and Devine, it is decided that Ransom should go to the Oyarsa. Like much of Lewis' work, belief is a major theme. The Oyarsa is similar to an archangel, and explains to Ransom that each of the inhabited planets in the solar system has its own Oyarsa, but the one who governed the Earth went to the bad and that is what has caused all the evil on the planet. The Malacandrans know it as the Silent Planet, and allow such evil people as Weston and Devine to exist. Lewis' main theme is the difference between good and evil, but unlike the other two books in the series, it never gets preachy. The descriptions of the Malacandrans and their planet are beautifully written, and despite some long philosophical discussions, the story is well-paced and enthralling.

C.S. LEWIS
1898 – 1963
Nationality: British
First Published: John Lane, 1938
Other Selected Titles:
Perelandra
That Hideous Strength
Of Other Worlds
The Dark Tower and Other Stories
Of This and Other Worlds
The Screwtape Letters
The Great Divorce

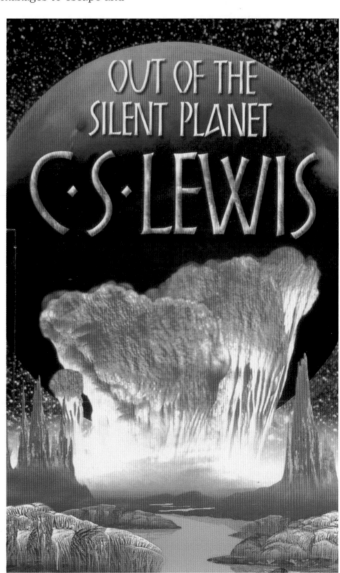

407

I Am Legend

RICHARD MATHESON
1926 –
Nationality: American
First Published: Fawcett
Publications, 1954
Other Selected Titles:
The Shrinking Man
Shock!
Nightmare at 20,000 Feet
Duel
Offbeat
The Beardless Warriors
Now You See It
Unrealized Dreams

Richard Matheson in 2000.

In a suburb of Los Angeles in the late 1970s, Robert Neville is perhaps the last human alive. Everyone else on the planet has been turned into a vampire. During the day, when the creatures are comatose, he seeks them out and kills them with the traditional wooden stake, fixes the defences on his house, strings up the garlic again and clears dead vampires off the lawn.

At night, he barricades himself indoors and drinks himself into a stupor while they taunt him and try to break in. But these are not mythological vampires like Dracula; they include his neighbours and other people he knew. By conducting a variety of experiments Neville learns that the condition has been caused by a bacterium, to which he alone is immune. Further experiments explain all the 'facts' about vampires involving fear of light and garlic, invisibility in mirrors, need for fresh blood, immunity to bullets, susceptibility to wooden stakes and aversion to religious symbols. The true horror of the story does not lie in the fights with the vampires, but in what the life Neville is forced to lead does to him. He is totally alone, forced

to barbaric slaughter on a daily basis just in order to survive, hanging on to a life that he does not really want to live any more. The calm writing style does nothing to lessen the chill or the impact of Neville's pain as he describes the death of his wife and daughter. As he loses his grip on sanity and comes close to giving up, the reader comes to understand what one man can endure if he has to and what happens when he goes too far. The final twist in the tale brings about the realization that Neville, the last human, is now the monster of legend.

Dwellers in the Mirage

Leif Langdon has always felt out of place in the modern world and prefers to explore and hunt. Years earlier, he witnessed a peculiar religious ritual in Mongolia and one of the tribesmen informed him that he was descended from Dwayanu, an ancient Mongolian warrior-king. While on a hunting trip in the foothills of the Endicott Mountains in Alaska he and his native American friend come across a mysterious mirage, behind which is a hidden valley inhabited by two races of humans: golden-skinned pygmies and descendents of the same Mongol people as he is.

Langdon embarks on a hair-raising set of adventures involving civil war, warrior-priestesses, giant leeches and sieges. Most terrifying of all is the Khalk'ru, a Kraken-like god of entropy and nothingness from another dimension, which dissolves every living thing it touches. Langdon discovers that he is not merely the descendent of Dwayanu, but is sharing his head with him: the ancient king takes over periodically when he feels it is necessary.

But what is the Khalk'ru? Is Langdon/Dwayanu its slave or its master? This rip-roaring tale contains elements of different genres: fantasy, mythology, lost world novels and contemporary pulp fiction. Langdon encounters strange and often amusing side characters, including several scantily clad women, and is thrust from terrifying event to petrifying incident with sometimes mind-boggling speed. Even at this rapid rate, Merritt finds time to describe the strange flora and fauna that have developed in the isolated world behind the mirage, using exhaustive detail with adjective piled upon adjective to build up vivid images.

ABRAHAM MERRITT
1884 – 1943
Nationality: American
First Published: Liveright Inc., 1932
Other Selected Titles:
The Moon Pool
The Ship of Ishtar
Seven Footprints to Satan
The Face in the Abyss
Burn, Witch, Burn
The Metal Monster
The Drone Man
The Fox Woman

A Canticle for Leibowitz

WALTER MILLER
1922 – 1996
Nationality: American
First Published: Lippincott, 1960
Other Selected Titles:
*Saint Leibowitz and the Wild
Horse Woman
The Best of Walter M. Miller Jr.
Conditionally Human
The Darfstellar and Other Stories
The Science Fiction of Walter M.
Miller Jr.
The View from the Stars*

Spanning more than 2,000 years, this novel is divided into three parts: Fiat homo, Fiat lux and Fiat voluntas tua, which were originally published separately. Part 1 is set in the 26th century in the aftermath of a nuclear war – the Flame Deluge – which destroyed civilization 600 years earlier. The anti-technology backlash after the war led to the destruction of all knowledge and the slaughter of everybody with any learning. The only major organization to survive is the Church. Monks of the order founded by the 20th-century engineer Isaac Leibowitz, who tried to prevent this, devote their lives to finding, hiding, preserving and copying fragments of scientific and technical literature that they do not understand.

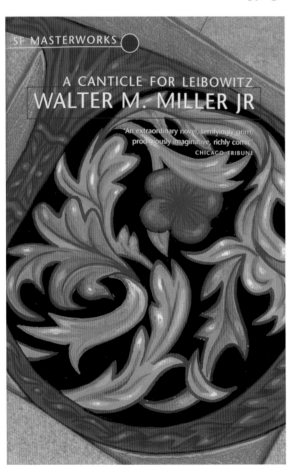

The second part of the story starts in 3174, when a new Renaissance is under way. However, advances in learning and technology are not just used for peaceful purposes: there are more and more wars. Part Three is set in 3781. Humanity's technological achievements are now beyond what they were at the time of the Flame Deluge, and it is obvious to many that another nuclear war is now imminent. The monks are debating how many of them should leave the planet. Miller examines several major philosophical themes in the book, including the nature of God; the human condition – whether mankind is doomed to a repetitive cycle of barbarianism, enlightenment and destruction; and the relationship between science and religion. Written when the US administration was anti-intellectual, fearful about the threat from the Soviet Union and paranoid about communism, this novel holds a stark warning about what Miller saw as the inevitable consequences of the nation's military build-up. In places grimly comic, in others deeply moving, with believable characters in all-too believable settings, this enthralling and thought-provoking book is one that does deserve the name classic.

Ringworld

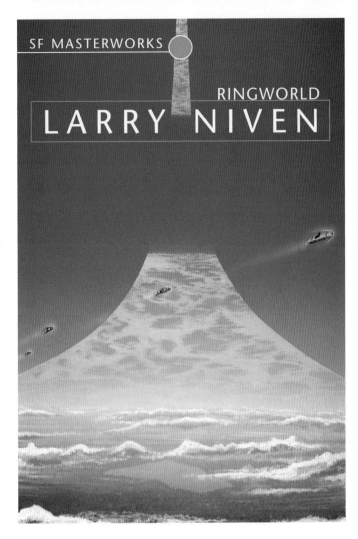

It is the year 2850, Luis Wu has just celebrated his 200th birthday, and he's bored. When he is approached by Nessus, a member of the two-headed Puppeteer species, with the offer of an unspecified expedition, he leaps at the chance. They find Teela Brown, who is genetically lucky, and Speaker-to-animals, an 8-foot-tall orange cat-like being. Nessus eventually reveals to Teela that the survival of humanity depends on a space ship that he will give her and Luis Wu if they succeed in their mission.

Eventually it emerges that they are travelling to the Ringworld, a 1,000,000-mile ring surrounding a planet, which the Puppeteers have recently discovered. When they reach the vast object, their ship is hit by its anti-meteor defences and they are forced to crash-land. The rest of the novel covers their exploration of just tiny parts of the terraformed artefact and their encounters with some of its 30 trillion inhabitants, its mechanisms, its flora and fauna and their search for a way to repair their spacecraft and leave. Who built the Ringworld, and are they still there?

The group's most astonishing encounter is with the descendants of humans brought to the planet thousands of years earlier by its creators. Their world is decaying; over millennia they have lost the knowledge of how it operates and now attribute its workings to divine power. When they mistake the visitors for gods, everything descends into violence. The relationship between the explorers constantly shifts, with first one in control, then another. Wu and Brown gradually become aware that Nessus is manipulating them, but to what ends? What was his motive for bringing them here and will they ever escape?

LARRY NIVEN
1938 –
Nationality: American
First Published: Ballantine Books, 1970
Other Selected Titles:
The World of Ptavvs
The Ringworld Engineers
Integral Trees
The Ringworld Throne
Ringworld's Children
The Convergent Series
Playgrounds of the Mind
The Magic Goes Away

"One of the most popular authors of our time."
—*Publishers Weekly*

BAEN

ANDRE NORTON

ANDRE NORTON
1912 – 2005
Nationality: American
First Published: World Publishing Co., 1958
Other Selected Titles:
The Defiant Agents
The Many Worlds of Andre Norton
Postmarked the Stars
Iron Cage
Lore of the Witchworld
Flight in Yiktor
The Monster's Legacy
The Mark of the Cat: Year of the Rat

Time Traders

In the first quarter of the 21st century, habitual offenders are 'rehabilitated' so when delinquent Ross Murdock is offered an alternative – to volunteer for an unspecified government project – he leaps at the chance, intending to escape as soon as he can. He is taken to a remote base where he is subjected to a battery of mental and physical tests. After encountering a badly injured man, he realizes that he's got himself mixed up in something both important and dangerous.

One of the other volunteers, Kurt, tells him that the US government is sending people back in time and Ross reluctantly agrees to escape with him. Kurt turns out to be a Soviet mole, so Ross overpowers him and returns to the base. On his return, he is told more about Operation Retrograde. The Soviet Union has found a way to travel in time and has acquired futuristic technology, including weapons, somewhere in the past. Naturally, the US government wants the technology for itself as well. The scientists at the base have constructed a duplicate time machine but have no idea where the Russians are in time. So they are sending volunteers, disguised as traders, to various periods in time to search for them. Ross is slated for Britain in 2000 BC.

When he and his mentor arrive at their destination, it is all too obvious that they have arrived at the right time: the Russians have bombed the trading station out of existence. What follows is a boys' own adventure, with good Americans, bad Russians and evil aliens. Lost in prehistory, the hapless hero must live on his wits, survive in a hostile environment and endure great hardship to defeat the enemy and make sure that neither one does anything to alter history.

Nineteen Eighty-Four

The ideas contained in Orwell's chilling dystopia have entered mainstream culture in a way achieved by only very few books, let alone science fiction novels. Concepts such as Big Brother, the Thought Police and Room 101 are instantly recognized and understood. In the novel, the world is divided between three regimes: Oceania, Eurasia and Eastasia. Winston Smith, whose job in the Ministry of Truth is to rewrite history in line with current political thinking, lives in a London still shattered by a nuclear war that took place not long after the Second World War.

Oceania is a totalitarian state, which resembles the more sinister aspects of the Soviet Union when Orwell was writing, at a time when he had become disillusioned with Socialism. The population is brainwashed into unthinking obedience, love of Big Brother, and hatred of Eurasia and Emmanuel Goldstein, the leader of the Brotherhood, an underground group of dissenters. They are also monitored for signs of deviance in behaviour or thought.

Winston and his girlfriend break the rules and, although they think they have got away with it, are being watched closely. When Winston is approached by O'Neill, who appears to be a member of the Brotherhood, the trap is sprung and they are sent to the Ministry of Love for a violent re-education. There are unanswered questions: do Big Brother, the Brotherhood or Emmanuel Goldstein exist or are they Party inventions? Even after 50 years, *Nineteen Eighty-Four* is still relevant: its depiction of a state where daring to think differently is rewarded with torture, where people are monitored every second of the day, and where Party propaganda tells people what to think, is a sobering reminder of the evils of powerful, unaccountable governments.

GEORGE ORWELL
1903 – 1950
Nationality: British
First Published: Secker & Warburg, 1949
Other Selected Titles:
A Clergyman's Daughter
Keep the Aspidistra Flying
Coming Up For Air
Animal Farm
Down and Out in Paris and London

The Narrative of Arthur Gordon Pym of Nantucket

EDGAR ALLAN POE
1809 – 1849
Nationality: American
First Published: J. & J. Harper, 1938
Other Selected Titles:
*Murders in the Rue Morgue and
Other Stories
The Prose Romances of Edgar A. Poe
The Raven and Other Poems and
Tales
Tamerlane and Other Poems
Tales of Edgar A. Poe
Tales of the Grotesque and
Arabesque*

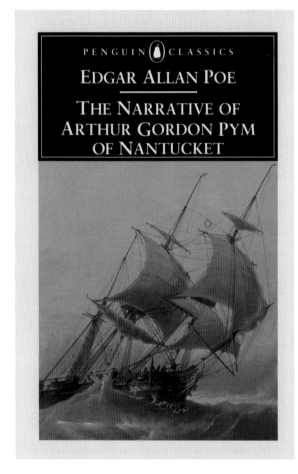

Almost from the beginning of Poe's only novel, what might be a straightforward sea-faring adventure is revealed to be anything but. Young Arthur Pym, with the help of the captain's son Augustus, stows away on a whaling ship, the Grampus, and is entombed without food or water in the hold for two weeks. From then on murder follows mutiny, with shipwreck and cannibalism in close succession. Neither the pace of the narrative nor the horror lets up. The story is written in the form of Pym's journal, and traces his gradual desensitization to the horrors that beset him, from terror early in the book to casual curiosity towards the end.

Aboard another ship, Pym and Peters (one of the mutineers who, despite his brutality, helps Pym) sail for the South Seas where they undergo and witness more trials and horrors, including ritual slaughter and live burials. Poe takes his characters to the limits of human endurance, risking their sanity, and brings in to question the sanctity of life and even the existence of God.

As well as being a rip-roaring yarn and coming-of-age story, *The Narrative* has been interpreted as a metaphysical tale: Pym undergoes allegories of shamanic initiation rituals, under the guidance of Peters, a sort of priest-guide. In the first part of the book, they descend to their worst depths, culminating in cannibalism, and in the second part, where the trials are spiritual as well as physical, each brings them farther out of their own darkness, with Peters gaining wisdom and Pym gaining his manhood, or perhaps something greater. In the abrupt, cryptic ending to the story contained in the preface and notes, Poe is playing with his readers. Is this a real narrative as it claims to be, or is it a novel?

The Inverted World

City Earth is governed by secretive guilds that run different aspects of its day-to-day functioning. Membership of a guild confers status and gives access to knowledge about the city and the planet. Helward Mann is a junior member of one of the guilds and through his work discovers that City Earth is, in fact, somehow being dragged northward on rails that are continually picked up from behind and relaid in front, in a never-ending attempt to stay as close as possible to the constantly-moving 'optimum'. The guilds have iron control over the population and social structure within the city is rigid.

Helward's wife, Victoria, is dissatisfied with her limited opportunities and status as a woman and persuades him to share the secrets he has learned, even though they are both aware the penalty for doing so is death. During Helward's visits to the outside of the city, which are forbidden to all but guild members, he learns more and more of the hideously distorted landscape through which the city is travelling, the nature of 'optimum', what the eventual fate of the city and the planet might be and why the guilds are so determined to keep the population in the dark. The sense of mystery and suspense build gradually throughout the story as, little by little, the secrets are revealed. Helward's adventures, and the frankly weird events that happen beyond the city, lead the reader to question their own perceptions and to re-examine the nature of reality, truth and illusion.

CHRISTOPHER PRIEST
1943 –
Nationality: British
First Published: Sidgwick & Jackson, 1973
Other Selected Titles:
The Affirmation
Existenz
The Space Machine
The Separation

The Green Child

HERBERT READ
1893 – 1968
Nationality: British
First Published: William
Heinemann, 1935

*English art critic and poet,
Sir Herbert Read.*

The word most often used to describe this book is 'strange', and
it is probably no coincidence that the author had close links to
several Surrealist painters. The only novel by this art critic and
poet, it is set in the 1830s. It concerns the return of a man called
Oliver to his childhood village in Yorkshire, after many years as
the benevolent dictator, Dr Olivero, of a South American
country. Arriving late one evening, he notices that the village
stream is running uphill and in the wrong direction and sets off
to investigate. When he arrives at the abandoned water mill he
sees a man carrying a dead lamb indoors to where a woman is
tied to a chair. He rushes in to untie her and suddenly notices
that her skin is green and translucent and her blood is green and
gold, rather than red and blue. The narrative then breaks off,
turning into a surreal flashback of his travels, how he became a

South American dictator and why he decided to fake his own death and return to England.

The story then picks up again with his rescue of the Green Child and their escape from her abusive husband to the underground realms of her own people. The story works on several levels: as well as being an exciting tale, it is a deeply philosophical journey through the self and an exposition of Read's anarchist ideas on the balance between freedom and order, totalitarianism and choice. This is particularly evident in the last section of the book, set in the underground crystal caves of the Green Child's society. It has been described as the most beautifully written piece of science fiction ever created.

The Laxian Key

First published as a short magazine story and later in book form in the collection *The People Trap and Other Pitfalls*, this is a hilarious cross between the myth that the salt in the sea is made by a perpetual salt mill, and the Greek fable of Pandora's box. It is one of several of Sheckley's stories to feature Arnold and Gregor of the AAA Ace Agency planet decontamination service, who, for a fee, will remove just about anything from anywhere.

Arnold always has an eye to the main chance, so when he comes across a bargain in the form of an alien artefact called a Free Producer at Joe's Interstellar Junkyard, he cannot resist. The machine seems amazing: it runs forever (which breaks at least one law of physics), taking its energy from around it (which breaks another); and it does not need servicing as it never breaks down.

Despite not knowing what the machine produces, Arnold turns it on, only to discover that all it produces is a worthless grey powder, called Tangreese. And then he finds out that there is no off-switch, and the only way to prevent it churning out the powder until the end of time is to find the Laxian Key. As witty as anything written by Mark Twain, and bitingly satirical, Sheckley's shaggy dog story of the ne'er-do-well Arnold and his long-suffering partner Gregor also packs a moral punch: don't meddle with what you don't understand.

ROBERT SHECKLEY
1928 – 2005
Nationality: American
First Published: *Galaxy* magazine, 1954
Other Selected Titles:
The Man in the Water
Citizen in Space
The People Trap

City

CLIFFORD D. SIMAK
1904 – 1988
Nationality: American
First Published: Gnome Press, 1952
Other Selected Titles:
Cosmic Engineers
Ring Around the Sun
Way Station
All Flesh is Grass
The Werewolf Principle
The Goblin Reservation
A Heritage of Stars
Highway of Eternity

This collection of interlinked short stories was originally published in magazines in the 1940s, then in book form when Simak added the introduction and the linking passages. The story unfolds with a group of dog scholars thousands of years in the future, debating whether humans ever existed or were in fact a myth created by ancient dog scholars. Most come to the conclusion that no species that selfish, materialistic and irrational could have survived long. The myths they discuss trace the slow decline of human civilization and their disappearance from the planet, and relate particularly to the Webster family. In the early stories, improved transport and communications technology means that the cities are abandoned and people live in the country, becoming increasingly isolated, agoraphobic, indolent and useless.

It is one of the Websters who gave dogs the power of speech, while another man, Joe, made it possible for ants in Wisconsin to survive the winter, which allowed them to evolve and spread across the planet. Humans had also developed the ability to transform themselves and a scientist who is studying Jupiter changes himself and his dog into the seal-like Jovian natives, and finds that Jupiter is a paradisiacal place. He eventually returns to Earth to persuade the remaining humans to leave Earth and join them.

One character who appears throughout the book is the Websters' old robot, Jenkins, and it is he who hides all knowledge of humans from the dogs, on the grounds that it is better they have no example of our corrupting, evil influence. The end Simak foresees for mankind is a hopeless one and, although written in his lyrical, pastoral style, in places the story is very creepy. An epilogue in some later editions adds the fate of the dogs and ants.

Donovan's Brain

Patrick Cory is a young doctor who is becoming increasingly obsessed with the idea of keeping the human brain alive outside its owner's body. Pushing the limits of science and ethics, he has succeeded in keeping a monkey's brain alive for a few hours. When he finds a man dying after a plane crash, he takes the man's brain and forces his colleague, Dr Schratt, to help him to cover up the crime. They put the brain into a vessel at Cory's private laboratory and keep it alive in a solution of nutrients.

CURT SIODMAK
1902 – 2000
Nationality: German-American
First Published: Alfred A. Knopf, 1942

Cory keeps the man's brain under observation, monitoring its sleep patterns and activity. He decides to try to communicate with the brain – which belonged to a powerful, ruthless millionaire businessman called Donovan – to the concern of his wife, Janice, and Schratt. Eventually, he and the brain begin to communicate telepathically, but that is not enough for the megalomaniac Donovan, who realizes that he can use Cory to achieve his aims. Soon the young man finds himself in Los Angeles doing Donovan's murky financial deeds. As the brain grows in strength, it gains more and more control over Cory's mind and body, seeing the world through Cory's eyes, speaking through him and making him carry out his wishes even hundreds of miles away. This chilling novel is compulsive reading, full of suspense, with a creeping sense of horror that intensifies as Cory takes on the tycoon's aggressive character and descends into the hell of being imprisoned in his own brain and culminating in the inevitable fight for control.

THE CLASSIC SCIENCE THRILLER BY CURT SIODMAK

Lest Darkness Fall

L. SPRAGUE DE CAMP
1907 – 2000
Nationality: American
First Published: H. Holt & Co., 1941
Other Selected Titles:
The Queen of Zamba
The Hand of Zei
The Continent Makers
The Tower of Zanid
The Hostage of Zir
The Prisoner of Zhamanak
The Swords of Zinjaban
The Venom Trees of Sunga

History professor Martin Padway is in the Pantheon in Rome in 1938, during a visit to study Mussolini's Italy. At the height of a huge thunderstorm, he is struck by lightning and regains consciousness to discover that he was been whisked back more than 14 centuries in time, to the last years of the Western Roman Empire, before Italy – and Western Europe – descended into the Dark Ages. Once he has come to terms with what has happened to him, he realizes that he will never get back to the 20th century and so determines to both carve out a life for himself and to try to prevent the fall of Rome.

A man of many talents, he starts out by building a brandy still and soon branches out into publishing a news sheet and mechanical semaphore. Not everything runs smoothly (his attempt to make gunpowder being one notable example) and for every problem that he solves, another springs up. But being the clever modern American that he is, he is more than a match for those around him and he is soon the power behind Emperor Theodahad's throne and making his attempt to thwart history.

This is a breezy, often funny, tale that is not meant to be taken seriously. The author refreshingly ignores the now widely accepted paradox that Padway's activities in altering ancient history will ensure that he probably will never come into existence. The background of late Rome is told in realistic detail, including stinks, muck, lice and all. The plot moves briskly and is always entertaining.

Last and First Men

This book is vast in scope. Its basic premise is that ours is just the first, and most primitive, of 17 species of humanity that will develop civilizations and then decline back into savagery over a scale of two billion years. Each succeeding species is more advanced than the previous ones, but each manages to contribute to its own destruction. It is profoundly spiritual and philosophical in nature, delving in to what it means to be human.

OLAF STAPLEDON
1886 – 1950
Nationality: British
First Published: Methuen, 1932
Other Selected Titles:
Last Men in London
Odd John
Star Maker
Darkness and the Light
Old Man in New World
Sirius
Death into Life
The Flames

Stapledon was a pacifist and a socialist, and these beliefs permeate the whole book, which has over the years been criticized for its apparent anti-Americanism, but this is in reality an early expression of anti-globalization. The story contains the seeds of many ideas that now form part of the canon of science fiction: the terraforming of planets; interplanetary migration; entire groups or species linked telepathically; and genetic engineering.

The demise of the first men is brought about through a western energy crisis, intellectual stagnation and nuclear experimentation, and each succeeding species emerges as a result of adaptation over millennia to the changes imposed on them by their environment.

In another controversial part of the story, in the far future, men settle on Venus, and in doing so wipe out the indigenous intelligent species. Debate raged about whether Stapledon was saying that man was entitled to do this or not. The great distances in both space and time that are explored in this book put mankind and its fragility into perspective. As the 17th, and last, men reach their apogee on Neptune, their ultimate fate is becoming obvious. While exploring the pain and angst of life in the universe, Stapledon still manages to find beauty and hope in the human condition.

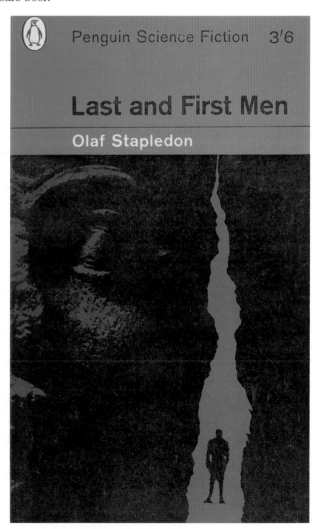

More than Human

THEODORE STURGEON
1918 – 1985
Nationality: American
First Published: Farrar, Straus &
Young, 1953
Other Selected Titles:
Godbody
Venus Plus X
Without Sorcery
The Dreaming Jewels
To Marry Medusa

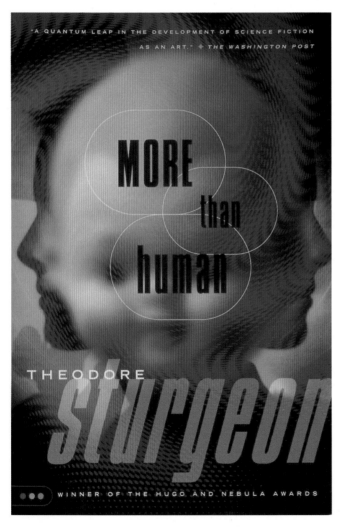

More than Human is made up of three novelettes: *The Fabulous Idiot, Baby is Three* (which was originally published in 1952 in *Galaxy* magazine) and *Morality*. Its theme is the next evolutionary stage of humanity. Lone is the idiot of the first part: ignored by everyone and shunned, he unknowingly uses telepathy and mind control to obtain food. Janie is a neglected girl who has seemingly limitless telekinetic abilities; the toddler twins, Bonnie and Beannie, can teleport but only speak two words between them; and Baby is superlatively intelligent but has severe disabilities and can communicate only telepathically via Janie. As individuals, they are outcasts; together, they form one whole being, *Homo gestalt*.

Despite the joined superhuman strengths of the children, because they were, through no fault of their own, social misfits, the new unity is both flawed and lonely for contact with others. As it struggles to come to terms with itself, it makes mistakes, with devastating consequences. But it learns from its mistakes and as the bonds within it strengthen, it begins to search for a purpose in life and a reason for its existence. In the last part of the book, Sturgeon explores the being's urgent need to develop a morality to protect both itself and those around it from its actions and their consequences.

In places this enthralling examination of the social implications of a massive leap in human evolution is deeply melancholic, in others chilling or even amusing. The story of the children's struggles and the emergence of the new being twists and turns right to the end.

Slan

Originally published in *Astounding Science Fiction* magazine, *Slan* is set in the 24th century. In the 22nd century, Samuel Lann genetically created Slans, mentally and physically superior mutant humans, to help their 'normal' counterparts. Now, however, Slans – who have tentacles in their hair that emerge when they are using their powers – are feared and loathed. They are believed to harm human children, and are shot on sight.

Despite this, Jommy Cross goes with his mother (both Slans) to the capital, Centropolis, where they are caught. She is killed, but the nine-year-old escapes. He hides out until he is old enough to make use of the knowledge his father left him to save the Slan, despite the dictator, Kier Gray's, sworn aim to exterminate them.

What Jommy does not know is that there is another type of Slan; tentacle-free, their only psychic ability is to hide themselves from tentacled Slan, by whom they are oppressed. One such Slan is Kathleen Layton, a young girl imprisoned by Gray. As Jommy grows up, he learns to put into action the knowledge his father had accumulated, including building himself a space ship.

Action is piled on action, and gradually the history of the Slan and truth behind humanity's hatred of them is revealed. The plot is complex, and there are several surprising twists. Who is behind the plot to assassinate Gray? Why is he obsessed with Kathleen, and is he less intolerant of Slans than he appears? Van Vogt's obvious theme is the irrationality of race-hatred and the ease with which it can be ignited through rumour. This is bound up in a fast-paced classic science fiction tale of enormous scope. Although it is dated in style, it is still a compelling read.

A.E. VAN VOGT
1912 – 2000
Nationality: Canadian-American
First Published: Arkhan House, 1946
Other Selected Titles:
The Weapon Makers

A Journey to the Centre of the Earth

Axel Lidenbrock lives in Hamburg with his uncle, Professor Otto Lidenbrock. The story opens as the latter rushes home to show Axel his latest acquisition: a runic manuscript by the renowned Icelandic explorer Snorri Sturluson. Hidden within its pages, they find a separate note which, when translated into Latin and read backwards, appears to be the Icelandic alchemist Arne Saknussem's tale of his discovery of a passage leading to the centre of the Earth from Snaefell, a dormant volcano. The passage is only revealed at noon during the last few days of June, just a month later.

Otto rushes off to the area, dragging a very reluctant Axel with him. There was a great deal of debate in France at the time about the teaching of science – especially science that questioned the teachings of Christianity – and one of the major aims of Verne and his publisher, Hetzel, in his *voyages extraordinaires* novels was to make science available to children through the medium of literature. This is why Axel is a 16-year-old and why he regularly contradicts his uncle's hypotheses with arguments based on then-current scientific thinking.

Despite Axel's hopes, they locate the crater and, together with guide Hans Bjelke, descend into the crater and find the passage. What follows is a hair-raising series of adventures involving giant mushrooms, underwater oceans, storms, plesiosaurs, ichthyosaurs, mastodons, a hidden race of giants (Axel, typically, questions their existence when they are patently there) and the magma chamber of an active volcano. For its time, the story is groundbreaking, and makes a gripping adventure. Later translations may include material dropped from early versions for being anti-British, too scientific, or too long.

JULES VERNE
1828 – 1905
Nationality: French
First Published: Griffith & Farrar, 1871 (first English translation)
Other Selected Titles:
The Children of Captain Grant
The Black Diamonds
Around the World in Eighty Days

Jules Verne.

Slaughterhouse-Five, or The Children's Crusade

KURT VONNEGUT
1922 –
Nationality: American
First Published: Delacorte
Press, 1969
Other Selected Titles:
Pearls Before Swine
Goodbye, Blue Monday
Lonesome No More

Using his own experiences as a prisoner of war in Germany, Vonnegut's deeply satirical 1969 novel explores the human condition through the medium of science fiction. The protagonist, Billy Piper, is 'unstuck in time', and never knows which part of his life he is going to experience next. In 1967, he is kidnapped by aliens, the Tralfamadorians, and exhibited in a zoo. During his stay on their planet, he learns that they have a completely different concept of time: for them, every moment, whether in the past, present or future, has always existed, always will, and will occur over and over again.

They are able to revisit any part of their lives at will, and so to them an individual's death does not matter as they are still alive in the past. One of the most important events in Piper's life was witnessing the Allied carpet- and fire-bombing of Dresden (which killed 130,000 civilians and flattened 90 per cent of the city) and the descriptions of that horror bring home in gripping fashion Vonnegut's eloquent anti-war message. The Tralfamadorians are

American writer Kurt Vonnegut Jr.

fatalists, and realize both the necessity of changing what it is possible to change, and the need to be wise enough to know what they cannot change. Billy Piper adopts this fatalism, and eventually he spreads it to millions of followers.

Despite its bleak message, *Slaughterhouse-Five* is a deeply, if very blackly, funny novel. The direct style of writing leaves the reader free to get to grips with both the non-linear story and the results of Vonnegut's brilliant imagination.

The Island of Dr Moreau

H.G. WELLS
1866 – 1946
Nationality: British
First Published: Sweetman, 1896
Other Selected Titles:
When the Sleeper Wakes
The Time Machine
The War of the Worlds
The Invisible Man

H.G. Wells broadcasting from the BBC in 1929.

Like several other lost-island novels of the era, Wells' story takes the form of a manuscript found by accident, in this case by the nephew of the protagonist Edward Prendick. After being shipwrecked, he is rescued and put ashore on a remote island with the other passengers on the boat. Here Prendick meets Dr Moreau, a scientist who was hounded out of Britain some years earlier because his unethical work with animals was unacceptable to the scientific establishment. It soon emerges

that his work on the island is even more gruesome as he is performing experiments on live animals, trying to turn them into something approximating humans, with the ability to think and speak. Their behaviour is continually reinforced by laws about what they must and must not do and strict obedience to Moreau which are 'woven into the texture of [their] minds'.

As each experiment fails, the victim is released into the wilds of the island to revert to beasthood. The book can be read on several levels; in addition to being a suspense-filled, compelling adventure, it has a number of points to make. At a time of great scientific advances, there was a great debate on medical and scientific ethics, much as there has been about cloning, stem-cell research, abortion and genetic modification in our own time. Wells' chilling accounts of the effects of Moreau's experimentation on the animals can be seen as part of the burgeoning anti-vivisection movement of the late 19th century, and a criticism of man's aim to shape the world into his own image. Prendick's narrative ends with a stark warning for society: after his eventual return to Britain, he cannot shake off the impression that the people he meets are reverting to beasthood just like the animals on the island.

H.-G. WELLS

50c.
L'OUVRAGE COMPLET

L'ILE DU DOCTEUR MOREAU

(Traduit de l'anglais par Henry-D. DAVRAY)

F. ROUFF, Éditeur,
Rue de Vaugirard, PARIS

ISLANDIA

THE EPIC UNDERGROUND CLASSIC

"Fabulous ... there has never been anything like it."
—THE NEW YORKER

AUSTIN TAPPAN WRIGHT

AUSTIN TAPPAN WRIGHT
1883 – 1931
Nationality: American
First Published: Farrar & Rinehart, 1942

Islandia

As a Harvard student, John Lang was friends with Dorn, a citizen of the remote nation of Islandia on the isolated southern continent of Karain. Within a few years, he becomes US consul to the country – one of only 100 outsiders allowed there at any one time – and discovers a culture very different from that of 1920s America. It is a hierarchical agrarian society governed by a few patrician families, where men and women are equals and free love common, but social mobility is non-existent.

It is a utopian place, everyone is content with their lot and the way of life is slow and peaceful. However, there is a cloud on the horizon: Germany is threatening invasion (today, the anti-German polemics and racist attitudes are jarring notes but were common at the time). Lang's tenure coincides with the run-up to a referendum on how to react, and he becomes deeply involved in the ensuing political machinations. It is through Lang's reactions that the plot progresses; through his reactions to the different ways of the Islandians, how the challenges these make affect his attitudes and, ultimately, to the choices he makes about his life. This is particularly obvious in his very dissimilar treatment of American and Islandian women.

This thought-provoking, uplifting novel has led many readers to step back from their own lives and re-evaluate the choices they have made and the values they hold. Wright conceived the idea for Islandia as a child and over the next 40 years developed for it a complete geography, social structure and language, which are impeccably carried through the book's thousand-odd pages. Unpublished in his lifetime, the book was put into coherent form by his wife, daughter and editor after his death.

The Day of the Triffids ✓

This post-apocalyptic novel starts the evening before the main character, Bill Masen, is due to have the bandages covering his eyes removed. As he listens, he hears hospital staff and other patients exclaiming at the beauty of the spectacular meteor shower outside. The following morning, he discovers that almost everyone else has been blinded by the lights. The fortuitous event that resulted in Bill being spared was a sting by a triffid – a genetically engineered, mobile, carnivorous crop plant that he farmed. He had previously been attacked by one as a child, so he had some immunity. His eyes had only temporarily been damaged, whereas most people would have been blinded and killed.

With the vast majority of the population incapacitated, those who retain their eyesight have the moral dilemma of whether to try to look after as many blinded people as they can or flee, leaving them to be eaten by the triffids. Much of the novel is an exploration of how people would survive an apocalypse. During his search for Josella, a sighted woman with whom he has fallen in love but from whom he has become separated, Masen encounters groups who organize themselves on a variety of models, including Christian, feudal and paramilitary.

He also looks at the function of women in such a society. The chilling realism of the book lies in the appalling realization that the vast majority of the population will have to be abandoned to their fate to allow the minority to survive and rebuild the human race. The horror of this gripping novel deepens when it becomes obvious that the triffids are communicating with each other and beginning to hunt cooperatively.

JOHN WYNDHAM
1903 – 1969
Nationality: British
First Published: Michael Joseph, 1951
Other Selected Titles:
The Crysalids
The Secret People
Stowaway to Mars
The Kraken Wakes
The Midwich Cuckoos
Trouble with Lichen
Chocky

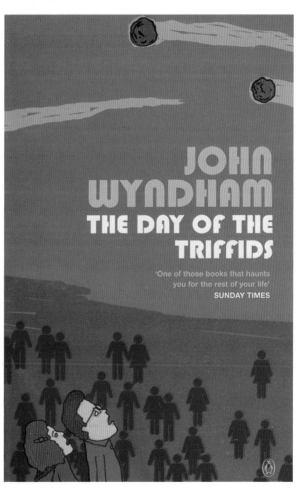

THRILLERS

More Work for the Undertaker

MARGERY ALLINGHAM
1904 – 1966
Nationality: British
First Published: William Heinemann,
1948
Other Selected Titles:
Mystery Mile
Death of a Ghost
The Tiger in the Smoke

Margery Allingham is regularly classified as one of the 'Big Four' novelists of Golden Age detective fiction. Along with her contemporaries, Christie, Sayers and Marsh, Allingham did much to ensure the continuing popularity of the thriller, but where she differs from them is in her deceptively entertaining approach and in the greater versatility of her detective, Albert Campion.

Campion is an upper-class eccentric whose colourless appearance belies his resourcefulness. His man-servant, Magersfontein Lugg, is as implausible a personality as his name suggests, being a reformed burglar with a heart of gold and a real, if rough, loyalty for his master. As the series progresses, Campion gains a wife, Lady Amanda Fitton, while his police connections extend from Inspector Stanislaus Oates to young Charlie Luke, who appears in this novel only to be completely outdone by Campion.

In *More Work for the Undertaker*, Allingham gives one of her finest performances. In quiet Apron Street, the intellectual Palinode family have been reduced to boarding in their own home. The kind of people who do crossword puzzles in Latin for fun, they may be eccentric but probably harmless. So when Ruth Palinode is murdered, Campion comes in to investigate her seemingly motiveless death. Allingham often uses Dickensian naming to reflect character or role and this work is no exception. The cast of characters includes the eponymous undertaker, Jas Bowels, who not only happens to be Lugg's brother-in-law but is, despite his name, a jolly rogue; while the bewildering events include poisoning, further murder, anonymous letters and a disappearing coffin.

The dialogue is witty and delightful and therefore entertainingly satiric but, underneath, the novel has a satisfyingly intricate plot, supporting Allingham's place as one of the most accomplished and influential writers of her day.

Devil Take the Blue-Tail Fly

John Franklin Bardin wrote thriller fiction
under more than one name, often in quite a
conventional manner, but it was as himself
that he was most inventive and experimental
and *Devil Take the Blue-Tail Fly* is
usually considered the finest example
of this creativity.

World War Two is over and life should be
getting back to normal, but normality is
exactly what eludes the female protagonist
from whose perspective the novel is told.
Ellen is anticipating going home to her
husband, Basil, having had a spell in hospital
after a mental breakdown. She is a
professional harpsichord player, he is a
conductor, and everything indicates there
should now be a happy future ahead of them
as she picks up her career again. However,
Ellen suffers from a personality disorder,
having an evil alter ego called Nelle who
becomes increasingly dominant as the novel
progresses. Ellen's confusion over happenings
past and present is a consequence of the
suppression of her memory when Nelle is
uppermost. For this reason, neither Ellen nor
the reader can be sure exactly how she was involved in Jim
Shad's death years before, an incident which nags away at her
like the irritation from the bite of a blue-tail fly.

Ellen's descent into a kind of madness provides an
extraordinary detective challenge to the reader: the clues to the
past can only be accessed through her fractured mind. Under
Bardin's deft handling, the inevitability of Nelle committing the
ultimate crime becomes almost secondary compared to the
horror of the crime Nature has played on Ellen. *Devil Take the
Blue-Tail Fly* is as remarkable today for its painful intensity as it
was shocking and agonizing to read in its own time.

JOHN FRANKLIN BARDIN
1916 – 1981
Nationality: American
First Published: Macfadden, 1948
Other Selected Titles:
The Deadly Percheron
The Case Against Myself
So Young To Die

Trent's Last Case ✓

E.C. BENTLEY
1875 – 1956
Nationality: British
First Published: Thomas Nelson & Sons, 1913
Other Selected Titles:
Trent's Own Case

Despite its title, *Trent's Last Case* was actually the first of the only two novels to feature this world-worn detective. E.C. Bentley's creation in 1913 was an early reaction to some of the conventions of crime fiction that had established themselves following on from the appearance of Sherlock Holmes. In this lampoon, Philip Trent's involvement in solving the murder of millionaire, Sigsbee Manderson, breaks all the so-called rules of detective fiction as they existed at the time.

Trent himself is actually a gentleman dilettante and occasional reporter, rather than a policeman, but he has all the ferreting instincts required for investigation. So when Trent is commissioned by the owner of the *Record* to look into Manderson's shooting on his country estate, he sets about the task with single-minded thoroughness. Trent makes the heinous mistake, however, of falling in love with the most likely candidate for murderess: Manderson's widow. The reader's sympathies are drawn towards Mrs Manderson as it becomes clear that Sigsbee Manderson was, in fact, an unattractive and scheming character – a victim who is hard to like. Trent comes to all the wrong conclusions and it is only at the very end of the novel that the evidence is explained for him, and for the reader.

Eschewing the melodrama which had been a common feature of mystery novels thus far, Bentley gives more attention to characterization. The reader's expectations of an invincible and unknowable detective are shattered – Trent is just an ordinary man who can love and who can fail. In taking this approach, Bentley's mystery anticipates the more realist style of the Golden Age detective fiction to follow.

Trial and Error

Anthony Cox wrote under several pseudonyms. As Anthony Berkeley, he based the underlying premise of *Trial and Error* on a true legal case where two men were separately found guilty for the murder of the same person. The humour of this story is Berkeley's own and his trademark dry wit is put to good use.

When Lawrence Todhunter is told he could die any minute from an aortic aneurism, he wants to do something with his last remaining months which will benefit humanity, so he steels himself to shoot Jean Norwood. Norwood is a rude, hostile and extremely unpleasant actress-manager, whose removal from the world would make many people's lives sweeter. Todhunter meticulously plans the murder and all goes well until the police arrest her son-in-law, Vincent Palmer, as their clear suspect. Todhunter has to confess to the murder in order to save the innocent man but the police are sure they have an airtight case and don't believe him.

Todhunter has, therefore, to make a case against himself, to prove himself guilty. In fact, he has to crack the perfect crime.

The novel is ingenious in the way it turns the comic tables on conventional Golden Age expectations for, although it tests the credulity in terms of the actual scenario, Berkeley's clever depiction of his characters is wholly believable.

In the book, the initial philosophical discussion about the sanctity of human life gives way to questions about the justice of the English legal system and this is tested out through the ramifications of an increasingly intricate storyline. The final twist of the story does much to answer these questions, however, while at the same time stretching the limits of the genre.

ANTHONY BERKELEY
(ANTHONY BERKELEY COX)
1893 – 1971
Nationality: British
First Published: Hodder & Stoughton, 1937
Other Selected Titles:
The Piccadilly Murder
Death in the House

PENGUIN BOOKS

MYSTERY & CRIME

TRIAL AND ERROR

ANTHONY BERKELEY

MYSTERY & CRIME

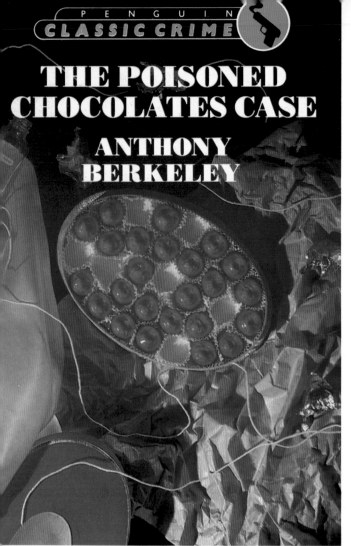

PENGUIN
CLASSIC CRIME

THE POISONED CHOCOLATES CASE

ANTHONY BERKELEY

ANTHONY BERKELEY
(ANTHONY BERKELEY COX)
1893 – 1971
Nationality: British
First Published: Collins, 1929
BOOK TITLES
The Layton Court Mystery
Murder in the Basement

The Poisoned Chocolates Case

This is another novel by Anthony Cox, writing under the pseudonym of Anthony Berkeley, featuring the series detective, Roger Sheringham.

Sir Eustace Pennefather, a louche and immoral character, is anonymously sent a box of chocolates. He gives the untouched box away to Graham Bendix, and soon his wife, Joan Bendix, is dead and he is seriously ill. Other than discovering the poison used in the chocolates, the police are only able to conclude that Sir Eustace was the intended victim but cannot take the case any further.

The problem comes to the attention of Roger Sheringham's 'Crimes Circle'. The members of this club each have an amateur interest in real crime and, among themselves, take on the challenge of solving the case. Rather than working together, however, they each come up with independent solutions arrived at by different methods. Meeting up night after night, they take it in turns to relate their findings, all of which are different.

The Poisoned Chocolates Case is noted for this multiple-solution scenario, as mixed as the centres of the chocolates themselves. The style is a bit tongue-in-cheek and, certainly, Berkeley's 'sleuths' unintentionally satirize classic modes of detection when they each fail to provide the correct solution.

The emphasis of this interesting story is more on the intellectual cleverness of each possible plot rather than on a desire for justice, but at the end of the tale the amateur sleuths do succeed in pinning down the real, if least likely, perpetrator. This is humorous, armchair detection at its best, relying on inventive wit and mental action, rather than the thrill and danger of the physical chase.

The Beast Must Die

Nicholas Blake's series detective, Nigel Strangeways, is the amateur sleuth of *The Beast Must Die* but the reader's attention is firmly fixed on his friend, the murder suspect Frank Cairnes, right from the beginning.

Cairnes is actually a writer of detective fiction, using the pseudonym Felix Lane to ensure his anonymity. Ironically, Cairnes forfeits that anonymity by taking up Part One of the novel, constituting almost a third of the whole, with a confessional diary. We are therefore let into his thoughts, feelings and motivations, unmediated and raw. For six months earlier, Cairnes's little son, Martin, was knocked down and killed by a hit-and-run motorist. Cairnes's wife died in childbirth and he is now left completely bereft, filled with terrible parental guilt and the desire for revenge – a revenge which must be to track the motorist down and kill him, using his writer's experience to plan a foolproof murder.

Although the police have been exceedingly thorough in their investigations, they have made no headway in finding the driver, but Cairnes, the detective story writer, succeeds where they do not. Unfortunately, when the driver is found murdered and Cairnes' intentions become known, he is naturally the chief suspect. The intricacies of the plot that follow in the remaining third-person narrative exemplify the best of Golden Age writing, but *The Beast Must Die* is chiefly remarkable for the very personal approach which overlays the puzzle. Questions of justice are often subordinated to the actual interest of solving the crimes, but here the reader is left in no doubt as to Cairnes' moral position, not only from the sheer impact of his emotional trauma, but also from the knowledge that the law would only deal out an unsatisfactory 'abstract justice'.

NICHOLAS BLAKE (CECIL DAY-LEWIS)
1904 – 1972
Nationality: British
First Published: Collins, 1938
Other Selected Titles:
Malice in Wonderland
The Case of the Abominable Snowman
The Private Wound

Psycho

ROBERT BLOCH,
1917 – 1994
Nationality: American
First Published: Simon & Schuster, 1959
BOOK TITLES
The Scarf
The Deadbeat
The Night of the Ripper

The chilling reputation of Robert Bloch's 1959 thriller has been somewhat overshadowed by Alfred Hitchcock's renowned film adaptation, but *Psycho* is worth reading for its relentless build up of psychological horror. Having stolen a large sum of money, Mary Crane arrives at Bates' Motel on her way to meet her lover. The initial interest is firmly focused on Mary's story and whether she will return the money or not. Norman Bates, the middle-aged motel manager, seems to be quite ordinary, if slightly odd and somewhat of a drinker, but this could be put down to his lonely lifestyle. When Mary is murdered – in a rather different, but just as horrific, way to that made famous by the film – the interest is shifted onto her killer, which becomes the first major twist in this shocking plot.

Bloch was influenced by some of the horrific practices which were revealed when multiple-murderer, Ed Gein, was caught. The Wisconsin farmer dismembered the bodies of his victims but had kept his mother's dead body in the house. The idea of having a double identity, of being a 'normal' member of the community and yet a crazed psychopath at the same time, was fused into Bloch's novel.

With *Psycho,* Bloch was reflecting the growing contemporary interest in the complexities of the human mind and the ways in which it can go wrong. This example of the thriller genre marked a move away from concern with horror from external factors to the internal horrors of the mind. The novel gives us a far more detailed and, for that reason, more frightening insight into Norman's psychopathic condition than a film can render and is, in its own medium, just as memorable.

Double Indemnity

James Cain's contribution to the hard-boiled thriller genre is perhaps nowhere better realized than in the mounting tension of *Double Indemnity*. Narrated in the first person by the insurance salesman, Walter Huff, the story is fast-paced and dark. Phyllis Nirdlinger, a beautiful *femme fatale*, seduces Huff into helping her murder her husband. They have to plan the perfect murder in such a way that Phyllis will be able to benefit from a double indemnity clause in the insurance package that Walter sold her husband. The majority of the novel is taken up with the account of their attempts to sidestep the growing suspicions of the police and of Mr Keyes, head of the Claim Department of General Fidelity Insurance. Additional complications pile up in the storyline around Phyllis' step-daughter, Lola, as Walter's guilt about killing her father overlays the guilt he also feels about his growing personal affection for her.

The great interest of this novel is Cain's masterly use of perspective: we see everything from Huff's point of view. Initially he seems to be the seducer and instigator. However, as his 'witness statement' develops, so does the truth emerge. Walter's surrender to Phyllis' allure and his subsequent puppet-role at her hands becomes apparent as the weakness of his character and the evil strength of hers is unmasked and the reader's sympathies are engaged in a different way. Billy Wilder's film version of 1944 gives a different ending to the story, but it is not so much the outcome that is at stake here – rather, Cain has created an engrossing situation and the reader's thrill comes from seeing it through Walter's helpless eyes as it spirals out of control.

JAMES CAIN,
1892 – 1977
Nationality: American
First Published:
Liberty Magazine, 1935
Other Selected Titles:
The Postman Always Rings Twice
Mildred Pierce

James Cain signs his autograph for a fan.

Thus Was Adonis Murdered

SARAH CAUDWELL
(SARAH COCKBURN)
1939 – 2000
Nationality: British
First Published: Collins, 1981
Other Selected Titles:
The Shortest Way to Hades
The Sirens Sang of Murder
The Sibyl in Her Grave

Thus Was Adonis Murdered was Sarah Caudwell's first of the mere four novels she wrote, all of which featured the Oxford Professor of Medieval Law, Hilary Tamar. Tamar is a first-person narrator who addresses the reader as though presenting a case. The Professor's gender is undisclosed and this supports the style generally, being neutral, detached and scholarly yet providing the thorough and satisfactory detail required for a detective story.

From the very beginning we know that Julia Larwood, a childlike, inadequate young woman but very competent tax-law barrister, is to be the unjustly-accused party whose innocence has to be proved. Julia is a member of Chambers whose senior partner was a past student of Tamar's. Julia travels to Venice for an art-lovers' holiday tour, but she is also hoping to indulge in the reputation of that city and have a romantic fling. The letters Julia sends back from Venice are read out among her colleagues with much wry amusement, until she is arrested for murder.

The Adonis Julia had in mind to seduce, 'the lovely Ned', is found dead and she is implicated when her copy of the latest Finance Act is found near his body. Luckily Julia continues to write home, as does her colleague Timothy who goes out to Venice too, so Tamar can unravel the case while comfortably ensconced back in London.

The letters add colour to Tamar's genderless narrative voice, as well as providing the basis for the colleagues' witty commentary. The novel's structure then its gentle humour and its academic approach all tend to distract the reader from the actuality of the murder, thus Caudwell gives an updated and enjoyable take on the traditional English puzzle thriller.

Farewell, My Lovely

Farewell, My Lovely is an exciting and fast-moving novel, constructed around two complicated narrative strands which eventually fuse themes of drugs, gambling, blackmail and murder. Moose Malloy, a slow-witted giant of a man, newly out of prison, is looking for his erstwhile girlfriend, Velma, at Florian's bar where she used to be a singer. Private eye Philip Marlowe comes across him here and witnesses Malloy's killing of the bar owner. Uninterested in this murder, the police inveigle Marlowe into tracking Malloy down for them, so his first quest is to find Velma and, through her, Moose. At the same time, Marlowe is hired to retrieve a jade necklace stolen from the wealthy Grayle family and this is where his troubles start in earnest, as he starts to fall for the attractions of *femme fatale*, Mrs Grayle.

Raymond Chandler was an admirer of 'hard-boiled' thriller author Dashiell Hammett, but his own detective, Philip Marlowe, is made of a different moral fibre. Chandler gives us a panoramic view of contemporary society, setting Marlowe up as the incorruptible hero of the people who can move easily through both the seedy, hustling atmosphere of Central Avenue as well as the upper reaches of Montemar Vista. Although Marlowe's narration shows the action through his character of wise-cracking, heavy-drinking tough guy, he also has a softer side, one which responds to the domestic temptations held out by women like Anne Riordan, a sweet young girl who becomes Marlowe's accomplice. Marlowe represents Chandler's iconic idea of the kind of 'man of honour' needed to protect the 'mean streets' of 1940s California.

Raymond Chandler in 1954.

RAYMOND CHANDLER
1888 – 1959
Nationality: American
First Published: Knopf, 1940
Other Selected Titles:
The Big Sleep
The Lady in the Lake
The Long Goodbye

**JAMES HADLEY CHASE
(RENE RAYMOND)**
1906 – 1985
Nationality: British
First Published: Jarrolds, 1939
Other Selected Titles:
*The Guilty Are Afraid
You Have Yourself A Deal
You're Dead Without Money*

No Orchids for Miss Blandish

Inspired by the hard-boiled American school, *No Orchids for Miss Blandish* was James Hadley Chase's first attempt at thriller writing and was an instant success. Chase did not set up a series detective, although occasionally characters reappear in other books. Rather, his mysteries typically revolve around a brutally frank view of the world which seems to make crime inevitable and the heroes less than heroic.

No Orchids for Miss Blandish was indebted to the story of real gangster, Ma Barker and her sons. The heiress, Miss Blandish, is kidnapped but her kidnappers are then themselves killed by a larger and more murderous gang. Ma Grissom, their leader and organizer, extracts half a million dollars in ransom from John Blandish but does not release his daughter. She keeps back the girl as a kind of plaything for her sadistic son, Slim, and the details of the girl's confinement are horrific. However, when the private eye, Dave Fenner, eventually finds her and attempts her rescue, the ending of the story is open to moral and psychological interpretation.

For its time, the content of the novel is shocking. The mixture of sex, violence and torture seems, indeed, to have been part of its appeal – as its alternative title *The Villain and the Virgin* suggests too – but where the book supports the morals of its period is that the scenario is meant to be disgusting, rather than pornographic, although 'Miss Blandish' could be any faceless victim. However, Chase does not express any strong disapproval for the crimes that are committed. The police only win because they have more power which, perhaps, reflects the sensibilities of a world on the brink of war.

The Murder of Roger Ackroyd

Although the best-selling and prolific career of the 'Queen of Crime' lasted right up to her death in 1976, this early book bears all the characteristics of Christie's deft handling of the genre. Featuring her famous Belgian detective, Hercule Poirot, who had appeared in her very first novel *The Mysterious Affair at Styles* (1920), and using an idealized English village for the setting, it is in the complexities of the plot that Christie shows her mastery.

In the absence of Captain Hastings, his usual Watson-like companion and chronicler, the recently retired Poirot is assisted by the local doctor in unravelling what is apparently a locked-room mystery. The rich manufacturer Roger Ackroyd is found murdered in his own study and the cast of suspects is limited. Like Hastings, Dr Sheppard assumes the role of chronicler, so Christie only allows us to see Poirot using his 'little grey cells' through Sheppard's narrative perspective. Christie is able to confound the reader's expectations with a plot twist that caused some shock and indignation among readers and critics alike on its first appearance and which still surprises today.

AGATHA CHRISTIE
1890 – 1976
Nationality: British
First Published: Collins, 1926
Other Selected Titles:
The Man in the Brown Suit
Murder at the Vicarage
Murder on The Orient Express
Crooked House

Agatha Christie at her typewriter in her home in Devon, 1946.

WILKIE COLLINS

THE WOMAN IN WHITE

NOW A HAUNTING NEW MUSICAL

The Woman in White

The Woman in White has been characterized as the first of the Sensation novels, a genre which became very popular in the latter half of the 19th century. Collins' work generated intense interest and encouraged many imitators.

The title and idea behind the book was inspired by a true incident. As Collins, his brother and the artist, Millais, were walking home late one night they fleetingly encountered a young woman, dressed in white, who seemed to be in a state of terror. In the novel, Collins marries this incident to aspects from another, real-life case of wrongful imprisonment. He gives us the convoluted story of Anne Catherick and Laura Fairlie, whose identities are stolen from them and who are both incarcerated in order that the villain, Sir Percival Glyde, may secure his financial future, while protecting a secret about his own identity.

The hero of the novel, Walter Hartright, falls in love with Laura and, with the courageous assistance of her half-sister, Marian Halcombe, he becomes the detective of the piece, working to unravel the mystery surrounding them all and restoring sanity – both literal and metaphorical – to their lives.

The Woman in White, like Collins' later masterpiece, *The Moonstone*, is structured around several different narrative voices, including that of Glyde's sinister co-conspirator the zestfully rendered Count Fosco. As each eye-witness account is given in turn, not only does Collins build up the fictional suspense, but he also makes clear the very real lack of autonomy experienced by women of the period.

WILKIE COLLINS
1824 – 1889
Nationality: British
First Published: Sampson Low, 1860
Other Selected Titles:
The Moonstone
The Law and the Lady
No Name
Armadale

Unnatural Exposure

PATRICIA CORNWELL
1956 –
Nationality: American
First Published: G.P. Putnam's Sons, 1997
Other Selected Titles:
Postmortem
Cruel and Unusual

Patricia Cornwall, shown here in March, 2000.

In Dr. Kay Scarpetta, Chief Medical Examiner of Richmond, Virginia, Patricia Cornwell has created a new kind of detective for a chaotic modern world, a world in which serial killers seem to be on the increase, their psychology unfathomable and their methods ever more gruesome.

While Scarpetta is on a lecture tour in Ireland she investigates whether there are any links between a series of unsolved murders there and a spate of murders that have been discovered in the USA. Back home, another mutilated body has turned up which differs slightly from the previous ones, but the next murder becomes the most shocking when it is discovered that the serial killer is using a modified form of smallpox on his victims. It is imperative that Scarpetta now finds and prevents any outbreak of the deadly virus.

The serial killer's need to gloat to Kay about his work leads him to contact her by email and show off his handiwork. With the help of her lover Benton Wesley, who is an FBI psychological profiler, the computer expertise of her genius niece, Lucy, and faithful Detective Pete Marino, Scarpetta has the support she needs to complete the job, both emotionally and professionally.

The smallpox virus is analogous to the serial killer who uses it. Unseen and deadly, the serial killer can disappear in the anonymity of the city, and only a forensic pathologist has the skill to catch him out or find him. Nor is crime limited any longer to the immediate community but stretches across the world. Cornwell has created a form of thriller in which the medical mystery itself provides just as much tension as the more classic race-against-time component of the novel.

The Moving Toyshop

Edmund Crispin's detective stories feature Gervase Fen, Oxford Professor of English Language and Literature and amateur sleuth, as and when required.

When poet Richard Cadogan needs a change of scene, he sets off for Oxford, arriving late at night after a protracted journey. Curious about a toyshop door being left unlocked, his urge for adventure does not prepare him for finding the dead body of an elderly woman inside. Cadogan is knocked out as he looks around the place and when he comes to several hours later he goes off to get the police.

However, when they return to the shop it has mysteriously become a grocer's and the toyshop has disappeared. The police are inclined to disbelieve Cadogan and, in indignation, he turns to his old friend Fen for help in solving the puzzle. Cadogan has forgotten that he picked up a scrap of paper with a telephone number on it which he slipped into his pocket while he was in the shop. When this comes to light again, Cadogan and Fen have some real evidence to work from.

The resulting investigation brings them up against a sprinkling of quirky characters and some farcical situations, but Fen puts his considerable intellect to what turns out to be a very serious crime and, under the amusing romp of the surface, Crispin constructs a tight plotline. Not surprisingly, literary allusion abounds: from limerick legacies, to games to pass the detectives' time, to quotations from unexpected quarters and, indeed, to the title reference itself. The style of Crispin's confections generally is a blend of the light-hearted and the erudite but *The Moving Toyshop* is probably the most fanciful in its premise and the most delightfully amusing classic for that reason.

EDMUND CRISPIN

**EDMUND CRISPIN
(ROBERT BRUCE MONTGOMERY)**
1921 – 1978
Nationality: British
First Published: Gollancz, 1946
Other Selected Titles:
Holy Disorders
Buried For Pleasure
The Glimpses of the Moon

In the Last Analysis

**AMANDA CROSS
(CAROLYN GOLD HEILBRUN)**
1926 – 2003
Nationality: American
First Published: Macmillan, 1964
Other Selected Titles:
The James Joyce Murder
Death in a Tenured Position
(UK title: *A Death in the Faculty*)

In the Last Analysis is the first thriller novel by Amanda Cross, introducing her series detective, Kate Fansler. Like her creator in real life, Fansler is a Professor of English Literature at a New York University and, also like her creator, an early feminist, a character who is unmarried, middle-aged and self-contained.

At the student's request, Kate Fansler refers Janet Harrison to Dr. Emanuel Bauer, a psychoanalyst who is a close friend of Fansler. A few weeks later, Janet is found stabbed to death on Bauer's office couch, with his fingerprints on the carving knife. It is as unreasonable for Kate to think of Bauer as a killer as it is to think anyone might have a motive to kill the secretive loner, Janet. Kate's dismayed interest that justice should be done rouses her detective spirit and she works her way through the seemingly impossible with the knowledge and help of Assistant DA, Reed Amhearst, another old friend.

Set in American academia, the Fansler novels draw upon the Oxbridge tradition of detection, but Cross gives it a very modern twist. We see Fansler working with her students in a way none of the English academic detectives do, and it is an attribute of Fansler that she uses that close involvement with her students and friends to assist in her investigation.

Fansler's detective methods rely on the same skills she uses as a professor: she talks through problems, paying close attention to detail and she is certainly not a female version of the all-action detective. Cross also uses that professor-student interaction to show up the treatment of female academics in the male establishment and it is this particular feminist element that makes the novel so innovative for its time.

'Twenty-five years ago Amanda Cross delighted readers with Kate Fansler ... the hero we'd been waiting all our lives for'
–Sara Paretsky

Amanda Cross
In the Last Analysis

Rose at Ten

Marco Denevi is best known in his own country for short stories and plays, although *Rose at Ten* (sometimes translated as *Rose at Ten O'Clock*) is his award-winning detective story.

The shy painter, Camilo Canegato, has been living in a small family-run hotel for the last twelve years and is on good terms with his landlady, Dona Milagros, and her family. During all that time Camilo has never said anything about his past life nor received any outside communications of any kind. Six months prior to the start of the novel's events, Camilo starts to receive letters; their envelopes are pink and scented and they have obviously been sent by a woman. Eventually Camilo explains to the surprised family that they are from Rosaura, a beautiful woman with whom he fell in love and she with him, but whose father wanted her to marry elsewhere and she and Camilo parted. One night, at ten o'clock, Rosaura actually appears at the hotel looking for Camilo and now he is put into the position of being expected to marry her. When she is murdered on their wedding night, Camilo naturally becomes the prime suspect.

It is through the investigation that follows that Denevi's mastery of psychological processes becomes clear. The remainder of the thriller is structured around the other characters' accounts of how they construe the events that have led up to the crime. Everybody has a different version of what occurred and Rosaura is seen to have a different personality with each account. Each narrative perspective assists in the painstaking reconstruction of character traits, actions and intentions until, at the last, a final letter ties up the threads.

MARCO DENEVI
1922 – 1998
Nationality: Argentinian
First Published: Catalayud-DEA Editores, 1955
Other Selected Titles:
Secret Ceremony

451

Vendetta

MICHAEL DIBDIN
1947 –
Nationality: British
First Published: Faber, 1990
Other Selected Titles:
The Last Sherlock Holmes Story
Ratking
And Then You Die

Michael Dibdin's series detective, Aurelio Zen, first appeared in *Ratking* but with this second book, *Vendetta*, Dibdin's skill seems even more assured, as is his ability to immerse the reader in all levels of the Italian setting.

On the surface, Inspector Zen of the Criminalpol section of the Ministry of the Interior seems as nonchalant as his world is violent. He is, however, a complex and sophisticated man whose private life, as he deals with his aging mother and embarks on a love affair with Tania Biacis, starts to infiltrate his professional reserve, putting his judgment at risk.

The story starts with the seemingly impossible massacre of millionaire Oscar Burolo, along with his wife and guests, at his impregnable retreat in the Sardinian mountains. Although the most modern of closed-circuit television systems was in place, the killer managed to get in and gun down the gathering without his own identity being caught on camera. Burolo's dubious business connections with certain influential members of the Italian government mean that Zen receives orders from the highest police levels to hunt down the murderer. Given the victim and his kind of world, Zen finds himself up against a great number of suspects, but the longer he investigates and the closer he gets to the killer so it appears that the killer in his turn is getting closer to Zen.

Vendetta is an extremely adroit and intense novel, whose very title is a reminder of Italy's reputation for the passionate and menacing intrigue which goes hand-in-hand with a disregard for the law. Zen's character is all the more interesting then, as the calmness of his own name belies that reputation, while his position as a law-enforcer becomes almost unrealizable in the irony of that context.

MICHAEL DIBDIN
VENDETTA
AN AURELIO ZEN MYSTERY

ff

The Glass-sided Ants' Nest

PETER DICKINSON
1927 –
Nationality: British
First Published: Hodder and
Stoughton, 1968
Other Selected Titles:
Sleep and His Brother
The Poison Oracle
The Yellow Room Mystery

Jimmy Pibble, Dickinson's police superintendent, is faced with the murky depths of both murder and anthropology in this darkly witty novel. Within an up-and-coming London area in the late 1960s, Flagg Terrace is a Victorian relic providing a home for the last survivors of an ancient New Guinea tribe. The Kus and their tribal customs provide the challenging and unsettling background for Pibble's investigation into the murder of their chief, Aaron Ku. Meeting with obstacles to understanding on all cultural fronts, Pibble must work out the motivation behind the killing which, from the available evidence, would appear to have been the work of one of the tribespeople themselves. Dr Eve Ku, a white Englishwoman and anthropologist who has married into the tribe, is Pibble's interpreter and go-between.

It soon becomes clear from Eve's sociological explanations that Pibble's extensive professional experience may not be sufficient in this case. He will have to take into account rituals and taboos that suggest that it was, in fact, impossible for the murder to have been committed by the logical suspect. The nature of truth itself becomes problematic.

At a time when racism still went largely unquestioned, *The Glass-sided Ants' Nest* addressed issues of prejudice through showing a variety of attitudes towards the Ku tribe, not just in the Western response to these supposedly childlike people but with reference to their own internal divisiveness. This is a recurring motif in Dickinson's work and he tackles it here with an inventive and imaginative humour and a wry nod to the rise of academic sociology. Nevertheless, Dickinson lets nobody off the moral hook and keeps the atmosphere taut throughout.

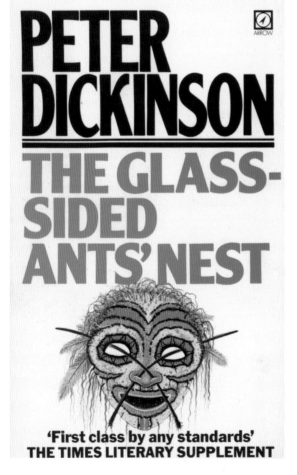

PETER DICKINSON
THE GLASS-SIDED ANTS' NEST

ARROW

'First class by any standards'
THE TIMES LITERARY SUPPLEMENT

He Who Whispers

John Dickson Carr was an extremely prolific thriller writer, who also wrote under the name Carter Dickson, and who was particularly known as a master of the locked room or impossible crime puzzle. One of his main serial detectives, Dr Gideon Fell, features in *He Who Whispers*. In this novel, Carr evokes a quite surreal and threatening atmosphere as background to Dr Fell's ingenuities, thrilling the spine as well as the intellect.

Miles Hammond is invited to a dinner of the Murder Club. He arrives late through the pouring rain, to be baffled to find only the invited speaker, Professor Rigaud, and one other guest, Barbara Morell, in attendance. Rigaud nevertheless relates his story of a strange murder in Chartres a few years before, which centres around the figure of an apparently dangerous woman. It turns out that this woman has a connection to Barbara Morell, and the story then moves to present-day England and another attempted murder. Complexities build up and only Dr Fell can get through to the truth by going back to the past and unravelling the earlier mystery.

Elderly and overweight, Fell cuts an eccentric figure which Carr is said to have based on G.K. Chesterton, the writer whose 'Father Brown' detective stories he so admired. And, indeed, Carr's detective has a moral attitude and sympathetic understanding similar to that of Father Brown. Fell is supposed to be a lexicographer, although he appears to spend more time defining people than words, hence the fact that much of the final reconstruction of events relies on his unparalleled knowledge of psychology. The novel ends on a triumphant act of unmasking which turns the tables on both the villain and the reader.

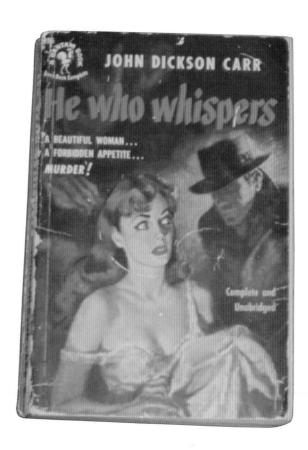

JOHN DICKSON CARR
1906 – 1977
Nationality: American
First Published: Harper, 1946
Other Selected Titles:
The Mad Hatter Mystery
The Plague Court Murders (writing as Carter Dickson)
The Crooked Hinge

The Big Clock

KENNETH FEARING
1902 – 1961
Nationality: American
First Published: Harcourt Brace, 1946
Other Selected Titles:
Dagger of the Mind
Clark Gifford's Body

Kenneth Fearing worked mostly as a freelance writer and poet but sidetracked into a few examples of thriller fiction, of which *The Big Clock* probably remains the best known. Referring to the idea that we all have to adjust our lives to an overriding clock, or ruling principle, *The Big Clock* is a metaphor for the guiding reins of society. George Stroud, cynical editor of *Crimeways* magazine, is only too aware of how his decisions help shape public thought and this position of influence becomes central to the novel when George needs to exploit it.

His employer, Earl Janoth of Janoth Enterprises publishing empire, turns to George for help when his girlfriend, Pauline Delos, is found murdered shortly after Earl had visited her. What Janoth does not know is that George himself had enjoyed an adulterous liaison with Pauline just prior to Earl's own visit.

George must be seen to put the investigative wheels of *Crimeways* into motion without calling attention to his own presence at the crimescene. Yet it can only be a matter of time before his identity as a material witness comes out. George has to conduct his own race against the Big Clock as the various threads he has started up begin to tighten. The novel is structured on the accumulation of first-person narratives from several of the characters in the case. This use of eye-witness accounts harks back to the earliest thriller novels and it does indeed enhance the sense of tension, while also showing the process of detective reasoning from more than one perspective. But Fearing's technique makes *The Big Clock* entirely modern in both its style and content.

Blood Sport

After retiring in 1957 from a successful career as a jockey, then working for a spell as a racing journalist, Dick Francis started writing thriller novels, making the most of his knowledge of the world of horse racing to provide an intriguing background for his fast-paced mysteries.

In *Blood Sport*, the hero figure is Gene Hawkins, a man whose qualification for this position is that while he seems ordinary, even nondescript, he also happens to be an intelligence agent who is suffering from a suicidal frame of mind. His employer, Keeble, invites him for a day out on the river, only to introduce him to Dave Teller, millionaire racehorse owner, whose prize stallion Chrysalis disappeared three weeks earlier. A 'specialist in arranging accidents' himself, Gene becomes interested in helping track down the horse when he saves Teller's life in a boating accident which Gene recognizes as a murder attempt. The story moves to America and the novel is packed with scenes of intrigue and suspense, finally leading up to murder.

Like most of Francis' many novels, *Blood Sport* uses horse racing as a vehicle for the mystery. The main characters may not necessarily be directly involved with the turf itself, but just have some indirect interest – Gene, for example, only has the merest connection with racing through his father, who was a trainer. The first person narrative, however – a feature of many of Francis' books – allows us inside the mind of the hero, and so enhances the reader's enjoyment of the specialized environment. In using the world of horse racing, Francis is in some ways harking back to the self-contained settings of Golden Age detective fiction, but bringing it up-to-date and making the sport of kings accessible to the ordinary reader.

DICK FRANCIS
1920 –
Nationality: British
First Published: Michael Joseph, 1967
Other Selected Titles:
Dead Cert
Whip Hand
Come to Grief

Dick Francis in London, 1967.

Quiet as a Nun

Antonia Fraser, better known for her historical biographies, featured Jemima Shore in a number of detective stories, of which *Quiet as a Nun* was the first.

Jemima Shore has a successful career as an investigative television journalist. As an 'old girl' of the Blessed Eleanor's Convent, she is called in to investigate the suicide of Sister Miriam. When they were schoolgirls, the nun had been Jemima's close friend, heiress Rosabelle Powerstock, a girl whose teenage cry had been that she 'wanted to find herself'. It appears that Miriam's death coincided with her desire to relinquish ownership of the convent land for, having been inspired by one of Jemima's programmes, she wished to sell the land to help the poor rather than giving it to the convent as expected. So concerns of public life intrude into the unworldly environment and murder is the outcome.

The theme of identity is always present in a 'whodunnit' but is particularly pertinent in this novel where, having given up their individuality, the nuns' habits make them appear as so many 'identical black crows'. By contrast, Jemima Shore's identity is one of an independent, liberated working woman, but is nevertheless somewhat in conflict with the demands of her married lover, Tom Amyas, MP.

Not only will Jemima's investigation open up the identity of the murderer, but she will also address her own identity in doing so. In the 1970s the conflict between feminist demands and those of the conventional life of a housewife were very much in the air and Fraser reflects that social conflict in the personal choices that face her detective heroine.

LADY ANTONIA FRASER
1932 –
Nationality: British
First Published: Weidenfeld & Nicolson, 1977
Other Selected Titles:
Oxford Blood
Jemima Shore's First Case

Lady Antonia Fraser in 1974.

The Sunday Woman

CARLO FRUTTERO
1926 –
Nationality: Italian
FRANCO LUCENTINI
1920 – 2002
Nationality: Italian
First Published: Harcourt Brace
Jovanovich, 1972
Other Selected Titles:
The D. Case
An Enigma By the Sea

*Italian writers and translators
Carlo Fruttero and Franco
Lucentini
co-write and sign their
books together.*

Carlo Fruttero and Franco Lucentini collaborated for many years and, although *The Sunday Woman* was their first crime fiction book, it was an immediate success, being highly regarded for its literary qualities to which, for many critics, the detective element seemed somewhat secondary. The book gives an incredibly full and detailed picture of Turin, evoking the variety of lifestyles of its inhabitants, as seen from their unique and different perspectives, and thus becoming an almost universal portrait for city life. However this city, just as any other, also harbours criminals.

The architect, Signor Garrone, an unpopular and unpleasant man, is found murdered by a stone weapon of obscene shape and Sicilian Inspector Santamaria finds himself in a very difficult and embarrassing position when suspicion lands on a member of the upper classes and his lady friend. With a broad array of suspects, much of the interest of the investigation comes from the closely observed interaction and contrast between the different ranks of society, for the nobles are as much fascinated by Santamaria as he is by them. When Lello Riviera, a homosexual friend of Garrone, is also murdered, Santamaria finally gets close to the answer. *The Sunday Woman* is a suspenseful whodunnit, working through all the possibilities as detective fiction requires, but it is also a fine

piece of writing that has depth of character and an intense atmosphere provided by the depiction of the city. The fact that the enduring elegance of Turin also masks extreme poverty and criminal malignancy is only to be expected, but that the authors delight in the city no matter what is clearly conveyed, constitutes a major strength of the novel.

Death in the Wrong Room

Anthony Gilbert was the pseudonym of prolific thriller writer, Lucy Malleson. Although she also wrote mainstream fiction under another name, as Gilbert her real identity was kept secret for many years, thus allowing her to develop her highly idiosyncratic serial lawyer-detective, Arthur G. Crook.

Colonel Anstruther's daughter has led a quiet and reclusive life at The Downs, the strange house built by her father. Reduced by the exigencies of World War Two to make ends meet as best she may, she is forced to take in paying guests.

In *Death in the Wrong Room* the mystery revolves around the death of Lady Bate, an aristocratic lodger who has only recently come to The Downs. It appears that Lady Bate knew something about her hostess' past life and the reason why she has kept herself to herself – a seemingly dangerous knowledge which Arthur Crook has to unravel, with increasing hazard to himself.

For the period, Crook is one of the most unusual detectives to have been created, ironically stepping across boundaries of class and decency in order to restore law and order. As his name suggests, this London lawyer is prepared to do whatever it takes to help his clients and this can include making up evidence to suit the case and bullying his way around the suspects.

His main quality, however, is that in complete contrast to his clients and, in particular, to other fictional detectives, he comes from a very different social background, being represented as lower-class, loud, greedy, vulgar and in many ways obnoxious. However, he is also wily, shrewd, brave and refreshingly different. In Crook, Gilbert has created a new kind of detective, a man of the people who works for the people.

**ANTHONY GILBERT
(LUCY BEATRICE MALLESON)**
1899 – 1973
Nationality: British
First Published: Collins, 1947
Other Selected Titles:
*The Man Who was Too Clever
Murder by Experts
The Looking Glass Murder
A Nice Little Killing*

rimemasterworks

Dashiell Hammett

'An acknowledged literary landmark'
ROBERT GRAVES

Red Harvest

DASHIELL HAMMETT
1894 – 1961
Nationality: American
First Published: Knopf, 1929
Other Selected Titles:
The Dain Curse
The Maltese Falcon
The Glass Key
The Thin Man

Red Harvest

Dashiell Hammett wrote many short stories for pulp fiction magazines but only five novels, of which *Red Harvest* was the first. Hammett had himself worked as an investigator for the Pinkerton's Detective Agency and he was therefore able to bring a strong sense of realism to his construction of the nameless narrator here – the Continental Detective Agency Operative.

This realism reflects the bleak background of the Depression in America and the Age of Prohibition. The town of Personville – dryly and aptly pronounced 'Poisonville' – is run by the local magnate, Elihu Willsson, who finds his dominion challenged by the very gangsters he employed to quell a strike in his Mining Corporation. Elihu's son, Donald, calls in the Continental Op but is murdered before the operative can see him. Elihu hires the Op to restore order in the town and return power to his own hands.

The novel is structured around the machinations of the private detective as he plays off each group of corrupt players against the others, including the police. The dark picture of contemporary American life is further enhanced by the fact that the Op himself is morally ambiguous. His flirtation with Dinah Brand, a hustling *femme fatale*, and the dubious circumstances of her death, result in his reflecting on some of his own practices. However, the approach he takes to sorting out corruption is as gritty and as lawless as it needs to be to get the job done and the Op's no-nonsense attitude and the pithy, wry language he employs come out of his own need to survive in this harsh world. In *Red Harvest*, classic formulae of detective fiction – including that of the 'heroic' investigator – are dispensed with, as Hammett develops the characteristics of the 'hard-boiled' genre he is credited with creating.

Suicide Excepted

Inspector Mallett of the CID is the central figure of *Suicide Excepted*, an early novel by Cyril Hare, a County Court judge in real life, who drew upon his legal experience in the creation of several detective stories. Hare also wrote articles for the humorous journal, *Punch*, and his detective fiction is characterized by a similar, stylish wit.

The local police come to Pendlebury Old Hall Hotel to investigate the unexpected death of Leonard Dickinson, a guest, when it appears he may have committed suicide by taking an overdose. Mallett himself, on holiday in the area, was one of the last to speak to the eccentric Dickinson in the hotel lounge and his statement as to the gentleman's frame of mind only helps confirm the verdict and that would seem to be the end of the matter.

However, it is in the interests of the immediate family that the cause of death should not be suicide because they will only be able to claim the considerable life insurance if it can be proved that Dickinson died through an accident or was murdered. To that end, his children take up the challenge to overturn the inquest ruling and the main concern of the novel is to make the case that murder was committed.

What is most interesting about *Suicide Excepted* is that Hare moves his professional detective largely out of the picture – Inspector Mallett does not take the central role. Rather, he supplies a supportive framework for a very amateur collaborative effort by family members under the authority of Stephen Dickinson, Leonard's son, but although they have no experience in detection that effort nevertheless builds up to a most surprising, yet justly satisfactory, result.

CYRIL HARE
(A.A. GORDON CLARK)
1900 – 1958
Nationality: British
First Published: Faber, 1939
Other Selected Titles:
Tragedy At Law
An English Murder
He Should Have Died Hereafter

Bones and Silence

REGINALD HILL
1936 –
Nationality: British
First Published: Collins, 1990
Other Selected Titles:
A Clubbable Woman
On Beulah Height
Death's Jest Book

Reginald Hill's Mid-Yorkshire detectives, Andy Dalziel and Peter Pascoe, first appeared in 1970 and, while they have developed a mutual respect over the years, they retain their very separate identities and approaches to policing. Pascoe provides qualities of college-educated, reserved sensitivity to be offset against Dalziel's blunt, but intelligent, policing. While this undoubtedly makes for humorous contrast, there are deeper points to be drawn from their characters. Dalziel epitomizes old Yorkshire – being the backbone of his team, solid, stubborn, curmudgeonly and altogether real – while Pascoe represents a more modern version of police in the community, having the softening influence of a wife and a far more liberal stance than Dalziel.

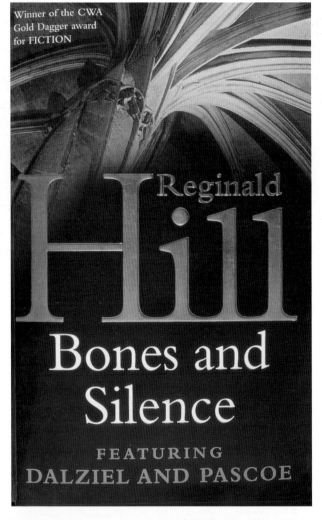

Winner of the CWA Gold Dagger award for FICTION

Reginald Hill

Bones and Silence

FEATURING
DALZIEL AND PASCOE

Bones and Silence is a very complex novel, belonging to the police procedural genre in that there are many lines of enquiry being followed simultaneously. The prime one of these is that Dalziel believes he has witnessed a murder. He saw a naked woman across the street both immediately before and then soon after she was shot, but his team thinks it was suicide. He is also receiving anonymous letters from a woman who threatens to commit suicide but he's undecided how seriously to take it, and the county is suffering from a spate of football hooliganism. Finally, he's been marked out to play God in a revival of the Yorkshire Medieval Mystery Plays, a piece of potential casting which seems wantonly mischievous.

Yet despite all the humour, Hill's novel confronts problems of identity for more than one character and the regional flavour of the series as a whole works in this particular book to make us think about the ways in which we understand what actually constitutes the identity of a criminal, a victim or a policeman.

A Rage in Harlem

Chester Himes adapted the hard-boiled thriller tradition of writers like Hammett and Chandler, translating it from West Coast America to East Coast Harlem and trading white loner detectives for black members of the ghetto society. In doing so, he provided an inspirational new template for later writers such as Walter Mosley to investigate the position of the black community through this form of fictional expression, a form which is violent and yet absurd at the same time.

Naive Jackson is so enamoured with the beautiful Imabelle that he parts with all his savings to a conman who claims he can return it tenfold. In order to buy off a Marshal who catches him during the counterfeiting operation, Jackson now has to steal money from his boss, the undertaker H. Exodus Clay, and trouble snowballs as Jackson's brother Goldy steps in to help, only to be murdered himself.

A Rage in Harlem introduces detectives Coffin Ed Johnson and his partner Gravedigger Jones, the toughest police in Harlem, who will go on to feature more effectively in further stories in the Harlem cycle. They are mean-looking men who are wedded to their Colt pistols because that is the only way they can command respect in their community.

The story is complex and the motivations in many ways seem farcical, but the consequences are far from amusing. That violence frequently coincides with a grim humour is unsettling, but it does shake up preconceptions, while Himes' minutely observed characterization lends a cynical realism to the writing which brings it home all the more.

Chester Himes.

CHESTER HIMES
1909 – 1984
Nationality: American
First Published: Fawcett, 1957
Other Selected Titles:
The Real Cool Killers
Cotton Comes To Harlem
Run Man, Run

PETER HØEG
1957 –
Nationality: Danish
First Published:
Rosinante/Munksgaard, 1992
Other Selected Titles:
Borderliners

Miss Smilla's Feeling for Snow

Peter Høeg's second novel, *Miss Smilla's Feeling for Snow*, is an unusual and enthralling addition to the thriller genre. Starting off in Denmark but then moving up to Greenland and the Arctic circle, the cold, dangerous yet beautiful environment becomes a character in the novel itself, literally breathtaking. This innovative setting is always more than a background to the story of Smilla Jasperson and her personal investigations into the death of a little boy, Isaiah.

Smilla is a Greenlander by birth and she spent her early childhood there with her mother, an Arctic hunter. Smilla's father is a Danish doctor with whom she has a very strained relationship. As a result, Smilla is a misfit, albeit an extremely intelligent one, whose love of mathematics gives some kind of pattern or anchor to her life. When her neighbour's son, six-year-old Isaiah, falls to his death from the snowy roof of their apartment block, Smilla's Greenlandic understanding about movement through snow leads her to read Isaiah's last footprints differently to the police. Convinced his death was not an accident, Smilla's character of sheer stubborn determination drives her to uncover the truth. Initially she starts to untangle the dispassionate coils of big business to which Isaiah appears to have fallen victim, but the novel then moves into an altogether larger arena and Smilla becomes caught up in all sorts of dilemmas, both of the adventurous and of the moral kind. *Miss Smilla's Feeling for Snow* is an unusual and compelling thriller and Smilla herself is an intriguing detective figure, a combination of modern, feminist qualities contrasted with the enduring mythology of her Greenlandic inheritance.

Malice Aforethought

Anthony Cox wrote under several pseudonyms. As Francis Iles, his innovative novel, *Malice Aforethought*, is a lasting testament to his skill and invention.

FRANCIS ILES
(ANTHONY BERKELEY COX)
1893 – 1971
Nationality: British
First Published: Gollancz, 1931
Other Selected Titles:
Before the Fact
As For the Woman

Insignificant Edmund Bickleigh, a country doctor living in the select community of Wyvern's Cross in Devon, has married slightly above his station and his wife, Julia, does not let him forget it. Her constant nagging and snobbish attitude grind him down, but she holds the purse strings in the marriage and he tries to ignore the hurt to his feelings. Bickleigh indulges in little flirtations to console himself for Julia's unconcealed contempt, but when he really falls for his neighbour, Gwynfryd Rattery, he decides he must murder his wife: the one power this doctor does have, after all, is over life and death.

This is not a whodunnit. The reader knows who the murderer is from the start of the novel. We also know the means to be used – slow poison. When the novel was first published, this approach was completely new. Up until then, detective fiction had always concentrated on the puzzle element, but here that was replaced with the focus on the perpetration of the crime and the psychological motivation behind it.

The fact that Bickleigh is in many respects quite unprepossessing makes the intensity of Iles's study all the more of an achievement, as the reader remains gripped nevertheless by the details and the suspense of not knowing whether the doctor will get away with it. This break with customary practices and the emphasis on psychology led some critics to hail the novel as leading the way for a modern form of detective fiction and it still makes an impact today.

Hamlet, Revenge!

**MICHAEL INNES
(JOHN INNES MACKINTOSH
STEWART)**
1906 – 1994
Nationality: British
First Published: Gollancz, 1937
Other Selected Titles:
*There Came Both Mist and Snow
The Daffodil Affair
Operation Pax
Appleby's Answer*

Hamlet, Revenge!, Michael Innes's second foray into detective fiction, is subtitled 'A Story in Four Parts', taking its structure from the progress of a play and, indeed, the outcome is a theatrical spectacle which thrills as much as it delights.

Innes's series detective, John Appleby, takes centre stage when he is called in to Scamnum Court to investigate the murder of the Lord Chancellor. Lord Auldearn had been acting the part of Polonius in a private – if grand – amateur production of *Hamlet*, when he was stabbed to death for real.

In addition to the huge audience of 300 people, there is a cast of nearly 30 key characters, all of whom are to be considered as suspects at one stage or another. The array of characters and their interactions make the logistics of the investigation very complex, as they cast up numerous red herrings in their wake, among which the theft of an important secret document has to be resolved, as do further murders. Innes also supplies a choice of several reconstructive solutions to add to the apparent mayhem.

Appleby's penchant for the apt, if sometimes absurd, literary quotation is put to good use here, the whole novel constituting both a scholarly understanding of, as well as a tongue-in-cheek nod to, *Hamlet* and 'the play within a play'. Yet the intellectual rigour of Appleby's investigation is never in doubt as, bearing in mind his more humble origins, he goes about questioning some of the most powerful politicians in England. The final scenes are both fun and exciting, a trait that Innes was to continue. *Hamlet, Revenge!* is an admirable example of the stylistic balance between farce and erudition that Innes made his own.

The Murder Room

P.D. JAMES
1920 –
Nationality: British
First Published: Faber & Faber
Limited, 2003
Other Selected Titles:
*Cover Her Face
An Unsuitable Job for a Woman
A Taste for Death*

Although Adam Dalgliesh first appeared over 40 years earlier, *The Murder Room* exemplifies P.D. James' continuing development of her featured detective. The Murder Room in the Dupayne Museum is devoted to telling the stories of, and displaying artefacts from, notorious, real-life crimes. The museum is owned and run by the Dupayne family but its future is in some doubt. However, when Neville Dupayne is burnt to death and so the only person wanting to close the museum has been removed, it seems it should be simple to pin down which suspects had the motivation to kill him. A member of the museum staff, James Calder-Hale, has connections with MI5 and it is through him that Commander Dalgliesh is called in to investigate, over the claims of the local police division.

Dalgliesh is an interesting amalgam of sensitive, published poet, a loner whose personal life is kept at bay much of the time, and a successful, intelligent detective working for the public good. Although similar in many ways to other fictional policemen, it is Dalgliesh-the-poet's keen insightfulness which lifts him above the crimes he investigates, yet at the same time keeps the moral imperative of his work clear.

Dalgliesh is supported by a strong team to do the investigative legwork and, in this sense, James gives the reader a police procedural novel as we follow Detective Inspectors Kate Miskin and Piers Tarrant through their paces. Yet *The Murder Room* is also strongly rooted in the elements of classic detection: the slightly old-fashioned, secluded community, the small cast of suspects and the slow burn towards crime. However, James' distinguishing strength lies in her creation of complex personal histories and relationships which encourages the reader to care for all her characters.

P.D. James, the award-winning mystery and suspense writer.

The Sleeping-Car Murders

**SEBASTIEN JAPRISOT
(JEAN BAPTISTE ROSSI)**
1931 – 2003
Nationality: French
First Published: Doubleday,1963
(First English translation)
Other Selected Titles:
Trap for Cinderella
One Deadly Summer

A best-selling thriller author in France, Sébastien Japrisot is less well-known outside his own country, yet his work is highly accomplished. He has strong links with cinema, both directing and writing for the medium, and the influence of this other interest can be found in his novels.

The Sleeping-Car Murders starts off as a single sleeping-car murder. The night train from Marseilles arrives in Paris and a young woman is discovered in her compartment in the sleeping-car, lying murdered in her berth. Inspector Grazzi heads up the investigation, with a view to questioning the other five occupants of the sleeping car as the only really possible suspects. All of them, however, have to be tracked down first and during this process the suspects are killed off, one after the other, until only two are left. Grazzi must solve the growing dilemma before his last two suspects fall victim as well.

*Sébastien Japrisot in
Paris, 1977.*

Japrisot is skilful at manipulating what in many ways has become one of the traditional settings for crime fiction. From the Golden Age onwards, the train has provided a modern environment for the locked-room mystery with a restricted community of suspects. Of course, the train also represents a means of speedy escape, while railway stations themselves have become emotionally-charged arenas for dramatic scenes.

Japrisot takes all of these elements and combines them with his writer's eye for the atmosphere of another thriller genre: the hard-boiled or *noir*. As Grazzi discovers more and more of the tangle of the suspects' lives so the dark, yet realistic, style of writing becomes all the more telling and suspense is built up relentlessly.

Death of My Aunt

Clifford Kitchin's first attempt at detective fiction, *Death of My Aunt*, was such an instant success that he came under pressure from the public to produce more of the same – which he undertook reluctantly and at increasingly longer intervals.

The initial success of *Death of My Aunt* may be attributed to several factors, not least of which is the amusing figure of its detective 'hero', Malcolm Warren, a stockbroker who is interested in both money and people. Both those interests are excited when his Aunt Catherine, who is the wealthiest and most influential member of his extended family, summons him to look into her considerable investments. However, Warren's arrival at her country home is followed the very next day by his aunt's death from poison.

Aunt Catherine's second husband, Hannibal – disdained by all the family save Warren owing to his lower-class background as a garage owner – comes under suspicion from Inspector Glaize. A series of revelations about the family ensues, which Warren, with his keen interest in human nature, endeavours to untangle.

Warren is rather younger – 26 years old – than the majority of amateur sleuths who had featured hitherto in detective fiction. His youthfulness and modern attitude, then, reflect some of the changes in society between the World Wars, making him a very empathetic character. There is a candour about psychological motivation which is very fresh in style and all the characters are three-dimensional, if a little quirky, but this only adds to the charm. Kitchin has contrived to present the reader with the crime-puzzle that was required at this era, but he has given it a greater psychological depth and this lifts the book out of the ordinary among its contemporaries.

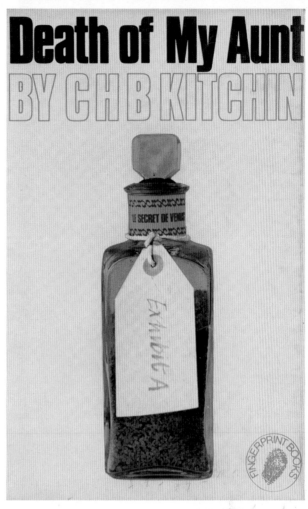

**C.H.B. KITCHIN
(CLIFFORD HENRY BENN)**
1895 – 1967
Nationality: British
First Published: Hogarth Press, 1929
Other Selected Titles:
*Crime At Christmas
Death of His Uncle
The Cornish Fox*

471

John le Carré.

JOHN LE CARRE
(DAVID CORNWELL)
1931 –
Nationality: British
First Published: Gollancz, 1963
Other Selected Titles:
Tinker, Tailor, Soldier, Spy
Smiley's People
The Constant Gardener

The Spy Who Came In From the Cold

The Spy Who Came In From the Cold set new standards for modern spy thrillers, becoming a classic example of contemporary Cold War fiction, yet it has since lost none of its capacity to enthral and excite.

The Spy Who Came In From the Cold tells the story of British spy, Alec Leamas. He leaves the British Secret Service, or 'Circus', to defect to East Germany, only to find out that he is still being monitored and used by the Director of the Circus, aptly known as 'Control'. Leamas has been framed in order to get at an East German agent, Fiedler, and he feels increasingly like a pawn in this elaborate scheme which involves double-crossing, dubious loyalties and personal betrayals. Leamas desperately wants to get out of the Cold War and the story's growing tensions reflect the sense of helpless entanglement. The book also uses the character of George Smiley, who would appear in later novels, but le Carré puts the personal focus on Leamas.

With this book le Carré addresses a more realistic state of world affairs. Rather than portraying an Ian Fleming school of glamorous spying where James Bond always wins out, he shows Leamas as lonely, demoralized and, above all, afraid. Retaining the element of deadly thrill, le Carré nevertheless injects a moral chill which was missing from the traditional, adventure-led spy stories. He makes it clear that there can be no simplistic reduction to us-and-them and that the West is as much at fault as the Eastern bloc. Although the plot of the novel is very complex, the personal stories are driven by basic human motives and le Carré makes us care about the real people caught up in the world of spies.

The Mystery of the Yellow Room

Although his lasting reputation rests upon the melodramatic *The Phantom of the Opera*, Gaston Leroux's earlier *The Mystery of the Yellow Room*, in which he recounts the 'extraordinary adventures' of Joseph Rouletabille, is a classic addition to early murder-mystery fiction.

As had rapidly become the norm after Doyle's Dr Watson, the story is related at third-hand by a friend of the protagonist. Rouletabille was a junior reporter when several years previously, aged only 18, he had given evidence at the Assizes which dealt with the case of attempted murder of Mlle Stangerson, daughter of an illustrious scientist. At the time, Rouletabille only divulged enough information in order to secure justice, but the full extent of his amazing investigation can be revealed after this discreet passage of time.

The Yellow Room mystery starts out as a locked-room puzzle, owing its antecedents to Edgar Allan Poe's *The Murders in The Rue Morgue* (1841), as is acknowledged, but it pushes the intellectual demands on the detective even further. When Mlle Stangerson retires to her room and shots are heard, people rush to her assistance only to find her room locked and no sign of any possible escape, while she herself is alone and barely alive. Rather eerily, a man's bloody handprint stains the wall and at first it seems that the supernatural must be involved.

The novel is most concerned with detailing the reporter's convoluted investigation which rests upon a combination of logistical intricacy, secret personal histories and a series of dramatic revelations. *The Mystery of the Yellow Room* draws the reader into one of the most bewildering and challenging cases to have been written at that time and it remains one of the great stylistic examples of the locked-room thriller.

GASTON LEROUX
1868 – 1927
Nationality: French
First Published: Brentano, 1907
Other Selected Titles:
The Phantom of the Opera
The Secret of the Night

DEDALUS EUROPEAN CLASSICS

The Mystery of the Yellow Room

"A masterpiece."
Maxim Jakubowski
in Time Out

GASTON LEROUX

The Last Detective

PETER LOVESEY
1936 –
Nationality: British
First Published: Scribners, 1991
Other Selected Titles:
The Detective Wore Silk Drawers
The False Inspector Dew
Bloodhounds

Peter Lovesey's experience with historical crime fiction in his Victorian detective series lends authority to this invocation of Peter Diamond, the eponymous last detective of this novel. For Diamond is the last of the old breed of detectives who, since the founding of the CID, had to use their quick wits and abilities to nose out criminals. In the modern world, where computer databases have taken over from personal knowledge of criminals, Diamond's preference for traditional methods is outmoded and, ironically, seen as non-conformist and disadvantageous for his career.

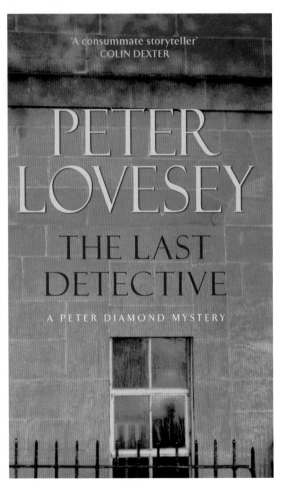

'A consummate storyteller'
COLIN DEXTER

PETER LOVESEY

THE LAST DETECTIVE

A PETER DIAMOND MYSTERY

The story opens with the discovery of a woman's naked body in a lake. She is identified as a retired TV soap actress and her husband, Professor Gregory Jackman, naturally comes under police suspicion. When Jackman saves the life of a drowning schoolboy and becomes friendly with the boy's mother, Dana Didrikson, she also comes forward as a suspect for other reasons. Both Jackman and Didrikson are given their own, first-person narrative sections within the overall third-person framework and this helps in bringing out the reader's sympathy for these characters – which only makes the final result the more upsetting, once Diamond arrives at the correct conclusion. First, however, in the wake of the mistakes which result from modern police methods, he makes a moral decision to resign and carries on his investigations unofficially.

Although the setting is modern-day Bath, Lovesey is still concerned with history. Part of the plot revolves around the theft of two letters supposedly written by one-time Bath resident, Jane Austen, and towards the end of the novel Diamond himself is nearly killed in the Roman Baths: the historic city gets to make its impact on the pattern of this complex and satisfactory thriller.

Final Curtain

Final Curtain is representative of the best of Ngaio Marsh's detective fiction. Drawing upon her experience in the world of New Zealand theatre and particularly on her love of Shakespeare, Marsh structures many of her detective stories around a theatrical theme. Her Scotland Yard detective is Roderick Alleyn, the younger son of a baronet, who is married to Agatha Troy, RA. In *Final Curtain*, set at the end of World War Two, Troy is commissioned to paint the portrait of aging Shakespearean actor, Sir Henry Ancred in situ at Ancreton Hall.

Ngaio Marsh (right) talking to Agatha Christie at The Savoy Hotel, London, in 1960.

As is customary with Marsh, the first part of the novel is spent in introducing the cast of characters, familiarizing the reader with their idiosyncrasies and the minutiae of their lifestyles, in this instance as witnessed through Troy's painterly eyes.

Ancreton Hall accommodates three generations of Sir Henry's family, all of whom have some expectations that he may support them financially in his will, and all of whom are suspicious of the influence the young gold-digger, Sonia Orrincourt, may have over him. The situation at Ancreton Hall becomes increasingly uncomfortable as a series of practical jokes culminates in the suspicious death of Sir Henry.

Troy has been waiting for Alleyn to return from three years war-work overseas but now their reunion has to be played out against the inhibiting backdrop of murder. Stylistically, Marsh sets the logical and fastidious workings of Alleyn and his colleague, the impervious Inspector Fox, in gentle, but humorous, contrast with the histrionics of the Ancred family. *Final Curtain* leads the reader through a satisfying deductive process, but Marsh's insistence on acquainting us with the emotional life of her detective lifts the novel above a mere puzzle.

NGAIO MARSH
1895 – 1982
Nationality: New Zealand
First Published: William Collins & Sons, 1947
Other Selected Titles:
Enter a Murderer
Death and the Dancing Footman
Clutch of Constables

An Oxford Tragedy

J.C. MASTERMAN
1891 – 1977
Nationality: British
First Published: Gollancz, 1933
Other Selected Titles:
The Case of the Four Friends

The detective in the case of *An Oxford Tragedy* is Viennese lawyer, Ernst Brendel, who is also a Visiting Lecturer in Law at St. Thomas' College, Oxford. When an unpopular tutor, Mr Shirley, is found shot dead in his rooms, Brendel's hobby of the study of crime and detection makes him the obvious person to turn to for discreet help. The elderly Senior Tutor Francis Wheatley Winn, who approaches Brendel for that help, is also the Watson-like narrator of the tale. Intelligent but fussy, Winn is anxious to restore order to the calm, if occasionally eccentric, life of the Oxford College and to do so with the minimum of public intervention.

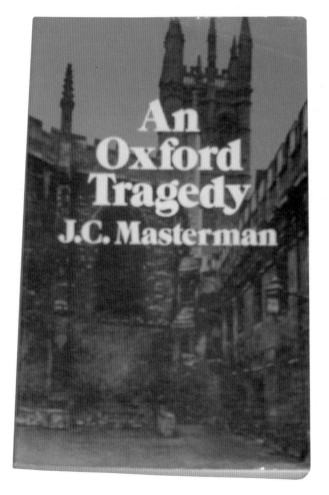

Having come up with this variation on the Golden Age convention of an enclosed community for the setting of the story, Masterman is less interested in addressing the moral questions of crime in that community. This may be hinted at in the title, for the 'tragedy' is not so much the murder of the unpopular victim than the unseemly disruption to College life. In fact, the perpetrator is allowed to commit suicide to ensure a neat and private closure.

John Masterman wrote only two novels of detection, but *An Oxford Tragedy* could be said to have initiated a sub-genre of thriller fiction where the detective figure is an Oxford-based academic, an approach used by Dorothy L. Sayers but particularly adopted by the popular writers Michael Innes and Edmund Crispin.

The Steam Pig

The Steam Pig is a politically-incorrect detective novel in which racism, sexism and violence are casually and unapologetically rife. As such, it is completely at one with the time and place in which it was written: the wrongs of apartheid in South Africa, pre-feminist chauvinism and police corruption are all represented here. James McClure very neatly wraps these up in a slightly deadpan style which only makes the social problems more devastating by contrast.

When undertaker, George Abbott, makes yet another mistake in tagging the bodies that pass through his mortuary, Theresa Le Roux's body is sent for a postmortem. However, had she been cremated as expected, Dr Styrdom would not have spotted the mark in her armpit that shows Theresa was murdered.

Yet the situation worsens, for the weapon that caused her death – a bicycle spoke – is the sort routinely used by Bantu gangsters. The big question is why a girl like Theresa – by all accounts a quiet, pretty, blonde music teacher – should apparently be mixed up with black gangs, and further questions about her identity have to be asked.

Lieutenant Tromp Kramer of the Trekkersburg Murder Squad has no qualms about using whatever violent method he may need to extract information and is just as racist as anyone else. Yet Kramer relies on his Bantu Detective Sergeant, Mickey Zondi, for the invaluable insights he can offer into white men's lives from his experience as a houseboy before he joined the police. Public interaction between black and white can only be countenanced as far as the law permits. In *The Steam Pig*, McClure addresses issues about identity and social worth because crossing the cultural divide by being of mixed race is not always readily detectable on the surface.

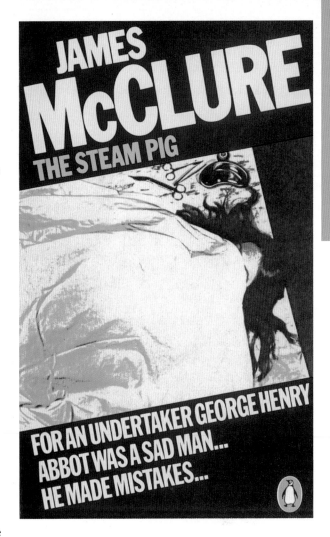

JAMES McCLURE
1939 –
Nationality: South African
First Published: Gollancz, 1971
Other Selected Titles:
The Gooseberry Fool
Rogue Eagle
The Artful Egg

477

The Seven Per Cent Solution

NICHOLAS MEYER
1945 –
Nationality: American
First Published: Dutton, 1974
Other Selected Titles:
The West End Horror
The Canary Trainer

The Seven Per Cent Solution is both a homage to and pastiche of Doyle's master-detective, Sherlock Holmes. It occupies a peculiar position with regard to its readers in that an intimate familiarity with the famous character would be useful, although not absolutely required, to appreciate the possibilities proposed here. Nicholas Meyer himself has produced several historical detective novels as well as other, more general, pastiches but *The Seven Per Cent Solution* is one of the more remarkable works of Holmesian scholarship to be found in fiction.

It is hard to realize the intense interest that the figure of Holmes himself generated, both in its time and beyond, and this

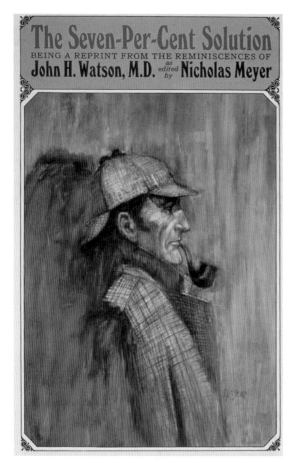

novel responds to the personal appeal of the character. For rather than just inventing another amazing tale of detection, Meyer presents his novel as the true version of what happened between Holmes' supposed death at the Reichenbach Falls and his reappearance three years later. The account which Dr Watson published is revealed as an exercise in protecting Sherlock's personal reputation becuase, as the title suggests, Holmes' addiction to cocaine was responsible for his disappearance. Watson and Mycroft Holmes actually took him to Vienna to consult with Sigmund Freud about a cure for his addiction and the novel traces some of the biographical surprises which emerge from his progress and recovery, taking a minor detour into detection at the end.

Stylistically, the novel is very persuasive, achieving a degree of authority in the impersonation of Watson-the-narrator. The voice is remarkably accurate and the details well-observed, although it is possible for aficionados to quibble. Of greatest interest, however, is the interaction between the real Freud and the fictional Holmes: a close relationship between the processes of psychoanalysis and detection is indicated, for both practitioners work to reveal true identity through attention to detail.

How Like An Angel

How Like An Angel is an excellent example of Margaret Millar's mystery writing in its subtle weaving together of apparently disparate strands and with its style, which lies somewhere between the mildly comic and the darkly sinister, making the effect all the more mysterious yet enjoyable.

Joe Quinn himself is somewhat less than an angel. A licensed private detective from Nevada, he is also an inveterate gambler who has just lost everything and literally stumbles into an off-beat religious community in the desert. Here he is offered charity in the form of basic board and lodging by Sister Blessing of the Salvation, who indicates that the community has some internal problems. She then goes on to hire Quinn personally to undertake an investigation, violating rules of communal property by offering him her own, illicitly-hoarded money. He is to find a man called Patrick O'Gorman, but Sister Blessing gives Quinn no reasons for her interest and no clues what to do if and when he does find him. Quinn soon discovers that O'Gorman is thought to have died several years before and finds himself attracted to O'Gorman's widow, Martha, though he remains unsure whether O'Gorman's death was caused by accident or murder.

Despite his dubious background, in honouring Sister Blessing's commission, Quinn emerges as a man who rediscovers his own moral worth. However, the novel cannot be categorized as a mere whodunnit for the question then arises as to whether O'Gorman is actually dead at all and Quinn must track through complex paths of embezzlement and cover-ups, love and more death, before he can arrive at an answer.

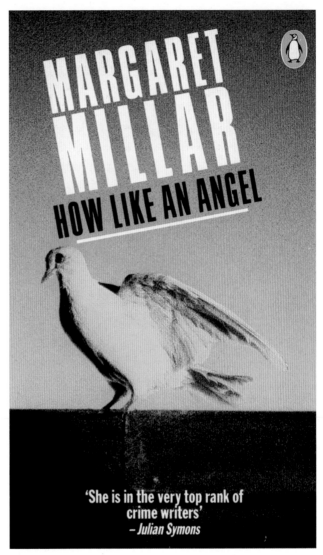

'She is in the very top rank of crime writers'
– *Julian Symons*

MARGARET MILLAR
1915 – 1994
Nationality: Canadian
First Published: Random House, 1962
Other Selected Titles:
The Invisible Worm
A Beast in View
Ask For Me Tomorrow

A portrait of A.A. Milne, around 1916.

A.A. MILNE
1882 – 1956
Nationality: British
First Published: Methuen, 1922

The Red House Mystery

A.A. Milne made only one foray into the thriller genre in his early *The Red House Mystery*. Like many other 'Golden Age' detective stories, the setting is the secluded environment of a country house and purports to take on another classic feature – that of the locked-room murder mystery. The field of suspects is restricted to the household and the members of Mark Ablett's house party. Ablett's brother, Robert, is expected to turn up, having been absent in Australia for 15 years: an unknown quantity, then, to all those present in the house. When a man assumed to be Robert is found shot dead in Mark's locked office and Mark himself has disappeared, it would seem that Ablett has committed fratricide.

Anthony Gillingham arrives at the Red House just as the murder is discovered, having come to visit his friend, Bill Beverley, who is one of the guests. Milne's enthusiasm for detective fiction had made him critical of the kind of scientific detective whose specialized knowledge remains unavailable to the reader, so Gillingham is introduced as an objective – if eccentric – outsider, whose main qualification to be an amateur detective is that he 'was born noticing'.

Bill becomes his amiable 'Watson': not his chronicler, but the person to whom Gillingham can expound his inductive reasoning as each layer of the problem is unfolded. In *The Red House Mystery*, Milne's intention was to set up a puzzle which the intelligent reader should be able to unravel for themselves. The book provides a variation on contemporary detective fiction which thus far had considered the reader more in the light of a bemused Watson, than as a potential Holmes.

A Red Death

A Red Death is the second book in the series by Walter Mosley which features the detective character, Ezekiel, or Easy, Rawlins. The sequence starts in 1950s Los Angeles and the background for *A Red Death*, then, is the era of McCarthyism and the Communist witch-hunts.

Easy is neither a committed amateur nor a professional paid detective as such – any investigating he has undertaken in the past has usually been bartered for or done purely as a favour. Although he apparently earns his living from odd janitorial jobs, his main source of income is from rental payments. In a period of white expansionism after the Second World War, Easy is a black capitalist, a property owner, but he is also a criminal in the eyes of the Internal Revenue Service as he has never paid tax on his properties. Thus he can be easily blackmailed by FBI Agent Craxton into investigating Chaim Wenzler, a white Jew suspected of Communist agitation.

Wenzler is working as a volunteer with the First African Baptist Church and Craxton needs Easy to infiltrate this community for him. As Easy delves deeper into what proves to be a much more complex set of circumstances involving corruption and murder, he relies on the help of his disconcerting friend, the psychopathic Mouse, and struggles with his attraction for Mouse's wife, Etta.

A Red Death paints a vivid picture of 1950s America, divided along lines of race but also divided over what actually counts as crime. The novel is most memorable, however, for the slick action and the marvellous rendition of the extended community in which Easy lives – not as a hard-boiled loner, but not always comfortably either.

WALTER MOSLEY,
1952 –
Nationality: American
First Published: W.W. Norton & Co.
Inc., 1991
Other Selected Titles:
Devil in a Blue Dress
Fear Itself
Little Scarlet

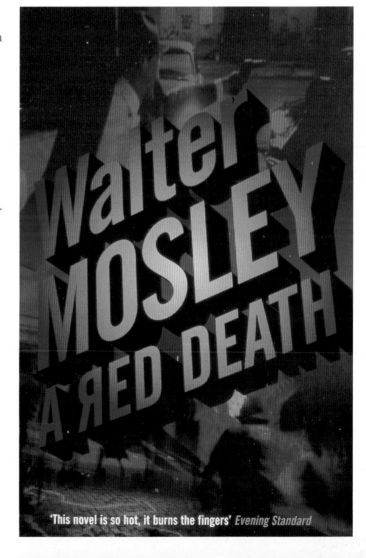

'This novel is so hot, it burns the fingers' *Evening Standard*

Deadlock

SARA PARETSKY
1947 –
Nationality: American
First Published: Dial Press, 1984
Other Selected Titles:
Indemnity Only
Total Recall
Blacklist

Sara Paretsky at the Edinburgh Book Festival.

Sara Paretsky created the character of V.I. Warshawski in the early 1980s. Known as Victoria to a very select few, as Vic to a slightly wider circle of friends, but as the anonymous V.I. to the world at large, Private Investigator Warshawski seems to be a female version of the tough or hard-boiled detective. V.I. has a background in the police force and this, along with her physical courage, hard-drinking and smart-talking, make her very similar to the traditional male loner. However, it is V.I.'s character as a woman that makes her as successful as she is because she also has concerns of family and community. These concerns command and direct her detective skills in a more than purely professional way, her emotional connections making her a stubborn, committed and resourceful investigator.

In *Deadlock*, V.I. is required to look into the murder of her own cousin, retired ice-hockey star, Bernard, or 'Boom Boom' Warshawski. They had been very close, both as family members and just as friends, trusting each other to the extent that Boom Boom made V.I. his executor. At first it appears that his death at the quayside of the Eudora Grain Company is just an accident, but Vic's knowledge of her cousin's personality makes her sure that this could not have been the case.

Soon she is embroiled in a fast-paced and dangerous undertaking and, when further deaths occur, her feelings about the case – not feminine intuition, but shrewd judgment – prove to be true. Although V.I. may occasionally step over to the shady side of the law herself, *Deadlock* shows her moral determination to uncover crime in big business and to find justice for her cousin.

Dover One

Joyce Porter's detective fiction series, which starts with *Dover One*, sets itself apart from the run of thriller novels largely for the unusual depiction of the central character, Chief Inspector Wilfred Dover. Dover is unlike any other sleuth. Although he is a professional, he scarcely professes to do any work, being lazy, bad-tempered, a martyr to stomach-ache and reliant on others to do the spadework. He often seems to be out of his depth intellectually: how he came to be Chief Inspector is a mystery which Porter keeps unsolved.

By contrast, his sergeant, Charles MacGregor, is young, fit, handsome, energetic and well-educated and looks set to have a good career in the police. Porter subverts the traditional premise of a wise, older sleuth training up a younger colleague, in order to extract as much humour as possible from the disparity between the two men.

Juliet Rugg, a 16-year-old maid, has been missing for two days and Dover's job is to find her. It is hard to see how Juliet could have vanished into thin air as she is described as having a very recognizable stature and appearance. The initial tone of the novel is slightly farcical and this continues even after it appears that Juliet has been murdered. In the long run, Dover comes up with an acceptable motive for Juliet's death, which will also satisfy the Chief Constable's desire for respectability in the public eye.

However, *Dover One* also broaches a really horrific alternative solution, which Porter slips in from a most unlikely source, leaving the reader uncomfortable in this gruesome knowledge. Porter plays with many of the clichés of detective fiction to produce her comic version, but the humour has its own startling and sardonic bite.

Dover ONE

JOYCE PORTER

JOYCE PORTER
1924 – 1990
Nationality: British
First Published: Jonathan Cape, 1964
Other Selected Titles:
Dover and the Unkindest Cut of All
Who the Heck is Sylvia?
Dover Beats the Band

The Chinese Orange Mystery

**ELLERY QUEEN
(FREDERIC DANNAY)**
1905 – 1982
Nationality: American
(MANFRED B. LEE)
1905 – 1971
Nationality: American
First Published: Frederick Stokes,
1934
Other Selected Titles:
The Roman Hat Mystery
The Tragedy of X
Inspector Queen's Own Case

Ellery Queen is the detective protagonist of the series which started with *The Roman Hat Mystery* (1929). As with Sherlock Holmes, we are detached from the workings of Ellery's mind by the narrator, a fictional friend. Ellery's inductive powers, therefore, seem almost impenetrable and the reader stands back and admires the great sleuth at work. However, unlike Holmes and his derivatives, Queen-the-author always plays fair and, at a critical point in the narrative, a challenge is presented to the reader to solve the case, all the necessary clues and information having been set forth.

The Chinese Orange Mystery is an excellent example of the Queen flair. A man is murdered while waiting to see Donald Kirk, a wealthy publisher and collector and an old college friend of Ellery's. The circumstances are bizarre: the furniture of the waiting-room has been turned back-to-front and the door has been locked from the inside. The only clue as to the actions of the murdered man is that the remains of a tangerine, or Chinese orange, are found in the wastebin. Nobody knows who the victim is; there are no clues on his person to identify him and nobody was in the vicinity. All the statements from the range of potential suspects must be sieved for details of opportunity and the mass of information mounts up.

Manfred Lee and Frederick Dannay, co-authors of the Ellery Queen mystery novels, 1950.

The identity of the dead man remains a mystery throughout the novel: Ellery's methods are almost more interesting than the answers. Ellery works alongside the police with his father, Inspector Richard Queen, who will ensure that legal justice is done. But Ellery is fundamentally an intellectual loner and many of the Queen novels are indebted to the traditional puzzle story structure, but rework it with a more modern feel.

The Man in the Net

The Man in the Net is a taut and well-crafted example of a Patrick Quentin mystery thriller. Quentin typically sets up an unexpected scenario or unusual premise and this is more than fulfilled in this novel.

John Hamilton left his lucrative job with a New York advertising agency to move to the country and try his hand at painting. His first show is not a success and he is under some pressure from his wife, Linda, to return to the city to make some money. Linda is having increasing difficulty coping with the dullness of life in the country and has succumbed to her alcoholism, although she is able to keep this completely secret from everybody except John.

So when John returns from a business trip to find his paintings slashed and Linda missing, later to be found dead, he cannot prove how unstable and violent she had become and the suspicions of the locals put him firmly in the frame for her murder.

As the net closes ever more tightly around Hamilton, he receives assistance from an unlikely source – a group of small children who give him shelter and run errands for him. Yet Quentin makes this seem perfectly believable as Hamilton's circumstance makes him desperately dependent on whatever tools he can use to find the real killer and so prove his own innocence.

Written in the third person but from Hamilton's point of view, the nightmare quality of his predicament is the key feature of this novel. Quentin's craft is particularly successful in being able to persuade the reader to overlook the improbability of the initial scenario and to get caught up in the increasing tension of the situation and the protagonist's dilemma.

'Drastic domestic mystery story verging on nightmare'
– Tatler

PENGUIN BOOKS

The Man in the Net

Patrick Quentin

COMPLETE & UNABRIDGED

2/6

PATRICK QUENTIN
(HUGH CUNNINGHAM WHEELER)
1912 – 1987
Nationality: American
First Published: Gollancz, 1956
Other Selected Titles:
A Puzzle for Fools
My Son, the Murderer
Suspicious Circumstances

Ruth Rendell, who also writes as Barbara Vine.

A Judgement in Stone

Ruth Rendell is a past master of the more traditional detective story, as is evident in the popularity of her series featuring Chief Inspector Wexford of Kingsmarkham. However, she also has an interest in the psychological thriller, writing both under her own name and as Barbara Vine.

A Judgement in Stone is a crescendo of a tale, building up its morbid intensity even though we know the perpetrator of the crime from the very beginning. Eunice Parchman goes as cleaner to the wealthy and intelligent Coverdale family: George and Jacqueline and two of their children, Melinda and Giles, who still live at home. More than half the novel is concerned with setting up a detailed contrast between the family's problems and interactions and their cleaner's lifestyle and state of mind. Rendell describes Eunice as a 'stone-age woman' and 'a stone that breathed' because Eunice's secret – and one which influences her moral sense – is that she cannot read. At all costs she must keep this secret, even from Joan Smith, the only person she can look upon as a friend. So when the Coverdales find out she is illiterate she has no choice but to shoot them, and her friend Joan becomes her neurotic companion in murder.

Rendell's achievement is one of sustained psychological truth – as readers of the tale and therefore literate ourselves, we can never fully appreciate Eunice's position and yet, at the same time, Rendell allows us to enter into the closed world of Eunice's life and to see just how damaging her illiteracy becomes. An unfortunate inadequacy spins out of control to become a tragic defect and, once again, Rendell's insight shows us how close we could all be to losing the veneer of civilization.

RUTH RENDELL
1930 –
Nationality: British
First Published: Hutchinson, 1977
Other Selected Titles:
A Guilty Thing Surprised
Murder Being Once Done
Simisola

Gaudy Night

The secluded, almost convent-like, environment of a women's college in 1930s Oxford provides the claustrophobic setting for *Gaudy Night*. Harriet Vane, a one-time murder suspect (the story of her acquittal owing to the detective work of Lord Peter Wimsey is told in *Strong Poison*) and a successful author of detective stories herself, returns to Shrewsbury College for the first time since graduating. A spiteful and vicious drawing is planted on one of the female graduates during the Gaudy weekend and this prefaces a spate of further poison-pen incidents and room-ransackings which the College Faculty ask Harriet to investigate.

The novel is tautly-plotted as well as tense in atmosphere. While the criminal action of the novel never actually descends to murder, Sayers makes much of the tensions which can arise among groups of women living in close proximity. The contemporary cultural conflict between the dependent, feminine housewife and mother, and the independent, academic celibate is played out here in *Gaudy Night*.

However, as the spitefulness and violence escalates, it becomes clear that Harriet herself is caught up in the crossfire as her own academic objectivity is compromised by her relationship with Lord Peter Wimsey, to the extent that he has to step in to assist her in her detective task. More than a mere puzzle-solving problem, Sayers concerns herself with character development and psychological study, thereby introducing a more realistic element into her version of Golden Age detective fiction.

DOROTHY L. SAYERS
1893 – 1957
Nationality: British
First Published: Gollancz, 1935
Other Selected Titles:
Strong Poison
Murder Must Advertise
The Nine Tailors
Busman's Honeymoon

Dorothy L. Sayers is appointed a warden of St. Thomas' Church, in London's Regent Street, 1952.

Mr Hire's Engagement

GEORGES SIMENON
1903 – 1989
Nationality: Belgian
First Published: A. Fayard & Cie,
1933
Other Selected Titles:
Maigret and the Killers
Madame Maigret's Own Case
Maigret and the Headless Corpse

*Georges Simenon
at home in Lausanne,
Switzerland, 1981.*

Georges Simenon was an incredibly prolific and speedy writer, producing several books per year, and was most famous for his writings about Commissaire Maigret. *Mr Hire's Engagement* is, however, an early non-Maigret story, a dark psychological thriller where the focus is not so much on the crime itself but on the prevailing atmosphere and characterizations.

In the small town of Villejuif, Mr Hire is an outsider, not so much because he is regarded as an actual foreigner, but through being a solitary person and keeping himself to himself. In a community where people expect to know about each other, he is suspicious because he doesn't talk to anybody. Then a girl is found murdered on a patch of wasteground, seemingly the victim of a violent robbery as her handbag is missing, and the police are looking for a sadistic killer. Hire's janitor declares that he saw a bloody towel in the odd man's flat and both police and community are prepared to jump to conclusions about him. Those suspicions are further supported by Hire's antisocial habit of watching his beautiful neighbour, Alice, across the way, but when Alice catches him at his voyeuristic practices she makes contact with him out of curiousity.

From the relationship that ensues between Mr Hire and Alice, Hire is put in a position where he becomes one of the strangest and most unsettling heroes in the thriller genre. Simenon concentrates, however, on that bleak and pessimistic, small-town atmosphere and the novel's outcome rings true psychologically, making us question justice, fairness and prejudice.

The Laughing Policeman

Husband-and-wife writing team, Maj Sjöwall and Per Wahlöö, collaborated on a police detective series starting in 1965 with *Roseanna*, which was received to great acclaim, and going on until Wahlöö's early death in 1975.

The Laughing Policeman is a key example, both of the style they made their own and of the working methods of their leading detective protagonist, Superintendent Martin Beck of the Central Bureau of Investigation in Stockholm.

One wet night, the passengers on a bus are machine-gunned down by an unknown killer and the police have to track him down with very little to go on. The public and the press assume it can only be the work of a motive-less madman but the police think there may be a sane, if dark, motive behind it.

Structured by looking back into the past lives of the victims and building up their characters and lifestyles for clues as to why they were shot and how they all came to be on the bus in the first place, the style of the novel is carefully realistic and grips the attention. Martin Beck and his detectives are also handled in a realistic manner, and the series could be categorized as belonging to police procedural fiction, where teamwork and painstaking police routine are minutely observed.

There is no omniscient, Holmesian work here, so the novel can be truthfully grim in its treatment of the professional setting, where the police are constantly struggling with administrative frustration and politically-created bureaucracy. This attention to the larger influences on the work of the police force makes *The Laughing Policeman* not only satisfyingly convincing, but also reflects the social conditions in Sweden at the time.

MAJ SJÖWALL
1935 –
Nationality: Swedish
PER WAHLÖÖ
1926 – 1975
Nationality: Swedish
First Published: Norstedt,1968
Other Selected Titles:
The Man on the Balcony
The Abominable Man
Cop Killer

Rex Stout (left) at a War Relief lunch in 1941.

The Red Box

Rex Stout introduced his series detective, Nero Wolfe, in 1934 and so created one of the more unusual thriller investigators to come into the arena. In *The Red Box,* Stout shows the talented Wolfe working his detective magic in his own inimitable style.

Molly Lauck, a show girl, dies quickly and horribly from potassium cyanide poisoning when she eats a piece of candy from a two-pound box of mixed sweets, although her friend's choice of sweet from the same box is unadulterated and safe.

The theatrical producer, Llewellyn Frost, needs Wolfe to solve the case and save the reputation of his fragile and overstretched business. Soon Wolfe suspects Frost's cousin, Helen, of the crime, and Llewellyn wants the case to be solved as quickly as possible, but that is only the start and more murder is committed.

While Wolfe shares some basic attributes with other detectives, it is in the particular form of those attributes that he is so different. Wolfe is an eccentric genius – a trope that goes back to Poe's Dupin – but his extremely misogynistic character, when coupled with his passion for cultivating orchids and for his indulgence in beer and gourmet cuisine, makes him an overweight and indolent man, who refuses to leave his home on business. He is thus very reliant on his hard-boiled sidekick, Archie Goodwin, to bring him information and do much of the work-on-the-street for him. Goodwin has more impact on the outcome of a case than the usual Watson-like helpers, being actually a detective by profession himself. Surrounded by his live-in helpers, Wolfe seems to live the life of one of his own hot-house flowers but, between them, Wolfe and Goodwin together make up the perfect detective figure.

REX STOUT
1886 – 1975
Nationality: American
First Published: Farrar & Rinehart, Inc., 1937
Other Selected Titles:
Fer-de-Lance (also entitled *Meet Nero Wolfe*)
Too Many Women
Please Pass the Guilt

The Man Who Killed Himself

JULIAN SYMONS
THE MAN WHO KILLED HIMSELF CRIME

Julian Symons was highly regarded for his work as both critical historian and author of detective fiction, and *The Man Who Killed Himself* is a fine example of his scholarly invention and wit when it comes to melding the psychological with the socially satiric.

The short novel revolves around a very ordinary man, Arthur Brownjohn. Brownjohn seems a typically hen-pecked husband so when he rebels and decides to murder his wife, the scenario is not original but Symons gives it a twist. Brownjohn wants to get his crime just right so he carefully researches the topic but, in the event, his attempt fails miserably as he makes various mistakes. Resolved to do better, he comes across Major Easonby Mellon, a man of striking confidence who nevertheless needs to abandon his own business, a rather dubious matrimonial agency. Together the two men plan to commit what they envisage as the perfect murder.

The set-up certainly has comic overtones but where it differs from conventional expectations is in the fact that Brownjohn's domineering wife, Clare, is actually right in her assessment of his capabilities. For Arthur would be one of life's losers, no matter his intentions: he was born incompetent. Symons' interest in the psychology of his criminals makes the juxtaposition of meek Arthur with irrepressible Mellon a source of humour but also of some serious social comment. A man like Brownjohn can never really make his satisfactory way in society, for the anonymity of city life has no time for his inadequacies. The complexities of the plot give rise to some clever surprises but the whole premise has an undercurrent of satiric discomfort.

JULIAN SYMONS
1912 – 1994
Nationality: British
First Published: Collins Crime Club, 1967
Other Selected Titles:
The Immaterial Murder Case
The Colour of Murder
A Three-Pipe Problem

A Pin to See the Peep-Show

F. TENNYSON JESSE
1889 – 1958
Nationality: British
First Published: Heinemann, 1934
Other selected titles:
The Solange Stories

F. Tennyson Jesse was a prolific mainstream novelist in her day who also took a great interest in real-life crime, even editing some volumes of the 'Famous Trials' compilations which were so popular in the 1930s. She wrote two collections of short stories which feature a psychic French detective, Madame Solange, but only wrote one crime fiction novel, *A Pin to See the Peep-Show*, which thus combines her two main interests.

A Pin to See the Peep-Show has probably remained her most famous novel and yet, interestingly, its premise was lifted from a true case which had had huge publicity several years earlier. F. Tennyson Jesse was only one among several writers who used the real case as the basis for fictional treatment. In 1922 Edith Thompson and Frederick Bywaters were on trial. They had had an adulterous affair and Edith's husband was murdered. Dorothy L. Sayers herself had written a version entitled *The Documents in the Case* (1930), with collaborator Robert Eustace, so the details of the trial would be fresh in the public's memory.

Jesse's lasting success with this true-crime thriller comes out of her aptitude for sympathetic characterization. In contrast to Sayers's two-dimensional depiction of a hard-as-nails, scheming woman, Jesse's construction of Edith Thompson as Julia Almond gives a more complex psychological explanation for her actions. Jesse shows us a woman who is led unintentionally into a crime of passion by her 'peepshow' daydreams of a life happier than could ever be available to her in her circumstances at that period. Jesse's novelistic techniques result in a piece of fiction which virtually presents a mitigating case for the defence.

The Daughter of Time

Although better known during her lifetime as the playwright Gordon Daviot, Josephine Tey's contributions to mystery fiction have probably earned her longer-lasting fame and in *The Daughter of Time* she presents an unusual perspective on the thriller genre. Inspector Alan Grant of Scotland Yard, who also appears in *The Man in the Queue*, is recovering in hospital after an operation which has sapped his strength but not his curiosity. Various visitors try to distract Grant from his boredom but his friend, the actress Marta Hallard, brings in a collection of pictures of historical characters for his amusement which then gives him the impetus for doing what he calls some 'academic investigating'.

Grant becomes particularly absorbed by a portrait of King Richard III – the English king whom history and Shakespeare have credited with the murder of the little princes in The Tower. This 'murder' and its motives intrigue Grant as he lies incapacitated in his bed. Enlisting the aid of Marta and a young American researcher, Brent Carradine, to bring him such books and evidence as he needs, Grant becomes bent on uncovering the truth – that daughter of Time – behind the historical incident and he brings all his detective abilities to bear upon the 'case'. Tey has given us a historical mystery, not because the novel itself is set in the past, but because it delves into the past. The methods of the detective and the historian are equally exacting and, unusually, this novel takes us inside the detective's thought processes as they occur and reveal the logic on which he develops his remarkable conclusions.

JOSEPHINE TEY (ELIZABETH MACKINTOSH)
1896 – 1952
Nationality: British
First Published: William Heinemann, 1951
BOOK TITLES
The Man in the Queue
Miss Pym Disposes
The Franchise Affair

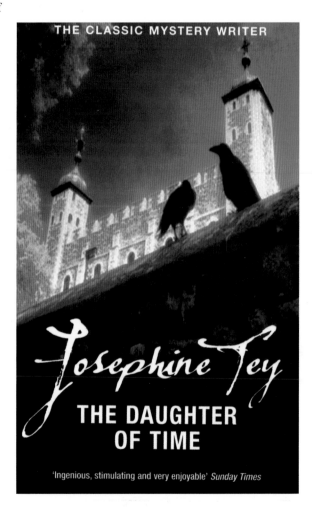

THE CLASSIC MYSTERY WRITER

Josephine Tey

THE DAUGHTER OF TIME

'Ingenious, stimulating and very enjoyable' *Sunday Times*

Above the Dark Circus

SIR HUGH WALPOLE
1884 – 1941
Nationality: Britsh
First Published: Macmillan, 1931
Other Selected Titles:
The Inquisitor

Hugh Walpole was prolific in many areas of writing but in the thriller genre he is better known for his tales of horror and the supernatural, rather than the crime-and-detection variety. *Above the Dark Circus* constitutes Walpole's main venture into incorporating the two elements.

It is narrated in the first person by Richard Gunn, an ex-soldier who is in dire straits after the First World War. Like many others at the time, he had no job to come home to and has tried his hand at most things, only for them to fail. He finds himself in Piccadilly Circus, faint with hunger and in a desperate frame of mind, when he encounters Leroy Pengelly, a nasty character from his pre-War existence. Pengelly had helped to trap and betray Richard's friend John Osmund, sending him to prison for a burglary to which John, however, would not confess. Richard was not only cut off from John by Pengelly's act but also from John's fiancée, Helen Cameron, whom Richard secretly loved.

Above the Dark Circus is concerned with unravelling the truth of what actually happened before the War when Osmund went to prison without saying a word in his own defence, and the result is to change people's lives. Piccadilly Circus is almost a character itself in the story, dominating the atmosphere as its crowded environs reveal the presence of all the players from the earlier stage. Yet the familiarity of Piccadilly Circus is in stark contrast to the unease of Richard's state of mind. The result is a novel which combines elements of the horror and supernatural – at which Walpole was so skilled – with the puzzle element of the whodunnit – all wrapped up in one unsettling and uncanny whole.

Born Victim

Chief of Police Fred Fellows and his team, which includes Detective Sergeant Wilks and Officer Raphael, feature in several of Hillary Waugh's thriller novels. 1960s Stockford provides a small-town setting where the police know nearly everybody, being themselves part of that community with families of their own to protect.

In *Born Victim,* Fellows is called out to investigate the disappearance of a 13-year old girl. Barbara, or Bobbie, Markle does not return from her first dance and her mother Evelyn's fears turn to the worst – that Bobbie may have been assaulted and even killed. Those fears are equally entertained by the police and *Born Victim* is a masterpiece of tension as Waugh piles up item upon item of evidence.

The novel could be categorized as police procedural writing. Although written in the third person, the case is viewed from Fellows' perspective and his mounting anxieties and suspicions drive the police action. The thoroughness with which Fellows and Wilks between them cover all the angles and discuss all the possibilities represents a typical police-led case, while also providing the reader with the full range of 'red herrings'.

One by one, as Fellows delves into Bobbie's background, her family and friends are investigated until the meaning of the 'born victim' of the title is revealed, but only at the very end. This thriller has a disturbing yet sad quality which puts a magnifying glass to the small-town, class-created hypocrisy of the period and the psychological damage it can cause.

HILLARY WAUGH,
1920 –
Nationality: American
First Published: Doubleday, 1962
Other Selected Titles:
That Night It Rained
Parrish for the Defence (UK title:
Doctor on Trial)
The Billy Cantrell Case

The Bride Wore Black

CORNELL WOOLRICH
1903 – 1968
Nationality: American
First Published: Ace Books, 1940
Other Selected Titles:
The Black Angel
I Married a Dead Man
Death is My Dancing Partner

Cornell Woolrich was a prolific short story and novel writer. After an apprenticeship in pulp-magazine writing, along with Hammett he became one of the first recognized writers of hard-boiled or *noir* thrillers. Woolrich is particularly associated with the suspense thriller form and *The Bride Wore Black* is a good example of this, his best field. Woolrich is probably remembered today, however, for his short story, *Rear Window*, which was made into a tense film by Hitchcock.

The eponymous 'bride' of *The Bride Wore Black* is a beautiful young woman called Julie – her surname changes as necessary – whose appearance in a town always spells trouble for one of its male inhabitants. For Julie is on a mission to find and kill certain men and as the novel progresses she commits five cold-blooded murders, none of her victims apparently having any connection with any of the others.

Only Lew Wanger, the detective figure, believes there is a link and that Julie herself is that common factor. Woolrich moves between the different perspectives of the *femme fatale* and her targets, which makes penetrating Julie's motives difficult and helps maintains the suspense. The reader is more knowledgeable than the police, who think the murders are accidents, but we are kept in the dark about the causes behind Julie's devastating effect until the surprise ending.

The novel shows both Woolrich's strengths and weaknesses as a writer. The plotting is unsophisticated, in that there are no real sub-plots or sidelines to enrich the overall tale, and his characterizations have no great complexity or depth. However, he does have mastery over the art of suspenseful delay and maintains the reader's engagement for this reason, wrapping up the whole in typical 1940s thriller language and atmosphere.

CORNELL WOOLRICH

THE BRIDE WORE BLACK

AMERICA'S MASTER OF SUSPENSE

STERANKO

TRAVEL WRITING

Travels

IBN BATTUTA
circa 1304 – 1368
Nationality: Moroccan

This is an enchanting travelogue of the 'civilized' world in the 14th century experienced by a unique explorer. Ibn Battuta was brought up in Tangiers, Morocco, an educated Islamic scholar and a freelance judge. His travels began when he was 20, when he set out on a pilgrimage to Mecca. Once started on his journeys, he just kept going with an almost insatiable wanderlust. His travels took him not only to Mecca but also to North Africa, Syria, Iran, Iraq, Turkey, India and then onward as far as Vietnam and China. Along the way Ibn takes interesting detours, for example stopping in the Maldives where he married into the Royal Family and set up shop as a local judge. After several decades of wandering and many tens of thousands of miles, he decides to return home to Tangiers.

At the request of the Sultan of Morocco, Ibn dictates his memoirs. Narrated in the first person, Ibn gives us his view of the world – people, customs, food and so on. This is not just about ancient places it is a window into the medieval world.

The Scorpion-Fish

NICHOLAS BOUVIER
First Published: 1981
Other Selected Titles:
The Japanese Chronicles
China (as a contributor)
Geneva, Zurich, Basel
(with Gordon A. Craig, Lionel Gossman)
Way of the World

Written as a travel novel, Bouvier takes us on a journey to an island close to India, thought to be Sri Lanka. The main character and narrator is a Swiss artist who introduces us to an exotic world of heat, humidity and an infinite variety of insects. He also describes a range of characters, including the Buddhist priests who explode buses on a regular basis, inert shop keepers, and even a levitating Roman Catholic priest who has been dead for years. It is a world of magic and mystery.

The narrator also tells us of the loneliness and solitude of a traveller, in his case seeking the company of a dung beetle and other bugs for amusement.

Witty and amusingly written by Bouvier, and skilfully translated into English by Robyn Marsack who won the 1988 Scott Moncrieff Prize for this work, *The Scorpion-Fish* was also the inspiration for Joanna Dudley's musical theatre piece of the same title.

The boat of Ibn Battuta, Arabic traveler, taken by pirates. Engraving XIXth century.

'A MASTERPIECE'
Bruce Chatwin

THE ROAD TO OXIANA

Robert Byron

ROBERT BYRON
1905 – 1941
Nationality: British
First Published: Macmillan, 1937
Other Selected Titles:
The Station
The Byzantine Achievement
The Appreciation of Architecture
First Russia, Then Tibet

The Road to Oxiana

Byron spent some 10 months travelling in Persia and Afghanistan during 1933–1934. This book is a record of his travels and thoughts on this journey. It is the quintessential travelogue and one that has set the standard for those to follow. An oft quoted tribute is that of Paul Fussell who wrote 'what *Ulysses* is to the novel between the wars and what *The Waste Land* is to poetry, *The Road to Oxiana* is to the travel book'.

One of Byron's great loves was monuments and architecture, and another history. His descriptions of the natural environment and the buildings he finds around him are written in lush prose, at times almost extravagant. His comments on politics and some of the individuals he comes across are incisive and can be both funny and acerbic.

This is a book of its time, both in content and in style. Byron paints us a living picture of the Persia and Afghanistan of another era. His death in the Second World War was truly a loss to travel literature.

In Patagonia

This book established Chatwin's reputation as a travel author. It is not the usual travel guide, with descriptions of ancient monuments, best beaches and local cuisine. Rather it reflects the author's own archaeological and artistic interests in people.

Chatwin writes in a Postmodernist style, often described as multi-threaded and somewhat fragmented. *In Patagonia* is a wonderful evocative book that gives a feeling for this region at the bottom of the world: the gauchos, pioneers, native peoples and its haunting, often isolated landscapes. Chatwin inspires us with descriptions of Butch Cassidy's life, which he researched extensively in the United States and in Patagonia, interviewing those still alive who knew or remembered Butch and his gang. Chatwin also reminds us of the earlier explorers and travellers, such as Charles Darwin. In a charmingly personal touch he searches for his own roots, his grandmother's cousin who had gone to Patagonia and acquired a bit of sloth hide.

This is a travel journal not to be missed, giving a unique view of Patagonia and a window into the life of a fascinating man.

BRUCE CHARLES CHATWIN
1940 – 1989
Nationality: British
First Published: Cape, 1977
Other Selected Titles:
The Viceroy of Ouidah
On the Black Hill
The Songlines

English travel writer and journalist Bruce Chatwin at his home in 1984.

The Voyage on HMS Beagle

CHARLES DARWIN
1809 – 1882
Nationality: British
First Published: Henry Colburn, 1839
Other Selected Titles:
The Origin of Species

This historic travelogue describes Darwin's five year voyage on HMS Beagle between the years 1831–1836. It was a world-changing odyssey which provided Darwin with the inspiration and evidence for the theory of evolution based on natural selection. The journal is written in the form of a diary in the first person, with dated entries written in chronological order. The content of the journal reflects the scientific nature of the trip, including detailed descriptions of the wildlife, the geology, the geography especially as it relates to water, and local inhabitants he finds on the way.

These careful, analytical descriptions are interspersed with personal anecdotes and opinions. Darwin writes in a well-paced and delightful style, at times a bit Victorian, but overall it is an interesting read. One travels with him to the Cape de Verde Islands, along the South American coast, the Galapagos, Tahiti, New Zealand, Australia and Mauritius. It is a lengthy book but one that lends itself to dipping in and out.

Charles Darwin.

My Journey to Lhasa

All the best travel books are written by true explorers, and this is no exception. The author amazed the world in 1924 by secretly entering the sacred capital of Tibet, forbidden to foreigners. No less astonishing is that she travelled across China from East to West dressed as a poor traveller accompanied by a monk called Yongden. They succeeded in slipping over the border undetected by the Tibetan officials and stayed in Lhasa for two months. At the time, Alexandra was 55 years old.

This was David-Néel's fifth sojourn into Tibet. By this time she was an accomplished Oriental scholar and conversant with the language and culture. Her journal brings this clandestine adventure to life. Written in the first person, her style has magical prose and descriptive dialogue. The experience is exquisite as one is transported to Lhasa in the 1920s and David-Néel brings to life all its splendour and squalor. She also shares with us her emotions, both those of the excitement of arriving, and those of the peace in being there.

ALEXANDRA DAVID-NEEL
1868 – 1969
Nationality: French
First Published: Harper and
Brothers, 1927
Other Selected Titles:
Magic and Mystery in Tibet
The Superhuman Life of Gesar of Ling
Tibetan Tale of Love and Magic

*Alexandra David-Néel dressed
as a Tibetan nun, 1928.*

On the Narrow Road to the Deep North

LESLEY DOWNER
Nationality: British
First Published: Jonathan Cape, 1988
Other Selected Titles:
Geisha: the Secret History of a Vanishing World
Women of the Pleasure Quarters: the Secret History of the Geisha
Madame Sadayakko: the Geisha Who Seduced the West

This is a travel journal within a travel journal. In the 1980s, Downer retraced the steps of Matsuo Basho's journey recorded in his famous *On the Narrow Road to the Deep North* (1694). Basho was a Japanese haiku poet and teacher, who is still greatly revered. Basho travelled extensively, often on foot, to gain inspiration. In 1689 he went with a disciple on a journey to the Northern Provinces. This culminated in *On the Narrow Road to the Deep North*, considered to be his greatest work. In this diary he writes his poems, gives a narrative of his feelings and views, as well as presenting a unique view of 17th-century Japan.

Lesley Downer uses Basho's book to walk in his footsteps, visiting the same shrines, ancient monuments and landscapes. She moves Basho's work on three centuries, adding her own unique perspective on the events and changes time has wrought.

This book was short-listed for the Somerset Maugham Travel Book of the Year award in 1988. It is out of print but is available at specialist bookshops and many libraries. It is well worth the search.

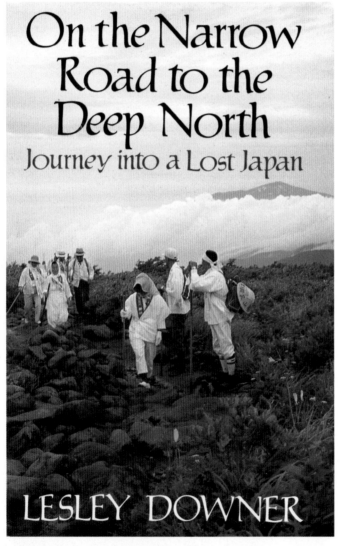

On the Narrow Road to the Deep North
Journey into a Lost Japan
LESLEY DOWNER

The Traveller's Tree

Patrick Leigh Fermor in Brittany, 1992.

One of the joys of reading travel books is that one meets such interesting people! Paddy Fermor is no exception to this. As a young man he travelled the length of Europe, particularly getting to know Greece and Greek. He is a gifted linguist, as well as an adventurer and war hero. *The Traveller's Tree* depicts his post-War travels in the Caribbean during the 1940s.

Fermor's journal is a detailed snap shot in time when the old social order based on African and European cultures was still recognizable, complete with Voodoo and allusions to darker practices. It was also when the colonial influences were waning and the American overtones were on the ascendancy.

The book takes us via every kind of transport from island to island. It observes the blend of cultures, the variety of natural environments, all types of people and all aspects of the arts, particularly music. Fermor, an accomplished raconteur, writes in a style that is rich, evocative and at times very amusing.

PATRICK LEIGH FERMOR
1915 —
Nationality: British
First Published: John Murray, 1950
Other Selected Titles:
The Violins of Saint-Jacques
A Time to Keep Silence
Roumeli
A Time of Gifts
Between the Woods and the Water
Three Letters from the Andes

Heinrich Harrer with the Commander of the Tibetan Army in April of 1954.

Seven Years in Tibet

This is not so much a travel book as an amazing adventure story, one that is so exciting that it was made into a movie starring Brad Pitt (1997). Harrer, an Austrian, was an accomplished mountaineer and skier who found himself in Karachi when World War Two broke out. He was interred with other Europeans in India and, after several attempts, managed to escape. The book charts his trek through the jungle and over the Himalayas to Tibet. This arduous journey took many months without the right equipment or clothing, all the time Harrar being a fugitive. Once he arrived in Tibet, he travelled to the Holy City of Lhasa. Here he was accepted and stayed for seven years. Harrer became an expert on the language and culture, eventually becoming a friend of the Dalai Lama.

This is a tremendous read; Harrer writes in a fast-paced narrative style which brings his extraordinary adventure alive.

HEINRICH HARRER
1912 – 2006
Nationality: Austrian
First Published: Granada, 1953
Other Selected Titles:
The White Spider
Return to Tibet
I Came From the Stone Age

Kon Tiki

This is a travel book with a twist. It is the tale of a scientific experiment which set out to prove that early peoples could have travelled from South America to Polynesia. This was initiated by an Incan legend of an exiled high priest king, Kon Tiki, who is said to have escaped by sea, heading westward. Heyerdahl was of the 'diffusionist' school of thought to explain the movement of populations and their technology and architecture. He therefore sought to prove that people were able to travel over long distances. He was later to try a similar experiment between Africa and the Americas.

Whether or not this hypothesis is true is of little importance in enjoying this amazing adventure. Six men travelled on a balsa raft from Peru to the Tuamotu Islands, in French Polynesia, taking 101 days and covering 4,300 miles. Heyerdahl writes in a lively story-telling manner which makes this book irresistible.

THOR HEYERDAHL
1914 – 2002
Nationality: Norwegian
First Published: Allen and Unwin, 1950
Other Selected Titles:
*American Indians in the Pacific:
the Theory behind the Kon-Tiki
Expedition
AKU-AKU: the Secret of Easter Island
The Ra Expeditions
Sea Routes to Polynesia
The Tigris Expedition
In Search of Our Beginnings*

Norwegian explorer and writer Thor Heyerdahl.

PENGUIN
BOOKS

THE BODLEY HEAD

THE
PURPLE LAND

W. H. HUDSON

THE BODLEY HEAD

COMPLETE

UNABRIDGED

The Purple Land

Hudson had American parents from British ancestry and was born in Argentina. He felt close associations to his English ancestry, while at the same time having a great love of South America. As well as being a novelist, he was also a naturalist and ornithologist who conducted professional research and was extensively published. The combination of his lively creative writing style and his thorough knowledge of his native land gave birth to the much acclaimed *The Purple Land*. One of its subtitles is 'Being the Narrative of One Richard Lamb's Adventures in the Banda Oriental in South America, As Told by Himself'. It is often classified as both fiction and travel.

The Purple Land is the tale of a capricious young Englishman travelling in Uruguay during a time of political change. Lamb's romantic adventures are very amusing and a bit 'Flashman'. However, these are truly brought to life by the descriptions of the geography, the fauna and flora, the climate and the people. The reader is effortlessly transported to 19th-century South America.

W.H. HUDSON
1841 – 1922
Nationality: Argentine-British
First Published: 1885
Other Selected Titles:
A Crystal Age
Idle Days in Patagonia
Hampshire Days
Green Mansions
A Romance of the Tropical Forest
Land's End: a Naturalist's Impressions in West Cornwall
A Foot in England
Tales of the Pampas

The Last Place on Earth

This book revisits the 1911 expeditions to Antarctica, the great race to reach the South Pole between Robert Scott of Great Britain and Roald Amundsen of Norway. This was the end of an era for great explorers, when you did not need the Starship Enterprise 'to boldly go where no man has gone before'. Huntford presents these two competing expeditions in graphic spine-tingling detail. He refocuses attention on and gives praise to the less well remembered success of Amundsen. It is even reported that in his quest for accuracy he researched the original sources written in Norwegian. Amundsen's small contingent was the first to reach the South Pole and returned alive, unlike the ill-fated Scott who died along with four of his companions.

Huntford is renowned for his polar biographies, providing historic fact and an understanding of the complex personalities in the exploring fraternity. *The Last Place on Earth* was the first of a trilogy, followed by *Shackleton* and *Nansen*.

ROLAND HUNTFORD
1937 -
Nationality: British
First Published: Hodder and Stoughton, 1979
Other Selected Titles:
Shackleton
Nansen
The Shackleton Voyages

Video Night in Kathmandu

PICO IYER
1957 –
Nationality: British
First Published: Alfred A. Knopf,
1989
Other Selected Titles:
The Recovery of Innocence
*Lady and the Monk: Four Seasons in
Kyoto*
Cuba and the Night
*Salon.Com's Wanderlust: Real-Life
Tales of Adventure and Romance*
*Imagining Canada: an Outsider's
Hope for a Global Future*
*A Sun after Dark: Flights into
the Foreign*

Perhaps Iyer realized earlier than most the impact of pervasive communications, cheap travel, and rock 'n' roll. The beginnings of the Global Village were already emerging in the mid 1980s. The internet was there lurking, waiting for everyone to get a computer and then broadband.

This wonderful travelogue takes us around Asia. The book's chapters are Bali, Tibet, Nepal, China, The Philippines, Burma, Hong Kong, India and Thailand. This is not a passive, serene view of landscapes and ancient gentle cultures. It is about 'today's world', as it was in the 1980s. In this time capsule, Iyer observes how different cultures were absorbing and morphing with the American/Western influences. For example, he analyzes the differences in impact the movie Rambo had in China, India and the Philippines. *Video Night in Kathmandu* is Postmodern in style and content; it is about globalization and how it feels around the world. Amid the humour and the adventure, there is also a great sense of loss.

'A wild and wonderful tour through the Westernized East'
ANITA DESAI

Journey to the Hebrides

This is a compilation of Samuel Johnson's *A Journey to the Western Island of Scotland* (1775) and James Boswell's *A Journal of a Tour to the Hebrides* (1785). These two journals document Johnson and Boswell's famous touring holiday in Scotland during the summer and early autumn of 1773. The two protagonists in this adventure could not have been more different. Johnson in his mid-sixties is nearing the end of his literary career and indeed his life. Boswell in his mid-thirties is just starting a less than successful career in law.

Johnson is motivated to journey to Scotland to experience for himself this wild land over the border. His account is considered a social history of Scotland at this time. For Boswell this was more of an adventure. His journal, published after Johnson's death, is considered more anecdotal, providing insights into Johnson's life. Together these documents give us a priceless view of two extraordinary men, how they perceived each other and the world they lived in. The whole is very much greater than the sum of its parts.

PENGUIN CLASSICS

SAMUEL JOHNSON
AND JAMES BOSWELL

A Journey to the Western Islands of Scotland
and *The Journal of a Tour to the Hebrides*

SAMUEL JOHNSON
1709 – 1784
Nationality: British
JAMES BOSWELL
1740 – 1795
Nationality: British
First Published: Canongate Books, 1996
Other Selected Titles:
JOHNSON:
Life of Richard Savage
A Dictionary of the English Language
The History of Rasselas, Prince of Abissinia
The Plays of William Shakespeare
Lives of English Poets
BOSWELL:
Dorando, a Spanish Tale
Account of Corsica
The Life of Samuel Johnson

A.W. Kinglake

EOTHEN

Introduction by Jonathan Raban

Eothen

One of the early travel books, this is subtitled 'Traces of Travel Brought Home from the East'. Kinglake was an historian, as well as a travel journalist. Educated at Eton and Cambridge he devoted his life to his studies. *Eothen*, like its author, is a wonderful piece of Victoriana; it is a fulsome account of all aspects of Kinglake's journey through the 19th-century world of Turkey, Cyprus, Palestine and Egypt.

He depicts the modes of transportation, the trials with petty bureaucrats, and the variety of food and accommodation. Writing in the first person he shares with us his motivations for travelling and his feelings for the people he meets and his travelling companions. Kinglake provides unique descriptions of the cities, landscapes, and monuments; one can almost see, hear and smell these exotic scenes. *Eothen* is a charming book that will transport you to a Victorian world full of eastern promise.

A.W. KINGLAKE
1808 – 1891
Nationality: British
First Published: Ollivier, 1844
Other Selected Titles:
Invasion of the Crimea (8 volumes)

The Seasick Whale

Emphraim Kishon was a well-known and admired Israeli satirist. He was born in Budapest, Hungary, into a Jewish family. During the Second World War he was imprisoned by the Nazis in several concentration camps, but through a series of fortuitous circumstances he survived. After the war he emigrated to Israel and worked as a columnist for a newspaper.

The Seasick Whale, with the apt subtitle 'An Israeli Abroad', tells of Kishon's travels through Europe and America. It is rich in descriptions of the people he meets and peculiarities of the different nationalities. They are insightful, amusing, ironic and seen from his very special perspective. Kishon is satirical but never bitter, his work is particularly revered in Germany where he had many friends. It may be difficult to find an English version of this book, but it is well worth the search.

EMPHRAIM KISHON
1924 – 2005
Nationality: Israeli
First Published: Tversky, 1965
Other Selected Titles:
Look Back Mrs Lot
So Sorry We Won
Woe to the Victors

A Rose for Winter

LAURIE LEE
1924 – 1997
Nationality: British
First Published: Hogarth Press, 1955
Other Selected Titles:
Cider with Rosie
As I Walked Out One Midsummer's Morning
A Moment of War

Laurie Lee is most famous for *Cider with Rosie*, a tale of his idyllic childhood in Gloucestershire. However, Lee's first foray into autobiographical writing was *A Rose for Winter*. Exuding his love of Andalusia, this travel book tells of his return to Spain after 15 years. It has been stated that when in his twenties, Lee spent four years travelling through Spain and fought in the Spanish Civil War. *A Rose for Winter* brings to life a country in the aftermath of the civil war, but which still has retained its cultural identity – bullfights, flamenco, a strong religion, deep passions and a pride in itself. Written in Lee's lyrical and evocative prose, one can smell the herbs, see the morning break and feel the heat. It is a book that you will love to read and re-read, and perhaps it will even entice you to visit, or re-visit, Spain.

Poet and author Laurie Lee in 1960.

Golden Earth: Travels in Burma

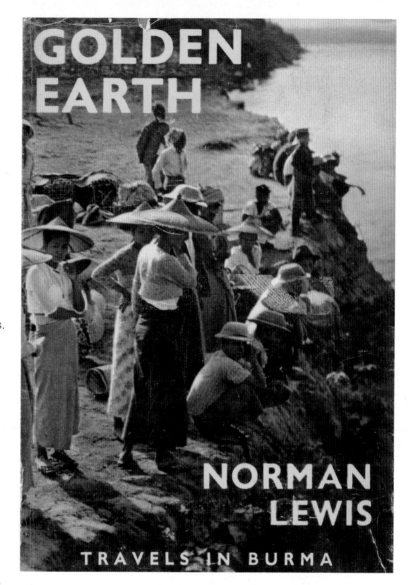

Published in the early 1950s, this book relates Lewis' travels in Burma. He paints a world that is mystical, spiritual and yet still has colonial influences. Lewis is an observer and a social commentator, often citing very amusing anecdotes. There are wonderful pagodas, temples and seedy hotels in Mandalay, with walls that have heat seeping through them. He delights us with descriptions of theatrical shows, monks and fishermen, and tales of dangerous jungle hunts. He depicts the trials of travel, illness and the vagaries of transport with a sense of fun. All this is written in an evocative style that is lyrical without being over-powering.

Graham Greene has been attributed with saying that Norman Lewis is one of the best travel writers, not of any particular decade but of the 20th century. This is a travel classic.

NORMAN LEWIS
1908 – 2003
Nationality: British
First Published: Cape, 1952
Other Selected Titles:
Sand and Sea in Arabia
A Dragon Apparent
The Honoured Society
Naples '44
Jackdaw Cake
The Missionaries
The Empire of the East
Sicily

Jack London writing aboard ship.

JACK LONDON
1876 – 1916
Nationality: British
First Published: Macmillan, 1913
Other Selected Titles:
The People of the Abyss
Call of the Wild
The Sea Wolf
White Fang
The Road

The Cruise of the Snark

This is both a travel log and an adventure story. London was already a famous author, having published *Call of the Wild* and *The Sea Wolf*, when he, his wife Charmian and a few friends decided to build a boat and sail around the world. The foreword of the book reveals London to be a bit of an Indiana Jones character. His motivation for the voyage was about feeling alive and taking on Herculean challenges. Having built a 45-foot sailing yacht, the group leave California and set off for Hawaii. Along the way London learns to use a sextant.

This entertaining journal gives an insider view of the dynamics of the group, as well as presenting descriptions of the people and places that they visit. The visit to the Lepers of Molokai and London's reaction to the disease create a fascinating vignette of the early 20th century before antibiotics. London writes in a style that will hold your attention as the Snark cruises on to the Solomon Islands and Tahiti.

Arctic Dreams

Winner of the National Book Award, this magical treatise invites us to explore and experience the artic in all its beauty. Lopez has extensively researched many aspects of this fascinating region: geology, geography, fauna and flora, and the peoples. His descriptions of the North Pole and the northern sky are not just informative but also hauntingly beautiful. Lopez brings to life what it is like to be involved in the scientific exploration in this wonderful and dangerous world: the driving sense of purpose, the shared love of the natural environment, the dangers and the camaraderie. This is not a 'boy's own' adventure, this is a real grown-up experience.

Arctic Dreams is quite rightly subtitled 'Imagination and Desire in a Northern Landscape'. If you have never wanted to visit the Far North with its aurora borealis and midnight sun this book might just make you change your mind!

BARRY LOPEZ
1945 –
Nationality: American
First Published: Charles Scribner's Sons, 1986
Other Selected Titles:
*Of Wolves and Men
Crossing Open Ground
The Rediscovery of North America
About this Life: Journeys on the
Threshold of Memory
Vintage Lopez*

ARCTIC DREAMS

BARRY LOPEZ

IMAGINATION AND DESIRE
IN A NORTHERN LANDSCAPE

The edges of any landscape – horizons, the lip of a valley, the bend of a river around a canyon wall – quicken an observer's expectations . . .

PANTHER

The Danube

CLAUDIO MAGRIS
1939 –
Nationality: Italian
First Published: Garzanti, 1986

Claudio Magris' 1986 book, *The Danube*, is an astonishing journey through the history, culture and geography of Central Europe. Magris follows the Danube from its source, at the very centre of what was the Austro-Hungarian Empire in all its ethnic diversity, through the Balkans to the Black Sea.

Magris brings to his writing the curiosity, authority and scholarship of a distinguished academic and polymath, the heart and lyricism of a poet, and the narrative skills of a novelist. *The Danube* is not so much a travel guide, more an epic 'novel-ogue' with the mighty river coursing through Vienna, Budapest and Bratislava, as its central protagonist.

This book is like travelling with the most charming and educative companion, one who feels the spirit of this magnificent river and how it both colours and takes on the unique character of the countries through which it passes.

The Danube inspires the reader to follow in Magris' footsteps, and yet it is an entirely satisfying experience for both the armchair traveller and the student of literature, architecture, ethnography, politics, art or history.

Claudio Magris at a café in Barcelona, 1999.

The Snow Leopard

Peter Matthiessen – novelist, short story writer and superb writer of non-fiction – combines his incomparable descriptive talents in his much acclaimed 1978 travel memoir, *The Snow Leopard*. Winner of the National Book Award in 1979, this transcendent work recounts Matthiesen's five-week quest through the Himalayas with naturalist George Schaller, in search of the Himalayan blue sheep (which they found to Schaller's evident delight), and the mystical and rarely seen snow leopard.

For Peter Matthiessen, this journey became a meditation too, upon, life, death and our relationship with the natural world. 'Why is death so much on my mind when I do not feel I am afraid of it?', Matthiessen asks, while walking a sheer Himalayan ridge. 'Between clinging and letting go, I feel a terrific struggle. This is a fine chance to let go, to "win my life by losing it."

At the time, Matthiessen was also coming to terms with grief at the loss of his wife to cancer. However, this is not a book about death or loss, it is a memoir of an unforgettable experience searching for peace and one of the most elusive creatures on earth, in one of its most fascinating lands.

Anyone acquainted with the author's fiction will be aware of the beauty of his writing, but it is in the synthesis of the art of the novelist with the science of the naturalist, and the intellect of the philosopher that *The Snow Leopard* truly transcends the confines of genre.

The Snow Leopard

Peter Matthiessen

'Matthiessen's book is a triumph
that will outlive him. It is a masterpiece'
John Hillaby

PETER MATTHIESSEN
1927 –
Nationality: American
First Published: Viking Press, 1978
Other Selected Titles:
Wildlife in America
The Cloud Forest: a Chronicle of the South American Wilderness
Blue Meridian: the Search for the Great White Shark
The Tree Where Man Was Born
Nine-headed Dragon River: Zen Journals 1969–1982
Men's Lives: the Surfmen and Bayen of the South Fork
African Silences

JAN MORRIS

DESTINATIONS

'very close to being pure magic'
Jonathan Raban

JAN MORRIS
1926 –
Nationality: British
First Published: Oxford University
Press, 1980
Other Selected Titles:
Coast to Coast
Sultan in Oman
The Market of Seleukia
Venice
The Presence of Spain
Pleasures of a Tangled Life
Ireland: Your Only Place

Destinations: Essays from Rolling Stone

In the early 1980s, writer Jan Morris was commissioned by hip magazine *Rolling Stone*, to write a series of interesting travel articles with a twist. Better known for her discursive, descriptive writing, Morris adapted very successfully to the more journalistic style required to fulfil her commission, which was to visit cities and countries at a time of transition, and write about them in that context.

The result is *Destinations*, a fascinating work, part history, part travelogue, and part political commentary. Morris visited such places as Delhi under Indira Gandhi, when a state of emergency had been declared; Istanbul, as the Middle East was wracked in conflict; Washington after Nixon's Watergate conspiracy was discovered, and many more. In retrospect, South Africa under Apartheid, and Rhodesia as the emergence of revolutionary Zimbabwe was on the horizon, are especially interesting and in a way, poignant. Panama as the canal was about to be handed over to the Panamanians also features, as do many others.

Jan Morris' incisive intelligence, singular powers of observation and elegant style, pared down to combine reportage with narrative, make this anthology a collection of historic moments, which resemble complete snapshots of time and place rather than postcards from abroad.

Never Cry Wolf

Concern for the environment and maintaining the balance of nature is not the preserve of the 21st century. More than 50 years ago, naturalist Farley Mowat was employed by the Canadian government to investigate the predatory activities of the wolf population of the Keewatin district of Northern Manitoba. Mowat spent the summer observing and being observed by the wolves, and the local Innuit tribe who showed him great kindness.

The worldwide success of *Never Cry Wolf* led ultimately to the Soviet government banning the hunting of wolves, and introduced countless readers to concern for the natural world.

This first-person account of his experiences is a serious work, but Mowat writes with self-deprecatory humour and punctuates his account with very funny incidents. He found that the wolves lived mainly on field mice (there is a recipe for creamed mouse in the book), culling only the old and weak caribou and thus strengthening the herd.

This book is more than an account of Mowat's experiences, since he uses his considerable talent for storytelling to accentuate the message of his work.

FARLEY MOWAT
1921 –
Nationality: Canadian
First Published: McClelland and Stewart, 1963
Other Selected Titles:
People of the Deer
Lost in the Barrens
The Dog Who Wouldn't Be
Ordeal by Ice
Owls in the Family
The Serpent's Coil
And No Birds Sang
Sea of Slaughter
My Discovery of America

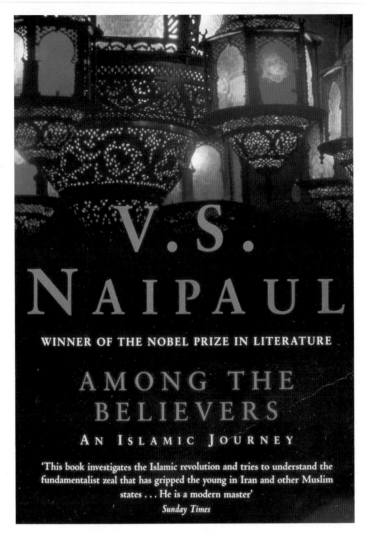

Among the Believers: an Islamic Journey

Nobel Prize-winner, V.S. Naipaul is perhaps generally better known for his novels than for his distinguished travel writing. Here he combines his great skills as a novelist – characterization and narrative pace – with the observational insight of the outsider, and descriptive power of a seasoned travel writer. To this he adds his great intelligence as a commentator on politics, history and religion.

In 1979, in the wake of the fundamentalist revolution that led to the overthrow of the Shah of Iran, and the return of Ayatollah Khomeini, an event that seemed to carry implicit Western approval, Naipaul spent seven months in Iran, Pakistan, Malaysia, Indonesia and Iran again. The West, it seemed, imagined that events in Iran would usher in a new period of reform. Naipaul warns that Islamic fundamentalism is never going to be modernizing in government and that the values of Islam are always going to be diametrically opposed to those of the West. His views were not well received at the time of publication, though tragically they have been proved chillingly accurate since.

This is a book of time and place, written in a world caught at a point of transition. It is a must-read of inestimable value for anyone who is concerned with trying to comprehend contemporary world events.

V.S. NAIPAUL
1932 –
Nationality: Trinidadian
First Published: Alfred A. Knopf, 1981
Other Selected Titles:
Beyond Belief: Islamic Excursions Among the Converted Peoples
Bombay: Gateway of India
India: a Million Mutinies Now
India: a Wounded Civilization
Island Voices: Stories from the West Indies
The Loss of El Dorado: a History

A Short Walk in the Hindu Kush

ERIC NEWBY
1919 – 2006
Nationality: British
First Published: Popular, 1958
Other Selected Titles:
The Last Grain Race
Slowly Down the Ganges
Love and War in the Apennines
The Big Red Train Ride
A Traveller's Life
On the Shores of the Mediterranean
Round Ireland in Low Gear
A Small Place in Italy

This wryly amusing, first person account of a spontaneous journey to the remote mountains of the Hindu Kush, north east of Kabul, can have done nothing to dispel the reputation of the eccentric, but game, Englishman when it was published in 1958. Newby, wearied by his years in a Mayfair fashion house, set out on his journey, accompanied by an equally inexperienced friend, after only a few days in Wales learning mountaineering.

A Short Walk in the Hindu Kush was Newby's second travel narrative and the start of an exceptional and illustrious career. In his preface, Evelyn Waugh described Newby as displaying 'the longing, romantic, reasonless, which lies in the hearts of most Englishmen, to shun the celebrated spectacles of the tourist and without any concern with science or politics or commerce, simply to set their feet where few civilized feet have trod'. It is easy to see how Newby became essential reading for the backpackers who were to follow.

His understated prose is interspersed with outstanding descriptions of the breathtaking landscapes and an unusual introduction to the Kaffir people of the region. Quoting from the phrase book he carried, he was able to open conversation with useful phrases such as 'a dwarf has come to ask for food', and 'a lammergeyer came down from the sky and took off my cock.'

Eric Newby in France, 1992.

Cees Nooteboom.

Roads to Santiago

The overwhelming impression left by Dutch poet, novelist and travel writer Nooteboom's *Roads to Santiago* is that it is in the spirit of its destination, a spiritual word pilgrimage on the road to Santiago de Compostela.

Consisting of 25 essays on Spain, it is also a kind of love letter to a country, which held for Nooteboom an evident deep fascination over many years and about which he is exceptionally knowledgeable.

Roads to Santiago reflects the themes that inform Nooteboom's fiction and poetry; a search for self and the relationship between fantasy and reality are present in these erudite essays, in which he explores art and the landscape, people and architecture, history, religion and culture both past and present. He sees Spain as the trustee for, and guardian of, Europe's history.

Critics have noted especially his marvellous meditative discussion of Velasquez and his digressions into Spain's post-civil war politics. Nooteboom's many written digressions are those that a spiritual pilgrim might make, on the long walk to Compostela, but there is a wealth of inspiration for the less erudite visitor in his beautiful descriptions of the sights, smells, sounds and even the soul of Spain.

CEES NOOTEBOOM
1933 –
Nationality: Dutch
First Published: Harvill, 1997
Other Selected Titles:
The Knight has Died
Rituals
In the Dutch Mountains
Philip and the Others
The Following Story
The Captain of the Butterflies
A Song of Truth and Semblance

La Salle and the Discovery of the Great West

Between 1682 and 1687, René-Robert Cavelier de La Salle, legendary French explorer of the New World, made three ill-fated attempts to find the mouth of the Mississippi and to explore its course from the great lakes to the Gulf of Mexico. On the first attempts La Salle and his men suffered dreadful deprivations: hunger and disease, encounters with hostile natives, and were even gored by buffalo. On the third attempt, La Salle tried to discover it by an overland route and was killed by his own mutinous men.

His body was never discovered.

This book, by one of America's foremost historians, is a vibrant, detailed and scholarly account of that third, ill-starred attempt. Parkman was a tireless academic. With a personal fortune derived from his wealthy Boston family, he was able to finance the in-depth research which was the basis of his works, and indeed could afford to travel to the locations about which he was writing. Perhaps it is this that gives *La Salle and the Discovery of the Great West* its authenticity as a work of travel narrative as well as an erudite history.

FRANCIS PARKMAN
1823 – 1893
Nationality: American
First Published: John Murray, 1869
Other Selected Titles:
The Oregon Trail
The Conspiracy of Pontiac
The Book of Roses
*The Jesuits in North America in the
Seventeenth Century*
The Old Régime in Canada
Montcalm and Wolfe
A Half Century of Conflict

American historian Francis Parkman.

Into the Heart of Borneo

**RAYMOND (REDMOND)
O'HANLON**
1947 –
Nationality: British
First Published: Salamander Press,
1984
Other Selected Titles:
*Charles Darwin 1809–1882: a
Centennial Commemoration
Joseph Conrad and Charles Darwin:
the Influence of Scientific Thought on
Conrad's Fiction
In Trouble Again
No Mercy: a Journey Into the Heart of
the Congo
Trawler*

The natural history editor of the *Times Literary Supplement*, Raymond O'Hanlon, and his friend, poet James Fenton, were at a party in 1981 when Fenton suggested to O'Hanlon that they take a jungle-walking holiday together. Fenton needed someone who could identify the flora and fauna of the jungle of Borneo. O'Hanlon, suffering depression after finishing his thesis on Conrad and Darwin, agreed. After SAS survival training, they set off with £2000 worth of excess baggage on a trip which was to turn into a highly dangerous quest by canoe into uncharted territory. With faithful native guides to lead them, O'Hanlon was hoping to find the possibly extinct, and certainly rare and elusive, white rhino.

Into the Heart of Borneo is an extraordinary story, reminiscent of those of amateur 19th-century explorers. Hapless Fenton and O'Hanlon might be, but O'Hanlon proves to be a brave, resourceful and fascinating guide. He shares his experiences with an honesty and humour that make this an anthropological monograph without condescension, a cracking adventure story, a morally uplifting tale, and a fantastically detailed guide to the birds of Borneo.

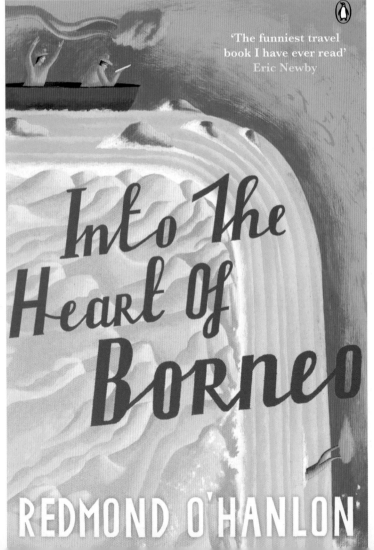

'The funniest travel book I have ever read'
Eric Newby

Into The Heart Of Borneo

REDMOND O'HANLON

The Travels

The Travels of Marco Polo, contained within the book *The Million*, is probably the most famous and influential travelogue in history, recounting the travels of Marco Polo and his uncles from Venice in 1271 to become the first Europeans to reach China. Marco Polo also gives an account here of the 17 years he spent in the service of the great Kublai Khan.

The Travels is divided into four books. The first gives a description of the Middle East and Central Asia on the outward journey to China. The second is a detailed account of China and the court of Kublai Khan. The third describes some of the coastal regions of the East: Japan, India, Sri Lanka, Southeast Asia, and the east coast of Africa. The final book gives an account of some of the recent wars between the Mongols and some of the regions of the far north, like Russia.

Polo was a gifted linguist, he had a good grounding in the Bible and Latin literature, he was an enthusiastic amateur historian and naturalist and a keen observer as well as a merchant. The text is rich in vibrant detail and impressionist description.

Allegedly written when Marco Polo was a prisoner of war, captured during a battle between Venice and Genoa, the veracity of the work and its contents has been a matter of some contention. True or not, *The Travels* is the most complete account of the Silk Road ever published. Without it we might never have known about many of the interesting new and exotic things he discovered in the Imperial court of the Kublai Khan: coal, asbestos, paper money and the Imperial post to name but four!

MARCO POLO
1254 – 1324
Nationality: Italian
First Published: 1298–99

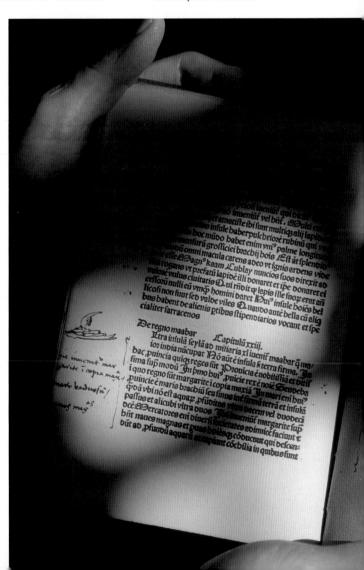

The edition of the travels of Marco Polo that belonged to Christopher Columbus.

DEAD MAN'S CHEST

TRAVELS AFTER
ROBERT LOUIS STEVENSON

'A most
enjoyable
travel-book'
Graham Greene

'Enchanting'
New Yorker

NICHOLAS RANKIN

NICHOLAS RANKIN
1950 -
Nationality: British
First Published: Faber, 1987
Other Selected Titles:
Telegram From Guernica

Dead Man's Chest: Travels after Robert Louis Stevenson

Nicholas Rankin is a well-travelled man and has lived in Bolivia, Kenya and Catalonia. He travelled even further afield when researching this fascinating book, *Dead Man's Chest: Travels After Robert Louis Stevenson*. Famously energetic and eccentric, marvellously inventive and a matchless writer of adventure and spinner of yarns, the great Scots author Robert Louis Stevenson died of a brain haemorrhage in Western Samoa in 1894, at the age of 44. He was already a legend.

Nicholas Rankin was inspired by the words of Jorge Luis Borges, who said 'I like hourglasses, maps, eighteenth century typography, the roots of words, the taste of coffee and the prose of Stevenson'. His own newly discovered passion for the life and works of Stevenson led Rankin to follow the author's journey from Edinburgh to the South Seas. Critics have called this work deliciously gossipy and meticulously researched, and indeed it is a joy to read the pithy yet informative text, containing as it does all the author's enthusiasm and a great deal of fascinating information about the great man.

Sailing Alone Around the World

Captain Joshua Slocum had the sea in his veins. He was born in Nova Scotia in 1844, and by the time he reached his 16th birthday he was aboard his first ship as an able seaman, working his way up to captain. He married in 1871 and his wife accompanied him on all his voyages, bearing four children on board. After many adventures, the death of his wife and the arrival of steam to challenge the power of sail, he found himself in Boston without a command. He took to writing about his adventures, but his first efforts were not successful.

Then in 1892 he started to build his own small sloop, the Spray, from a derelict hull and in April 1894 at the age of 51 he set off from Boston to circumnavigate the world, a total of 46,000 miles, alone. The first man to achieve this remarkable feat, he arrived in Newport, Rhode Island in June 1898.

The breathtaking account of his epic voyage, told in the style of a born storyteller, was first published in a magazine, and his inspirational story was an instant success and achieved bestseller status in book form in 1900. This fascinating book has remained in print ever since, a handbook for would-be round the world yachtsmen and a fine travel adventure for those of us who prefer dry land.

Joshua Slocum (left) on board his sloop Spray in 1897.

JOSHUA SLOCUM
1844 –1909
Nationality: Canadian
First Published: The Century Company, 1900
Other Selected Titles:
The Voyage of the Destroyer
The Voyage of the Liberdale

English explorer John Hanning Speke poses in front of a painted backdrop.

J.H. SPEKE
1827 – 1864
Nationality: British
First Published: 1863

Journal of the Discovery of the Source of the Nile

John Hanning Speke was an English Imperial adventurer and explorer. On an East African expedition to discover the source of the Nile, Speke and his travelling companion Richard Burton became the first Europeans to discover Lake Tanganyika. Both men fell ill during the expedition and Speke became first temporarily deaf, and then temporarily blind, and indeed could not see the great lake when they first found it.

They had heard of another lake nearby and Speke set off alone to find and name Lake Victoria. Speke returned to England before Burton and with Speke's famous speech before the Royal Geographical Society, claiming to have discovered the source of the Nile, began one of the most rancorous disputes in the history of exploration.

Speke was chosen to lead the next expedition, without Burton, which he claimed proved that Lake Victoria was indeed the source of the Nile. Burton continued to contest Speke's claims and the day before the two men were to conduct a debate before the Royal Geographical Society, Speke died of a self-inflicted gunshot wound. It is not known whether this was accidental or suicide.

This extraordinary work, illustrated with detailed maps and drawings, is a fascinating contemporaneous account of Speke's personal and literal journey.

Travels with Charley: In Search of America

JOHN STEINBECK
1902 – 1968
Nationality: American
First Published: Viking Press, 1962
Other Selected Titles:
Sea of Cortez: a Leisurely Journal of Travel and Research 1941 with Edward F. Ricketts
Bombs Away: the Story of a Bomber Team
A Russian Journal
Log from the Sea of Cortez
America and America

In the Autumn of 1960, just before his 60th birthday, one of America's finest 20th-century novelists set out on a road trip in a camper/tractor called Rocinante with only his poodle Charley and a full bar for company, to reacquaint himself with America. John Steinbeck explained 'I had not felt the country for 25 years'.

The result of his observations and opinions, conclusions and thoughts were published to great acclaim in this work of non-fiction, *Travels with Charley in Search of America*. Apparently, no one recognized him on his journey, which seemed to follow a random path from his point of departure in Sag Harbor, New York, and he tries to take back routes and stop in small towns. Steinbeck's observations on the America of 1960 and of its people are pertinent to their time and prophetic in ours, but at no time does he offer any suggestions for changes or improvements to anything he describes.

John Steinbeck with his French poodle, Charley, the hero of the book.

Needless to say this is a beautifully written travel memoir, and it is telling that even in this work of non-fiction he does not claim that his reality is shared. 'What I set down here is true until someone else passes that way and rearranges the world in his own style.' Like all the best road trips, this is also a personal journey for Steinbeck in which he is as frank in his observations about his own life and creativity as he is about the lives of others, which he sees so clearly and describes with such unique skill.

Travels with a Donkey in the Cévennes

ROBERT LOUIS STEVENSON
1850 – 1894
Nationality: Scottish
First Published: Nelson, 1879
Other Selected Titles:
An Inland Voyage
The Silverado Squatters
Across the Plains
The Amateur Emigrant
*From the Clyde to California: Robert
Louis Stevenson's Emigrant Journey
In the South Seas*

Robert Louis Stevenson is well known for his magnificent works of fiction and adventure, but less known perhaps for the non-fiction, especially travel writing, that forms an important part of his repertoire. This book is one of his earliest works.

Travels with a Donkey in the Cevennes is the tale of his 12-day solo hiking trip in the Cevennes mountains of southern central France, in which he covered 120 miles. The area was largely unpopulated and often impoverished, but the barren landscape seems to have struck a chord with the young Scot. The historical divide between, and the harsh restrictions of the day on the lives of the Catholics and Protestants of the region would also have been very familiar to him. In his early twenties, Stevenson undertook this book to raise money to support the woman he loved, and partly because, as becomes obvious both in his work and in his later life, he longed for adventure.

The book is part history, part travelogue and part adventure, but it was also the start of a new popular interest among the general public in outdoor activity as a form of recreation. Famously, it is in this book that Stevenson tells of commissioning the first ever sleeping bag, which was so heavy that he needed the donkey to carry it.

The Valley of the Assassins and Other Persian Travels

Freya Stark is one of those astonishing figures of the 1920s and 1930s who surprised her contemporaries and surprises us still today. An intrepid and extraordinary woman, she moved to Baghdad in her late thirties and set out alone to explore remote and undiscovered parts of the Islamic world, in the company of armed brigands and hospitable tribesmen. Stark was no Imperialist adventuress, though adventuress she was. She was ahead of her time assimilating tribal customs, reading the Koran, learning Arabic and insinuating herself into the local communities.

She travelled by foot, camel, car and donkey in order to reach the ancient fortress described by Marco Polo in the valley of the Secret Society of the Assassins. Since no maps were available of the area, Stark inveigled a local guide to take her across the mountains and plains until she found the tulip-covered ruins of the fortress. She then proceeded to chart the first maps of the area.

Freya Stark writes in the no-nonsense style in which she lived her life, with a sharp intelligence and great courage. *The Valley of the Assassins* is a truly fascinating travelogue and real adventure story vividly depicted, of a world now vanished forever.

British writer and explorer Freya Stark in 1950.

FREYA STARK
1893 – 1993
Nationality: British
First Published: John Murray, 1934
Other Selected Titles:
Alexander's Path
Ionia: A Quest
Dust in the Lion's Paw
Journey's Echo
East is West
Minaret of Djam
A Portrait of Turkey
The Southern Gate of Arabia

PAUL THEROUX
1941 –
Nationality: American
First Published: Hamish Hamilton, 1975
Other Selected Titles:
The Old Patagonian Express
The Kingdom By The Sea
Sailing Through China
Sunrise With Seamonsters
Riding The Iron Rooster
To The Ends Of The Earth
The Happy Isles Of Oceania
The Pillars Of Hercules

The Great Railway Bazaar

One day in the early 1970s, Paul Theroux, an American novelist living in London, set off on an epic journey from London's Victoria station, which took him by train to Japan, by way of Europe, Southern Asia, Southeast Asia, and East Asia. Then he crossed Russia to return at last to Victoria station.

This fascinating and unusual journey resulted in novelist Theroux's first travel narrative and was hugely successful. He writes with a slightly grumpy sense of heavy irony, which is nonetheless atmospheric and richly evocative.

Theroux leaves the reader with the impression that neither the destination nor the places through which he passes are of great interest to him. It is the journey itself, and especially the humanity in all its rich diversity that are really vital and important for him.

Consequently, *The Great Railway Bazaar* seems like a journey that one has taken oneself, sitting beside Theroux in the carriage, as he chats to people from all the countries he passes through and from all walks of life, captivated as he is by the romance of the railway bazaar.

Southern Cross to Pole Star

A.F. Tschiffely was considered to be completely mad when in 1925, at the age of 30, he decided to undertake a seemingly impossible journey. He was not a madcap adventurer, but a sober Argentinian who was moved to travel 10,000 miles from Buenos Aries to Washington D.C. on horseback. The journey took three years, from 1925 to 1928.

His mounts were two Criollo horses Mancha and Gato, direct descendents of the horses which the conquistador Pedro de Mendoza brought to Argentina in 1535. Tschiffely described the feral, tough intelligent pampas stock in a subsequent book published in 1949, in which the journey was recounted from the point of view of his mounts, entitled *The Tale of Two Horses*.

Southern Cross to Pole Star, sometimes called *Tschiffely's Ride* or *The Ride,* recounts this epic and unusual journey and was hugely successful when it was first published in 1933. Tschiffely was able to move to London and take up a permanent career as a writer.

Once again, this is a travel book inspired by the journey itself and the means of transport rather than the destination. The author's love of horses and riding, and his deep understanding of the animals, are palpable in his description of this great feat of endurance, and in his other travel narratives.

A.F. TSCHIFFELY
1895 – 1954
Nationality: Argentinian
First Published: William Heineman, 1933
Other Selected Titles:
Round and About Spain
Bohemia Junction
The Tale of Two Horses
Ming and Ping
This Way Southward
Bridle Paths: the Story of a Ride Through Rural England

Aimé Felix Tschiffely with his fiancée Violet Marquesita, in London 1933.

A Tramp Abroad

MARK TWAIN
1835 – 1910
Nationality: American
First Published: American
Publishing Co., 1880
Other Selected Titles:
Innocents Abroad
Roughing It
Old Times on the Mississippi
Life on the Mississippi
Following the Equator

Mark Twain is probably America's greatest novelist, satirist, social commentator and humorist and the author of many novels and works of non-fiction. In 1869 he achieved early success with *Innocents Abroad*, a humorous account of the travels of American tourists through Europe, The Holy Land and the Near East. It is a satirical view of his countrymen abroad, who confidently poke fun at the customs, people and places they don't understand. It became one of the most successful travel books of the century, selling 80,000 copies.

In 1880, Twain published the unofficial sequel to *Innocents Abroad*, *A Tramp Abroad*, which was based on a 15-month walking holiday through central Europe and the Alps which he took in the company of his friend the Reverend Joseph Twitchell in 1878. In fact, they managed to avoid walking as much as possible, taking a variety of modes of transport.

Although not as successful as his first book, it is a truly hilarious collection of observations and commentary on the people they met, the languages they heard (especially German) and the places they visited on the way.

The book is a lively and colourful collection of pieces written, as you would expect, with Twain's customary wit and panache. Mark Twain was a born travel writer, as he was a novelist and it is interesting to note that his masterpiece *The Adventures of Huckleberry Finn* is also a kind of travelogue, or at the very least a journey in more than one respect.

On Fiji Islands

Ronald Wright, award-winning novelist, essayist, historian and travel writer, brings all these disciplines to his 1986 work, *On Fiji Islands*. Wright gives a fascinating, considered account, in elegant insightful prose, of the transition of these islands, a former British colony, 'from cannibalism to Methodism'.

On Fiji Islands is neither a travel brochure nor an anthropological study, but in it Wright compares the experience of the Fijians to that of other post-colonial nations and notes none of the sense of inferiority which can be detected elsewhere, but instead a quiet dignity among its people.

He implies that on this occasion, whether by happy accident or design, the British allowed the islands a degree of autonomy, and a peaceful transition to a constitutional monarchy was achieved.

Ronald Wright brings an academic's attention to the history of Fiji and he is most interested in how Christianity and cannibalism have been merged to create a hybrid with which the people are perfectly comfortable. The problems faced by Fiji are centred in the tension between native Fijians and the Indian population, since there is no sense of integration or a melting pot of ethnic groups. This book is not a conventional travelogue, but from its sociological, political and historical perspective it is both instructive and unusual.

RONALD WRIGHT
—————————
ON FIJI ISLANDS
—————————

"THIS IS A FINE TRAVEL BOOK,
PERSONAL WITHOUT BEING PRETENTIOUS,
OPEN-EYED WITHOUT BEING NAIVE,
AND I'LL GLADLY TRAVEL WITH WRIGHT
WHEREVER HE GOES NEXT."—*WASHINGTON POST BOOK WORLD*

PENGUIN TRAVEL LIBRARY

RONALD WRIGHT
1948 –
Nationality: British
First Published: Viking Press, 1986
Other Selected Titles:
A Short History of Progress
Henderson's Spear
A Scientific Romance
Home and Away
Stolen Continents
Time Among the Maya
*Cut Stones and Crossroads: a
Journey in Peru*

AUTHOR INDEX

ACKNOWLEDGEMENTS

Octopus would like to thank the publishers and
organisations that have supplied material or granted us
permission to publish copyright images. Every effort has
been made to contact the copyright holders. Please
contact the publishers if any credits have inadvertently
been omitted.

Baen Books /cover reproduced by permission of Baen
Books; art © by Bob Eggleton 412.

Bloomsbury /Psycho by Robert Bloch 440; /Soldiers of
Salamis by Javier Cercas 260;
/Video Night in Kathmandu by Pico Iyer 512; /Stepford
Wives by Ira Levin 406; /Bliss by Katherine Mansfield103;
/The English Patient by Michael Ondaatje 335.

Bridgeman Art Library /Bibliothèque Nationale, Paris,
France, Giraudon 111; /Private Collection, Archives
Charmet 429.

Christie's Images /B W Huebsch, 1919 238.

Clarke, Irwin and Company /The Wars by Timothy
Findley, Toronto, 1977 278.

Corbis UK Ltd 8-9 detail 2, 10 top, 16, 61, 62-63 details
2 & 7, 68, 72, 95, 102, 119, 126-127 detail 1, 204, 217,
441; /Archivo Iconografico 62-63 detail 3,104, 110, 120,
125, 157, 186; /Tony Arruza 207; /Austrian Archives 74;
/BBC 428; /Eleanor Bentall 126-127 detail 3, 170;
/Bettmann 5 top, 10 bottom, 8-9 Main Picture & details 3
& 6, 11, 14, 17, 18, 34 Top, 62-63 Main Picture & detail
1, 67, 75, 80, 84, 86, 87, 94, 96, 98, 100, 108, 112,
114, 115, 116, 118, 122, 123, 126-127 details 5 & 6,
152, 153, 158, 168, 172, 174, 178-179 details 1 , 2 , 3 &
4, 192, 196, 198, 201, 208, 210, 221, 223, 226, 227,
228, 231, 242, 245, 252 top, 261, 263, 269, 279, 292,
299, 308, 318, 322, 323, 325, 328, 348, 351, 370, 376-
377 details 1, 2, 4 & 5, 381 bottom, 383, 387, 392 right,
401, 403, 432-433 Main Picture & details 1 & 4, 443,
445, 484, 490, 498-499 details 2, 5 & 6, 505, 508, 518,
527, 531, 532, 533, Illustration by James Hill/105;
/Stefano Bianchetti 247; /Blue Lantern Studio 23 bottom,
/Peter Pan illustration © Mabel Lucie Attwell 2006.
Licensed by Copyrights Group 13; /Christie's Images 39;
/Colita 371; /Dean Conger/Ivan Nikolaevich Kramskoy 62-
63 detail 5, 117; /Bob Daemmrich 232 detail 2, 314; /EPA
/Ivan Alvarado 180, /Nicholas Asfouri 320, /Julian Martin
520, /Frank May 234, /Enrique de la Osa 177;
/Christopher Felver 354, 427; /Allen Ginsberg 249; /Alex
Gotfryd 53, 465; /Philip Gould 277; /Louise Gubb 232-233
detail 5, 289; Rune Hellestad 8-9 detail 1, 41, 526;
/Historical Picture Archive 73, 81, 91, /Macmillan, London,
UK, Household Stories by the Brothers Grimm, 1892 23
top; /Arne Hodalic 232-233 Main Picture, 294; /E 0 Hoppé
78, 121, 194, 480; /Hulton-Deutsch Collection 5 centre,
8-9 detail 4, 12, 33, 46, 62-63 details 4 & 6, 76, 79,
89, 93, 124, 126-127 detail 4, 175, 178-179 Main
Picture & details 5 & 6, 184, 188, 189, 195, 212, 218,
258, 265, 281, 287, 301 top, 321, 331, 332, 333, 358
right, 373, 416, 457, 458, 475, 487, 498-499 detail 4,
516, 535, 537; /James Marshall 35; /Ed Kashi 336 right,
398, /for "Le Magazine Littéraire" 232-233 detail 4 & 243;
/Kipa /Sergio Gaudenti 132; /Stephane Klein 138; /Francis
G Mayer 126-127 Main Picture, 173; /Christopher J.
Morris 232-233 detail 1, 342 top; /Michael Nicholson 77,
82, 148, 193; /Louie Psihoyos 376-377 Main Picture,
397; /Roger Ressmeyer 378; /Reuters 498-499 detail 3,
509, /Kieran Doherty 232-233 detail 3, 366, /Forum 404,
/Handout/Albert Ferreira 304, /Jeff J Mitchell 302 bottom;
/Reza; Webistan 313 top; /Rykoff Collection 424; /Leonard
de Selva 224; /Touhig Sion 232 detail 7, 300; /Stapleton
Collection 498-499 detail 1, 504; Summerfield Press 183;
/SYGMA 301 bottom, /Sophie Bassouls 126-127 detail 2,
139, 161, 215, 240, 246, 251, 255, 268, 290, 298 right,
330, 376-277 detail 3, 379, 386, 390 bottom, 408, 432-
433 detail 2, 460, 469, 470, 472, 486, 498-499 Main
Picture, 503, 507, 525, /Annebicque Bernard 106, /Patrick
Durand 259, /Gianni Giansanti 310, /William Karel 432-
433 detail 3, 488, /Jessica Kovaks 432-433 detail 6, 448,
/DON MACLELLAN 8-9 detail 5, 42, /Jean Mascolo 273,
/Colin McPherson 232-233 detail 6, 283, 309, 432-433
detail 5, 482, /Pierre Vauthey 375; /Michael S Yamashita
529; /Zuma/Jonathan Alcorn 388.

ACKNOWLEDGEMENTS

Dedalus Books, Sawtry /Translation copyright @ Dedalus 1997 473.

Dover Publications, Inc /Suicide Expected by Cyril Hare 463; /An Oxford Tragedy by J C Masterman 476, both titles out of print.

Deutscher Taschenbuch Verlag, Munich/Germany /Alfred Dölblin: Berlin Alexanderplatz, 1965 © for the cover illustration by Celestino Piatti 270.

The Echo Library 181.

Ediciones Colihue S.R.L. /Rosaura a Las Diez by Marco Denevi/cover by Ricardo Deambrosi 451.

Éditions Gallimard /La Guerre des Boutons by Louis Pergaud, folio édition, Mercure de France; cover photograph from La Guerre des Boutons, a film by d'Yves Robert © Christophe L.-D.R 38.

Éditions Gallimard, Jeunesse /Les Malheurs de Sophie by Comtesse de Ségur; cover illustration by Danièle Bour 49.

With Permission of Faber & Faber Ltd 254, 274, 288, 305, 368, 453, 288.

Fremantle Arts Centre Press, Western Australia /My Place © Sally Morgan 1987 214.

Grove/Atlantic, Inc / © 1957 by John Calder (Publishers) Ltd/Cover design by Henry Sene Yee. Published by Grove Press 293.

Hachette Jeunesse Roman /Le Grand Meaulnes, Le Livre de Poche Jeuness, 2002 236.

HarperCollins Publishers Ltd /© 1997 John Brewer 133; /© 1991 Alan Bullock 135; /© 1984 Janet Frame 190; /© 2001 Jonathan Franzen 282; /© 1960 Alan Garner 1960 21; /© 1995 Peter Gay 147; /© 1989 Martin Gilbert 149; /© 1990 Reginald Hill 464; /©1938 C S Lewis, cover illustration by Jim Burns 407; /© 1995 Rose Macaulay 209; /© 2002 Carol Shields 355; /© 1938 T H White 59.

HarperCollins, Inc /Lost Horizon © 1933, 1936 James Hilton; renewed © 1960 by Alice Hilton/Published by Perrenial 296.

Peter Harrington Antiquarian Bookseller /Bloomsbury/Harry Potter and the Philosopher's Stone, Harry Potter and the Chamber of Secrets, Harry Potter and the Prisoner of Azkaban, Harry Potter and the Goblet of Fire, Harry Potter and the Order of the Phoenix and Harry Potter and the Half-Blood Prince by J.K. Rowling 45; /HarperCollins Publishers Ltd © 1954 J R R Tolkien 56; /Reprinted by permission of Houghton Mifflin, Portrait of a Lady by Henry James 1892 97; /Humphrey Milford/Oxford University Press c1930 55; /Macmillan, London, Uk Just So Stories by Rudyard Kipling 26; /Random House, Inc The Diary of a Young Girl by Anne Frank. Published by Doubleday & Co, Inc, 1952 191.

Hodder & Stoughton /Howards End by E M Forster 88; /The Seven-Per-Cent Solution John H Watson M D, as edited by Nicholas Meyer,1975 478.

Reprinted by permission of Houghton Mifflin /Rites of Spring by Modris Eksteins 141, /The Blue Flower by Penelope Fitzgerald 284; /The Great Railway Bazaar by Paul Theroux 536.

Ibooks.com /The Bride Wore Black by Cornell Woolrich/cover illustration and design by STERANKO 497.

International Polygonics /He Who Whispers by John Dickson Carr, Bantam, 1951 455.

Kingfisher Publications /From Black Beauty Copyright © Kingfisher Publications Plc. Reproduced by permission of the publisher, all rights reserved/cover illustration by Angelo Rinaldi 43.
Little, Brown & Co /Surfacing © 1994 Margaret Atwood, published by Virago 239; /In the Last Analysis © 1992 Amanda Cross, published by Virago 450; /The

Diviners © 1989 Margaret Laurence, published by Virago 307; /The Last Detective © Peter Lovesey, published by Time Warner Paperbacks 474; /Ornament of the World © 2003 Maria Rosa Menocal, 2003, published by Little, Brown & Co 164; /Interview with a Vampire © 1994 Anne Rice, published by Time Warner Paperbacks 341.

Luso-Brazilian Books 312.

Macmillan, London, UK /Jane Eyre by Charlotte Brontë 70; /Frozen Desire by James Buchan 134; /Cosmicomics by Italo Calvino 392; /Pandaemonium by Humphrey Jennings 155; /Among the Believers by V.S. Naipaul 524.

McClelland & Stewart Ltd /A Handmaid's Tale by Margaret Atwood 382; /A Fine Balance by Rohinton Mistry 326; /Running in the Family by Michael Ondaatje 219.

Octopus Publishing Group Limited /Ken Adlard /© E.H. Shepard, reproduced by permission of Curtis Brown Group Ltd, London 34 bottom, /Andrew Gardiner 399, /HarperCollins Publishers Ltd © 1952 Isaac Asimov 381 top, /Macmillan, London, UK/The Prime of Miss Jean Brodie by Muriel Spark 358 left, /Random House Group Ltd 400, 392 left; Ron Dixon /HarperCollins Publishers Ltd © 1937 Dr Seuss 51, /Frederick Warne & Co, 1902 40, /Random House Group 43; /Hodder & Stoughton /Bonjour Tristesse by Françoise Sagan, John Murray, 1955. Jacket design by F. Quilter 349; /Reproduced by permission of Penguin Books Ltd 253, 71; /Random House Group Ltd 338; /Tim Ridley/Nigel Williams/Random House Group 390 top, /Seymour Lawrence 426.

The Orion Publishing Group /Gollancz /A Canticle for Leibowitz by Walter M Miller JR 410; /Ringworld by Larry Niven 411; /Orion /The Big Clock by Kenneth Fearing 456, /Red Harvest by Dashiell Hammett 462, /Malice Aforethought by Francis Iles 467, /The Laughing Policeman by Maj Sjowall & Per Wahloo 489, /Sophie's World by Jostein Gaarder 20; /Weidenfeld & Nicholson History /Dead Man's Chest: Travels after Robert Louis Stevenson by Nicholas Rankin 530.

The Overlook Press /Islandia by Austin Tappan Wright. Copyright 1942, 1944 by Henry Holt and Company, LLC. Copyright © 1958 by Sylvia Wright. Copyright © 1970 by Sylvia Wright Mitarachi. Cover design by Yellowstone Ltd 430.

Oxford University Press /Front cover from Sense and Sensibility by Jane Austen (Oxford World Classics, 2004) 66; Front cover from Childhood, Youth and Exile by Alexander Herzen (Oxford World Classics, 1980) 199; Front cover from Destinations (1980) 522; /A Sicilian Romance by Ann Radcliffe (Oxford World Classics, 1998) 107.

Reproduced by permission of Penguin Books Ltd 27, 28, 29, 36, 44, 58, 60, 69, 83, 85, 101, 109, 130, 131, 136, 137, 142, 143, 145, 146, 150, 160, 163, 165, 166, 169, 176, 197, 200, 205, 229, 237, 252 bottom, 266, 272, 276, 303, 311, 319, 344, 350, 353, 360, 362, 365, 367, 372, 374, 384, 391, 413, 414, 420, 431, 434, 435, 436, 438, 446, 449, 471, 477, 479, 485, 491, 510, 513, 528, 539.

Penguin Group (USA) Inc /The Bloody Chamber © Angela Carter 1979. Cover design by Michael Ian Kaye and illustration by Roxanna Bikadoroff 256; /84 Charing Cross Road © Helene Hanff 1970, cover design by Chin-Yee Lai and photograph by Alec Bolton 197; /Dracula by Bram Stoker. Introduction and notes copyright © Maurice Hindle 1993 113; /The Wind in the Willows © Kenneth Grahame 1908 22.

Images courtesy Princeton University Press 167, 171.

The Random House Group 5 bottom,15, 24, 25, 50, 128, 129, 154, 156, 162, 182, 185, 187, 202, 213, 230, 248, 250, 257, 262, 264, 267, 271, 275, 280, 285, 286, 291, 295, 297, 292, 302 top, 306, 316, 317, 324, 327, 329, 336 left, 339, 340, 342 bottom, 343, 346, 352, 356, 357, 359, 361, 364, 380, 389, 405, 418, 419, 444, 454, 466, 483, 493, 502, 506, 514,

517, 519, 521, 523, 534, 538.

Random House, Inc /From The Three Stigmata of Palmer Eldritch, cover, by Philip K Dick, © 1964. Vintage Books 395; /From To your Scattered Bodies Go, cover, by Philip José Farmer, © 1971. A Del Rey Book 396; /From Sorrows of Young Werther by Wolfgang von Goethe, cover © 1971, Random House, Inc. Vintage Classics 90; /From The World According to Garp, cover, by John Irving, © 1997. Used by permission of Ballantine Books 298 left; /From I Will Bear Witness, cover, by Victor Klemperer, translated by Martin Chalmers, © 1998. Used by permission of Random House, Inc 206; /From The Cairo Trilogy, cover, Naguib Mahfouz, © Naguib Mahfouz. Everyman's Library 313 b; /From Reading Lolita in Tehran, cover, by Azar Nafisi, © 2002. Used by permission of Random House, Inc 216; /From The Messiah of Stockholm, cover, by Cynthia Ozick, © 1987. Vintage Books 337; /From The Human Stain, cover, by Philip Roth, © 2000. Vintage Books 345; /From More than Human, cover, by Theodore Sturgeon, © 1953, renewed 1981. Vintage Books 422; /From The Accidental Tourist, cover, by Anne Tyler, © 1985. Ballantine Books 369; /From The Conscience of Zeno, cover, by Italo Svevo. Vintage Books 363.

Jo Ann Reisler and her husband /Reynal & Hitchcock, 1943 47.

Royal Library, National Library of Sweden /Rabén & Sjögren 30.

Image courtesy of Self-Realisation Fellowship, Los Angeles, California /Image of Autobiography of a Yogi by Paramahansa Yogananda 222.

Serpent's Tail 235, 347, 481.

SPCK (Society for Promoting Christian Knowledge) 211.

By Courtesy of Stanford University Press 64.

Stella and Rose's Books of Tintern, Monmouthshire and Hay-On-Wye /With permission of Faber & Faber Ltd 48; /Reproduced by permission of Penguin Books Ltd 32; /Text and Illustrations © 1964, renewed 1992 by Roald Dahl Nominee Ltd. By Permission of Alfred A. Knopf, an imprint of Random House Children's Books, a division of Random House, Inc 19.

The Thames Publishing Company 54.

Topfoto /Roger-Viollet 501.

Wildside Press /digital collage by Alan Rodgers 394.

The Women's Press Ltd /A Good Man is Hard to Find by Flannery O'Connor/cover illustration Lauren Elder 334.

Reproduced by permission of Yale University Press /The Stripping of the Altars by Eamon Duffy 140.

544